W. VIRGINIA

VIRGINIA

UCKY

SEE

GEORGIA

NORTH CAROLINA

SOUTH CAROLINA

ATLANTIC OCEAN

FLORIDA

OF MEXICO

Clemmentown
Powhatan
Richmond
James R.
Appomattox Court House
Petersburg
Lynchburg
Amelia Court House
Southside R.R.
Richmond & Danville R.R.
Dan R.
Danville

Greensboro
Hil
High Point
Jamestow
Yadkin R.
Salisbury
Lexington
Concord
Yorkville
Charlotte
Fort Mill
Catawba R.
Chester
Cokesbury
Newberry
Camden
Broad R.
Abbeville
Columbia
Woodstock
Washington
Woodville
Atlanta
Madison
Augusta
Sparta
Crawfordville
La Grange
Sandersville
Savannah R.
Macon
Dublin
Ocmulgee R.
Oconee R.
Ogeechee R.
Hawkinsville
Alapaha R.
Irwinville
Suwannee R.
Milltown
Valdosta
Madison
Jacksonville
Monticello
Moseley's Ferry
St. John's R.
Waldo
Gainesville
Orange Lake
Fort Butler
Ocklawaha R.
Ocala
New Smyrna
Lake Weir
Cook's Ferry
Lake Harney
Carlisle's Landing
Indian R.
Fort Capron
Tampa Bay
Manatee R.
Jupiter Inlet
Fort Dallas
Bimini
Miami R.
Key Biscayne
Elliott Key
Cape Sable
Islandia
Nassau
Knight's Key
Indian Key
Key West

An
Honorable
Defeat

Frank –

Thanks for another
great year of golf and
friendship, with a great
year ahead of us.

John
Unrithers '01

WILLIAM C. DAVIS

AN HONORABLE DEFEAT

The Last Days
of the
Confederate Government

HARCOURT, INC.

New York   San Diego   London

www.harcourt.com

Library of Congress Cataloging-in-Publication Data
Davis, William C., 1946–
An honorable defeat: the last days of the Confederate government/
William C. Davis.—1st ed.
p.   cm.
Includes bibliographical references and index.
ISBN 0-15-100564-8
1. Confederate States of America—Politics and government.
2. Davis, Jefferson, 1808–1889. 3. Davis, Jefferson, 1808–1889—
Captivity, 1865. 4. Richmond (Va.)—History—Siege, 1864–1865.
5. United States—History—Civil War, 1861–1865—Peace. I. Title.
E487 .D277 2001
973.7'1—dc21   00-046143

Text set in Caslon 540
Designed by G. B. D. Smith

First edition
A C E G I K J H F D B

Printed in the United States of America

Our children may forget this war, but *we* cannot.
The war came and now it must go on
till the last man of this generation falls in his tracks,
and his children seize his musket and fight our battle.

—Jefferson Davis
President, CSA

This has been a magnificent epic.
In God's name, let it not terminate in a farce.

—John C. Breckinridge
Secretary of War, CSA

Contents

ACKNOWLEDGMENTS
xi

Introduction
ENDS AND BEGINNINGS
xiii

Chapter One
"THE RESPONSIBILITY OF ACTION"
1

Chapter Two
"LET IT NOT END IN A FARCE"
36

Contents

Chapter Three
"A VERY TROUBLESOME ELEPHANT"
70

Chapter Four
"THE SHADOWS OF MISFORTUNE"
95

Chapter Five
"I CANNOT FEEL LIKE A BEATEN MAN"
125

Chapter Six
"WE ARE FALLING TO PIECES"
169

Chapter Seven
"ALL IS LOST BUT OUR HONOR"
201

Chapter Eight
"THE CONFEDERATE GOVERNMENT
IS DISSOLVED"
242

Chapter Nine
"THIS, I SUPPOSE, IS THE END
OF THE CONFEDERACY"
265

Chapter Ten
"THIS MAZE OF ENEMIES"
286

Chapter Eleven
"THE LAST HOPE IS GONE"
313

Chapter Twelve
"WE ALL FELT PROFOUNDLY GRATEFUL"
349

Aftermath
"WHEN ALL THESE WOUNDS ARE HEALED"
384

NOTES
401

BIBLIOGRAPHY
459

INDEX
479

ACKNOWLEDGMENTS

Numerous friends and associates were generous with their time during the research for this book, and I would be remiss if I did not offer thanks for their invaluable aid now. A first word of gratitude must go to a man now long gone, the late Alfred J. Hanna, who thirty years ago engaged in a delightful and helpful correspondence with me, growing out of his work many years before on his still outstanding *Flight into Oblivion*. His encouragement led me three decades later to present this volume, which stands beside, rather than supplants, his own.

Gary W. Gallagher, Michael Musick, Richard McMurry, and David Coles were all helpful in tracking down sources not immediately available. At the same time, several descendants of the characters in this story provided materials from their family archives, including Walter Agard, Louisa Hill, Katherine Prewitt, and Peter Ten Eyck, all direct or collateral descendants of John C. Breckinridge, while Stephen Sands generously shared material on his great-grandfather Richard Russell. John S. Carbonne, Craig M. Morisak, and John R. Riddler all lent me manuscript narratives never before used from their family papers, and Charles Peery (Friends of the CSS *Hunley*) was very generous. John and Ruth Ann Coski of the Museum of the Confederacy were most kind with illustration requests.

And finally thanks to my wife, Jennifer Davis, who makes all things worthwhile.

Introduction

ENDS AND
BEGINNINGS

Virtually all wars have their winners and losers. To the vanquished the manner of being beaten may pose more peril than defeat itself, for the character of every peace is shaped by the close of hostilities that gave it birth. Never is this more the case than in a civil war. The generations of tensions and animosities that send brothers to battle each other beg for a solution, whereas wars seldom produce more than simple decisions. Force may result in victory, but rarely does it settle the differences that transformed shouting to shooting.

In 1865, as the American Civil War entered its last tormented weeks, perceptive men in the Confederate States of America realized that whether or not their side would fall was no longer the ultimate issue, but rather *how* it should fall. The tragedy of recent generations in central Europe, and in their own hemisphere in Mexico and South America, told them all too well of the retaliation, revenge, and the long dark night of oppression that could follow defeat in an internal struggle. They knew well enough that their own war of the past four years had certainly generated enough blood and anguish to guarantee no shortage of victors anxious for vengeance. At the same time, the realization of what they had sacrificed, and the commitment many still felt to the principles for which they struggled, made it imperative that thinking men look ahead and plan for the South after defeat. They felt a rich sense of their own and their ancestors' place in history. In their rhetoric they went to war to vindicate their forefathers' struggle for certain rights, including the right to hold slaves. Defeat would not mean that those rights were any less just, and even after the war they hoped to regain at least some of them in time, perhaps even win back in legislative halls what they had lost on the battlefield. If the Confederacy met its end the wrong way, however, it risked losing any hope for regaining those rights in the future, as well as the precious things they hoped to share with their victorious Revolutionary ancestors—dignity, pride, and honor. That they would lose the war such men did not doubt. The question now was, could they win their own posterity?

In the end it would come to a very personal struggle between two men, both of whom had fought for the cause, but from radically different motivations, and each of whom now faced the close with dramatically opposing hopes and ideas of how it should end. Their battle of ideas and emotions, and that of those who followed them, decided the verdict of their generation, and history itself rested on whether their cause should merely be lost or forgotten.

AN
HONORABLE
DEFEAT

Chapter One

"THE RESPONSIBILITY OF ACTION"

"**R**emember, 'mum' is the word."

The chief clerk of the Bureau of War, the principal office of the Confederate War Department in Richmond, Virginia, repeated those words more than once by the middle of March 1865. In ancient times a king or emperor might expect to be the very first to hear important news, direct from the lips of a messenger just arrived. Ironically, the advent of rapid communications technology, coupled with sophisticated administrative organization, meant that by the mid-nineteenth century, the latest bulletin, no matter how stunning in importance, might go through half a dozen people before it reached the top. On April 12, 1861, when Confederate batteries around Charleston harbor opened fire on Fort Sumter and commenced the Civil War in earnest, the news flashed to the interim capital in Montgomery,

Alabama, did not go directly to President Jefferson Davis, or even to his secretary of war. Instead, the first in the capital to know that war had broken out was William Griffith, the key operator on duty at the Southern Telegraph office in the Winter Building on Commerce Street. Within moments, however, the news was known all over jubilant Montgomery, helped along by a gaggle of journalists who occupied the room above Griffith just so they could hear for themselves the tune the wires sang for him.[1]

Four years later, though the phenomenon was the same, the handling of the news differed dramatically. In Richmond, the Confederate capital since late May 1861, the Confederate War Department had its own direct telegraph lines, and just as well, for by now the incoming news was so uniformly unhappy that it was best not released to the general public until the government chose the right time, framed to present as good a face as possible. War Department censorship of news from the fronts was already an accepted fact and had been for months, but still, in these most desperate hours, officials enforced every bit of caution possible lest something slip out. The first people to know the latest news were often the copyists in the Bureau of War, for even in its most desperate hours, the Confederacy embedded itself in that most typical of Anglo-Saxon mires, paperwork. Though they saw the most dire tidings in the letters and telegrams that they laboriously transferred into their copybooks before the originals went to their destinations, those clerks had to keep the news completely to themselves.

At sixteen Fannie Walker Miller was the only woman working in the bureau. Thanks to her neat hand most of the copying fell to her, and late on March 9, just as she was leaving for the day, the chief clerk handed her the latest letters received, carefully wrapped to prevent casual eyes from discerning their contents. When she opened the package, she saw immediately on top a letter with the signature of General Robert E. Lee and began copying despite the late hour. The general addressed the new secretary of war, General John C. Breckinridge, now in office scarcely a month, and the letter could not have been more depressing. "The military condition of the country," said Lee, "is full of peril." His army in the trenches and earthworks surrounding Richmond and neighboring Petersburg was underfed, ill clothed, undersupplied, and disintegrating from desertion. The men had not been paid in far too long, and they faced an ever-growing enemy army all but encircling them and the capital. "It seems almost impossible to maintain our present position," Lee concluded. "The army cannot be kept together, and our present lines must be abandoned."[2]

Fannie Miller was shocked. "If this is so, we are lost!" she blurted out before she caught herself. Once again the chief clerk admonished her to "remember, 'mum' is the word." Once she composed herself and finished her copying, neither she nor her superior said another word. When they finished their work for the night, each simply rose and left without comment, and in the days ahead they did not speak again of Lee's letter.[3] Had she been less surprised, or the chief clerk not so concerned about secrecy, they might have noted something even more shocking in Lee's letter. "I have received tonight your letter of this date requesting my opinion upon the military condition of the country," it opened, and in closing Lee added that he was succinct in his response "to enable you to make the use of my answer, which you desire."[4] Breckinridge had asked for this statement, knowing in advance what it would say, and because he had a specific purpose in mind for Lee's response. Incredibly, this foretelling of imminent and utter disaster for the Confederacy seemed to be exactly what the secretary of war wanted to hear.

By the winter of 1864–1865 certainly no one needed a clairvoyant to sense that the South was all but on its knees. The war appeared to start well with victory after victory in 1861 and 1862, but numbers and resources and time all worked against Jefferson Davis and his cause. Despite stunning and continuing successes in Virginia, the Confederacy steadily lost ground west of the Appalachians from September 1861 onward. In July 1863 the fall of Vicksburg on the Mississippi cut the South in two, while at the same time Lee's first great defeat at Gettysburg gave his army a savaging from which it never recovered. The following year Yankee armies under William T. Sherman first took Atlanta, then drove for the Atlantic coast, capturing Savannah late in December and cutting the eastern Confederacy in two yet again. Now Sherman marched north, having already taken Charleston and Columbia, South Carolina, and drove toward a junction with the Union army commanded by Ulysses S. Grant that now nearly encircled Lee and Richmond. Through it all the only hope had been that the Northerners might tire of the cost in blood and treasure and simply let the South go its own way, but that glimmer died in November 1864 when President Abraham Lincoln won overwhelming reelection, an affirmation that the Union intended to stand firm behind him to ultimate and complete victory.

After Lincoln's triumph, with Lee almost bottled up in his trenches and Yankee armies marching practically at will across the South, with desertions epidemic and Confederate civilian morale just as shattered as its industrial, economic, and agricultural infrastructure, most thoughtful Southerners recognized that an inevitable end was in sight. Indeed, many had expected it for some time, among them Vice President Alexander H. Stephens, who so despaired of any hope and so objected to Davis's policy that after March 1862 he simply went home to Georgia. Thereafter he only occasionally, and grudgingly, returned to Richmond, leaving his duties—such as they were—to be performed by others. By late 1864—like a small but vocal group of other dissidents, including his friend Robert Toombs, the old arch-secessionist Robert Barnwell Rhett of South Carolina, and even out-of-favor Generals P. G. T. Beauregard and Joseph E. Johnston—Stephens was convinced that their only hope lay in the assertion of the sovereign powers of the individual states to force Congress to change Davis's policy. Some thought they needed another revolution. Toombs favored the simple overthrow of the president, even if by violence. "Begone Davis," he bellowed, while Rhett openly called for deposing the president and installing Lee as an interim dictator.[5] As happened so often in the history of revolutions, in the tangle of disappointed ambitions and bitter disagreements on policy, the men who had made the rebellion were turning on one another.

The focus for most of the resentment was Jefferson Davis. "To these malcontents," his wife, Varina, complained, "the blighter's hand was the President's." Yet even she admitted that he had not the temperament or makeup of the executive. "He did not know the arts of the politician, and would not practise [*sic*] them if understood," she observed. Seemingly aloof to all but intimate friends, unwilling to relax his dignity to cajole when needed, and constitutionally unable to countenance any perceived threat to his prerogatives, or even simply to explain himself when misunderstood or questioned, he seemed naturally to repel those whose support he most needed. Sensitive to a fault, he felt the injustice of others' criticism, yet it only served to make him more distant and imperious. Knowing him and his quirks of personality better than any other, Varina Davis felt grave misgivings from the moment he assumed the presidency.[6]

Yet no one else available in February 1861 was better qualified to assume the office. Davis's service as colonel of Mississippi volunteers in the recent conflict with Mexico made him the South's greatest living war hero, an important asset for any would-be leader, and especially so since the framers in Montgomery envisioned the possibility of their president being literally commander in chief. His West Point education and four years as secretary of war under President Franklin Pierce made him intimately familiar with the organization and administration of an army—and the Confederacy looked to its armies for survival—while Davis's years as a senator from Mississippi acquainted him with all of the leading men in the South and, presumably, with the necessary workings of a congress. In fact, arguably only one Southern leader was better qualified to assume the newly created office, but that man was a Kentuckian, and the Bluegrass state had not seceded, nor would it, and the president of the Confederacy logically had to hail from one of its component states.

Given his personal limitations and the handicaps inherent in attempting to win independence from a larger, more populous, wealthier, industrialized Union, Davis had done as well as might have been expected from anyone. He personally built the army, and if he interfered with some commanders like Johnston, it was usually only when they idled or failed to keep him informed of their plans. Having found Lee, by contrast probably the finest field commander of the war, Davis interfered not at all but bent every effort to cooperate and give the general what he required. Critics complained that Davis did too little to secure diplomatic recognition from England and France, a first step to friendly military intervention, yet he was one of the first to foresee—as events were to prove—that foreign powers were never going to recognize the Confederacy until it had demonstrated that it could win its independence on its own. He also saw what many chose to ignore, that "King Cotton" had lost its crown, and that the threat of a cotton embargo would not sway England, which by now had both a surplus of the staple on hand, and also supply sources elsewhere. Of course he made serious mistakes, especially, perhaps, in failing to use cotton to fill the Treasury more amply at the outset, and quite certainly in several of his choices for high civil and military positions, yet the same could be said of Lincoln. If only Davis's personality and temperament had been more winning, and his grasp of human nature more keen like Lincoln's, those who became his enemies might have forgiven him a multitude of lesser shortcomings. But with this seemingly cold, distant autocrat, so inscrutable that one of his closest friends called him a "sphinx," opponents were not in a forgiving mood.

At least one thing none could deny was Jefferson Davis's wholehearted, all-consuming dedication to his cause. At first some doubted. He had been a moderate before the war, never a rabid secessionist, and a man who openly proclaimed his love of the Union and a wish to see it preserved so long as Southern rights to slavery and the opportunity to spread the institution into the newly forming territories of the West were not infringed. Indeed, extremists like Rhett suspected that Davis, even some months after his inauguration as Confederate president, was not entirely with the movement but rather hoped to achieve reunion with the North on the basis of constitutional guarantees on the slavery question. Davis soon disabused all but the most stubborn, however, that he was no reconstructionist. Instead, as the war went on, Davis demonstrated more and more that he saw himself and the Confederacy as one and the same, inseparable. Personally incapable of admitting error or accepting defeat, he transferred that same zealousness to his devotion to the cause. In spite of every new reverse, he preached hope. At every fresh disaster, he called only for renewed dedication and sacrifice. Even when Lincoln won reelection, Davis refused to be discouraged. Rather, he argued, this proof that the North would never compromise or give up should only make Confederates redouble their determination. The language of apocalypse began to echo in the executive office as occasionally he hinted that the South must have either complete independence or complete destruction. A few days before Lee's letter to Breckinridge came to the War Department for copying, Davis made public speeches in Richmond—which he rarely ever did during the war—promising new victories in the spring, even predicting that by the summer, Lincoln would be on his knees suing for peace. One opposition editor thought Davis's expressions "boastful, almost to the point of grotesqueness," while Vice President Stephens, on a rare visit to the capital, suggested that the president's optimism was "the emanation of a demented brain."[7]

Neither was an objective evaluation of the president's state of mind or of his dedication to the cause, yet within each there still lurked ominous shadows of portent. Much of the criticism of Davis that gave rise to his vocal but largely impotent opposition centered on the presumption that he sought to aggrandize himself with dictatorial powers. Certainly he dominated his Congress, which in four years only overturned one meaningless veto. Certainly, too, he surrounded himself in the executive branch of government with men largely sycophants or ciphers, especially in the all-important War Department. No one in his administration challenged him, and any who tried did not stay long in office. The Congress granted him every extraordinary power he requested, from suspensions of the privilege of the writ of habeas corpus, to national conscription, press censorship, military impressment of slaves, and even seizure of crops and livestock for the armies. Davis did it all under the plea of necessity, and rightly so if the Confederacy were to continue to resist, and yet every act seemed to trample on the very constitutional rights and liberties that Confederates thought they had gone to war to preserve. Accusations of tyranny and dictatorship from his critics were so common now that they appeared even in the capital press.

More moderate heads knew that Davis was no tyrant, but they had also seen the great mass of the Confederate people follow him this far in spite of every sacrifice, and in the face of growing signs that the cause was doomed. They watched Congress bend to his will despite a growing and vehement opposition that would have been more powerful but for the jumble of cranks and blowhards like Rhett and Toombs and Senator Louis T. Wigfall in its forefront, men so besotted with their own importance and pet grievances that they could never organize themselves or attract a substantial following. In the face of the ruin they had suffered already, how much further would the people go? More frightening still, with his by now absolute unwillingness to countenance anything but independence, through how much more death and desolation was Jefferson Davis willing to lead them?

If Congress showed no willingness to curb him, it had been painfully evident that his cabinet exerted little or no influence, either. Rather, from the very outset the powerlessness of his appointees was a subject of private resentment among the incumbents, and public sport for the press. Everyone remembered that Davis himself had been a very dominant secretary of war for his friend President Franklin Pierce, the only executive job he had ever held. Yet many also recalled the stories of Davis's unwillingness to entrust authority to others, what one called his attitude of "big man me and little man you" in dealings with subordinates, and his obsession with doing everything himself, even when it came to counting the number of lines of copying his clerks did per hour to make certain they were working hard enough.[8] It was no wonder that when word of his election to the presidency in 1861 went abroad in the new Confederacy, some agreed with the wag who suggested that his cabinet appointments would be "for Secretary of State, Hon. Jeff. Davis of Miss.; War and Navy, Jeff. Davis of Miss.; Interior, ex-Senator Davis, of Miss.; Treasury, Col. Davis, of Miss.; Attorney General, Mr. Davis, of Miss."[9]

Davis's critics always leapt for the nearest hyperbole, and yet in every cabinet department in which he took any interest at all, he dominated. More than one of his secretaries resigned out of pure frustration at having nothing to do, starting with his first secretary of state, the bibulous Toombs, who got the post chiefly as a sop for his not getting the presidency. Davis himself made all foreign policy, and Toombs derisively quipped that he could carry all the remaining duties of his department in his hat. He was followed by R. M. T. Hunter of Virginia, best known for his fawning sycophancy in the president's presence and for his political machinations behind Davis's back, as Hunter had hoped to replace Davis when his provisional incumbency expired in February 1862. When Davis won reelection to a full six-year term in November 1861, however, Hunter stayed on only a few months before going into the Senate, where he could flirt with the opposition. Even three years later Hunter was still intrigued by those who hoped to force Davis's resignation and install the Virginian in his place. Since 1862 the secretary of state had been Judah P. Benjamin, a permanent cabinet fixture who had started as attorney general with nothing to do and then served a brief and controversial incumbency at the War Department. The public outcry at reverses suffered when Benjamin was in the War Department forced Davis to remove him, but the unctuous Louisianian had become so necessary to Davis personally that he simply shifted him to secretary of state. Of his three successors as attorney general, none had anything to do, and the current incumbent, George Davis, got the post only after two others turned it down.

Other cabinet members came and went. No one knew or cared about the attorneys general, while no one ever seemed to approve of the men in charge of the Treasury. Christopher G. Memminger, the first incumbent, lasted three years before resigning in the summer of 1864, exhausted from criticism over a fiscal policy in large part imposed on him by Davis and Congress. Davis appointed George A. Trenholm in his place, but then Congress repeatedly refused to enact any of his proposed reforms. By March 1865 Trenholm had already tried more than once to resign, but Davis would not accept, and so another cipher remained in office. The War Department, meanwhile, seemingly devoured secretaries. Leroy P. Walker resigned in disgust at being treated like a clerk by Davis. Benjamin came after him, and then his successor, George W. Randolph, actually tried to exercise independent judgment. When Davis disciplined him for overstepping bounds, Randolph resigned so suddenly that Davis had to put an out-of-favor general in his office for a few days until he appointed Virginian James A. Seddon. Little more than a clerk himself, Seddon at least lasted more than two years before public and congressional protest at the course of the war led to his removal.

Just two men actually carried the same portfolios from the outset. Stephen R. Mallory of Florida, the secretary of the navy, held the dubious distinction of being the only cabinet member whose own state delegation opposed his confirmation. Followed by rumors of being a drinker and womanizer, he took over a Navy Department that he and Davis virtually created from nothing. His was always a hopeless task, yet he achieved as much as was possible, making his ironclads on the rivers and his commerce raiders such as the *Alabama* and the *Tallahassee* on the high seas a constant nuisance to the Union. Yet Davis always regarded the conflict as first and last a land war, and he paid little attention to Mallory, once reputedly saying in derision that he wanted no navy.[10] Mallory's counterpart in glamourless posts was John Reagan, postmaster general. Three men turned down the position in 1861 before Davis finally persuaded this hard-bitten old

Texas Indian fighter to take it on. By dint of ingenuity and bullying, however, Reagan actually made his system work, creating the only Post Office Department in American history to pay its own way. But Davis had left him almost entirely on his own, having neither time nor interest in postal affairs.

Of all of these men, however, only Benjamin had any real influence with the president, and that troubled Davis's friends and enemies alike. Born on the island of St. Thomas, Benjamin made his fortune as a lawyer and planter in Louisiana. His being a Sephardic Jew immediately attracted the enmity and distrust of anti-Semites, but in spite of that he enjoyed a solid rise in politics, representing his state in the United States Senate by the time of secession. He was an engaging little rotundity, with a seemingly perpetual Mona Lisa smile behind his whiskers. When he took the ever present cigar from his mouth, he spoke with a slight French accent and a bit of a lisp that seemed effeminate to some and put off more than a few men who met him. He gambled seriously at cards, and vague stories told of his ejection from Yale for theft when a young man. Everyone knew of his unusual marriage to a New Orleans girl many years his junior and from whom he had been separated for more than twenty years. Rumors spoke of her notorious infidelity, with insinuations that she sought sex outside the marriage because she found none in it. Some speculated that the lisp and effeminate manner were more than an affectation. Charles E. L. Stuart, once a journalist and now a Post Office Department clerk, suggested that Benjamin was "only a quarter man," one destined by birth for bachelorhood. "Nature had made him the safest of creatures, in manly mould," he charged, adding that Benjamin would have made a perfect guard in a harem. Richmond's common but whispered speculation was that he was either impotent or a homosexual.[11]

Regardless of gossip, none could deny Benjamin's hold on Davis. For one thing, the president gravitated toward those who, like himself, were the object of what he thought unjust criticism, and critics vilified Benjamin, especially during his inept tenure in the War Department. More than that, however, the secretary of state was easily the most obvious and accomplished sycophant in the government. Always calm, always pleasant, he never challenged or disagreed with the president. Rather, as other cabinet members like Mallory saw to their disgust, Benjamin had a talent for reading Davis's moods and prejudices and then played to them. When Davis fell out with Generals Johnston and Beauregard, Benjamin thereafter lost no opportunity to condemn them in his presence, likely helping to prevent either officer from being as useful to the Confederacy as he might have been otherwise. Seeing Davis's opinion that the North would never negotiate an armistice or peace short of capitulation, the secretary of state fed that conviction, and thereby, thought some, prolonged the war. Benjamin "never lost an occasion or opportunity to express his want of confidence," Mallory complained. Unlike most of the cabinet secretaries, Benjamin's office was in the same building as the president's, and Davis spent more time with him than with most of the others combined. "They were daily & much together," Mallory observed, and Davis's prejudices became what the navy secretary called "Benjamin's favorite theme." Toward any man or issue that the president was inclined to oppose, "Mr. Benjamin's influence, constantly exerted, kept his feelings against them constantly re-freshed," even by intentionally misconstruing the evidence.[12]

Unfortunately, for all his many strengths, Davis was never a sophisticated judge of men. Repeatedly he placed his trust in those whose talents lay chiefly in telling him what he wanted to hear. Himself disdaining to flatter, he could not recognize it when others aimed that art at him. To his mind a man who agreed with him was simply and obviously right, and thus en-titled to trust, and no one agreed with the president more than Judah Benjamin. As a result, by 1865 there was no one in the government whom the president trusted more. Davis never saw the other side of his confidant, the Benjamin who openly made fun of some of the president's proclamations and public papers in front of his staff in the State Department, or the Benjamin who ridiculed Davis for being vacillating and slow to make de-cisions. "I never saw such a man in my life," Benjamin would exclaim of Davis in exasperation behind his back, but to his face he was ever the loyal toady.[13] Many wondered just where Ben-jamin's true loyalties lay, and the general conclusion was that his first and foremost allegiance was to himself. Most ominous of all, Benjamin habitually seconded and reinforced Davis's determi-nation to seek no accommodation with the Union, but to fight on to victory or annihilation. Whether he meant it or not, his en-couragement was sufficient support to keep Davis from waver-ing on a path increasingly likely to lead to oblivion.

Out of the sticky web of a vocal but impotent opposition, a subservient Congress disenchanted with the conduct of the war, the vacuum of influence among all but one of the cabinet, and too much influence for ill on the part of that one, the legislative branch of the government spun for the first and only time in the war a confrontation with the executive, and Congress demanded changes. By late 1864 several of Davis's military appointees were vastly unpopular. The outcry to put Joseph E. Johnston back in command of the major army facing Sherman had also risen to more than just a mantra among the opposition and Johnston's friends. The country at large wanted changes, even if change for its own sake. Perhaps everyone was tired most of all of Seddon and his lackluster administration, for he, too, seemed to devote himself assiduously simply to not crossing Davis.

The change came in mid-January, first with a threat of a House vote on a resolution of no confidence in the cabinet. Meanwhile a series of measures went on the floor, one after another, calling for Benjamin's resignation, reducing Davis's control over military affairs, calling for reinstatement of Johnston and Beauregard to army commands, and demanding the creation of the post of general-in-chief—obviously for Lee—in order to place in his hands more control of the armies, and perhaps even as a first step to making him the dictator that Rhett wanted. Davis still had more than enough support in Congress to defeat most of the proposals, but in sum they revealed the depth of disenchantment. Obviously, after yielding none of his prerogatives for four years, Davis was at last going to have to give way at least a little. No counterrevolution, still this action was the biggest show of resistance from Congress since its creation. Even then, Davis made the best of it all. He got Beauregard entirely written out of the resulting bills, and reduced the call for Johnston's reinstatement to a simple expression of its desirability. He assented to the general-in-chief legislation, recognizing that Lee was by now so exalted in the Confederacy that elevating him to a supreme command could only do good for the country's morale and determination. Even then, the final legislation failed to specify the extent or definition of Lee's power, with the result that Davis could still cling to much of it himself. Benjamin remained secure, but to circumvent the no-confidence vote on the cabinet, Davis willingly sacrificed Seddon, who was himself so ill and angered by criticism that he wanted to resign, anyhow. On January 18, 1865, he did so, though Davis sat on the resignation for almost two weeks before formally accepting.[14]

Even before Seddon resigned, the rumors of who should succeed him flew through Richmond and revealed an unaccustomed unanimity between administration supporters and the opposition. Indeed, only one name was bandied about, as it had been for some time even before Seddon actually quit. Coincidentally, Davis himself seems to have been thinking the same man for several months, just as rumor said he toyed with it way back in the fall of 1861 when Walker resigned. On September 20, 1864, tired of Seddon, Davis sent his aide Colonel William Preston Johnston with only verbal instructions on a secret mission to southwest Virginia to see the commander of that military department, Major General John C. Breckinridge.[15] None of those involved ever revealed the purpose of the mission, but most likely Johnston's task was to sound the general on taking over the War portfolio. If so, probably no one, least of all Davis, realized what a sea change it represented for the president's hold on power.

Breckinridge turned forty-four just two days before Seddon resigned, yet he had already packed more into his career than most men twice his age. Born in Lexington, Kentucky, the grandson of Thomas Jefferson's attorney general, he was almost certainly destined for prominence as the scion of one of the most distinguished families in the Bluegrass state. Following legal studies at Transylvania University and at Princeton, he practiced law in Lexington until the outbreak of war in 1846, after which he was elected major of the Third Kentucky Infantry and went with his regiment to Mexico. He saw no action but came back with that all-important military title affixed to his name and easily won a seat in the state legislature in 1849, when he broke with the family's Whig tradition and ran as a Democrat. Two years later, perceived as the anointed successor of Henry Clay in spite of his being a Democrat, Breckinridge won the first of two terms in Congress from Clay's old district, during which he attracted unusual attention and regard despite his youth. As a result, in 1856 when his party nominated James Buchanan for the presidency, it chose Breckinridge as his running mate, even though the thirty-five-year-old Kentuckian had been constitutionally eligible for only five months.

He spent four years as the youngest vice president in the nation's history, but they were years that removed him from the public debate as the sectional crisis sped on toward 1860. Like his family and most in his state, Breckinridge was an instinctive moderate. He supported slavery in principle, because the Constitution sanctioned it, and sometimes owned one or two house servants himself, yet he occasionally emancipated one of his blacks, and to friends confided his inner discomfort with the institution. Critics in the South sometimes accused him of being secretly an abolitionist. Never an actual proponent of secession, he nonetheless believed it to be an implicit right in the national compact but something to be applied only as a last resort. He upheld the doctrine of state sovereignty and limited government, while favoring a stronger and more progressive central authority in Washington than did men like Davis. Above all, he believed in the Union and compromise, showing himself a true heir of Henry Clay despite their party differences.

As a result, when the crisis came he found himself right in the middle. His party split in 1860 over the issue of slavery's extension into the territories. The Northern wing backed Stephen A. Douglas, while the South and a number of delegates from other states met separately and nominated Breckinridge against his wishes. The split virtually guaranteed that Abraham Lincoln, the Republican candidate, would win by a simple plurality, while the more numerous Democrats divided their votes between their two candidates. In the end Breckinridge only accepted the nomination when persuaded that doing so would show Douglas the hopelessness of his own candidacy, opening the door to the withdrawal of both in favor of a compromise candidate acceptable to North and South, who would then stand a real chance of beating Lincoln. But Douglas refused to budge, and Breckinridge found himself trapped, with no choice but to go on with what he admitted to friends was "a forlorn hope." In November he polled 850,000 votes, well behind both Lincoln and Douglas, though their votes were heavily sectional: Lincoln's entirely in the North, and Douglas's predominantly from the free states as well. By contrast Breckinridge polled strongly in every section, evidence of his moderate appeal despite the perception that his wing of the party was in the hands of the secessionists. He carried eleven states to Douglas's two, putting him second in the electoral count.

As incumbent vice president and president of the Senate, it was Breckinridge's duty to supervise the counting of the electoral

ballots to declare the actual winner, and though there were sus-
picions that Southerners in the chamber might attempt to dis-
rupt the proceedings, the Kentuckian ruled with an iron hand
and refused to allow interruptions, attracting the admiration
even of Republicans on the floor. Meanwhile Kentucky's legislature had already elected him to a seat in the Senate, and on
March 4, 1861, after swearing in his successor as vice president,
he stepped from the podium to his new desk on the floor. He
immediately became an outspoken opponent of the Lincoln administration, especially after the outbreak of war at Fort Sumter,
and thereafter Breckinridge condemned all of Lincoln's actions
in raising an army to put down the rebellion. He still hoped for
some compromise that would bring the seceded states back into
the Union, and feared that every step toward war and coercion
only made that goal more difficult. When more moderate slave
states like Virginia, North Carolina, and Tennessee seceded in
the wake of Lincoln's raising an army, Breckinridge's position
became increasingly untenable.

Lincoln, a fellow Kentuckian and an old friend, greatly feared
that strategically located Kentucky, which currently maintained
a precarious pose of neutrality, would secede. If it did, he believed, the Union might well be lost, which made him apprehensive about Breckinridge, the most popular Kentuckian of his
time, who could use his influence to lead the state into secession. As a result, even though Breckinridge had not committed
a single disloyal or illegal act, as soon as Kentucky abandoned
neutrality in September and sided with the North, Union military authorities swept into the state and, among their first acts,
ordered Breckinridge's arrest. Warned in advance, he faced a
choice between evils. Other outspoken opposition politicians

were being arrested and held without habeas corpus, for how long no one could predict, in order to silence their voices. If he allowed himself to be arrested, that would be his fate, too. Or he could flee to the South and throw in his lot with the Confederacy, even though he confessed to friends that he had little expectation that the rebellion could succeed, and was not certain in his own mind that he thought it ought to succeed. In the end, given the choice of submission or resistance, he decided to resist. Unsaid was his hope that there might still be a settlement between the sections, though it appeared the South had to make a show of determination on the battlefield to force the North to the negotiating table. Thus, by fighting for the Confederacy, he would be like a number of others in the South, perhaps even Stephens, fighting in the end for a reformed Union.

On reaching Richmond in late October, Breckinridge immediately heard rumors that Davis would appoint him secretary of war to replace Benjamin, who was always intended as a temporary incumbent after Walker's resignation. But Davis saw a better use for Breckinridge—giving him a brigadier's commission and sending him west to the army forming in southwestern Kentucky. The influence that Lincoln feared, Davis coveted. He hoped that Breckinridge in Confederate uniform would be a powerful inducement to fellow Kentuckians to side with the South and enlist, while the mere political influence of having one of the most popular men of the times behind Confederate banners was hailed as worth a whole division of soldiers in itself. Though the enlistments were not forthcoming, as most Kentuckians remained doggedly on the fence or attached to the Union, the new brigadier proved an able soldier. He commanded his army's reserve corps at the Battle of Shiloh and won promotion to major general, and thereafter gave a distinguished performance on battlefields of the western theater from Baton Rouge and Vicksburg to Chickamauga. By late 1863 he led a corps of the Army of Tennessee commanded by General Braxton Bragg, who had a history of trying to shift his own battlefield failures to the shoulders of his subordinates. He tried it once with Breckinridge at the beginning of the year, and after the Confederate debacle at Missionary Ridge on November 25, he did it again.

Though Bragg's charges against Breckinridge were unfounded, and Davis himself seems not to have believed them, during the ensuing general shake-up in that army's high command, Breckinridge was reassigned. But he went to what amounted to a promotion, an independent department command of his own in southwest Virginia. For the next year he shone, turning back one Federal raid after another, and at New Market, Virginia, on May 15, 1864, he won one of the most stunning small battles of the war, in the process winning kudos from Lee himself. Thereafter Breckinridge seemed to be everywhere, reinforcing Lee as he faced Grant outside Richmond, then off to organize the defenses of Lynchburg, then commanding a corps in General Jubal Early's small army as it invaded the North and reached the environs of Washington itself, where some Confederates joked about installing Breckinridge in the Capitol once more. Battles in the Shenandoah Valley followed, and then in the fall, when Colonel Johnston came on his mission, Breckinridge was back in his department once more, preparing for the next Yankee raid. By January 1865 the Kentuckian was the twelfth senior-ranking major general in the army, and had seen service in more states of the Confederacy than any other general in the service, led a division or corps in three different field armies, and commanded his own small army as well. People of the Shenandoah hailed him as the new Stonewall Jackson. If only Kentucky had seceded at the start with the others, some lamented, Breckinridge would have been president from the start, and there was talk that if the Confederacy lasted until February 1868, when Davis's term as president expired, Breckinridge should be his successor.[16]

When Davis offered Breckinridge the portfolio of secretary of war that January and the Kentuckian accepted, it marked much more than a simple change of bureaucrats. This man was no Walker or Seddon, to be casually overridden by the president or treated dismissively as a clerk. He had led ten thousand and more in battle. He was still the beau ideal of the thousands of Kentuckians who had sided with the South, while in both of the major armies now in Virginia and South Carolina he was highly regarded by rank and file, and with the single exception of Bragg, not one high commander in the service failed to hold him in high esteem. Every bit the diplomat that Davis was not, Breckinridge by simple personality got along with almost all factions, from the prickly Joseph E. Johnston and Beauregard to the slippery Hunter, and even the erratic Toombs, in part no doubt because they all recognized his popularity and sought his influence for their varying schemes and causes. Even the radical opposition, with whom Breckinridge never felt sympathy, somehow came to think that he might stand with them. Privately Toombs declared in 1864 that he believed Breckinridge sympathized with himself, Johnston, Beauregard, and others, in dreaming of launching a counterrevolution to oust Davis.[17]

That was nonsense, but it revealed how even the extremists wanted Breckinridge on their side, and when some heard of his appointment they were stunned. Gustavus Smith knew from his own experience how impossible it could be to work with Davis. "How is it that Breckinridge is Secretary of War?" he asked Toombs. "I can't even guess how it came about." Toombs agreed that it was hard to believe, but they concluded that "the President has changed his nature."[18] As for the mainstream, Lee's high opinion of Breckinridge was on public record after New Market, and on hearing that the office had been offered, Lee himself wrote to Breckinridge urging him to accept. Half a million men who were now Confederate citizens had voted for Breckinridge in 1860; in some states that was more than had bothered to turn out to vote for Davis himself in his uncontested reelection in November 1861. Nor had Breckinridge stayed entirely aloof from politics as a general. From the start he was a powerful member of the influential Kentucky lobby in the army and in Richmond, pressing always for renewed efforts to occupy their home state and free it of the Lincoln yoke. Except for his dispute with Bragg, which was promulgated far more by Bragg than by Breckinridge, he adroitly stayed out of the numerous feuds that almost crippled the high command in the Army of Tennessee, and unlike others, he refused to politick against Bragg behind his back. His standing was such that in late 1863, several generals who were launching a potentially explosive proposal to Davis—that slaves be enlisted in Confederate armies in return for their freedom—successfully sought his support in the hope that his prestige would earn them a fair hearing. They even asked that he go to Richmond to make their case in person. In desperation Davis was ready to act, but the almost scandalous request struck at the very core of the Confederacy by suggesting that a black man could be a soldier and might therefore be implicitly the equal of a white. The outcry over the officers' involvement in the proposition probably stunted further advancement for some, including the enormously popular and capable Patrick R. Cleburne, but still somehow no stigma attached to Breckinridge. In an unprecedented move, the Confederate Congress even gave Breckinridge an open invitation to take a seat in its deliberations whenever he chose, despite his holding no elective office whatsoever.

In short, here was a powerful man of a sort never before seen in the cabinet, his prestige in the army at least equal to Davis's, and his popularity with the people probably greater. Charming and engaging, diplomatic, the least egotistical or confrontational of men, he never sought conflict, and yet even Davis, so often undiscerning, saw well enough that this was a man he could not dominate. As if to punctuate the fact that the new secretary would be his own man, Breckinridge placed conditions on his acceptance. He told Davis, before he would agree to take the post, that he intended to be "a positive, and not a passive, chief of the Department." It was rumored that he insisted on Davis removing the odious Bragg from his current post of chief military adviser, and though that was untrue, Breckinridge did demand that the controversial and all but incompetent commissary general, Davis's old friend Lucius B. Northrop, be dismissed. Davis had stood by Northrop through almost four years of outcry over his ineptitude and the hardship it had caused in the armies, but now he gave in. Breckinridge's record and following said silently to the president what the Kentuckian would never have declared himself: In the big-man-me–little-man-you sweepstakes, spirited debate might ensue over which of them was which.

The reaction to news of the appointment confirmed not only the esteem felt for Breckinridge but also Davis's wisdom in his choice, for immediately morale got a much needed boost. "He is a noble fellow, with a good strong golden thread of patriotism running through him, composed, courageous, and cautious," declared General William Preston. The change proved immediately popular with the civilians in Richmond, who hailed it as an omen of hope for the cause.[19] As a sign of what they expected him to achieve, they reflected on what he might have done at an earlier day. "If we had had Breckinridge in Walker's place at the beginning," mused the wife of General James Chesnut, "what a difference it might have made."[20] In the War Department itself there was almost jubilation. Assistant Secretary of War John A. Campbell feared at first that Breckinridge was not a happy choice, since he was not by nature a bureaucrat and seemed disinclined to bury himself in detail like his predecessors, but Campbell kept an open mind and soon it changed. Robert Kean, the head of the Bureau of War in which Fannie Miller worked, soon appreciated Breckinridge's direct manner of approaching problems like Northrop, while General Josiah Gorgas, head of the department's Ordnance Bureau, actually took heart from Breckinridge's refusal to shirk the big picture for paperwork. "Breckinridge carries his duties cheerfully," he observed a few days after the change of secretaries. He would "I hope make a good Secretary *because* he evidently intends to push work off upon others, & not involve himself in details, which is right."[21] Elsewhere in the government, Robert Tyler, register of the Treasury, expressed his pleasure, while John B. Jones, a War

Department clerk, saw in the wake of the appointment that "every effort will be made to popularize the cause again."[22] On hearing of Breckinridge's acceptance, Lee expressed his pleasure warmly, declaring that from his personal experience of Breckinridge's character and ability, he thought him the ablest man in the Confederacy to oversee its armies.[23] Over in the Post Office Department, however, the ever acidic Stuart, though elated with the change, complained that it was "like sending for a competent physician when the patient was already physicked and poulticed to death by quacks."[24]

What the new secretary of war encountered on taking office could hardly have encouraged him, for several of the component bureaus were a mess.[25] He set about his task indefatigably. Indeed, one of his shortcomings as a general had been his tendency to work himself endlessly without rest until he collapsed for a day or two out of exhaustion. He did not pace himself now, and during the first two weeks worked until well after 2 A.M. before going to bed.[26] There were changes to make in personnel and organization, information to gather, and new procedures to implement, yet within three weeks Lee advised him that his once nearly starving army had not been so well supplied in months. In another few weeks the flow of supplies actually overloaded the capacity of the railroads to get them to the troops, while across the Confederacy, where once armies often had to forage from week to week, War Department depots had nearly three million rations on hand.[27]

But even before he attacked the problems within his department, Breckinridge's very first act was something at once more fundamental and far reaching. As a general in the field he had seen enough on his own to confirm his fear of four years earlier that the Confederacy could not succeed. Even if Davis refused to see the obvious now, the evidence was abundant to most thoughtful men that the end was near. No sooner did he take office than Breckinridge called Campbell to him for a lengthy private interview. Himself a fellow moderate who opposed secession and the war, Campbell had been assistant secretary for more than two years now and could offer the most trenchant views of any in the department on the state of the Confederate armies. Breckinridge asked more than that, however. He wanted Campbell's view on the state of the Confederacy itself, and Campbell responded that in his estimation the cause was hopeless. They had neither the finances, the resources, nor the manpower to continue with any chance of success.

It was what Breckinridge expected to hear, but Campbell's response helped him to determine his course thereafter. More convincing still was what Campbell told him of a mission from which he had only just returned two days before. Davis had authorized Campbell, Stephens, and Hunter to meet with Lincoln under truce flag at Hampton Roads on February 3 to discuss possible terms of peace. It was a cynical act by the president, for he fully expected that reunion would be a sine qua non for Lincoln, just as he would himself refuse to yield on Confederate independence. Davis had even intentionally altered the wording in the instructions Benjamin gave Campbell and the others, specifically deleting a reference to "one common country" and substituting a statement that the two "nations" would have to negotiate. Privately Benjamin expressed his irritation, predicting that the change would of itself kill their chances.[28] Thus there was no basis for compromise between the two sides, nor would Lincoln even countenance an armistice pending further negotiations. Stephens and others hoped that a cease-fire could be a first step to eventual independence, expecting that once the guns stopped, the North would not have the will to start fighting again. If the Confederates then just dragged out the negotiations long enough, the Union might in the end let them go. Not surprisingly, the commissioners came back with nothing to report, which was exactly what Davis expected and wanted. Bedeviled increasingly by a growing peace movement, and with Stephens himself backing a current resolution in Congress calling for a convention of all the states to formulate a peace policy, Davis needed Lincoln's refusal to negotiate. It would send abroad through the Confederacy the message that they would get no concessions from the Yankees and that there could only be total victory or total defeat.

Lincoln's basic demand, in fact, was simply that Southern armies cease fighting and the seceded states return to the Union. That left a host of other issues of vital concern still subject to negotiation, including confiscation of property, possible prosecution of the South's leaders, compensation for slaves freed due to emancipation, and even the possibility raised by Lincoln that the Emancipation Proclamation itself, being a war measure, might cease to be effective when the war ended, meaning Southerners in a reunited nation could conceivably remain secure in their slave property. Faced with almost certain defeat, anyhow, Confederates might come out of defeat with much better terms by negotiating now than if they continued on and forced the North to beat them into definitive subjugation when they no longer had anything, even surrender, with which to bargain.

In reporting his mission's results on February 5, Campbell

proposed to Davis instead that the best they could do now was stop the bloodletting and propose peace on terms of reunion and acceptance of emancipation. The president refused to countenance such a suggestion, saying somewhat sarcastically that, among other things, he had no constitutional power to negotiate for his own official suicide. The states in their sovereignty created the Confederacy, and only they could agree to its surrender and dissolution.[29] So saying, he neatly ducked the more central question. Even if he did not have the constitutional authority to surrender, unquestionably as president he did have the moral authority to call on the states to act to stop the pointless killing. While others in the cabinet, like Mallory, were willing at least to consider further negotiations on Lincoln's basis, Benjamin typically changed his tune. Now he was the only one who adamantly backed the president's refusal to even consider the terms laid down by Lincoln, sometimes parroting Davis's exact words. As angry as he had been at Davis for altering the commissioners' instructions, to make immediate negotiations impossible, now he spoke even more bitterly of Lincoln's proposal as "suicidal folly." Mallory felt that Benjamin bore the blame more than any other for sustaining and encouraging the president's refusal to seize the opportunity, unhappy though the alternative was to all of them.[30]

Campbell explained all this to Breckinridge during their interview, and it was disheartening because Davis's determination, encouraged by Benjamin, only promised more death and destruction before the inevitable. Campbell's own bitterness showed. "The idiosyncrasy of one man defeated the design," he grumbled. Davis was unfit either to be a revolutionary or a chief executive. "Slow, procrastinating, obstructive, filled with petty scruples and doubts, and wanting in a clear, strong, intrepid judgment, a vigorous resolution, and a generous and self-sacrificing nature, he became," a disgusted Campbell concluded, "an incubus and a mischief." It was evident to Campbell that unless something was done, Davis would have his armies continue to fight until they disintegrated, and then call on the survivors to go to the hills and continue resistance as guerillas until they were all hunted down, perhaps prolonging the agony for years and only visiting further devastation and bitterness on their already ravaged land and people. "The action of Mr. Davis in refusing all negotiations upon the basis of Union," Campbell concluded, "compelled conservative men to act independently of his authority."[31] The problem facing the Confederacy in its fatal crisis now was that it did not appear to have "the man or men who would take upon themselves the responsibility of action."[32]

Campbell was wrong, for sitting there with him in that office as he made his report was perhaps the only man in the Confederacy who could change Davis's course without a coup and still hope to bring the war to an honorable end short of humiliating defeat or absolute subjugation. Campbell handed Breckinridge a draft of a plan for an armistice that he had prepared immediately after returning from Hampton Roads, hoping that the secretary of war might be able to use it as a basis for bringing Davis around. He also expressed his belief that Richmond would fall to the Yankees within a matter of weeks and that when it did, Lee's army would probably disperse.[33]

Breckinridge began taking that action almost at once, though not perhaps as Campbell expected. Knowing Davis's resolution, the secretary decided that the best way to approach him was not by direct confrontation but rather a steady accumulation of persuasions. No sooner had Campbell left his office than Breckinridge ordered the heads of each of the bureaus of the department to submit to him "a succinct but clear statement" of their current condition and an estimate of their ability to continue operations.[34] Within two days he had his responses, and they painted a portrait of disintegration, inadequate funds and resources, and insufficient manpower. It was no worse than he expected, but now he had actual statements in hand that he could use when ready. He gave them to Kean and ordered him to keep them in his personal care, separate from department files, until Breckinridge was ready to act.[35]

Meanwhile there was opinion to sound and support to build. Breckinridge visited Lee's headquarters on Valentine's Day, and two days later Lee came to the War Department. Thereafter they met frequently, and soon after their first discussion Breckinridge forthrightly asked the general for his views on the possibility and consequences of evacuating Richmond and Petersburg, and where to concentrate supplies for the retreating army. By February 25, in response to Lee's suggestions, Breckinridge was giving orders for the removal of stores to points on Lee's anticipated line of retreat, while at the same time offering advice on a concentration between Lee's army and the Confederate forces in South Carolina, now again under the command of Johnston.[36]

Breckinridge also continued meeting with Campbell, who gave him advice on February 23 for the evacuation of Richmond itself, raising the questions of where the government should relocate in such an event, what to do with official archives, what transportation to have available, and the other resources needed for an orderly removal.[37] Two days later Breckinridge ordered the heads of all his bureaus to prepare their offices for evacuation at a few hours' notice, at the same time actually commencing the removal of commissary stores from the capital, and a day or two after that met again with Lee. Expecting to have at least another ten days before Richmond would have to be abandoned, Breckinridge wanted to be prepared for less.[38] On February 25, during a cabinet meeting, he brought up for the first time the subject of evacuating Richmond. Davis refused to discuss it, but at least Breckinridge got it on the table. Meanwhile, even without the president's involvement or permission, the secretary already had plans for the eventuality well under way. He warned friends in his old department of southwest Virginia, the line of Lee's anticipated retreat, that their region might "soon become of vast importance," though cautioning that "I cannot say more now."[39]

Finally on February 26 or 27, Davis relented enough to meet with Lee and Breckinridge to discuss evacuation if it became necessary, of which Lee and Breckinridge were long since convinced. At this same meeting yet another peace plan proposal came forth in a rather bizarre suggestion from a Union general in the army facing Lee that there should be a cease-fire during which officers and their wives would call on each other between the lines. Presumably it based its hopes on the prewar fraternity between the families of many of the opposing commanders, thinking that somehow out of their renewing acquaintances they would be less willing to continue fighting each other. Meanwhile their generals-in-chief should conduct discussions looking toward a military surrender short of defeat that might lead to a general peace. Breckinridge thought the idea at least worth an effort, not so much out of hope for any direct result but rather because it would keep alive the basic idea of a negotiated peace and honorable ultimate surrender. Davis expressed little hope, and proved to be right when he allowed the generals to go ahead and try to no avail, but it served his purpose in giving him yet another example of Yankee recalcitrance to publicize. Lee himself left the conference all but shaking his head at the president's "remarkable faith in the possibility of still winning our independence."[40]

At least Davis did not stop Breckinridge from getting all the departments, not just his own, started on the sorting and boxing of nonessential records for shipment to safety—in itself a tacit admission that at some point Richmond *might* have to be abandoned—and that was a beginning.[41] But the secretary of war and Lee did not give up. They continued meeting frequently, and spent March 4 closeted in Breckinridge's office for several hours while Lincoln was being inaugurated for his second term. Lee expected Grant to open a new offensive any day now, and confessed that his depleted army could not stop the Federals from completing their encirclement of Richmond and Petersburg. If the enemy reached and cut the last available lines of escape—the Southside and the Richmond and Danville Railroads—then even if the army withdrew from its trenches and retreated, the government would be cut off and trapped.[42]

Now, too, the general and the secretary stepped entirely out of the bounds of their positions and into the realm of politics. Breckinridge's office had been an almost daily gathering place for Richmond politicians ever since he took over. Every morning several members of Congress, many of them old friends, came for what a War Office clerk called an "audience" with the secretary of war.[43] Even though Breckinridge, at forty-four, was the youngest cabinet minister to serve on either side during the war, still the graying heads of senior statesmen looked to him now to gain the president's support for their bills, while a growing number of them sought his aid in their own efforts toward peace. Very likely with their encouragement, he and Lee discussed an attempt of their own to get the machinery of negotiation rolling, this time looking to the Senate to initiate an effort that, if strongly supported, Davis might not be able to kill even by veto. It was nothing less than a scheme for Lee and Breckinridge to collude with the peace forces, to take "the responsibility of action."

Chapter Two

"LET IT NOT END
IN A FARCE"

L ee and Breckinridge chose their target well, or so it seemed. Virginia's was easily the most powerful and influential of the state delegations in Congress, and its de facto head was Senator Hunter. Moreover, though certainly associated with the peace movement, he had been very careful—deceptively so, some would have said—to distance himself from the outspoken Davis opposition. Thus, a proposition for renewed negotiations coming from him would not be dismissed automatically as just another blow aimed at Davis. It would at least get a full and fair hearing, and that was all Breckinridge and Lee needed for their plan to work. Lee called on Hunter first almost immediately after the March 4 conference with the secretary of war. He urged that if the Hampton Roads conference left Hunter with any hope that they could get better terms now than would be available if later forced to surrender at the enemy's discretion, then as one of the most influential men in Congress, and a leader in the peace movement, it was the senator's duty to make every effort necessary. It was more than a hint, for Lee forthrightly said that Hunter should initiate appropriate resolutions in the Senate. Without actually saying so, Lee made it clear to Hunter that he believed there was no hope of saving the cause. Then Lee offered the stratagem devised between himself and Breckinridge. He believed that if he, as general-in-chief, were publicly to recommend and endorse opening peace negotiations, then the armies and the people who so revered him would regard it as "almost equivalent to surrender."

In the most benign sort of "coup," Lee and Breckinridge would be using Lee's overwhelming prestige with the military and the people at large, not to overthrow their constitutional chief executive or in any way violate their oaths of office but to force Davis toward a desired end. It was simple, audacious, and would accomplish its goal not at gunpoint but through the power of public opinion. Soon afterward Breckinridge also called on Hunter, reiterating almost word for word Lee's entreaty—to the point that the senator suspected the two were working together. It might have worked, but Hunter refused to get involved, pleading that he was too wrapped up in a petty squabble of his own with Davis and would risk compromising his honor by participating in a scheme that his own enemies might attribute to spite.[1] It was the sort of response that might have been expected from a man whose whole Confederate career had been aimed at his own advancement without taking risks. In addition, one clerk in the War Department had noted already that Hunter did not seem overfriendly toward Breckinridge, and speculated that the senator saw in the secretary "a formidable rival for the *succession*—if there should be such a thing."[2] Obviously, if Breckinridge had his way, there would definitely be no succession, and thus if he cooperated Hunter would be cursing his own chances to be a future president, miniscule though they were. Unfortunately, Hunter was the best hope for success with the scheme, and his refusal effectively derailed the plan, though neither the secretary of war nor his general were ready to give up.

Instead they returned to the kind of more subtle persuasion that Breckinridge commenced when he called for the reports from his bureau chiefs. The day after his long conference with Lee, Breckinridge received a lengthy confidential letter from Campbell, one that the secretary may actually have solicited himself, just as he had sought his assistant secretary's views from the outset. Campbell said nothing he had not said before. The South's bid for independence was doomed, "but it is not necessary that she should be destroyed," he argued. He reiterated his plea for negotiating with the North on the basis of reunion and acceptance of emancipation, fearing that if they attempted to continue the fight, it must inevitably degenerate into a futile effort by partisan bands that could be as much a threat to their own people as to the Yankees. Then he suggested a means to accomplish much the same thing as Breckinridge and Lee's scheme, but by slightly different methods. If Breckinridge, in his official capacity as secretary of war, were to call on Lee for a formal statement of his views of his situation and prospects, and for his recommendations for remedy, if any, the general would have no choice but to obey. As if any hint were needed as to what

Campbell hoped Lee would say, he attached with his letter his own memoranda on the Hampton Roads conference, detailing Lincoln's few basic requirements for peace. Campbell hoped that Breckinridge could then get the president to put Lee's report and recommendations before Congress.[3]

That last, of course, was highly unlikely, for Davis had a history of withholding from Congress documents that he found offensive or contrary to his purposes, but Breckinridge knew without being told that it would be easy to notify a few sympathetic members of Lee's response and have them then enter on the floor of the House and Senate calls for Davis to turn it over, calls that he could not constitutionally refuse. That would be all that was needed to get Lee's views before the public, and if he forthrightly recommended opening negotiations as he hinted to Hunter, then their purpose might be achieved after all. On March 6 or 7 Breckinridge met again with Lee and discussed Campbell's suggestion. Seeing that it fit perfectly into the overall concept of their original scheme, they agreed that Breckinridge would formally call on Lee for such a report.

On March 8 the secretary of war addressed to him a short confidential note. "Since I assumed the control of the War Department," he said, "a more extended knowledge has convinced me that our condition is full of peril, and that it demands united counsels and prompt action." In language meant for Congress's consumption and not Lee's, Breckinridge suggested that if the legislature was not fully advised of the military situation—and his statement implied a belief that it was not—it ought to be "in order that its wisdom may co-operate in advising whatever further measures shall seem necessary to rescue the Confederacy from its present danger." Perhaps purposely he did not distinguish just what the danger he spoke of was, whether simply the prospect of defeat of the cause, or the possible forfeiture of property and rights, perhaps even liberty, if a vengeful Union were forced to conquer them in detail. Hidden within those words, "whatever further measures shall seem necessary," was the possibility of pressing for a negotiated surrender short of defeat. Breckinridge closed by promising that he would put Lee's report, accompanied by his own commentary, before Davis for him to communicate to Congress if he saw fit. The timing was crucial, for Congress expected to adjourn in just three days, but this, too, suited the secretary's purpose, for Lee's report coming before them at the last minute, whether submitted by Davis or demanded by a floor resolution, would ensure that it received full and undivided attention, as well as maximum publicity.[4]

Lee received the note that evening and immediately began his reply, having had plenty of time to reflect on what he would say. It did not go off to Richmond until the following morning, where Fannie Miller waited with her pen to copy it in spite of her shock at its content. Unfortunately, Breckinridge may have been shocked, too. Lee's letter was full of anticipated declarations that suggested hopelessness, but in almost every instance he stopped just short of categorically protesting that all was lost. He even said that while the abandonment of Richmond was a possibility, he did not think it necessarily fatal to their cause. Yet then he wavered back again, and went on to assert that their perilous situation was nothing worse than should have been anticipated from the beginning given their inferiority in manpower and resources. In fact, they had already forestalled what he called "the legitimate military consequences" of Yankee superiority longer than could have been expected. That easily read to mean that he thought Union military victory inevitable, but now he did not say so as he had said to Hunter.

And instead of calling in his own words for the opening of peace negotiations, he skirted the edges of that, too. Rather, everything depended on the sentiment of the people, he said, concluding that "their representatives can best decide how they will bear the difficulties and sufferings of their condition and how they will respond to the demands which the public safety requires."[5] For a military man supposedly unschooled in the ways of politics, Lee demonstrated that he could imply everything while saying nothing just as well as the most practiced candidate on the stump. Did "public safety" mean continued Confederate independence—which he implicitly suggested could be hopeless, and otherwise had admitted to be the case—or did it mean what was best for the Southern people in the long run, after Confederate defeat? Did his reference to the current sufferings of the people and to future demands on them imply that he believed they had taken all they could stand, and could endure no more? And how were their representatives to "decide" what was best for them? Congress could not of itself take an affirmative decision to make the war continue any longer, for it had not the power to create additional men or raise more money from a South already depleted of both. In fact, in this instance, arguably the only "decision" that Congress had the power to make was one in the negative, to end the war by calling for peace talks.

Still Lee's failure to come out and forthrightly say so seriously blunted the intended effect of his report. In the end, the old warrior simply could not bring himself to recommend surrender, despite his private convictions. That same day, the Senate finally approved a bill realizing what Breckinridge had advocated more than a year before, authorizing the enlistment of enslaved blacks as Southern soldiers, suddenly opening the door, at least hypothetically, on tens of thousands of fresh men who might fight in return for their freedom. Scattered forces in North Carolina were starting to concentrate on building a substantial army under Johnston once more, and Lee already envisioned a junction of his army and Johnston's, which could create a command numbering upwards of eighty thousand, almost equal to either Grant's or Sherman's. He would still face a massive but weary army under Grant, to his rear, and another led by Sherman, at his front, but so long as they did not combine themselves, he could hope to defeat one first, and then turn to face the other. The Virginian had pulled rabbits out of his hat for so long that he could hardly help thinking he might do it one more time. As a result, in the constant inner war between an intellect that told him he was beaten and a heart that never countenanced defeat, he found himself in the end caught between the lines.

Lee handed in a report that now fell short of the impact that the secretary of war hoped it would have. Robert Kean in the Bureau of War complained that Lee's reply was "cautious," while even Davis's private secretary, Burton Harrison, observed that the general was acting "very cautiously." Campbell simply concluded that Lee "declined to do more than perform his military duty and would not assume to counsel much less to act upon the question of peace."[6] That meant Breckinridge must act on his own to strengthen it himself. He called on his department heads for a new statement of their condition and got, as he expected, an even gloomier response than the last time. He attached these to Lee's letter and covered it all with his own assessment. Three weeks earlier, just ten days after taking office, he had warned Davis that "it is plainly impracticable for this Department to carry on any of its operations under such a condition of things."[7] Now he let the accompanying documents make that same case, but stopped short himself of recommending peace, very likely because attaching such an expression might prevent Davis from forwarding it all to Congress. Breckinridge spent almost all day Sunday, March 12, closeted with Davis and Benjamin, and the next day he returned to the president's office to hand him the package of reports. Most likely in person, as he did for his commentary on Lee's letter, he simply added that he concurred with Lee's sentiments and recommended that it all be laid before the legislature before it adjourned.[8]

This could still accomplish his purpose, though by this time Breckinridge must have been wearying of the seemingly endless machinations as he tried to usher chief executive and Congress toward a constitutional, and therefore honorable, solution to the crisis. It was no secret that what Kean called "a large part of Congress" felt fed up with Davis's management and wanted him to make a new overture to the Union to get peace on better terms now than they could expect later. Unfortunately, like Hunter, no one in the Senate either had the courage to make the proposal or felt confident that Davis and Benjamin would deal with any such move effectively, or even in good faith.[9] But the secretary of war was not beaten yet.

When Davis saw the bundle of reports handed him by Breckinridge, he accepted them at face value and ironically may even have welcomed them. Having seen both the failure of the Hampton Roads conference and the abortive generals-and-wives armistice result in brief surges of war spirit, in large part through his own engineering, he may have hoped that instead of inspiring gloom, these reports could serve to awaken Congress and the people to the new sacrifices necessary for victory. As a result, he sent a message to Congress as soon as his meeting with Breckinridge concluded, asking it to postpone its adjournment. "Our country is now environed with perils which it is our duty calmly to contemplate," he told them, but added that he was convinced they could still overcome the danger and win their independence. Indeed, he raised the specter of virtual slavery for themselves if they gave up. However, instead of actually presenting Lee's letter and the other reports in his message, he simply paraphrased their content and then put his own best interpretation on them, considerably dampening their effect. He got his postponement until March 18, but only so that Congress could act on more of his measures for continuing the fight. In a separate brief message received in the Senate the following day, Davis actually did send the package of reports but commented only that, with reference to what he said in his lengthy earlier message, Lee's letter dealt with "a contingency which, if it should occur, must seriously affect the opinions which I then expressed." Unfortunately, in his message Davis had so irritated Congress by chiding them for laxity and failure to meet his expectations, they devoted much of the remaining few days to drafting lengthy rejoinders redirecting toward Davis responsibility for current embarrassments. In the process, the message containing Breckinridge's package was tabled with no sign that it would be taken up before they adjourned. It was another round to Davis.[10]

The only hope now was to get someone in the Senate, whose charge included diplomatic affairs, to bring the reports to the floor and demand their publication, or else introduce resolutions to call on Lincoln for terms. Campbell had tried to put some backbone into Hunter and others, but none would take a chance, yet Breckinridge was ready to try one more time. A couple of nights after Davis sent the papers to the Senate, the secretary of war convened a meeting in the Richmond hotel room of Henry Burnett, of Kentucky. Hunter and Allen Caperton, of Virginia, were there, Louis T. Wigfall, of Texas, and two Missourians, George G. Vest and Waldo Johnson. All six of them were senators, yet with only fifteen members of the Senate remaining in Richmond despite the postponed adjournment, they represented a powerful bloc, and there were at least three or four others not present who were known to be favorable toward a peace overture.

Once they assembled, Breckinridge addressed them briefly, asserting frankly the conviction that the Confederacy was doomed and might indeed even now be in its last days. Then he turned his remarks to the representatives from Missouri and Kentucky. "If the Confederacy goes to pieces and our armies are disbanded without any formal action on the part of the Confederate Government, the soldiers from the cotton States and from that portion of our territory not occupied by the enemy will go to their homes and probably remain there unmolested," he said. But the Missourians and Kentuckians in uniform would be far from their homes and largely cut off by Yankee armies. Moreover, since both states had remained in the Union, those soldiers might meet a hostile reception if they did get home, especially in Kentucky, whose legislature had made service in Confederate arms a felony. He feared to speculate, he said, what proscriptions might await them if their rights were not guaranteed beforehand by a general and binding agreement with Washington.

It was an entirely new tack, as Breckinridge hoped now to induce those senators to take action before the adjournment, in order to protect their own fellow citizens, if they were not willing to do it for the country at large. "Our first duty, gentlemen, is to the soldiers who have been influenced by our arguments and example, and we should make any and every sacrifice to protect them," he argued. "What I propose," he said, "is this: That the Confederacy should not be captured in fragments, that we should not disband like banditti, but that we should surrender as a government, and we will thus maintain the dignity of our cause, and secure the respect of our enemies, and the best terms for our soldiers." He well knew that there were some top leaders like himself who ran serious risks by surrendering. Just two months earlier the Union general assembly in Tennessee had passed a joint resolution that Davis, Benjamin, Lee, and others, including himself, should be executed if captured, and there were indictments against him for treason in several other states, including his own Kentucky.[11] Nevertheless, he said, "I am willing to assume the risk, and to surrender as Secretary of War," though he confessed concern for Davis, whom he knew would not be willing to escape the country and would very likely face a rope if taken alive. But that was an issue that could wait. Now it was urgent that they do something, and it was in their power to do it, for their soldiers if not for their country. "This has been a magnificent epic," he declared, imploring them to "in God's name let it not terminate in a farce."[12]

Still, not one would act. Congress, it seemed, had been bested so often by Davis that it no longer had the spirit or will to stand up to him. Moreover, seeing the end coming, many a representative had already left, while others departed every day,

even before the end of the session, hoping to escape being captured with Richmond. Whereas before March 18 there were a
dozen or more influential men in the capital to form the loosely
knit cadre that the Kentuckian had hoped to use to overcome
the president and achieve a surrender before active campaigning commenced anew, after the adjournment there was only
himself. Though the forces in North Carolina had already met
in smaller engagements a week before, and more were surely on
the way, Breckinridge recognized that by now for most of the
people of the Confederacy, Lee and his Army of Northern Virginia really symbolized the cause, just as Richmond represented
its four years of determination to hold out. The blow from the
loss of their capital would be great enough. But if Lee, who had
brought them most of their great victories and who embodied all
of their hopes, were to have surrendered, Southern morale could
not have survived the blow. As soon as Lee started fighting
again, however, it would raise expectations, making it all the
more difficult to force Davis to accept the inevitable, even as it
lessened their chances of anything other than a surrender at Yankee discretion. This winter, indeed these seven weeks since
Breckinridge took office, had offered a small window of opportunity for the best terms they could hope to get, but Davis's
domination and congressional cravenness had managed to keep
it shut.

Breckinridge, however disheartened, kept his disappointment to himself and kept trying, but events were about to take
over, as he feared they would. The very afternoon of the day
that Congress adjourned, Breckinridge went to Lee's headquarters and remained for two days, then returned again for more
talks two days later.[13] Their discussions they kept private, but

they must have taken a fresh look at their situation in the wake of the Senate's failure in their program. Davis's strident opposition at this stage felt that only a palace coup could solve the problem, but Lee and Breckinridge were constitutional democrats to their core, and it is unlikely that either would have countenanced even speculating in that direction. Besides, to use the army to seize power from Davis would hardly help them in securing terms, for the Yankees would naturally then regard themselves as dealing with insurgents within an insurgency, with even less legitimacy than the existing government. Besides, such an act would propel the country toward that farce that the secretary so dreaded.

Nevertheless, it was readily apparent that Congress's failure made the army now their best hope, not for victory or extended life, but for the kind of peace they wanted. If Lee simply stayed in his trenches until surrounded and starved or battered into submission, it would be a part of that piecemeal conquest that Breckinridge predicted would only rob their cause of dignity and diminish their hopes for an honorable peace. However, now that spring weather made renewed campaigning and a push by Grant to overwhelm them inevitable, they needed to keep Lee's army alive and actively in the field. Richmond was doomed; all objectively knew that now—even Davis, though he could hardly admit it. If Lee could hold Grant at bay long enough to get the government's essential impedimenta out of the city, and as much in the way of materiel and supplies as possible, then he could pull out of his lines, head southwest, and try to make that junction with Johnston. There was no hope of winning overall victory, of course, but having one large army, or even the two smaller ones operating in the field and still presenting at least something of a threat, would give the Confederacy a stronger hand for terms if Breckinridge could find another constituency to back him in forcing Davis to the table, and the secretary already had that new backing in mind. Johnston, meanwhile, had assembled his now small Army of Tennessee, and on March 19, while Breckinridge and Lee met, he actually achieved a minor success at Bentonville, North Carolina, though he could do nothing definitive against heavy odds to stop Sherman. But at least he was in the field. That could be enough. They could still surrender as a nation with their tattered banners flying freely rather than face reconstruction as conquered prisoners of war.

That put the responsibility in Lee's hands now, and he took it. Five days after concluding his two-day meeting with Breckinridge, he organized and launched a substantial assault intended to break through Grant's encircling line at Petersburg and force him to pull one wing back to keep his own army together, at the same time relieving pressure sufficiently for Lee to take part of his army to reinforce Johnston and attempt to best Sherman before returning to deal with Grant again. The whole plan was desperate, but so was their situation, and Lee as much as admitted that it had only scant chance for success. Yet his initial attack almost succeeded before he encountered resistance that he simply had not the strength to push aside. Lee wired the news to the War Department at once, and when Breckinridge read it, he knew the message's import. The effort having failed, they could do nothing now to prevent Grant's steady drive to close off their last line of retreat out of Richmond. "Something must be done soon," the secretary told Gorgas when he read the telegram.[14]

Every day now, as clerks like Fannie Miller scratched away with their pens, they did so amid the packing of books and papers into crates for shipment west. "It never occurred to my happy, hopeful heart," she said, "that a move of Grant was anticipated or that Richmond would fall."[15] If so, then the teenager was almost alone in the capital, for practically everyone else knew or feared what was coming. All through the city people hung red flags from their windows, signifying that they had furniture to sell or houses to rent, signs of their intention to leave.[16] Cabinet ministers, perhaps including Breckinridge, packed what they could, to be ready. Perhaps only Davis refused to prepare for what he did not wish to admit was coming. Instead, he made himself seen about the city, riding out to the army camps or through the streets of town, leaving the citizens marveling at his apparent cheerfulness.[17] It was, to a degree, a pose for effect but reflected, too, a sort of serenity in a man who had made an all-consuming commitment and decision, and for whom there were no troubling doubts. "We are fighting for Independence," he had said earlier, "and that, or extermination, we *will* have." There could never be reunion, he maintained, for hatred and bitterness between North and South were now cemented in the soil of both by the congealed blood of hundreds of thousands of the slain. "Our children may forget this war," he said, "but *we* cannot." Rather, "now it must go on till the last man of this generation falls in his tracks, and his children seize his musket and fight our battle."[18]

Though Davis's talk of annihilation rather than submission was largely just rhetoric to stiffen public resolve, he certainly had death before dishonor on his mind. He told his wife, Varina, to pack for herself and their children, and detailed his private secretary, Burton Harrison, to accompany her on a train out of Richmond on March 31. Before she left he gave her a pistol and instructed her in its use. If she should be in danger of falling into Yankee hands, he said, he wanted her to use it to "force your assailants to kill you" before she suffered the humiliation of capture or worse. He may even have intended that she use it on herself. When he took her to the train depot that last night, he did not conceal his own fatalistic conviction. "If I live you can come to me when the struggle is ended," he said through his tears, "but I do not expect to survive."[19] Among the few officials remaining in Richmond by the end of the month, the common expectation was that when the collapse came, Davis would not flee the country, just as Breckinridge had warned, but that he would somehow try to get to Texas and continue the war with the scattered Confederate forces west of the Mississippi.[20]

Some determined to stay in Richmond and accept its fate. Indeed, Campbell hoped that by allowing himself to come under Yankee authority, he might yet be able to help with the inevitable peace. He met with Breckinridge now and told him that he would remain and attempt to see Lincoln himself. Interestingly, he also asked the secretary of war for permission to speak on behalf of the Confederacy regarding peace terms. Only Davis or Congress had authority to grant that, of course, but it is significant that Campbell sought it not from the president, who would never have granted it in any case, but from Breckinridge. The Kentuckian realized the official limitations of his position well enough to know that he could not formally grant such power to Campbell, but neither did he forbid his assistant from making the attempt. Campbell showed him a draft he had prepared for peace term proposals—the same suggestions he had made weeks before—and again Breckinridge did not try to deter him from presenting them to the Yankees. Any talks with Lincoln, whether sanctioned by Confederate authority or not, had the chance at least of being helpful.[21]

Meanwhile Breckinridge began to pursue that other avenue toward peace that he hit upon. It was no secret that some of the states felt disenchanted with Davis and his administration, and had for some time. Back in the fall of 1864 there were rumors that Governor Joseph Brown, of Georgia, toyed with making a separate peace with Sherman in order to save his state, and though he declined to enter negotiations with the Yankees, still Brown's antagonism to Davis and stiff-necked insistence on Georgia's sovereignty put spine into other governors who believed the president assumed too much power for himself. Among the more vocal was Zebulon Vance, of North Carolina. His state was slow to secede, with a heavy Union sentiment in its western counties, and the subsequent conduct of the war, during which North Carolina raised more regiments than any other state, only to see Richmond siphon most of them to Virginia and elsewhere instead of aggressively defending their own state, left thousands of Carolinians even more disaffected.

By 1865 one of the leaders of the admittedly spineless peace movement in Richmond was North Carolina Senator William A. Graham. He had suggested to Campbell and Breckinridge during the days of the abortive Senate scheme that his state's legislature might be in a mood to take action in calling for peace discussions.[22] Of course, eleven states had seceded all told, but of that number Texas and Arkansas were isolated and all but out of communication, being west of the Mississippi, while Louisiana, Tennessee, Mississippi, and now South Carolina were almost completely occupied by the Yankees and no longer had effective state governments in operation, and Georgia was badly overrun. The fall of Richmond would put Virginia's government either out of business or on the run as well, which left only three scattered states—Alabama, Florida, and North Carolina—with fully functioning governments. As the largest and most territorially intact by far of those three, Vance's state suddenly assumed an importance far beyond anything in its previous Confederate history, especially if Lee and Johnston made their junction and North Carolina were to become the new battleground. Thus a call for negotiations from its assembly could have a decisive impact on peace hopes.

In fact, when Vance heard of the package of reports and Lee's March 9 letter that Breckinridge turned over to Davis, he contacted the secretary at once, thinking that it signified the inauguration of the peace movement that Breckinridge himself had hoped to launch. The Kentuckian sadly apprised him of the reality, including Davis's failure to make any comment or positive recommendation based on the papers when he turned them over to Congress. "His published message embraces all that has occurred touching the question of peace," Breckinridge advised. Then, without specifying any particular topic on his mind, he closed by telling Vance that "I shall be happy to hear from you at any time and will be pleased to confer fully." The context of the rest of the letter made quite clear what he was hoping to discuss.[23] Vance himself was not of a mind to take any sort of lead in a peace movement, having recently won his office on a platform of unyielding resistance to the enemy. Still, Graham's report to him of conditions in Richmond and of the expressions by Lee and others of hopelessness were hard to ignore. Graham urged Vance to convene the legislature. Though he, too, saw the inevitable coming, Vance agreed to do nothing more than discuss the matter with his advisory council. When they met they were so divided that no consensus emerged, and thus the governor would not call the legislature. All he would do for the moment was to prepare his state capital for an evacuation of its own if necessary.[24] If Vance had any doubts that the war was coming to his doorstep, Breckinridge dispelled them at the end of the month when he advised the governor to have the track gauges on North Carolina's railroads adjusted to match those of Virginia so that "in the event of disaster" the government could run all of the Virginia rolling stock south.[25]

Vance would take persuasion, but for the moment there was no more time. Saturday, April 1 saw the people of the city, as usual, seizing on any pretext to inject some gaiety into their lives, and now indulging in April Fool's Day jokes.[26] Unfortunately, there was no joke in the dispatch Breckinridge received from Lee that evening. The Yankees had pushed him out of Five Forks, west of Petersburg, making the Southside Railroad untenable and reducing Richmond itself to the single line of the Danville Railroad, which now stood in danger of being cut by Yankee cavalry raiders. He could not hold out more than a matter of hours, rather than days, now. Lee asked to meet with Breckinridge and/or Davis to determine his course, and probably took time for a brief visit late that night.[27]

In Richmond there were almost no government officials left but Davis and the cabinet, and of the latter only the secretaries of war and the navy were still actually functioning, while the others simply attended to their packing. Mallory spent some of the day pacing on the pavement outside his home, a pistol in his hand, quite probably practicing in case he had to use it against

Yankees before long.[28] The president himself and his aides William Preston Johnston, Francis Lubbock, and John Taylor Wood were otherwise alone in the executive mansion on East Clay Street, surrounded by remnants of furniture and the several boxes of Davis's papers that Harrison had packed for him before leaving with Varina and the children.[29] Outside in the streets of the city the news of the loss of Five Forks sent a shock through the people, for everyone understood what it meant. Breckinridge spent most of the day at the War Department, alternately dealing with incoming telegrams, calling out the city's reserves to assume places in the defenses as Lee was forced to withdraw portions of his command to cover other threats, and himself taking a hand at packing the department's remaining archives in crates. During the evening Admiral Raphael Semmes, the now beached commander of the once notorious commerce raider CSS *Alabama*, joined him, as did a government clerk, W. H. Swallow, and together they passed the hours well into the night at their packing, each taking a hand at nailing the tops securely on the wooden boxes, and marking them for shipment.

When they finished, Breckinridge and the others walked over to the State Department offices and there found Benjamin, seemingly as imperturbable and cheerful as always, sitting atop a crate of his own records and singing a silly ballad of his own earlier composition titled "The Exit from Shocko Hill." It was, quite literally, graveyard humor, since their building on Franklin Street was in fact only a few blocks' walk from Shockoe Hill, site of the city hospital and one of its older graveyards. The aptness of the song's title seemed in rather poor taste. General Samuel Cooper, the adjutant and inspector general of the army, and thus its chief record keeper, came in and felt outraged at Benjamin's poor taste. "Nero fiddled while Rome was burning," he chided the secretary of state, but Benjamin only stopped singing in order to start whistling the tune instead, and the incensed Cooper walked out.[30] As the deathwatch continued into the night, none wanted to admit that by now there was nothing they could do but fiddle and wait for the burning to come.

Breckinridge went to an early service at the Broad Street Methodist Church the next morning, and while there he received the first in a series of telegrams from Lee intimating that this would likely be the last day he could hold his line.[31] At once he went to the War Department to await further news, but when the telegraph wires went silent for some time to come it seemed an evil portent to all. Benjamin, as well as Kean, Lubbock, and others, joined him at times in the vigil, and Reagan and Campbell stopped in on their way to church.[32] Then at 10:40 A.M. came the word that Lee must abandon his defenses that night, and perhaps even sooner. They had to get out of Richmond immediately, while Lee would try to pull his army back along the line of the Danville Railroad north of the Appomattox River.[33] At once Breckinridge sent a copy of the telegram by clerk to the president.

Davis had his own pew at St. Paul's Episcopal Church on Ninth Street. He was especially close to the Rev. Charles Minnegerode, who had recently helped him with his conversion and commitment to the church and was now in the pulpit, having finished his sermon, delivering a communion address prior to administering the sacrament. As he spoke, the church sexton, a pompous old fellow who wore an outmoded ruffled shirt beneath his fading blue suit, walked up the aisle from the back of the congregation. They had all seen him do this many times before; he enjoyed calling attention to himself as he delivered a message to someone during a service. Now he strutted with added pomp because he carried a note for the president. Stepping up behind Davis's pew, the sexton reached out and touched him gently on the shoulder to gain his attention, then handed him Lee's message, whispering in his ear that it came from Breckinridge.

At once all eyes in the church focused on Davis as he read. With that iron will that had characterized him for years, Davis did not let his face betray an inkling of the contents, though some thought he paled behind the impassive mask. Quietly, without disturbing Minnegerode as he spoke, Davis arose and followed the sexton back up the aisle and left the church. Nevertheless, all eyes followed him as he departed, and at least some maintained they knew then that something was dreadfully wrong. When the sexton returned a few minutes later and drew General Cooper out of the congregation, and soon came down the aisle yet again to call out another member of the government, then summoned two more, including Campbell, whispering broke out all through the congregation. Before long, and despite Minnegerode's attempts to keep them seated, they rose in groups of ten and twenty and simply walked out. On the porch of the church they gathered in a throng that spilled out onto the corner at Ninth Street, where they stood almost silently, staring across Grace Street at the Central Hotel, now the offices of the Confederate auditors. Piled in the street in front of the building were heaps of government documents being consumed in flames. No one had to tell them what that meant. Quietly, with neither expression of surprise nor despair, the crowd simply melted away.[34]

Davis and his aide Lubbock quickly walked across the capitol square, along the way meeting Reagan, who had gone looking for him. Once he reached his office Davis summoned all of the other cabinet ministers, as well as Governor William Smith and Mayor John Mayo. Before noon all assembled except the attorney general, George Davis, who had gone to a different church from his usual and could not be found. Mallory encountered Benjamin on the street as they approached, smiling as always, cigar in his mouth, twirling his gold-headed cane in his fingers as if he had not a care in the world. To himself Mallory thought the secretary of state rather like "the last man outside the ark, who assured Noah of his belief that 'it would not be such a h-ll of a shower, after all'." But it was bravado, for Mallory could see well enough that Benjamin was already shaken by the news, which had spread quickly.[35]

Without the informal conversation and reminiscences with which the president usually opened his cabinet sessions, he simply read Lee's latest telegram. It spoke for itself. That done, Davis told them to pack their remaining vital archives and prepare to be evacuated. They must also get the $500,000 or more of actual coin in the Treasury out of the city, and with it the deposits from the Virginia banks as well. Not being formally in the national service, the home guard and local reserves would stay behind to prevent looting and maintain some order after the evacuation. Mallory volunteered as escort and guard for the money the company of midshipmen forming the small Confederate Naval Academy, then quartered in a Richmond warehouse when not aboard their school ship *Patrick Henry*. That vessel, like the rest of Semmes's James River fleet, would have to be destroyed, and since the boys were actually sworn into Confederate service, unlike the locals, they were still under Mallory's orders. Before the meeting broke up, Mallory sent an order to their commander, Captain William H. Parker, to have his company waiting at the Danville depot by 6 P.M. There was no talk, at least in front of Davis, about this signifying the end of the cause. Rather, they assumed that the plan now was for Lee to make a junction with Johnston to continue the war. Thus when he turned the meeting over to Breckinridge, who either at Davis's request or simply by common assumption was to manage the evacuation, there was no talk of the leaders leaving the country. They would only move the government to some safer locale.[36]

Before the meeting assembled Breckinridge was already planning how to get them all away. In answer to his inquiry, Lee had assured him that he thought he could keep the enemy away from the Danville Railroad for the balance of the day, thus the secretary told the president and cabinet that he would have transportation for them at the Danville depot, ready to depart at 8 P.M. That done, as the others dispersed to pack or burn their remaining records, Breckinridge went back to the War Department to speed the final packing. Kean and others spent the balance of the daylight hours sending the boxes to the depot, sometimes even carrying bundles themselves, or organizing wagon trains to leave Richmond with the less vital archives and baggage. Fannie Miller met Kean on the street, and finding his arms loaded with as much as he could carry and tears filling his eyes, she asked him if as an employee she should join them in their flight. "I cannot advise a lady to follow a fugitive government," he told her sadly, then hurried on toward the depot. With nothing else to do, she went home and sat in her front window to watch the growing pandemonium outside as all of Richmond, it seemed, filled the streets, preparing to leave.[37]

When his cabinet left him, Davis himself remained in his office for a few hours, while Lubbock and Johnston moved as much of his personal papers as they could manage over to the executive mansion for final packing in a trunk along with what they found in his home office and other rooms of the house during a final hasty survey. George Davis arrived at last after the meeting had dissolved, yet found the president calm and composed. Davis told him what had happened and sent him on his way to see to his own preparations. Davis himself did not leave the executive office building until about 5 P.M., after Breckinridge sent him word that Lee's latest dispatch indicated the Danville line would be secure until morning. Then Davis finally walked over to his home on East Clay Street and began his own packing, with little time left before the train was to leave. Soon afterward Davis's old friend Clement C. Clay of Alabama arrived, perhaps the last man actually to enter Richmond on a day when, as Clay's wife later quipped, "the trend of Confederate travel just then was in an opposite direction." Just returned from a failed diplomatic mission to Canada, Clay found the president hurriedly packing a valise with some clothing and papers, while the signs of his last-minute sorting of essentials lay scattered all about him on the floor.[38]

Breckinridge spent most of the afternoon either at the War Department, overseeing arrangements, or meeting with Mayo and General Richard Ewell and others to determine what to do with military stores in the city that could not be safely gotten away. Ewell wanted to torch all the warehouses filled with tobacco and cotton and other items that the Yankees would find useful. Indeed, he had long-standing orders from Lee to do just that, and it had been Confederate policy from early in the war. Gorgas protested the order to Breckinridge, fearing that the fires could easily spread to the rest of the city. He felt even more concern when Breckinridge gave orders that all bridges across the James River should be burned once the evacuation was completed. Mayor Mayo added his voice to the protest, and in the discussion, Breckinridge relented so far as the warehouses were concerned. "It would be a disgrace to the Confederate government to endanger the destruction of the entire city," the secretary concluded.[39] In fact, Campbell had heard no discussion at all of burning warehouses in recent days in the War Department. Besides, Gorgas had already proposed to Ewell that simply pouring turpentine on all the goods in the warehouses would effectively destroy them without resorting to fire. Unfortunately, in the confusion and rush, Breckinridge apparently did not give Ewell a positive order countermanding the standing directive, or else Ewell decided for himself that Lee's earlier order should take precedence.[40]

Breckinridge had almost no time to go to his own residence, where he and his invalid wife, Mary, shared quarters with Kentucky Congressman Eli M. Bruce. He would have to leave her behind, for she was too ill to travel. By 6 P.M. the War Department archives that could be removed were at the station, and Breckinridge himself finally left for the depot. In all the rush, Breckinridge probably forgot completely that he and Benjamin were supposed to have been the guests of honor at a dinner party that evening given by Thomas Conolly, a British member of Parliament and now owner of a blockade runner.[41] Meanwhile, the president had finished his hasty packing and then taken a last look around the executive mansion, and finally passed the time before leaving by sitting in discussion with his aides. He seemed sad but calm, and when his carriage pulled up outside around 6 P.M., he quietly stepped outside to the sidewalk, lit a cigar, and got in for the short ride to the station.[42]

The scene at the Danville depot was almost pandemonium. None of the cabinet had arrived yet when Breckinridge rode up on his horse, but Parker and his one hundred midshipmen were there, among them Breckinridge's own son, nineteen-year-old Clifton. Earlier Breckinridge gave orders that no one without a pass from him personally was to be allowed into the depot, yet already a crowd had gathered outside clamoring to be let in.[43] When Davis arrived a few minutes later, he found Breckinridge already at work overseeing final preparations for loading the two waiting trains, one for the officials and one for the Treasury. Breckinridge took the president to the car in the first train, which he had reserved for him and the rest of the cabinet, and there they conferred privately for a few minutes before Benjamin and the others arrived. The ensuing hours after the cabinet meeting had not played well on Benjamin's nerves. His hands shook when he met with the French consul that afternoon. Always smooth and urbane, now the secretary of state stumbled over himself as he tried to say and do everything at once in his panic. "I have nothing in particular to say to you," he began in a quivering voice, "but I wanted to be sure to shake your hand before my departure." Even though Benjamin assured the diplomat that the evacuation was only a prudent precaution and they might even return soon, the Frenchman discounted it all as "illusion" or "lack of sincerity," noting that both characterized the secretary of state.[44] He may have suspected as well that Benjamin, who avowedly had no other motive for the brief meeting except farewell, may have been acting in his own interest, extending a last courtesy to the representative of a foreign nation to which he might have to flee for his life if affairs continued on their current course. One thing was clear. No one in the cabinet, least of all Benjamin, was exerting any authority or taking any responsibility now, none but the secretary of war.

Breckinridge told Davis that he would remain behind to direct the rest of the evacuation. That done, he would ride west with an escort and try to reach Lee and his retreating army. Just what directions, if any, Davis gave to him they kept between themselves, but Breckinridge's intent was seemingly twofold. With the government now on the run, and possibly soon to be isolated from Lee and his army, Breckinridge would be able to confer with the general and give direct orders to facilitate the hoped-for junction with Johnston, without losing vital time having to go through Davis, wherever he might be. For Lee, Breckinridge might have to be the government for a few days. The secretary could also continue his previous discussions with Lee on the best way to seek terms, in the event that Lee reached the conclusion that he could no longer maneuver or fight the pursuing Federals without senseless waste of life. They might still have some hope for their old plan of using Lee's surrender as a catalyst to bring a general halt to the war, on some kind of favorable terms for the peace to follow. Even if Lee, as general-in-chief, could not enter into political negotiations representing the government of the Confederacy, he could at least, if he chose, direct all its armed forces to lay down their arms.

Their private conference done, Breckinridge left the president and remounted his horse, riding along the length of the trains to inspect their continued loading. He had given orders that none but members of the government and vital personnel were to be allowed aboard. The bridges across the James were still intact, and citizens who wanted to leave could do so by that route. Still, there were those who felt they must get out on the trains, and they used every means they could conceive to get aboard. Mallory looked out a window with some amusement as he saw and overheard some of the attempts made to get a seat, but the train guards remained immovable.[45] Meanwhile, 8 P.M. came and passed, but as word from Lee indicated that he felt more secure about holding his position through the night, Breckinridge delayed sending the president's train out. Instead, from time to time he rode up to Davis's car window and the two renewed their deliberations. Much of the rest of the time he spent with Captain Parker, who meanwhile watched both president and cabinet with keen interest. Davis seemed calm as usual, and Breckinridge "was as cool and gallant as ever." The rest of the officials, however, looked rather anxious to be on their way.[46] When Parker pointed out that some of his young men were poorly clothed and that there were bales of army clothing and blankets in the station just arrived that morning, which Lee would never use now, Breckinridge allowed him to equip his command from them.[47]

Finally at 10 P.M., as Lee's telegrams grew less dire and more confident, Davis left the train and Breckinridge dismounted, and they went into the office of the president of the railroad in the station, where Mallory, at least, thought they were feeling last-minute hope for better news that might cancel the evacuation. In fact, Davis and Breckinridge simply discussed with the president of the line a possible route for one of the wagon trains that was also going out of town that evening, laden with supplies intended for Lee's army somewhere on his line of retreat. By eleven o'clock, however, the word from Lee did not improve, and Breckinridge could wait no longer. He escorted Davis back to his car, said a farewell to the rest of the cabinet, and then left and remounted his horse, again riding to Davis's window. A few more words and he gave the order for the train to depart, though not before allowing one last recuperating soldier to climb atop the already overburdened train.[48] Almost at the last moment, Davis sent one of his aides back to the executive mansion to get the family spoons and forks that he had forgotten to pack. The train could not wait for him to return, so the aide and the presidential cutlery would have to ride out of the capital in company with the secretary of war.[49]

Breckinridge and Parker watched the train clank slowly off into the night, then turned their attention to the second train, for the Treasury. It took more time than anticipated to get all of the gold and silver aboard, and the slowness of the Richmond banks in getting their deposits to the depot added to the delay. Parker became somewhat apprehensive, for now the streets around the depot began to fill with the more sordid elements of capital society—the scroungers, thieves, and deserters, until then in hiding. Provosts had broken in the heads of barrels of military whiskey to keep it from getting into the hands of stragglers or civilians, but a number managed to scoop enough from the gutters to get drunk, and thus made pot-valiant they began loot-ing businesses and warehouses. Inevitably it got worse. In the distance they heard the first explosions as Semmes's crewmen destroyed or scuttled their ships. That sent panic into a crowd already made skittish by drink. Then people saw portions of Lee's army that had been in or near Richmond start marching down to the James bridges and crossing. Some of the crowds lit small fires in the streets for warmth. Others gathered around the still burning piles of government papers on Ninth Street outside St. Paul's. An ammunition magazine went up with a thunderous roar. Surrounded by fires large and small, with the concussions from explosions shaking the ground, Parker thought it seemed "as though hell itself had broken loose." Through it all, he mar-veled at Breckinridge's composure in the crisis.[50]

Finally sometime after midnight Breckinridge at last got the second train loaded, its cars bulging with people even on the end platforms and roofs. He said good-bye to his son Clifton and sent Parker and the midshipmen on their way with the treasure carefully packed and sealed in wooden crates.[51] There was still a long night ahead, as more and more of Lee's troops would pass through the city and over the bridges. Fannie Miller stayed at her window for hours after dark. "O, the horrors of that night!" she remembered, and "the rolling of vehicles, excited cries of the men, women, and children as they passed loaded with such goods as they could snatch from the burning factories and stores that were being looted by the frenzied crowds." Even society matrons were caught up in the looting, several moving about town with their expensive shawls and bed sheets filled with pil-fered shop goods. One carried a dozen large boxes of tobacco away from a warehouse to her home, and one of the wealthiest men in the city was seen scurrying up Cary Street with a bolt of red flannel under his arm. Some men in uniform, either deserters or soldiers in town on sick leave, broke into a confectioner's to steal candy. Most ran at least some risk—if not from home guard, then from shattered glass sent flying as the explosion of the magazine broke windows all over the city. Officials had prudently shut down the gas works earlier that day, but now the looters used candles or burning bundles of papers to illuminate their work. When they found what they wanted, they dropped their burning papers on the shop floors, starting more fires. "No one dared to lie down or think of sleeping," said Fannie. Over at Bruce's house, Mary Breckinridge sat in complete darkness, not having the heart to light a lamp amid the surrounding tragedy.[52] Sallie Putnam observed with disgust that "Richmond was ruled by the mob," and Kentucky cavalryman Leeland Hathaway, one of the last to board the second train, declared that "drunkenness ran riot over the city."[53]

Breckinridge was too occupied at the depot, and then supervising the last wagon trains of ordnance and more archives and matériel as they set off across the bridges, to be able to prevent Ewell from setting fire to four warehouses in the city. The officer commanding the guard placed at Mayo's bridge, which would be the last left standing, had little to do but stand his post in the cool night air and "gaze on the terrible splendor of the scene." Richmond, he said, was "like a blaze of day amid the surrounding darkness." Shortly one after another of the bridges over the James went up, until there were three of them blazing. More magazines went off, some sending scores or even hundreds of shells into the air, whistling and shrieking until they, too, exploded, while thousands of rifle cartridges went off in the flames, peppering the night with their staccato rattle.[54]

As dawn approached, what Breckinridge and Mayo and others feared came to pass. A wind rose, or perhaps the several fires scattered about the city created a draft of their own. Some thought the firing of the bridges led to what followed, but almost certainly it was the well-packed warehouses that created one huge fire that began to spread from block to block, fed by the small blazes elsewhere. By daybreak more than thirty blocks of the city were in flames, and there was nothing anyone could do to stop the conflagration. The few Confederates remaining in the city did not even try, of course. Just after sunup, with almost all Southern soldiers safely across the James and advance parties of Federals starting to enter the northern outskirts, Breckinridge met Ewell and they spoke briefly. Breckinridge looked with distress at the growing fires, surely regretting that he had not given more positive instructions forbidding Ewell to set the warehouses afire.[55] But there was no time for recriminations, and soon he left to ride to Mayo's bridge. There he waited until the Seventh South Carolina Cavalry appeared, having made a final sweep of the city for stragglers. When the Carolinians thundered south across the bridge, their commander yelled back "all over, good-bye; blow her to h-ll."[56]

The bridge guards had already set their fires when Breckinridge and his staff galloped across amid the gathering blaze. As he reached the other side, where he was joined by his adjutant Lieutenant Colonel James Wilson recently exchanged from a Yankee prison camp, Colonel Walter Taylor of Lee's staff, and a few others, Breckinridge and the rest turned their mounts and watched the disaster on the other side for a few minutes. Flames erupted from the windows of the enormous Gallego Flour Mills. The four burning bridges cast brilliant reflections on the surface of the James, while overhead a dense cloud arose, illuminated from within by the lofting flames and millions of sparks carried up in the draft.[57] It was one of the most tragically impressive sights of the war, and Breckinridge had already seen more than his share. There was no minimizing the catastrophe before him, and for the Kentuckian it was especially upsetting, for Mary was back there somewhere between the fire and the Yankees, surely safe enough, but just as certainly frightened. There was nothing for it now, however, and after a few minutes the secretary of war turned his horse's head to the west and rode off. Though now he was a general in the field again, leading a motley but growing escort of men and officers, significantly he wore not the uniform of a soldier but the black broadcloth suit he had donned when he took over the War Department, with a dark cloak thrown over his shoulders. Exercising the command of a general, he dressed as a statesman. In the days ahead he would have to be both.[58]

Chapter Three

"A Very Troublesome Elephant"

By fits and starts, at ten miles an hour, the presidential train crawled through the night toward the west. Most of the cars were densely packed with people feeling the shock of the suddenness and enormity of the last few hours. Congressman Horatio Bruce found himself stuffed into a car with a host of people who looked almost dazed with exhaustion and depression. "I never knew so little conversation indulged by so large a number of acquaintances together," he mused. Even though almost all of the fellow government minor officials and employees on the car knew everyone else, still "very few words were interchanged." Some like Bruce, in their nervous exhaustion, simply fell asleep.[1]

More than thirty men crowded the seats in the cabinet car, and yet there, too, Mallory found that "silence reigned over the fugitives." Knowing as they did that the Danville line passed perilously close to the last known position of part of Grant's encircling army, and that Yankee cavalry were out raiding in force beyond Grant's lines, everyone felt the possibility that they might be "gobbled," as the secretary of the navy put it. In fact, all of them on the train felt the absence of conversation, as each sat lost in his private thoughts. It was more than mere personal fear, which most—except perhaps Benjamin—seemed to dismiss. The sense of impending finality oppressed them. The events of the last twenty-four hours seemed to many an abrupt jolt, awakening them to the probability that the cause was truly lost. Mallory, for one, could not help thinking back on the four years of carnage and sacrifice, all now for naught. He feared that he looked himself "like a man who had done his best and been whipped." Looking about him he saw his own turmoil mirrored in the "painful images" of the others, "reflected more or less distinctly upon every face."[2]

"Heads of Departments, chief clerks, books, & records, the Adjutant General Cooper, with the materiel and personel of his office,—all the essential means for conducting the government were here," mused Mallory. To divert his own mind, he studied once more his fellow ministers. Benjamin, whom Mallory clearly never liked, seemed to have regained his good humor. He alone of them seemed in the mood for conversation, as he chewed on a sandwich and chided the others around him for their long faces. Delving into history, he reminded them of other peoples who had recovered from darker hours than this. Mallory thought that had Benjamin been a more imposing character, he might have lifted their spirits, but sitting there "in form and feature, and expression, so jolly, the very picture of contentment, smiling sweetly," he failed to inspire, especially when he jovially spoke of his economy in recent months and boastfully pointed out that the coat and trousers he wore had once been an old but commodious shawl. Behind the pose, however, Mallory could not help but notice the flushed complexion that gave evidence of Benjamin's inner agitation, nor the incessant nervous fiddling with an ornament on his watch chain. Some thought that Benjamin looked not like a man resolved to see this cause through to the end but rather one who would soon be looking out for himself.

John Reagan seemed another matter. Mallory thought that their country could not boast of a man of greater heart or more conscientious dedication to his post, and regarded him as a man of wisdom and ability, faculties that belied the careless, almost slovenly appearance of the old Texas Indian fighter as he chewed a plug and with his pocketknife whittled little figures out of sticks. "Silent & sombre, his eyes as bright & glistening as beads," the postmaster general made no effort to conceal his anxiety. Recent Yankee penetrations everywhere in the Confederacy had so disrupted his mail service that there was little left of his once ingenious postal system but his clerks and his account books. Moreover, he viewed events with the undeluded fatalism of the frontiersman, and he knew well enough what likely lay ahead. Reagan himself confessed that his sorrow in that hour was oppressive.[3] Now, his jaw grinding away at the tobacco in his cheek, he sometimes gazed out the window or around the car, yet seemed to see nothing, meanwhile attacking stick after stick, with no attempt to fashion anything at all, but rather slivering each down to nothing before taking up the next.

Poor George Trenholm had to lie down across a seat much of the time, suffering from neuralgia and some internal complaint for which the morphine that he took only made him sicker. His wife, Anna, accompanied him as nurse, the only woman on the car.[4] Given his preference, he likely would not have made the trip at all but would have taken his chances in Richmond. However, with his treasury aboard the other train several hours behind them, he was now the only cabinet member besides Breckinridge who still actually had a department and resources to manage. Benjamin may have joined the austerity ranks and munched at a sandwich, but not Trenholm, still one of the wealthiest men in the South. With him now besides his wife were baskets of expensive delicacies and a few bottles of peach brandy, which he gladly shared with his companions.

No one seemed even to notice the attorney general, but several of the president's aides were there, though quiet. Wood and Johnston kept to themselves, yet when pressed into the limited conversation assured others that they remained confident of their cause. Lubbock, senior to the others at least in age, took it on himself to try to inject some cheer into the trip. When Benjamin was not holding forth with his forced bonhomie, Lubbock regaled them all with anecdotes from his years in Texas. Mallory thought them pointless, and had no doubt heard them before, as Lubbock told his stories on the slightest pretext and seemed himself to find them far more amusing than the others.

Jefferson Davis sat quietly through it all, and during the night the rest largely left him to himself, though he responded when addressed directly. By morning, while the mood in the car lightened somewhat thanks to Trenholm's brandy and a sense of relief after they had passed beyond any immediate danger from enemy cavalry, the president was still largely impassive. Word had spread along the line that the government train was coming. It had to stop often, twice at places where, earlier, trains had suffered accidents. On one occasion, as they slowly started off again after being stopped by a train that had derailed, Davis looked out his window and saw wounded soldiers lying beside the track where they had been thrown by the wreck of their train, and some of them horribly mangled. It was not a sight to cheer him or his companions.[5] Several times crowds met them as they passed through towns, begging the latest news and to know how dire the situation. Learning that Davis was aboard, everyone wanted to see him or shake his hand. Bruce thought the president kept up a bold front and spoke encouragingly to the people when he spoke at all, but when one crowd at Clover Hill cheered him from the platform that morning, Davis did not rise and come out. He just smiled and waved to them from his window, while out in the crowd some could see the exhaustion and anguish on his face. "I saw a government on wheels," recalled John S. Wise, a soldier on that platform. "It was the marvelous and incongruous debris of the wreck of the Confederate capital."[6]

Finally between 4 and 5 P.M. the government train pulled into the Richmond and Danville Railroad depot just across the Dan River from its namesake town of six thousand. A considerable number of those people stood around the station as the locomotive Charles Seddon brought the cars to a halt. When Davis stepped down, local dignitaries offered official greetings, and though the crowd seemed cordial and cheered the president, Mallory thought they lacked the enthusiasm of old. "There was that in the cheers which told almost as much of sorrow as of joy," he felt.[7] Mayor James Walker had already organized a citizens' committee to find lodgings for the dignitaries and some makeshift quarters for the government offices to recommence operation. Now he took Davis, Mallory, and the ailing Trenholm to the spacious home of Major William T. Sutherlin, where they and a few others were to be house guests.[8] Trenholm was so weak he could not walk, and the morphine he took for his neuralgia made him so nauseated that he was constantly in peril of being sick. Still his wife rejoiced. "We are safe & well, Thank God," she would write a few hours later. "Truly the Lord is merciful to us."[9] Reagan took quarters in a house on Main Street, and the rest found beds elsewhere throughout the town.[10]

While the clerks spent the next three hours unloading the archives and other impedimenta from the train, Davis's first concern was news. He had been seventeen hours on the train for what should have been an eight-hour trip at most, and during all that time he heard nothing. Now as he and the cabinet ate their first hot meal in a whole day, at Sutherlin's hospitable table, the president made inquiries about Lee's whereabouts. No one seemed to know, and no telegrams came in either from Lee or Breckinridge. All governments subsist on information, and the Confederates were no different. For probably the first time in the entire course of the war, Davis spent fully twenty-four hours in the dark about the state of his armies. Exhausted and apprehensive, he and the rest could do little more than go to their scattered beds and hope for some word on the morrow. Before retiring, Davis sent a brief telegram to Varina to let her know he was safely out of Richmond.[11]

Meanwhile, another locomotive finally came in behind them. The treasury train, with Parker, the midshipmen, and a crowd of government employees aboard, traveled no faster than the one before it and did not arrive until evening. Behind them came others in a procession of trains, some of which actually left before the president's but were shunted onto sidings until his had passed, while others were assembled in and near Manchester, just across the James from Richmond, after the bridge was burned. These carried a motley collection of civilians, mostly men, and every imaginable description of cargo, as people had rushed to get their prized possessions clear of enemy hands and the city's looters. One car pulling up at the depot yielded a box of tame squirrels, an African parrot, and a hunchback, all of them fevered with excitement, including the bird.[12]

The next morning Davis and his cabinet, all except the incapacitated Trenholm, began to survey the town they expected to make their new capital. The president hoped it would be only a temporary expedient, of course, before they could reclaim Richmond and finally drive the invader entirely from their soil once Lee and Johnston united. The people of Danville, however, rather hoped the leaders would make the city a permanent home.[13] Davis himself made a horseback tour of the city's defenses, finding them inadequate, and even gave some direct instructions for relocating works. Soon he assigned an officer to superintend the city's works, and then called a meeting of the cabinet, in the Sutherlin parlor, to discuss their immediate future. They were still isolated, all rail communication to the north and east now cut off, and telegraph connections at best sporadic, thanks to Union cavalry raiders. Only hours before, they heard the Danville rail line that brought them in had been cut behind them by Yankee raiders. Another day's delay in leaving Richmond and they would not have gotten out.[14] They still did not know the entirety of the fate of Richmond, though the late arriving trains brought reports of the devastating fire. In such a condition of almost complete uncertainty, it was impossible to make any definite plans. Davis simply asked them to get their departments into operation as quickly as possible pending further developments, an injunction that really applied only to Trenholm, Reagan, Kean, and Cooper in Breckinridge's absence. He also undoubtedly discussed with them the need to get some word of encouragement out to the Confederate people at large as quickly as possible, in an effort not only to put the best possible gloss on the fall of the capital but to encourage continued determination to resist.

After the meeting adjourned, Davis went into the Sutherlin library and seated himself at a marble-topped table to write an address to his people. Benjamin, having nothing to do, may have remained with him, but was certainly near at hand while Davis wrote. Davis's pen revealed that he had lost none of his ability to make silk purses of sow's ears. "It would be unwise, even if it were possible," he began, "to conceal the great moral, as well as material injury to our cause," he said of the loss of Richmond. The city and its defiance in the face of four years of Yankee attempts at conquest had become symbols of their cause. Having said that, however, the president immediately began to imply—it would have been fatuous to claim it outright—that the fall of Richmond was actually a benefit. "The loss which we have suffered is not without compensation," he asserted. Defending Richmond had kept Lee tied in his trenches for months. "We have now entered upon a new phase of a struggle," he claimed:

> Relieved from the necessity of guarding cities and particular points, important but not vital to our defence with our army free to move from point to point, and strike in detail the detachments and garrisons of the enemy; operating in the interior of our own country, where supplies are more accessible, and where the foe will be far removed from his own base, and cut off from all succor in case of reverse, nothing is now needed to render our triumph certain, but the exhibition of our own unquenchable resolve. Let us but will it, and we are free.

One could almost feel sorry for the plight of the Union armies as he depicted their disappointment to discover that the fall of Richmond did not, as they expected, signal the end of the Confederacy. Worse, he declared that the enemy's "failing resources" would force Lincoln to abandon the war entirely if it could not be won speedily. All they had to do was continue to hold out a little longer and the foe would simply give up. Refuse to be beaten, and they never could be. "It is my purpose to maintain your cause with my whole heart and soul," he said, promising that he would never agree to give up another foot of ground without a fight. Then he addressed Virginians in particular. For the moment forgetting—as did most people in the East and even the world—that most of the war had been fought west of the Appalachians and that out there the North had conquered all but scattered smallholdings of Confederate resistance, he spoke of the Old Dominion having taken "the main shock" of the war, and gave his pledge that it would be defended. "No peace [will] ever be made with the infamous invaders of her

homes by the sacrifice of any of her rights or territory," he declared. If force of arms drove Confederate forces from her bor-
ders, they would return again and again until the enemy gave up
trying to subjugate them. They must not despond, he declared.
They must meet the foe with renewed defiance, "with uncon-
quered and unconquerable hearts."[15]

Given that Davis was not ready to give up, there was little
else he could do but issue such a proclamation. However, if he
genuinely believed what he was saying, as he later suggested
that he did, then it was little short of delusional. Lincoln's reelection demonstrated that the Union had the moral and spiri-
tual resources to keep on fighting for another four years if need
be, and even Davis could not deny that the North had enjoyed
overwhelming superiority in material resources from the beginning. He knew better than anyone that Yankee arms had by now
swept almost every Confederate warship from the rivers and
seas, taken every major city and seaport but Mobile—which was
under siege and would hold out only another week—isolated
and rendered all but pointless the scattered army west of the
Mississippi, controlled virtually everything between that great
river and the Appalachians, and were chasing Johnston with
more than double his numbers while Grant was surely after Lee.
Indeed, for all Davis knew at the moment of writing, Lee might
have been run to ground already. In the face of all that, to suggest that the enemy was so tired and demoralized as to be on
the verge of giving up was scarcely better than ridiculous.

Davis also made it clear that just as he would never give up,
neither would he even entertain discussions for peace. At the
Hampton Roads conference Lincoln told Stephens, Hunter, and
Campbell that the separation of West Virginia from the Old

Dominion to form a new state at the end of 1862 was neither reversible nor negotiable. Now in promising Virginians that he would never make terms with the enemy that involved her losing territory or rights, it was Davis's veiled reiteration of what he had been saying all along. Lincoln insisted that West Virginia be forever separated from Virginia; Davis pledged that it should not. Lincoln's emancipation violated the rights of slaveholders throughout the Confederacy; Davis declared that he would never accede to such a usurpation. He would negotiate on neither point, and he knew the North would not, though in fact Lincoln had hinted that in return for immediate peace, the Union might recede from or even repeal emancipation. Davis was cannily trying to capitalize on that brief boost of enthusiasm and determination produced by the failure of the Hampton Roads conference and the generals' wives scheme, each of which he had skillfully—and cynically—manipulated, both before and after the fact, in order to bring the people to his preferred conclusion that entering into any negotiations was hopeless. Now he sought to do the same thing with the loss of Richmond. There could never be peace without independence.

New in this paper, however, was the implicit call for a different kind of warfare in their changed circumstances. The talk of living off the land, operating in the interior, and depending on their people to succor the armies, while the remnants of their forces would become essentially raiders sniping at isolated targets of opportunity, all could mean only one thing. He envisioned now turning the contest into a partisan conflict. Davis had hinted at this in the past. Even now he did not declare the policy openly, but it was the inevitable consequence of the scenario he projected. Confederate partisans had been very successful on a limited scale during the war, and he could look back to the Revolution and earlier conflicts for examples of determined irregulars holding out successfully against greatly superior and organized invaders.

The trouble was, in looking at history, Davis chose to learn all the wrong lessons, or rather to misuse it to support his own flawed expectations. No separatist movement in recent history had won out against heavy odds without being the client state of another power that could feed it material support or even manpower. Without substantial French support in money, arms and munitions, and actual armies, the colonies would likely never have won their independence, and they enjoyed the added advantage that Britain had to wage the war more than three thousand miles from its own soil while also contending with adversaries elsewhere in the world. Lincoln could concentrate exclusively on conquering the South, and had but to look out a White House window to see Southern soil across the Potomac. Moreover, there were absolute necessities like rifles, cannon, and ammunition that could not be gleaned from the civilian population of the interior, essentials that the land could not provide. With their own factories either destroyed or cut off from them, they could not make their own. Their seaports were all in Yankee hands, making importation through the blockade impossible, and with their rail infrastructure demolished or in Yankee hands, there would be no way for any such materiel from outside to be transported to the remnants of their armies, who by definition would be clinging to the more remote fastnesses of the hill country.

As for the success of Confederate partisans like Colonel John S. Mosby, while they won lots of adulation from the loyal civilians where they operated, the fact remained that they never stopped a single significant Union campaign or ever offered more than an—often embarrassing—annoyance to Yankee commanders. Even what Mosby and his like did achieve depended heavily on the willing support and subsistence of the civilians of his locale, which was just what Davis's scheme could not count on, for the high country of southwestern Virginia and western North Carolina, northeastern Georgia, north Alabama, and eastern Tennessee, the regions where his new partisan armies would have to take refuge, were also precisely those areas most heavily infected with Unionism and anti-Confederate sentiment since the beginning of the war. He would be placing his soldiers in a position where they could obtain almost nothing from outside, among a people who would not support them from within. Moreover, had he chosen to acknowledge it, Davis had before him the example of other Southern partisans, like the guerrillas of Missouri and eastern Tennessee, as demonstrations of how unmanageable such troops could become even for their own side and of how easily such a mode of warfare degenerated into mere plunder and barbarism.

Davis's proclamation, in short, promised fantastical results based on his misrepresentation of circumstances and possibilities that simply did not exist, and he more than anyone, except Lee and Breckinridge, was armed with information and experience more than sufficient to demonstrate the utter impracticability of his plans. Years later even he admitted that his expectations were "over-sanguine," which was as close to a confession of outright error as he ever came.[16] Yet he could not see, or refused to see, that folly then. What he did not say at that time or ever, probably because he could never admit so even if he recognized it, was that his call for continued resistance on this new basis also offered a prescription for the sort of farcical end to their epic that Breckinridge warned against weeks before. In that event, any inner doubts or fears the president may have had were of no consequence matched against his declared determination to continue the fight to the end, no matter how bitter, and apparently not one member of his cabinet raised a voice to urge him otherwise. Even though some of those on his train read into Danville's polite but reserved welcome the weariness and failing resolve of its people, Davis did not. He was more cut off and remote than ever from the true sentiment of the exhausted and dispirited Confederate civilian population. It would have broken his heart to know that this very day, as he sought to find new words to breathe fresh fire into his people, back in Richmond there were citizens so resentful of his escaping and leaving them behind that they spread a rumor among themselves and told the Yankee soldiers now marching through their streets that their president had actually fled town in a dress, disguised as a woman.[17]

Certainly the unctuous Benjamin said nothing when Davis handed him the draft. Indeed, he may well have contributed to it himself. Rather, he now acted as the president's messenger and took it to the office of the Danville *Register* to have it run off as a handbill and then included in the next issue of the paper as well. Benjamin, for the moment secretary as well as runner, even wrote out a clean copy of Davis's much edited text before the printer could set type.[18] The proclamation hit the streets that afternoon, and the immediate reaction showed just how far the president was drifting from the sentiment of the people. Colonel Robert Withers, commanding the small garrison at Danville when the government arrived, read it fresh from the press, and saw and spoke with others in town after they had given it a reading. "Evidently designed to neutralize the depressing effect of the surrender of the Capital," Withers recalled, he regarded the assertion that the new freedom given to Lee would be an advantage as transparently groundless. "I neither saw nor heard of anyone," he said, "who was much enthused by the assurance."[19]

In fact, the overwhelming majority of Confederate soldiers and citizens would never see the proclamation, for the collapse of communications meant that it could not even get out of Danville for some days. That, too, ought to have occurred to Davis, but most immediately it was meant for Virginian eyes, and he could reasonably hope that by hand and word of mouth it might circulate before too long through the ever decreasing part of the state still under his control. For now, there was little else he could do but wait to hear from Lee. The rest of the day he spent in renewed inspection of the defenses, as well as looking into the progress of his ministers in getting their offices running again.

"I do not know what we are going to do," Trenholm's wife confessed that afternoon, though she expected from what her husband could tell her of Davis's plans that they would be remaining in Danville at least a few days.[20] When they had felt like talking at all on the train from Richmond, the cabinet frankly discussed who should do what when they reached Danville. Benjamin and George Davis virtually constituted in themselves their entire departments, and since a government on the run could conduct no diplomacy, nor debate legal niceties, those gentlemen were largely at their leisure. Trenholm, of course, was too sick to do much, and in any case they had now to husband their specie, and there could be little or no disbursement of funds from the Treasury. Parker and his midshipmen simply kept their train under guard, while a few thousand dollars were shifted to the vault of a local bank to meet immediate local expenses and to sell specie to locals in return for inflated paper money in order to get some genuine medium of exchange in operation.[21]

The midshipmen and their treasure train remained on the siding at the Danville station, the young men setting up camp alongside the track. It was a pleasant bivouac in a grove of trees, but the young men, unlike the government officials, found the townspeople cold and inhospitable. Perhaps it was because of envy or suspicion at the young men's proximity to undoubtedly the greatest sum of money ever seen in the town. The boxes and kegs—"things" the young men called them—aboard the train contained gold and silver, double-eagles, Mexican dollars, some ingots, and even a fair quantity of copper pennies, totaling more than $327,000 in Confederate treasury specie, and perhaps $450,000 or more from the Richmond banks. Some boxes contained five sacks of $5,000 each in gold coin, weighing over seventy-five pounds per box. More than $143,000 of the money was in United States silver coinage, which was still the prevalent hard currency in the South since the Confederacy never put any specie of its own into circulation. It came in dimes, quarters, half and whole dollars, and weighed by itself more than four tons. There were fifty kegs of Mexican dollars, $4,000 in each, making nearly another five tons.[22] Beyond this there was some quantity of jewelry and precious stones, most of it having been contributed by patriotic ladies to finance construction of more ironclad warships, which of itself made it singularly appropriate that the keeping of all this now lay in the hands of youngsters who until recently had been in training to be naval officers.[23]

No wonder Mallory quipped that "this coin was felt to be a very troublesome elephant." Davis would not allow it to be used except as pay for the soldiers in the ranks, yet there was not enough to pay all of the men still in service, nor any way to get a fair share to men in Lee's army or in the other extended commands far to the west. Davis would not even allow the release of some of the coin to pay his cabinet, and a few of the government officials complained to no avail. Fixed in his resolve, the president would not accord one treatment to his leaders and another to those led, and so no one was paid.[24] By April 6, concerned by the fear that raiding Federals might sweep past the city's thin defenses and capture the treasure, Davis and Trenholm decided to send it by rail farther south to Charlotte, where a vault offered better protection than boxcars. When Parker got his orders, he went to Mallory and asked him to see Trenholm on his behalf. Neither the secretary of the treasury, the treasurer, nor any other senior department staff had been with the train thus far, and none seemed intent to go on with him to Charlotte. Instead, Walter Philbrook, merely the chief teller, represented the Treasury Department, which placed an enormous responsibility on Parker, who was not even answerable to Trenholm. He thought the secretary or some other senior person ought to take responsibility and accompany the train. "It was not a time to be falling sick by the wayside, as some high officials were beginning to do," Parker complained, perhaps referring to Trenholm himself. Mallory may have met with Trenholm, but if so the ailing treasury secretary was not up to making even such minor decisions now and bumped the question to Davis, who would appoint his own chief clerk, Micajah H. Clark, to take over from Philbrook. Meanwhile the remaining gold that had been moved to the bank vault in Danville was carted back to the train, the minor clerks and others connected to the treasury boarded, and that evening Parker and the midshipmen were on their way south once more.[25]

Because not all of them had been accommodated on the last train out, the midshipmen continued to arrive as late as April 6, just in time to board the train for Charlotte.[26] Indeed, Danville was becoming something of a navy town now. The number of unattached officers who came out of Richmond congregated at the local naval storehouse, and there every day from its opening at 9 A.M. until the paymaster closed the building, marooned captains and commanders and lieutenants lounged the days away sitting on barrels of hardtack and pickled beef, spinning yarns, packing and repacking their sea trunks, and displaying curious souvenirs from their voyages. "They were generally grave and silent," wrote their frequent companion and chief, Mallory, "& without ships, or boats, or duties, all adrift upon dry land, they presented a pretty fair illustration of 'fish out of water'." Many wrote letters on borrowed stationery or paper scavenged from one of the trunks, yet a single common inkwell served them all, while the rest idly practiced their knots, even making "sailor art" creations from rope and line, like Turks' heads and ornamental hangings. A few, with literal gallows humor, tied hangman's knots.[27] Late on April 4, when another train brought in some five hundred seamen from the scuttled James River fleet commanded by Admiral Semmes, Davis asked him to turn his men into an artillery brigade to man the batteries around the city. Two days later the president actually gave Semmes a commission as a brigadier general, an implicit statement that Davis had little faith in the local commander, Colonel Withers. At least one old sea dog would have something to do.

Only the War and Post Office Departments really swung into action. Kean and General Cooper were offered rooms in a former girl's school on Wilson Street, now owned by Ann Benedict. Kean thought it imperative to have his office operating, even though Breckinridge was out of touch, simply in order to give the appearance of business as usual for morale's sake. It appeared to work, for the next day when men with one of the wagon trains came into town, one of them found that "everything in Danville suggested at least the possibility that the Confederate Government would renew its customary work in a few days."[28] Kean and his assistants began opening and routing or filing the War Department mail they found accumulated in Danville awaiting shipment to Richmond, and attended to whatever other business they could.[29] Gorgas tried to get his Ordnance Bureau up and operating, though Mallory thought the effort "spasmodic" at best.[30]

Davis's aides themselves assisted in every office, young Johnston complaining that he had so much to do and was "in such a turbulent uproar all the time," that he could not even find moments to write a personal letter.[31] Even if a letter could be written, there was little likelihood of it getting anywhere, though Reagan and his clerks moved into the Masonic hall and converted it into an ersatz Post Office Department. There was civilian mail on the trains that had come into Danville from

Richmond, and other mail accumulated from other points.[32] With nothing else to do, they began sorting and postmarking to send them out again by rail lines now closed, toward destinations where postmasters no longer functioned, or to addressees which were mostly now behind Yankee lines. Yet it was important to make the show of doing business, and the bureaucratic instinct for paperwork would not be denied.

Reagan himself helped out in the routine work, and one of the most colorful subalterns in the whole fleeing government worked with him. In 1860 Charles E. L. Stuart had the temerity to publish a pro-secession newspaper, the *Volunteer*, in, of all places, New York City. Though born in Poland, he declared that he was descended directly from the royal house of Stuart and was in fact rightful heir to the English crown. Earlier in the war he repeatedly importuned Davis to make him a general or confer some high civil appointment on him. "A vile Bohemian," Davis's secretary, Burton Harrison, called him, "a free lance of a fellow." Stuart also fancied that he looked rather like Shakespeare, an appearance that he intentionally cultivated. Thus there was a delicious irony—that might have been charged to sense of humor if Davis had had one—in the fact that the only appointment Stuart ever got was a minor assistant clerkship in Reagan's department. Now that the would-be king of England was whiling away the Danville hours hand stamping envelopes and sorting the mail, he was at last genuinely like Shakespeare, a man of letters.[33]

Finding lodgings for everyone had proved something of a scramble, for the fine homes like the Sutherlins' could not accommodate all. Not a few of the lesser officials and their families took up residence in some of the boxcars emptied of their

contents after the evacuation trains reached Danville. There
was even a bridal party spending their first wedding nights in
one of the cars on a siding, and the local commissary undertook
to feed all of the refugees.[34] Benjamin actually walked Danville's
streets for some time on the day of his arrival, meeting a friend
from Richmond to whom he confessed he had no place to stay.
"It was a new thing, I doubt not, in his experience to be uncertain about his immediate movements," thought Dr. Moses
Hoge. "It had always been his good fortune to lay his plans skil-
fully and execute them as well." Hoge offered to share his own
room at the home of a local doctor, and after some persuasion
Benjamin accepted. Almost immediately he adapted himself to
the routine of the house, as Benjamin seemed always to accommodate himself to his circumstances. Despite his different—
and to some unwelcome—faith, he joined the family in church
and at prayers at home. Though other government departments
tried to function, most of the time when not closeted with
Davis, Benjamin had nothing to do but read and indulge his delight in stimulating conversation with his hosts. Indeed, while
Davis struggled mentally and emotionally with trying to keep
his nation afloat, Benjamin spent much of his time indulging in
literary debates on the merits of Tennyson and Shakespeare ver-
sus Dryden and Byron.[35]

In the Sutherlin house itself, Jefferson Davis passed his hours
in ignorance and uncertainty. At least he and his staff found their
quarters in the mansion comfortable.[36] From Tuesday April 4 on
he sent couriers to try to find Lee and bring back word of the
general's whereabouts and prospects, but none returned. At the
same time, realizing that they might be forced to retreat farther
south, he telegraphed to Greensboro, North Carolina, where

Beauregard commanded, to protect the necessary rail lines just in case. At the same time, no doubt sensitive to the irony that he was now having to depend on his most ardent enemies in the military for his own and his cause's future hopes, he sent word to Joseph E. Johnston near Smithfield, North Carolina, but could tell him nothing other than to conform his own plans to what he knew of Lee's earlier intention to make a junction. In the absence of any news at all from Lee, Davis could only assume that the general was trying to effect that objective.[37]

It was the waiting with nothing else to do that most wore on the president's already exhausted nerves. Not entirely sure where she would be, Davis wrote Varina a long letter telling her more of the flight from Richmond, including some meaningless domestic details about furniture and bedding, even groceries and their spoons. Starving for more important information himself, he felt compelled to tell her something, anything, however inconsequential at the moment. "I do not wish to leave Va, but cannot decide on my movements until those of the army are better developed," he complained, lamenting that "I weary of this sad recital and have nothing pleasant to tell." By April 6 he still had nothing more to tell, though at least a letter from Varina reached Danville and assured him that she and the children were safe in North Carolina for the moment. Aided by his chief clerk, Micajah Clark, Davis was setting up the executive office in the Benedict house. Though he continued to use the Sutherlin parlor for his cabinet meetings, the absence of information made them all but pointless for the moment.[38]

To fill some of those hours, Davis met a small stream of visitors, most of them refugees from Richmond, that passed through Danville, several of them congressmen like Bruce, or

Kentucky's Humphrey Marshall, now on his way home as he saw the end at hand.[39] Sometimes he sat with Sutherlin and talked of farming, the war with Mexico, even secession itself. "We have done the best we could," Davis said of the war effort.[40] But in the main, Davis busied himself looking over Danville's defenses and surveying the warehouses stuffed with provisions for Lee's army if the men and matériel could only be brought together.[41] He had hoped by now to meet face to face with Lee, yet not a word came, nor anything from Breckinridge, either. Benjamin tried unconvincingly to cheer his companions with clichés. "No news is good news," he told them, but he won few to his view.[42] In the Sutherlin house, the president's hostess could not help but see how little interest Davis took in his food. He remained ever agreeable and controlled, and even outwardly belligerent, but she detected in him what she called an "anxious state of mind."[43] In these dark hours ignorance was the nourishment of worry.

The waiting took a toll on Danville society, too, as well as on the other members of the government, excepting the now revived Benjamin. Davis's proclamation, hollow as it may have been, seemed to infuse some renewed spirit into the city's people, though they were likely unaware that they were almost the only ones in the dwindling Confederacy actually to read it in their newspaper. They all needed word from Lee, and yet none came, while scouts sent out to find the army did not return. Amazingly for a people who had thrived on gossip for years, scarcely even a rumor came into town, yet it was not hard to surmise that if word from Lee was not coming through, there could be only two explanations. One was that he had met with some shattering reverse; the other was that the pursuing Yankees had gotten between his line of retreat and Danville, and no word could get through. Some did say they thought the general, in fact, had won a smashing victory over Grant and was too busy pursuing him to communicate with Danville. Davis did not believe it for a minute. Mallory could see that the president expected no good news. "To a few, very few," he reflected, "they were days of hope; to the many they were days of despondency, if not of despair; & to all, days of intense anxiety."[44]

Finally, on the morning of April 7, Davis ordered that another scout be sent out, this time to establish a line of couriers to connect Danville with Lee, wherever he could be found. That evening the scout left by special train to go as far north as possible before setting off cross country, even as an alarming report came into town that Federal raiders were on their way. "This threw a chill over the scene, and each man looked into the face of his neighbor with a countenance that seemed to ask 'what next?'" said W. H. Swallow, himself just arrived. At once extra men went out to the earthworks on the hills surrounding the city, and Semmes, now General Semmes, as senior military officer present, took command. Before long they learned that the rumor was false, but it put an edge on the already nervous temporary capital, and by the next morning Swallow observed that the town echoed to rumors "producing as much anxiety as that at Richmond the week before."[45]

At the same time, the scouting party left their train and were on horseback, riding north until late on the night of April 8, when they came to the small hamlet of Red House. Still they learned nothing of Lee's whereabouts or movements, though the countryside around them had seen a lot of very recent raiding by Yankee cavalry. More ominous were the large numbers of deserters and stragglers from Lee's army. They had left the main body days before and knew nothing of its movements of the last three or four days. Indeed, some of them had been coming into Danville for the past day or two. Cumulatively, their number and demoralization did not bode well for Lee and the rest of his apparently dwindling command. When the scouts halted at Red House, they knew they must be getting close to more recent news. Very likely the next day they would finally learn something, but for now they bedded down for the night, just twelve miles south of Appomattox.[46]

Chapter Four

"THE SHADOWS OF MISFORTUNE"

Red House was too small a village for the scouts not to know that it had other visitors that night. Now six days out of Richmond, Breckinridge and his party were finally on their way to Danville. He had quite a following when the Kentuckian at last turned away from the sight of the burning city early on April 3 and rode west to find Lee. Besides his former adjutant Lieutenant Colonel James Wilson, his son Cabell, and others, he was accompanied by General Isaac M. St. John, the commissary general with whom he had replaced Northrop, and General Alexander R. Lawton, the quartermaster general. It was no accident that the secretary of war kept beside him the two men most intimately connected with supplying the armies. Lee's effort to get away from Richmond depended almost entirely on being able to feed and equip his men on the march. One of the few successes of the last few weeks had been the work of men like St. John and Lawton in assembling the necessary stores in supply depots such as Danville and elsewhere, but now they had to get that matériel to Lee, and at places governed not by his wishes but by the opportunities that the pursuing Yankees might afford. Indeed, the day he pulled out of Richmond and Petersburg, Lee had sent an urgent request to have rations for his army awaiting him at Amelia Courthouse, some forty miles southwest of the abandoned capital. Tragically, in the confusion and haste of the evacuation, the request never got to Breckinridge or St. John.[1]

It was only well into April 3, as Breckinridge and his party rode west, that he may finally have learned of Lee's request, and by then it was too late. Even though Breckinridge himself hoped to find Lee at Amelia, there was now no time for supply trains to get to Lee from Lynchburg or North Carolina, for Lee was moving fast to escape the Federals and probably could not wait. But as he rode along the road, Breckinridge encountered large numbers of quartermaster and commissary wagons that had left Richmond carrying what they could take out of the warehouses before they were burned, and now he and St. John gathered them as they proceeded and directed them to hasten toward Amelia.[2]

Organizing the scattered wagon trains slowed the secretary of war, but fortunately more and more retreating men and officers gravitated to his little party until he had at least a score riding with him to help in the work. Now Breckinridge faced an immediate problem. Lee had crossed to the south side of the Appomattox River soon after leaving his lines, but the enemy pursued so closely that Breckinridge and his party could not fol-

low. As a result, he and the wagon trains moved north of the
river, seeking a crossing that would allow them to join the army.
By April 4 he reached Powhatan, where he found more generals, separated from their commands, who attached themselves to
him, including Bushrod Johnson and the president's nephew
Joseph Davis. Amelia lay just fifteen miles southwest, but the
wagon train had grown so large now, it was bound to attract
the attention of Federal cavalry raiders skirting Grant's army.
Breckinridge tried to get the train across at Genito but found the
bridge burned and so proceeded on to Powhatan Courthouse,
due north of Amelia. Not only did the Appomattox still separate
him from Lee's army but also from any firm information as to
the army's whereabouts, and now the Kentuckian confessed he
could only guess where Lee might be. With Yankee cavalry now
on his own heels, Breckinridge pushed the wagon train on toward Clemmentown, the next bridge over the river, and just a
few miles northwest of Amelia. If Lee was still there, they might
yet get to him.

They pushed on all day, and by nightfall approached Clemmentown but dared not risk making the crossing in the darkness. Instead they bivouacked with the wagons for the night,
having now to protect the supplies from a growing number of
stragglers and deserters all along the road. "The more I see of
matters the less hopeful I become," one of Breckinridge's party
wrote in his diary that night. They crossed the next morning
but almost immediately got a report that a body of enemy cavalry already in front of Lee's army was believed to be heading
north from Jetersville to attack their train and keep it from
reaching the army. No one knew anything definitive, and finally
Breckinridge called for a half dozen volunteers from a cavalry

squadron temporarily attached to the column to make a recon-
naissance. Breckinridge himself rode with them to the front of
the wagon train and there watched them depart before he prepared the train to defend itself if need be. Already in the distance to the south he could hear sporadic firing indicating that
something was happening between his own position and Amelia.

Within minutes the scouts returned to report that only two
miles below them they found the artillery and supply train of
one of Lee's infantry divisions under attack by enemy horsemen
and just being captured. Almost immediately one of the quartermasters from the captured train came riding past at a panic
yelling that the Yankees were coming and would be upon them
in seconds. The teamsters on many of the wagons panicked and
ran away, while others began throwing everything they could
out of their wagons to lighten the load as they tried to make
speed back to the bridge. Some cut loose their teams and abandoned their wagons, riding the horses to the rear, while a few
men just swam the river. Even soldiers who had attached themselves to the train joined in the stampede, but Breckinridge refused to be spooked, and stood his ground with a few of his
original party.

He remained on the road for fully an hour, waiting to see
what developed, while trying to rally more about him by going
to the crowd of confused soldiers and civilians and calling for
volunteers to help him meet the foe. Finally he had a hundred
or more infantrymen and about twenty cavalry rallied, and then
led them forward, down the road toward Amelia Courthouse.
They went perhaps a mile when they found a few skittish officers from the captured artillery train firing into the woods and
warning that the trees were alive with Yankees. Breckinridge

soon discovered that there was not an enemy to be found, however. Then he heard firing in their rear. A small party of Union raiders had detached itself from the main column that captured the artillery and supply train, and had ridden to the Clemmentown bridge by a different road. Rushing to the rear, Breckinridge found his own train under attack, an assault made easier by the scattered and abandoned wagons and the bulk of the teamsters and others having fled to the north bank of the river. With his twenty cavalry, Breckinridge charged down the road and into the raiders, taking them somewhat by surprise, and driving them off, though not before they managed to set fire to some of the wagons.[3]

Had he had time to muse on the affair, Breckinridge might have pondered the fact that the skirmish made him the first and only serving cabinet officer in American history to lead troops in action. Now, however, having repulsed the raiders, he realized most immediately that the direct road ahead of him to Amelia was cut off, and moreover that it no longer mattered. One thing the secretary of war had learned from the skirmish was that Lee had indeed been in Amelia Courthouse that day, but also that the enemy cavalry, at least, had reached Jetersville on the Danville Railroad. That effectively cut off Lee's continued progress along that line, making it impossible to supply him by rail from the depots at Danville or further south in North Carolina. Without needing to hear from Lee, Breckinridge now reasoned that the only alternative was for Lee to abandon the Danville road and strike due west across country, through Amelia Springs, in an attempt to reach Farmville on the Southside Railroad. That track connecting Farmville directly with Lynchburg still lay in Confederate hands and represented the only remaining available supply line for the army. As a result, Breckinridge ordered the teamsters to reload what they had thrown out and hitch the teams back to the remaining wagons, and then move off to the southwest on roads that would take them to Farmville.

Meanwhile the Kentuckian, with St. John and a few others, decided to leave the train and strike out for Amelia Springs, hoping to meet Lee en route to Farmville. It was dangerous and difficult, for as he and his party rode on they passed all along the way evidence of the Yankees nipping at Lee's heels. Burning wagons loaded with rations and forage, even headquarters baggage, littered the road, telling their tale of disintegration, while Federal patrols were everywhere in the neighborhood. Still Breckinridge got through to Amelia Springs early the next morning, to find that Lee had been there as recently as 4 A.M. and was now only a few miles west near Deatonsville, just east of Sayler's Creek and about five miles short of Farmville.[4] Riding on without sleep, the secretary finally encountered General James Longstreet's corps about dawn and, at his temporary headquarters, at last met with Lee again.

There was not much time for conference, but Lee brought Breckinridge up to date on his progress during the past four days, sad a tale though it was. The principal task before them was supplying the army. St. John said he had some eighty thousand rations at Farmville and wanted to know whether to hold them there or send them to some other point on the Southside, but Lee confessed that he was so uncertain of his own movements that he could not answer, meaning it would be best to hold them at Farmville pending further notification. Even then his army was about to split accidentally into two columns from confusion about unfamiliar roads. Lee went on to Rice's Station on the Southside, where he attempted unsuccessfully to get a telegram through to Davis, while Breckinridge, St. John, Lawton, and the rest rode to Farmville to oversee getting the rations ready for distribution or removal at short notice. All day they waited to hear from Lee but no word came. Breckinridge sent couriers out every few hours to learn Lee's position and intention, but only late in the day did they hear anything, and it was news of disaster. The Yankees had cut off and attacked more than eight thousand men at Sayler's Creek and forced their surrender. In a stroke, Lee's army had been reduced by almost a third.

Breckinridge and his staff took quarters in a house on the edge of town and were there when Lee himself arrived late that night.[5] All through the night the remains of his army passed through, taking with them a portion of the rations St. John had on hand.[6] There was no time to rest, and as the skeletal regiments marched on westward toward Appomattox Station on the Southside, where St. John promised more supplies, Lee and Breckinridge met again. The general said he still hoped somehow to reach North Carolina and asked Breckinridge to get word to Johnston, though he confessed again that he had no idea what route he would be able to take, if any. Fresh reports coming in indicated that Lynchburg was under threat, and Lee issued orders to scattered Confederate cavalry in the area to try to hold the city, indicating that he may have expected to continue moving west through Lynchburg and then turn south for North Carolina. He might even have to move through southwest Virginia, justifying Breckinridge's foresight weeks before in putting his old department on the alert. Meanwhile, Lee told Breckinridge that besides the terrible loss at Sayler's Creek, the straggling from his remaining columns had been terrible. The army was gradually evaporating, and from what Breckinridge now knew he concluded with some understatement that "the situation is not favorable."[7]

If there was time, Breckinridge and Lee must have discussed at least the possibility that there was no way out. Their talks of weeks before, when Lee had seemed willing to use his influence to help force peace negotiations, must have haunted them now, for they were staring in the face the alternative he and the secretary had hoped to avoid: defeat in detail leaving no option but to take whatever terms Grant offered. Even now, they likely addressed the probability that if Lee could make a junction with Johnston, the combined army would be far too small to oppose either Grant or Sherman successfully, let alone both of them. Nevertheless, as a substantial combined force, they might pose enough of a threat that their existence could once again raise hopes that the Yankees would make favorable terms rather than be forced to fight them.

And Breckinridge had some reason to think that good terms were yet a possibility. Before leaving Richmond, he had ample opportunity to discuss with Campbell what the assistant secretary intended to propose to the Yankees when they occupied the town. No longer regarding himself as answerable to a government on the run, Campbell could speak his mind, but it is hardly likely that he and Breckinridge did not consult to formulate a general approach, nor that the Kentuckian, as both Campbell's superior and one of the most distinguished statesmen of his generation—and an old friend of Lincoln's as well—did not influence the assistant secretary's thinking. By the time Breckinridge and Lee met on the morning of April 7, Campbell in fact had already met with Lincoln when the president himself went to conquered Richmond three days earlier. The war was ended, Campbell said, echoing Breckinridge's expressed sentiments as well as his own. In his discussion, he confined his suggestions to Virginia, suggesting that if Lincoln showed magnanimity in dealing with the Old Dominion, other states would take heart and accept the same terms, virtually an echo of the discussions between Breckinridge and Lee about setting an example in Virginia first. Campbell proposed summoning the state legislature to have it use its recognized sovereign authority to pull all remaining Virginia soldiers out of Confederate service and put an end to all further acts in support of the rebellion. That, of course, would effectively dissolve Lee's army, while Virginia's abandonment of the Confederacy ought to be all that was needed to precipitate the other states doing the same. This stopped short of having the legislature actually vote to reenter the Union—which Lincoln, in any event, always maintained it had never lawfully left in the first place—but it would still achieve an end to the war and the Confederacy by the only means that Davis himself recognized, individual state action. He would not have to commit that "political suicide" that he maintained he had not the power to do.

Campbell asked Lincoln, in return, for "as much gentleness and forbearance as could be possibly extended." Lincoln agreed not to require oaths of allegiance to the United States, which many Confederates would find humiliating, and even seemed to leave open the question of allowing currently elected legislators to continue in office, running the state. Such matters of individual and political rights were always at the forefront of Breckinridge's own policy for the peace to come. He also felt concern for property rights, though he regarded slavery as ended, and just as well. Lincoln did tell Campbell that he would not retreat from his proclamations regarding emancipation, which Campbell certainly took to mean that slavery was a dead issue, but hinted that while he would not personally abandon emancipation, that did not mean that Congress might not act to rescind it in whole or part, probably a somewhat disingenuous attempt to plant false hope and secure cooperation.

When it came to other property of Confederate citizens now in Yankee hands, however, Lincoln agreed that anything not already condemned and sold by his government would be released and returned to its owners as soon as any state that promptly recognized the authority of the United States withdrew its troops from resistance. That made it clear that Lincoln was suggesting a policy for all the Confederate states, and that Virginia should be the pilot. Moreover, he assured Campbell that "scarcely any one" would be denied a pardon and restoration of full rights of citizenship upon application. There might even be a general amnesty. If Campbell interpreted Lincoln's words overoptimistically, still the offer represented about everything Breckinridge could have hoped for. Lincoln's only caveat was that if the Confederates persisted in fighting until they had to be beaten into submission, then confiscated property would not be returned.[8] Campbell had hoped to get an armistice out of Lincoln. The president refused, but that, though frustrating, was hardly a significant loss. Moreover, Campbell knew—as did Breckinridge—that others in North Carolina were attempting the same state action, particularly William Graham, who hoped to get a meeting between state officials and Sherman in order to make a separate peace. If their efforts came to anything, then the action of the two largest eastern states, with the most men in the service, would surely be all that was needed to bring about a general capitulation.[9]

Though Breckinridge could have had no communication with Campbell after leaving Richmond, still he knew that his assistant secretary was making some effort to get terms, and he knew the general lines agreed between them as to what they hoped those terms might be. Pending whatever resulted from Campbell's efforts, the best hope now for securing the most favorable settlement possible was to keep Lee in the field, though without fighting any more battles, which would only further deplete his strength and serve to make the Federals less amenable to leniency. Indeed, the disaster at Sayler's Creek already considerably compromised any bargaining power based on Lee remaining at large. Given that neither Lee nor Breckinridge had been able to get any word through to Danville as yet, it is unlikely that either was aware of Davis's April 4 proclamation of war to the last ditch, but both already knew the president well enough to know his position on surrender. If Breckinridge and Lee discussed the matter now, the only conclusion compatible with their previously expressed opinions was that Lee should try to keep his army intact and out of reach of the enemy long enough to join Johnston and then stay at large until Campbell's efforts or those in North Carolina could bear fruit. Should Lee fail and be surrounded and brought to bay by Grant, as appeared hourly more probable, then the best he could do would be to get any units that could escape the trap—most likely cavalry—off to Johnston and then strive for an honorable surrender of the remainder. In no event could he allow his remaining men to disband and take to the hills to heed the president's call for a partisan war.

Whatever passed between Breckinridge and Lee that morning, each kept to himself, yet clearly when they parted they were of one mind on the best future course for the Army of Northern Virginia, and probably for the Confederacy and the post-war South as well. Three years and one month later to the day, when Lee looked back on the war and discussed his army's successes and failures and the policy of the government itself, he singled out only one man for praise, and it was not one of his generals. Speaking to Davis's aide William Preston Johnston, he said he regretted that Breckinridge had not been made secretary of war earlier. "He is a great man," said Lee. "I was acquainted with him as Congressman and Vice-President and as one of our Generals, but I did not *know* him till he was secretary of war, and he is a lofty, pure strong man."[10]

Breckinridge last saw Lee that morning of April 7, when he left the general pushing his remnants through Farmville and on to the west. The secretary of war, with his party, rode out of town early when he received reports of approaching Federals. It was imperative that he rejoin Davis now, having done all he could in counseling Lee and seeing, through St. John, that at least ample supplies would be available if the general could reach them. With the sounds of skirmishing in the environs of Farmville in his ears, Breckinridge and his companions crossed to the south side of the Appomattox once more and rode westward toward Pamplin Station on the Southside line. As they left Farmville behind, the Kentuckian rode past Lieutenant Joseph Packard, an artilleryman without a command now, who observed that "his calm, buoyant manner was very impressive."[11] Breckinridge, it seemed, was one of those born to shine in a crisis.

He reached Pamplin's that evening, after riding twenty miles without molestation and noticing that the volume of firing back in the direction of Lee's army seemed greatly reduced. They found more supply trains waiting on a siding, and hearing reports that the enemy cavalry was nearby, Breckinridge and St. John at first suggested sending them west a few miles to Appomattox Station, where they expected Lee would be that evening, but again they were cut off from communication with Lee. With the situation changing hourly there was no way of knowing whether Lee might have changed the direction of his march and could even then be heading for Pamplin instead, meaning he would need the supply train where it was. Absent any definitive information, Breckinridge decided to leave the train where it was, and the next morning, April 8, rode onward to the southwest, toward Danville some sixty miles away. That night he stayed at Red House, just as Davis's own scouts arrived. Besides telling them the situation, he now for the first time had access to a secure telegraph line and dispatched a message to Danville, reporting the orderly evacuation of Richmond and a brief synopsis of Lee's movements through the previous morning, including the first terse news of the disaster at Sayler's Creek. Ominously, Breckinridge added that he had heard no firing at all in the distance that day, though he ventured no guess as to what that meant. He was on his way now and would join Davis as soon as possible.[12]

What the secretary could not know was that the silence heralded the opening of correspondence between Grant and Lee, initiated by the former just hours after Breckinridge bid Lee farewell. Lee at first refused to acknowledge his situation as hopeless, a natural opening response, but went on to ask what Grant's terms would be. With communication opened, Grant pressed Lee that day but did not launch an attack, and the next day responded that he required only that Lee's men put down their arms and give their parole not to fight again. Lee replied that he did not think his case yet hopeless, but it was mostly bluff, for by late on April 8 the Federal cavalry had gotten ahead of him, arriving in Appomattox Station, capturing the supplies waiting there, and cutting off the last line of retreat. There was nothing left to him now but to try to cut his way through the encircling blue band of steel, or surrender.

Lee responded that evening, even as Breckinridge wired Davis of the urgency of their situation, and now he was once again the Lee who had been discussing ending the war with Breckinridge all those weeks before. "The restoration of peace should be the sole object of all," he told Grant, but he would not discuss surrender. Rather, he proposed to meet his adversary the following morning to consult as to how Grant's proposal "may affect the C. S. forces under my command, & tend to the restoration of peace." The semantic distinction was significant. Lee would not discuss surrender of the Army of Northern Virginia but would talk about matters concerning "the C. S. forces under my command."[13] He could only be speaking, then, in his capacity as general-in-chief, which meant that he wanted to negotiate some agreement covering all Confederate forces in the field. It may have been Breckinridge's idea, or Lee's, or that of both, but it was the natural conclusion to the scheme they had framed in their private meetings back in March. As general-in-chief, Lee could treat on behalf of all armies without stepping outside his authority into the realm of politics, and if he ordered all Confederates to lay down their arms, then the war was over, the Confederacy was dead, and any further calls from Davis for resistance would be pointless. The president might not feel that he could euthanize the cause by executive fiat, but Lee could end it just as effectively by ordering an armistice for the armies that were all that kept the cause alive. It was yet another way to end the revolution by strictly constitutional means, as Breckinridge strove to do from the first, and if he could get a cease-fire from Grant, then there might be yet a chance for negotiations, especially if Campbell was having any success with the Lincoln administration. They could still end the war and come out of the peace deal with some guarantees of their rights, and their heads held higher for having been treated as equals, rather than being forced to surrender at discretion, to be treated as a conquered people.

Grant, however, was unwilling to play along. Lee's suggestion was months too late to have any practical allure. Grant knew Lee was mortally wounded. Lincoln had also made it clear at Hampton Roads, with Grant present, that there could be no armistice. The only way to stop Yankee guns was for the Rebels to put down theirs. Early on April 9 Grant sent a reply that he had no authority to treat for general peace, only Lee's surrender. The gray chieftain had no choice but to launch one last effort to break out, as well to show Grant that he still had teeth to force a route of escape. When that failed, he finally accepted the inevitable and agreed to discuss his surrender. For Lee, at least, the war was over, and once more Breckinridge's efforts to bring about a general peace had been foiled.

The morning of April 9, as Lee faced his last day in command, the secretary of war and his party set out for the temporary capital, crossing the Staunton River at Ward's Bridge that first day and moving on through Competition Courthouse the next. In all probability he was just as ignorant of what was happening behind him at Appomattox as he was of what was about to take place ahead of him in Danville. The days there had passed no more quickly after Davis sent out his scouts to find Lee. On the evening of April 8 Davis received Breckinridge's discouraging telegram about the condition of Lee's army, and though it was not disastrous, it was hardly encouraging. That same night Davis had called a cabinet meeting at the Sutherlin house and was meeting with his ministers around the dining room table when his secretary, Burton Harrison, newly arrived back from Charlotte, interrupted to announce that Lieutenant John S. Wise had just come with news from Lee. Like the other scouts who went out several days before, Wise had been ordered to find Lee, and now he told Davis and his cabinet that he had met the general as recently as the day before, and the news he imparted was even worse than Breckinridge's telegram. Confirming the loss at Sayler's Creek and the terrific straggling and desertions, he told them Lee had remaining perhaps only a third of the army that had been with him at Richmond.

He thought that Davis and the others seemed not to believe him, but he went on to express the opinion that Lee would be forced to surrender. The president determined to send the young man back the next morning with dispatches for Lee if he could be reached.[14] That night Davis and Sutherlin sat outdoors on the porch during a heavy rain, smoking cigars. His host warned the president that he ought to get away from Danville, and soon. "Major, I comprehend the situation exactly," Davis responded. "It is all clear before me and I would not evade it if I could. For myself I care nothing—it is my dear people that I am thinking of—what will become of my poor people?"[15] There spoke the beginning at last of realization, yet with it the same fatalism that made some fear the president would willingly take "my dear people" to the grave with him rather than yield. Meanwhile Harrison contrived to keep as a souvenir Breckinridge's telegram, written on a half sheet of cheap yellow paper torn from a pad at the telegrapher's office. It began to be evident that the war and the Confederacy might not last long enough for many more keepsakes to be created.[16]

The next day was Palm Sunday, and Davis went to church as usual. Now the breakdown in Confederate communications became more painfully evident, as an April 6 telegram from Lee finally got through, bringing news by wire that was obsolete, thanks to Wise's report. Still Davis fired off a return telegram that no doubt echoed the dispatches he sent that morning with Wise, expressing his hope to see Lee soon in Danville with his army. That evening over dinner the discussion inevitably turned to Lee's dire position, and though all were loath to broach the subject, someone mentioned the possibility of surrender. Mrs. Sutherlin asked if Lee's surrender did not mean that they were beaten at last. "By no means," Davis shot back. "We'll fight it out to the Mississippi River." The other members of the cabinet nodded in halfhearted agreement, though surely less from any confidence in the sentiment than from long accustomed habit of not gainsaying with the president. Davis himself seemed more confident than ever to the Sutherlins, perhaps in part because when Harrison arrived he had brought with him a letter from Varina written just the day before. "I know that your strength when stirred up is great," she said, "and that you can do with a few what others have failed to do with many." The Almighty would yet deliver them and their cause "through his own appointed agent," and she believed that agent was her husband. Now Sutherlin's wife concluded from Davis's manner that ultimate success was only a matter of time, that "he would fight to the end, beyond the end."[17]

The news came the next afternoon. Throughout the late morning and early afternoon stragglers from Lee's army, many of whom escaped the disaster at Sayler's Creek, began to come into town. None of them had any definitive information, but the tale they told only made Breckinridge's and Wise's news the more portentous. Davis was in his office in the Benedict house about 3:30 or 4:00 P.M., with a heavy and dispiriting thunderstorm raging outside, when finally the scouts he had sent out himself several days ago returned. The president and his ministers, excepting the ailing Trenholm, were just sitting to an early supper in their office when Captain W. P. Graves and his associates entered the building. Davis sat impassively as Graves reported having gotten as far as Pamplin's on the afternoon of April 9, where he met General Thomas Rosser, one of Lee's escaped cavalry commanders, who gave him news of the surrender meeting even then taking place. Graves could not wait to glean more, but immediately left for Danville. He also brought a written confirmation from Rosser or someone else in the know. Almost without comment, Davis heard Graves out, then brought him to the dining table to share the cabinet's meal, throughout which no one spoke of Graves's news.[18]

Yet it hit them all the same. Handed the written confirmation by Graves, the members of the cabinet passed it from one to another, each scrutinizing the paper, exchanging doleful looks and a few stunned comments. Then they all fell silent, a quiet that the navy secretary thought "more eloquent of great disaster than words could have been." Mallory, borrowing Thomas Jefferson's famed exclamation in 1820 when he learned of the Missouri Compromise over the extension of slavery, declared that Lee's surrender "fell upon the ears of all like a fire bell in the night." The news made it evident that with no armed forces now between Danville and Grant, they must pack up the government and move south at once, that evening even. Prepared for this eventuality, Davis decided that they should remove to Greensboro, North Carolina, where Johnston's nearby Army of Tennessee could afford at least temporary protection. Appointing 8 P.M., less than four hours hence, as the time for their train to leave, the president hastily adjourned the meeting, and Mallory and Reagan hurried to their offices to start the packing.[19]

Davis immediately got a wire off to Johnston informing him of Lee's surrender, ordered his aides Johnston and Lubbock and Harrison to oversee preparing the train, then returned to the Sutherlin house.[20] By now he no longer concealed his agitation over the news. After whispering to Mrs. Sutherlin that Lee had been forced to surrender and he and the government must leave immediately, the president hurriedly began packing some important papers and a few personal items in a valise. Just then Governor William Smith, who was himself attempting to reestablish the state government in Danville, came to call, and Davis told him the fateful news. The governor saw the president pacing back and forth, clearly nervous and agitated, and Davis had little to say to him other than to confirm Lee's surrender and declare that "I shall be off as soon as I can get ready."[21] He summoned Gorgas, Cooper, and other War Department staff, but when they arrived he had no instructions to give them. Gorgas thought the president "was evidently overwhelmed by this astounding misfortune," and when Davis could give him no directions, he said he would wait for orders until Breckinridge arrived on the morrow, evidence again that the officials looked increasingly to the secretary of war and not the president for guidance in the crisis. Kean, too, complained that neither Davis nor his cabinet gave any instructions to the several bureau chiefs like himself and Gorgas, "which caused great confusion" and no little resentment at their being effectively abandoned to their own devices until Breckinridge arrived.[22] Only Mallory showed any real energy as he went back and forth through the muddy streets giving orders and arranging transportation to the depot for the most vital naval property.[23]

As usual, Benjamin and George Davis had little to do. Benjamin returned to his lodgings and said nothing to his hosts, putting on the same carefree pose as usual and even discussing some Tennyson that he intended to regale them with later that evening. But then he motioned his friend Dr. Hoge to step out of the room with him. "I did not have the heart to tell those good ladies what I have just learned," he confessed. "General Lee has surrendered and I fear the Confederate cause is lost." Asked what course he might pursue now, the secretary of state said he would go with the fleeing government to Greensboro, but that was as far as his own fixed purpose stretched at the moment. Hoge suggested that the official party would now surely be the object of a concerted Yankee pursuit, making any escape the more difficult if Benjamin remained with Davis. Benjamin only responded with what Hoge thought a pitiless smile, saying "I will never be taken alive."[24]

At once all was bustle and rush. Officials and clerks and confused soldiers filled the streets. What could not be loaded hastily on the few trains at the depot had to be abandoned, and commissaries threw open the doors to their warehouses to the people, who gathered in a dense crowd to collect what they could and then leave for the countryside before rumors of approaching Yankee cavalry were realized. People took whatever they could, with little thought of practicality. One ragged veteran, his uniform and shoes falling to pieces around him, eschewed new apparel and even rations in favor of a heavy box of tobacco he could scarcely carry.[25]

Somehow no one at the Benedict house thought to notify Trenholm, who only got the news when he asked about all the commotion outside his sickroom window at the Sutherlin house. He then learned that he had but an hour to get to the depot. "This was the most dreadful and trying part of the journey," Anna lamented. Her husband dressed quickly despite his persistent nausea, but there was no time or energy to pack their baggage. Moreover, the spring rain had been falling heavily now for two days, turning the red clay of the streets into a perfect morass. When the Trenholms left the house and tried to walk to the station, they sank at every step to their ankles in the mud. Unable to make any progress in his condition, Trenholm hailed a rickety farm cart and they rode in the back of it a third of the way to the depot until they met an ambulance that someone finally thought to send for them. Even then, the remaining trip, though short, was so rough in the mud that Trenholm became violently ill before they reached the depot and discovered that there appeared to be no passenger cars at all. No one knew if Davis and the rest had already left, or even if any trains were going to go out after all. Trenholm could barely stand, and there was no place in the depot for him to sit, so Anna found him a spot on the floor of a boxcar and laid him on some blankets and one of her shawls. An hour or so of rest, some of the peach brandy that Anna thought to bring along, and liberal inhalation of a strong cologne as a stimulant finally revived the Treasury secretary sufficiently that he could face the trip ahead. Even then, Anna told him nothing of what she had learned of Lee's surrender, fearing the news would prostrate him. Trenholm soon heard it for himself from those bustling around the train as it loaded.[26]

Davis had sent orders to the depot at 5 P.M. for an engine to be coupled to a passenger coach; two boxcars for horses, vital records, and whatever else could be loaded; and a flat car for the rest. Train master J. H. Averill got it ready, but then the delays commenced. Mallory, Reagan, Kean, General Cooper, and others each insisted that a boxcar be attached for the impedimenta of their departments, and Averill obliged, but it slowed their departure. Eventually there were ten cars hooked to the engine, and despite the train master's protest that the dilapidated locomotive could handle no more, Davis's staff authorized adding two more cars.[27]

The president and cabinet packed in such a hurry that each took little more than a valise with essential toiletries and a few changes of shirts and underclothes. Everything else they would have to leave behind in the rush to get to the depot by the appointed hour.[28] As bad as the short journey was for the Trenholms, it was little better for the rest. Mallory thought the mud knee deep, and when he reached the depot it seemed a bedlam. By now it was dark, and out of the gloom came a cacophony of yells from teamsters, swearing soldiers, panicked civilians shouting to find missing companions, and the snorts and squeals of horses spooked as handlers tried to force them aboard the stock car. "Nothing seemed to be ready or in order," Mallory complained. It was the very opposite of the essentially calm and organized scene of a week before at the depot in Richmond, and evidence of the need of Breckinridge's calm guiding hand. Now no one seemed to be in charge. In the melee, especially with Trenholm incapacitated, it is even possible that no one thought to retrieve some of the silver coin that had been deposited in the local bank vault.[29]

As a result, 8 P.M. came and went without their departure. Two hours later the cabinet and principal staff, excepting Trenholm in his boxcar, still stood or sat in a little group near the train, huddled on or around their meager baggage to protect it in the crush. Reagan stood atop his trunk, while George Davis and Benjamin sat on their luggage, bags that in Benjamin's case included a cooked ham given him by his recent hosts.[30] Around them swirled a sea of jammed quartermaster wagons bringing supplies and department baggage, soldiers and stragglers trying to push past the train guard Harrison had placed there to stop those without authorization forcing their way onto the cars, and a general press of civilians now panicked by reports that enemy cavalry had already cut the rail line to Greensboro, trapping them all. People besieged Harrison with pleas to allow them on the train, but no matter how many cars he had added to the engine, they were not enough. General Gabriel Rains, an assistant to Gorgas responsible for land mines and other so-called "infernal machines," came to Harrison and announced that he had with him an assortment of his devices and that he and they, as well as his two daughters, ought to be placed on the presidential train. Harrison refused him politely, especially since he was not anxious to have explosives as baggage despite Rains's assurances that they were harmless. But Rains somehow got to Davis and played on their old prewar association to get himself and family aboard.[31]

The rain at least had tapered to a light drizzle, still adding to the gloom of the dark, moonless night. Listening to all the uproar around them, the cabinet actually saw very little except the constant red glow from Benjamin's cigar. Finally at eleven o'clock Davis himself arrived, after an emotional parting with the Sutherlins. He had eaten a light evening meal to make up for the one so brutally interrupted earlier that afternoon. During the course of the strained conversation, the others at his table including Benjamin and Reagan raised the question of what to do if they had to retreat all the way to the coast and take ship for Texas and the Trans-Mississippi department. They would need money, but between them they had no more than a thousand dollars, and Davis confessed that he had not a cent except in now worthless Confederate money. As the president was leaving for the depot, Mrs. Sutherlin handed her husband a bag with a thousand dollars in gold that they had carefully hoarded through the war, telling him to give it to Davis. Sutherlin tried to do so as Davis entered his carriage, saying it was "a mere trifle of gold—take it, and ask no further questions." Davis tearfully declined. "I cannot," he said. "You may need it more than I."[32] Saying farewell to Sutherlin on the platform, the president and the others took their seats in the passenger coach.[33] One of his last acts had been a letter of thanks to the mayor and town council of Danville for their hospitality. "I had hoped to be able to maintain the Confederate Government on the soil of Virginia," he lamented. Instead, "the shadows of misfortune which were on us when I came have become darker."[34]

Though Harrison had reserved an entire seat for the president, Davis now found that his kindness to General Rains resulted in there being no other place for one of the daughters except next to himself. "That young lady was of a loquacity irrepressible," Harrison realized when it was too late. "She plied her neighbor diligently—about the weather, and upon every other topic of common interest." The train had not even started yet, for the recent rain soaked much of the cord wood for the locomotive, and it would not burn. "There we all were, in our seats, crowded together, waiting to be off, full of gloom at the situation, wondering what would happen next, and all as silent as mourners at a funeral," said Harrison, "all except, indeed, the General's daughter." Everyone else could see on Davis's face his annoyance and impatience at her tedious prattle, but not the girl herself. She only stopped briefly when a loud report near their seat startled them all. One of Rains's assistants had also gotten on the car and carried in his coat pocket a small contact fuse that accidentally exploded when he sat down rather too vigorously on the top of the unlit iron stove at the end of the car. As the officer jumped up and everyone else leapt to their feet in surprise, he began comically trying to smother the smoking embers alarmingly close to his posterior.[35] Harrison filed the episode away as one of "some sad and amusing stories" that he intended to regale Varina Davis with when next they met.[36]

At last the train began a halting movement out of the station sometime around 11 P.M., but it was destined to be a short trip at first. The track proved bad, which slowed them considerably, and then no more than five miles south of Danville, virtually on the North Carolina border, the overtaxed engine simply broke down. Someone had to get a horse off the stock car and ride back to Danville, and they lost more time while waiting for another engine to arrive to continue their journey.[37] Thereafter it took them another two hours or more to make the comparatively short forty miles to Greensboro, a journey that Anna Trenholm found tedious and that must have been even more tiresome for Davis with his garrulous seat companion.[38] It became positively uncomfortable at one point when smoke from the woodstove backed up in the flue and filled the car. The occupants cried out as their eyes watered, and a few like Reagan probably swore eloquently until they got windows open and the car emptied of the clouds, only to let in a cold breeze that chilled them all. They may not have known that the cause was a small group of nine soldiers who could not get a pass from Davis's staff to board the train. Instead, they had shoved past Harrison's guard and climbed atop the presidential car. As the train moved out of the station, they felt the cold of the night air made worse by the soaking drizzle, and so for warmth they huddled around the stove flue where it emerged from the roof of the car. To trap more of the escaping heat, they piled their blankets over the pipe and sheltered themselves underneath, and even when they heard the passengers' outcry below they kept the flue covered, the smoke below only making those dark shadows surrounding the Confederacy even blacker.[39]

Behind them the fleeing government left another town in shock. Danville had seen almost nothing of the war directly, and then for the past week it had been the capital of the Confederacy. Suddenly that was gone as abruptly as it had come, and in its place was the fear of imminent enemy attack. Another engine with additional archives and government staff went out after the presidential train, while the crowds went on to loot more storehouses, and then early the next morning the arsenal accidentally exploded, killing fifty or more of the townspeople who had been rummaging through it, too, in search of anything worth taking.[40] A last troop train departed at noon on April 11, and Kean managed to get himself and his remaining employees and boxes of office archives aboard. Just how near a thing the removal of the government was became evident when this train covered barely half the distance to Greensboro before it was stopped at the Haw River by a bridge burned the night before by Union cavalry raiders.[41] In fact, they struck not more than five minutes after Davis and the cabinet train passed over the span. Told of the narrowness of his escape when he reached Greensboro, Davis only replied that "a miss is as good as a mile."[42] The old bravado was returning after his recent shocks, and as he faced finding a new capital and the new circumstances created by Lee's surrender, the president felt once more ready to accept the challenge. William Preston Johnston, with him as they detrained in the North Carolina city, perceived that the president was "as collected as ever."[43]

And yet the government was not entirely gone from Danville. Sometime in the late morning of April 11, Breckinridge and his party rode into town. Expecting to find Davis and cabinet, the secretary of war found instead that virtually everyone of importance had left. He took heart from at least one of those who remained, however, for here he met his son Clifton. "I saw that the time had come for those who loved our leaders to gather around them," the young man said. As a result, five days earlier, when the rest of the midshipmen were ordered south with the treasure train, he requested a month's leave of absence so that he could wait for his father to arrive, and tendered a resignation that would take effect thereafter.[44] Parker could hardly object, since there was no longer a navy.

There was little for Breckinridge to do in Danville, and he could have moved on immediately once Clifton joined him, but he stopped to do what he could for the soldiers remaining in town, both those still under some semblance of discipline and those clearly on their way home. Taking quarters in the recently abandoned Benedict house, he cared for these men as best he could, doling out any supplies remaining in the plundered government warehouses. Several dismounted Kentucky cavalrymen, cut off from their command, trudged in that afternoon and called on the general. One of them he immediately recognized as Leeland Hathaway, whom he had met years before at home. "His memory of faces & names was phenomenal," Hathaway recalled. Breckinridge saw worn-out men who had literally walked through the soles of their boots till their feet bled. He stood at once to welcome them "with that immaculate grace & charm which never left him," and greeted a startled Hathaway by name, asking what he could do for them all. The soldiers wanted to get to Johnston's command in North Carolina, and at that Breckinridge gave them orders for new army shoes, saddles and bridles, and leave to take any horses they could find.[45]

Late that morning General Rosser and staff rode into town, having escaped the surrender at Appomattox and sent his remaining cavalry troopers to Lynchburg. He had hoped to find Davis here in order to give a better report than he had been able to send back through Captain Graves, but now he met with

Breckinridge and passed along a full account of Appomattox. Breckinridge ordered Rosser to return to central Virginia to try to gather as many stragglers, detached commands, and other soldiers not covered under Lee's surrender and parole terms. He wanted the cavalryman to organize them and then report to Governor Smith.[46]

Rosser had hoped to get authorization to continue to fight as a partisan, but Breckinridge had entirely different plans for him. The Kentuckian had heard enough of what happened in Richmond after the evacuation, and now with his own eyes saw in Danville the results of a similar breakdown in law when the authorities left. He wanted to prevent such looting and destruction, not to mention accidental loss of life, occurring again. Admitting as he had for some time that the cause was hopeless, he could have had no purpose of continued resistance in mind for Rosser, especially guerilla warfare, which the secretary always repudiated. Lee's surrender meant that the Yankees held virtual sway over the entire state, making any small command of a few hundred—or even a few thousand such as Rosser might assemble—futile in opposition.

But placing such soldiers under civilian control of the governor would make them state troops rather than Confederate. They might then function as normal militia to maintain civil order during the vacuum between the collapse of Confederate control and the transition to Union rule. Breckinridge probably had an even more subtle end in mind, however, one consistent with the discussions he and Campbell and others had been having for some time. If Campbell succeeded in getting authorization for the legislature to convene and exert some degree of civil authority as the sitting, rightfully elected representatives of the people, then it would be consistent for Lincoln to recognize Smith as an equally lawfully elected governor. In effect, Breckinridge and Campbell combined would be attempting to direct a form of Confederate "reconstruction," with a state civil government that recognized the end of slavery and the resumption of national authority, while fielding a perfectly legal state militia to enforce it. If the Union let them get away with it, it would be the gentlest sort of reconstruction they could hope for, and far better than they had a right to expect. Once again Virginia's example could spread easily to North Carolina, and thereafter no Confederate state could hold out.

Soon after Rosser left, General Lunsford L. Lomax came in from the west for a similar consultation, and likely left with similar instructions.[47] Unfortunately, Breckinridge did not know that Smith, who had left Danville, was not returning to Virginia any time soon, which would have seriously weakened the tenuous scheme, nor could he know that while Campbell had achieved some seeming concessions from Lincoln, political opposition in the North forced Lincoln to reconsider, even as Lee's surrender virtually ended the war in Virginia and made Campbell's proposals irrelevant after all. It would be a few days yet before Breckinridge learned enough to realize that any hope for "Confederate reconstruction" of Virginia was gone, but by then he was already walking on the next potential stage for enacting peace without defeat. After a long day of acting as the only official of the Confederacy in the town that had until the day before been its last capital, he rode out with Clifton and the others late that night for North Carolina and the government on wheels.[48]

Chapter Five

"I CANNOT FEEL
LIKE A BEATEN MAN"

No welcoming committee met the presidential train at the Greensboro depot that cold and rainy morning. Most of the town was asleep, and when awakened, officials were none too forthcoming. Former Governor John Morehead offered the comfort of his substantial house to Trenholm and his wife, while Davis found lodging at the temporary home of his aide and kinsman John Taylor Wood. But the town had nothing to offer to the rest of the cabinet or Davis's staff. In the end they had no recourse but to make do with living in a broken-down passenger coach with a leaking roof.[1] The fact was that western North Carolina had never been strongly committed to the cause, its hilly reaches harboring strong pockets of Unionism just as did the high country throughout the South. Moreover, in the current state of disaster, the arrival of Davis and his government could only result in making Greensboro itself a target for Yankee raiders who, until now, had spared the city. No wonder "they found very few sympathizers," as the clerk Charles E. L. Stuart observed.[2] William Preston Johnston, who wrote to his wife that "we had a good time at Danville," could only say of Greensboro that they "got along," though when he sent Varina Davis a note, he sought to alleviate any concern she might feel for her husband and his official family by saying that "we are a fixture for the present and are comfortable fixed." Looking back on the last few days, young Harrison confessed that "an age seems to me to have passed."[3]

Mallory was more forthright about Greensboro. "Off hand, generous hospitality has ever been regarded as a characteristic of the South," he wrote, "but at Greensboro it was the old story, of which political history presents so many chapters; the ship was sinking and, in their haste to desert her, the expeditious rats would not even see those who still stood by her Colors." Johnston was in retreat before Sherman, the capital at Raleigh might soon fall, and Greensboro itself could soon be in Yankee hands. Vengeance might then find any who showed undue charity or support to Davis and his ministers.[4] Those who could not get aboard the train but had to ride to Greensboro met the same reception. Indeed, along much of the way the North Carolinians seemed unfriendly, some even pleased to hear that Richmond had fallen and the war must be nearly over. Moreover, most seemed to blame Davis himself for their misfortunes. In Greensboro itself some townspeople forthrightly and repeatedly asked the visitors "how long are you going to stay?"[5]

The best the government would get from Greensboro was what Wood himself described as "sullen indifference."[6] Indeed,

Wood's own landlord protested initially at the notion of housing Davis even temporarily in Wood's rented lodgings. He relented enough for the president to move into a small second-floor room with little but a bed, a writing desk, and a handful of chairs, but Davis did not protest. It was likely the same room occupied by Varina just five nights before on her way to Charlotte, and she may have left letters for him with Wood.[7] More than that, however, in the face of disaster, Davis felt the return of even more of his resolve, the sort that could be sustained only by unrealistic optimism. He had received no report from Lee himself of the surrender, and as a result he was no sooner off the train and established at Wood's than he began to look for a silver lining. He wired Governor Vance that afternoon that reports of Lee's surrender were unofficial. Confessing that the disaster must have been such that the Army of Northern Virginia no longer existed as an organized force, he began still to indulge the hope that Lee and his senior officers and large numbers of the men in the ranks might somehow have escaped capture. Such men, with Lee at their head, could be the nucleus of renewed resistance. "An army holding its position with determination to fight on, and manifest ability to maintain the struggle, will attract all the scattered soldiers and daily and rapidly gather strength," he declared. They must redouble their efforts. Seeing the evidences of demoralization and outright disloyalty evident in Greensboro's surly welcome, he warned the governor that "moral influence is wanting," and urged him to do what he could to revive public spirit.[8] Young Johnston echoed his chief's sentiments when he declared the next day that "the loss of an army is not the loss of the cause" and that "there is a great deal of fight in us yet."[9]

This same spirit animated Davis when Beauregard, summoned from Raleigh, arrived by train not long after the government train itself came in. The general and Davis thoroughly detested each other, though at least the president gave Beauregard credit for being a fighter, unlike the timorous Joseph E. Johnston. Making his headquarters in a boxcar of his own, Beauregard immediately went to the government train, where he found the cabinet and their staff in good cheer and quite hospitable in their ludicrous quarters, though he thought they looked rather pathetic—helpless bureaucrats roughing it. They pumped him relentlessly for his assessment of their prospects in the state, scarcely giving him a chance to answer until Davis himself stepped onto the car and took him aside to speak in private.

Beauregard gave Davis an unvarnished account of the situation, if anything shaded even darker by his own conviction that they were beaten. Sherman had more than ninety thousand men marching on Johnston's fraction of that number, perhaps no more than twenty-four thousand. Reports from Georgia and Alabama told of deep enemy penetrations that Confederate forces were too weak to resist. Men from their armies were absent without leave, scattered all across the country, and though he was attempting to collect those within his area of command, he thought they faced an inevitable end, and soon. Davis paid him the courtesy of attentively listening, but it was evident to the general that the president was not interested in his conclusions. Instead, he said exactly the same thing to Beauregard that he wrote that day to Vance. West of the Mississippi, with E. Kirby Smith's army reputed to be sixty thousand strong, they could hope to "prolong the war indefinitely." Beauregard was shocked at what he called

Davis's "visionary hope," but perhaps not surprised, as he never placed much faith in Davis's military judgment.[10]

Later that day Davis wired Johnston to come to Greensboro to confer with himself, Beauregard, and Breckinridge, whose arrival he expected hourly. Johnston's train pulled into the yard the next morning, but instead of going directly to the president he met first with Beauregard. Besides sharing a loathing of Davis, they were alike agreed in their conviction that the fighting must end and quickly, and now they consulted on how best to present a united front when they met the president. Shortly after midday Davis asked them to come to his ersatz cabinet room in one of the boxcars, but instead of having them lay their views before the gathering, Davis simply lectured generals and ministers alike. Their cause was not defeated, he told them. They would merely shift the scene of resistance west of the Mississippi where General E. Kirby Smith still commanded a large, though scattered army, and remnants, like those of Lee's men who escaped Grant, would migrate west and rally to their standard. He refused to countenance any of their protests to the contrary and postponed further discussion until Breckinridge should arrive.[11]

That afternoon Davis returned to his room at Wood's, and there welcomed several visitors, including the son of General Lee, who had managed to escape before the surrender. Happy to be talking with patriots willing to continue the fight, rather than pessimists like Beauregard and Johnston, Davis warmed to his theme and calmly predicted to them that though they were sorely pressed, still they could prevail. As he was speaking, General Lee's formal notification of the surrender and the magnitude of the loss arrived. There were no remnants of the Virginia army

other than scattered and disorganized clumps of cavalry. Lee himself was on parole as a prisoner of war and would never lead Confederate arms again. Davis read the news quietly, then handed it
over to young Lee and Wood to read while he turned his head
away that they might not see his tears. "He seemed quite broken at the moment," said Lee as he and everyone else but Wood
left the president's room.[12] Wood himself remained with his kinsman, his own spirits shattered. The news was overwhelming, he
soon wrote in his diary. "It crushes the hopes of nearly all."[13]

That evening Breckinridge finally arrived after a hard ride
from Danville, having to skirt Yankee raiders along the way. Preston Johnston saw him when he arrived at Wood's house to report to Davis, and found him "quite well & bright" despite the
rigors of his journey.[14] But he came on no cheerful mission as
he went to Davis's room and had the sad duty of confirming the
day's earlier dispatch, as well as giving Davis his first intimate
eyewitness picture of affairs with Lee in the last days before the
surrender. Davis heard the news in his usual manner, no doubt,
then notified Breckinridge of the cabinet conference scheduled
for ten o'clock the next morning. The secretary of war's work
was not over for the evening, however. He met with some of the
other cabinet ministers in their car, and likely from them learned
of the views expressed by Beauregard and Johnston. Certainly
the cabinet knew that the generals thought the cause was lost,
and now either Breckinridge sought out Johnston, the senior
general, or Johnston came to him.

Johnston frankly told Breckinridge that further resistance was
futile and would only add to the sufferings of the Confederate
soldiers and people without benefiting a cause that was now
dead. He outlined for the secretary what he knew of the more

recent movements of their forces in the Carolinas and on west to the Mississippi, developments from which Breckinridge had been largely cut off for the past ten days, though it hardly surprised him to learn of the continuing dissolution of their various armies. Johnston argued that the only power remaining in Davis's hands now was that of ending the war by giving up resistance, which he ought to do at once. Breckinridge, of course, agreed and had felt the same for weeks. He asked Johnston if he would be willing to express his views before Davis and the cabinet, and when the general agreed, Breckinridge pledged to get him an opportunity to do so.[15]

Soon after leaving Breckinridge, Johnston met with Mallory, who volunteered his own anxiety to end the war speedily. "What, in your judgment, do the best interest of our people require of the Government?" asked Mallory in phrasing that sounded rather as if designed to elicit an answer as testimony for the record. "We must stop fighting at once," Johnston replied, "and secure peace upon the best terms we can obtain."

"Can we secure terms?"

"I think we can," said Johnston. "At all events we should make the effort at once, for we are at the end of our row." Knowing that he had an ally now, Mallory replied that

your position as the chief of this army, & as the military Commander of this Dept. demands from you a frank statement of your views to the President. You believe that our cause is hopeless, & that further resistance, with the means at our command, would not only be useless but unjustifiable, and that we should lay down our arms & secure the best terms we can get for our people. I will, if you please, state all this to the President, but I think you had better do so at once, and explicitly.

Mallory had seconded Breckinridge in asking the general to place his frank view before the president, perhaps even acting at his urging. Supported by Beauregard, Johnston would add one more witness for the prosecution against continuation. Both Breckinridge and Mallory already knew that to date the cabinet would not stand up to Davis, Mallory himself having gone along until now. Breckinridge's own voice would be but one, however powerful; the more men he could parade before the president to argue the same case, the stronger it became, and the greater also was the chance that in a growing collective opposition to continuing the war, the rest of the cabinet might find the spine to speak up, especially Reagan, who showed independent spirit, at least in private. Indeed, Reagan himself may have been visited by Breckinridge or Mallory that night, for when the time came he would suddenly stand in agreement with them.[16]

They gathered once more in the room at Wood's house the following morning—Davis, Breckinridge, Mallory, Reagan, Benjamin, George Davis, Beauregard, and Johnston, with only the ailing Trenholm absent. During the night Breckinridge had gotten to Davis and impressed on him the necessity of all the cabinet hearing Johnston's report; it only remained for the general to do his part to get the necessary discussion in train.[17] Clearly Breckinridge did not warn the president as to the extent of Johnston's views or that he would be suggesting negotiations, for when Davis told his cabinet beforehand of his purpose in calling the meeting, he told them that it was only to hear the generals' report on the condition of their armies and what future course they could advise with reasonable expectation of success. "I was fully sensible of the gravity of our position," he said later, but in spite of that he immediately reverted to his old habit of opening cabinet sessions with irrelevant recollections and anecdotes.[18] The others, most of whom had a different expectation of what they should be doing, looked on in wonder as he reminisced. Observed an incredulous Mallory,

> At a time when the cause of the Confederacy was hopeless, when its soldiers were throwing away their arms and returning to their homes, when its government stript of nearly all power could not hope to exist beyond a few days more, and when the enemy, more powerful & exultant than ever, was advancing upon all sides, true to his habit, he introduced several subjects of conversation unconnected with the condition of the Country, and discussed them as if at some pleasant ordinary meeting.[19]

Reagan, too, caught the feeling that perhaps no one wanted to introduce the subject for which they were really gathered, as if postponing bad news would make it evaporate.[20]

Most probably, of course, Davis simply hoped to forestall facing the inevitable reality of what he was about to hear. Even then, when finally he called on the generals to speak, he tried to preempt the impact of what he knew they would say. They all felt the gravity of the situation, he said. There was no denying their recent reverses. "But I do not think we should regard them as fatal," he went on. "I think we can whip the enemy yet if our people will turn out. We must look at matters calmly, however, & see what is left for us to do. Whatever can be done must be done at once. We have not a day to lose." It was the old mantra yet again. Renew their spirit, bring their stragglers and deserters back into the ranks, and they could yet achieve their independence.

Johnston did not speak at first, perhaps dumbfounded by Davis's optimism, or simply not certain that the president had finally finished his small address. "We should like to have your views General Johnston," Davis prompted. Only then did the general speak, and as he started, the president purposely avoided looking him in the face but began to fiddle with a scrap of paper on the table.

> My views are Sir, that our people are tired of the war, feel them-selves whipped, & will not fight. Our country is overrun, its military resources greatly diminished, while the enemy's military power & resources were never greater, and may be increased to any extent desired. We cannot place another large army in the field, and, cut off as we are from foreign intercourse, I do not see how we could main-tain it in fighting condition if we had it.—My men are daily desert-ing in large numbers, and are stealing my artillery teams to aid their escape to their homes. Since Lee's defeat they regard the war as at an end. If I march out of North Carolina her people will all leave my ranks. It will be the same as I proceed South through S. C. & Geo., & I shall expect to retain no man beyond the bye road or cow path that leads to his home.—My small force is melting away like snow before the sun & I am hopeless of recruiting it.

Johnston spoke deliberately, the expression on his face mirror-ing the somberness of his words, and revealing as well the utter detestation he felt for Davis. Indeed, Mallory thought the gen-eral sounded almost spiteful as he spat out his concise sen-tences, pausing between each for greatest effect. It would be a crime to continue the war, Johnston concluded. The president should immediately open peace negotiations.[21]

Davis never took his eyes off the paper in his hand but re-peatedly folded and unfolded it, either as a studied rudeness to Johnston, whose loathing he reciprocated, or because he sought to lose himself in abstraction rather than face both Johnston's

scorn and his words. For a minute or two after the general finished, no one spoke. Then Davis, his face still impassive, said
to Beauregard in a deliberate yet strangely muffled tone, "What
do you say?" That general only replied that he was in full agreement.[22] Another silence followed, one that Reagan recalled as
funereal in tone, as "it was apparent that we must consider the
probable loss of our cause."[23]

Davis continued to stare at his folded paper while the rest
watched him intently. Finally he spoke again, turning to the
cabinet and asking for their reaction to what the generals had
said. This was the moment Breckinridge had been working toward since he first asked Lee for his own report, and the same
from his department heads, some two months earlier. In the
end, Lee had been unable or unwilling to stand to the mark. But
Johnston, perhaps helped in part by his hearty hatred of Davis,
had done so now and gladly—and with Lee out of the equation,
Johnston spoke as their senior field commander, and Beauregard
the next senior.

One by one they agreed with the generals. Reagan spoke
first, advising that they capitulate and suggesting that they seek
much the same terms that Campbell and Breckinridge had been
working toward. Given that until this moment Reagan had
shown no predilection to get involved in the peace question,
and that he had backed Davis until now, there is every probability that Breckinridge—with whom he would associate closely
in the days ahead—managed to persuade and prompt him before the meeting. Now he proposed disbanding their army and
acknowledging the authority of the United States in return for
the preservation of their existing state governments, no inter-
ference with personal and property rights of Southern citizens,

amnesty against prosecution for participating in the war, and the privilege of their soldiers marching to their home states under arms and their own colors, and once home, to turn over their weapons. He said nothing about slavery, though it must have been implicit to them all that their regional institution would have to die with their hopes for independence. Breckinridge spoke immediately to second Reagan's proposal, then Mallory followed, and finally George Davis, and their only substantive difference with the terms outlined by Reagan was a general agreement that Davis and themselves would probably have to be excluded from any amnesty. Only Benjamin, sycophantic to the end, urged that they were not beaten and ought to carry on the fight, despite his own expression of defeat when he was leaving Danville. Indeed, the secretary of state actually made an impassioned plea for continuing the war that surprised even those accustomed to his toadying to Davis.[24]

Very likely stunned by the seeming rebellion in his cabinet and the way the discussion had gotten beyond his control, Davis asked Johnston what he proposed to do, reminding him that at least twice in recent months, the enemy had refused to discuss terms with them. That refusal to negotiate, based as Davis knew it would be on his own insistence that Confederate independence was a sine qua non, had twice so far defeated the peace movement, and likely he counted on it again now. But Johnston countered with a variation of the generals' wives scheme that Breckinridge had favored, and with which the Kentuckian might well have prompted him the night before. He suggested that he and Sherman open discussions for terms regarding only military forces, which easily fell within common military usage and could involve no political stumbling blocks. Davis agreed that it could be tried, and then went on to display probably the same feigned willingness with which he had duped the Hampton Roads commission into thinking that he was actually open to serious negotiations. "We can easily try it Sir," he said before the cabinet. "If we can accomplish any good for the country, Heaven knows I am not particular as to form."

Johnston suggested sending a note to Sherman to propose an interview between them, with an armistice pending the outcome. It was the old story so far as Davis was concerned. Nothing would come of a meeting because neither Sherman nor his government would negotiate with the Confederate government itself on any basis including independence, and as chief diplomat, it would be up to Davis himself to determine Southern terms. Naturally he would never approve any cartel arranged between Johnston and Sherman that proposed the terms Reagan outlined, but an armistice in the meantime only served his purpose by allowing more time for him to inspirit his soldiers and his people. Indeed, a failure of military negotiations might have the same salutary effect on Southern will as the civil rebuff at Hampton Roads. In short, Davis had nothing to lose by letting Johnston have his way, because he knew that he could himself prevent anything coming of the meeting. Such a failure would also serve to admonish his wavering cabinet that their only alternative was to continue. In his own obsession with independence or nothing, he simply could not grasp that, for the rest— probably even Benjamin—independence had for some time ceased to be a consideration. "Well, Sir, you can adopt this course," Davis said to Johnston, "though I confess I am not sanguine as to ultimate results."

While Mallory took down his words, Davis himself dictated a

brief note to Sherman on behalf of Johnston, and typically it said nothing of the possibility of defeat or surrender. It only acknowledged that Lee's surrender had "changed the relative military conditions of the belligerents," and on that basis asked for a "suspension of active operations" not only by Sherman but also from Grant, "to permit the civil authorities to enter into the needful arrangements to terminate the existing war." Davis was trying to buy time, for a suspension of operations would mean no movement at all by the Yankee armies, thus stalling a junction between Grant and Sherman, and halting Union forces everywhere else in their tracks. This was more than a mere cease-fire—and Davis surely knew well that the Yankees would never agree to that—but then his statement about "the civil authorities" taking over once the armistice was in place was his anticipated jugular blow to anything coming of this approach. That would end this little palace coup and show them they must follow his lead. Breckinridge, at least, should have seen what the president was trying to do. More likely, all of them did. Certainly Mallory saw that all of them recognized that "no further military stand could be made." That being the case, what was left them but capitulation? That no one objected to the president's self-defeating wording of the note to Sherman, signified only the logical expectation that at this stage the momentum of events would surely propel any military talks beyond just the arena of the generals, by which time Davis would be powerless to halt their progress.[25]

That did not quite end the meeting, for after Johnston signed the note and sent it off for immediate delivery to Sherman, Davis went on to ask Johnston what line of retreat he currently projected for getting his army to the southwest, ultimately to join with remaining forces in Alabama and elsewhere. That alone demonstrated Davis's expectation that nothing would come of a meeting with Sherman, and moreover his own intention that the failure of such a meeting would not eventuate in a surrender of Johnston's army, let alone the Confederacy.[26] What Johnston thought when he left that evening to return to his army was another matter.

When the generals and ministers departed, Davis remained at Wood's and allowed the iron mask to fall from his face. The rejection by his cabinet mirrored his treatment at his lodging, where his hosts repeatedly asked Wood when he and the president would leave, even insisting that they must go, as they were fearful that Yankee cavalry raiding the region would exact revenge upon them for harboring Davis. They were only the more alarmed to have Johnston and Beauregard and almost the entire cabinet in their home. Seeing the mood revealed on Davis's face, Wood wrote in his diary that "depression is universal and disorganization is setting in."[27]

That evening Breckinridge and the rest of the cabinet stood around a fire outside their rail car lodgings discussing the meeting and what it meant. Despite their initial chagrin at being refused hospitality in the town's homes, the ministers and clerks did not find their passenger car existence entirely uncomfortable, thanks chiefly to the good cheer with which most of them met their adversity. In fact, Mallory thought the "Cabinet car" proved to be what he called "a very agreeable resort." They even welcomed visitors with an exaggerated hospitality in inverse proportion to the humility of their lodgings, and here at least the perpetual good humor of Benjamin, the jolliest of the bunch, served a good purpose in uplifting and stimulating the flow of good cheer amongst them all and as a counterbalance to General Cooper's persistent disgust with their conditions. Benjamin may well have exaggerated his own bonhomie specifically to tease old Cooper, continuing a less than friendly relationship between them that dated back years to Benjamin's' brief tenure as secretary of war.[28] Mallory's car of naval stores provided them with abundant stores of bacon and bread, while others managed to forage eggs, biscuits, and coffee locally. "With a few tin cups, spoons & pocket knives, & a liberal use of fingers, & capital apetites," said Mallory, they ate their fill.

It often presented an amusing prospect. The habitually serious attorney general George Davis looked entirely comical holding in one hand a crude corn cake, baked on a hoe held over the fire, while in the other he grasped a chunk of fat bacon semi-broiled over the same coals, his face all the while showing the exertions required to chew the tough meat. Benjamin perched above a bucket of stewed apples, alternately reaching into a bag filled with hard-boiled eggs, his Danville ham long since gone. The whittler Reagan, most at home with a knife, plied his Bowie blade over a ham of his own "as if it were the chief business of life," while the necessity of sharing a tin cup for coffee meant that Mallory had to swallow his scalding hot in order to pass it along to the others before it cooled. He observed with amusement that officials until then accustomed to discussing the great affairs of state, from secession to foreign intervention, now devoted their conversation to whether or not there would be dinner, and if so, what and where. The same debate also ensued when they tried to sleep in the cramped seats and on the floor of the cabinet car, turning on the geometric problem of a six-foot man lying comfortably on a four-foot seat. As a result,

Mallory impishly observed that "the times were 'sadly out of joint' just then, and so was the Confederate Government."[29]

As they stood around the fire that evening, gnawing at their bacon and dreading the nightly contortions on the coach seats, the government clerk W. H. Swallow, just arrived on horseback from Danville, approached out of the gloom, recognizing Breckinridge's voice. When he asked what was happening, the Kentuckian took him aside. "We shall not be here long," he confided, "but will move on to Charlotte in a day or so." He may not have told the others yet, but he had reports that Yankee cavalry raids had cut the railroad and burned bridges below them. The enemy might not yet know just where Davis and his government were, but they must soon learn, especially given the temper of the townsfolk of Greensboro. The city would inevitably be a Federal objective, and soon. Moreover, since he and the other secretaries now believed that events had been put in motion leading to a surrender—and by common assent they expected that no amnesty or pardon would apply to them—it was imperative that they not risk being taken. "From this point I shall ride southward on horseback," Breckinridge continued, there being no alternative.[30]

He and the rest felt special concern for Davis, whom they were sure would take no special precautions for his own safety. Apparently after the cabinet meeting that day, Breckinridge and Benjamin, despite their differences on the prospect of further resistance, approached the president either singly or together and suggested that it was time to consider plans for his escape from the country. That presented a challenge, for Davis told them both that no matter what happened, he would not leave Confederate soil so long as there was an organized band of men anywhere still willing to resist. Before they left Greensboro, Davis's attitude was common knowledge among all the cabinet. "He shrank from the idea of abandoning any body of men who might still be found willing to strike for the cause," mused Mallory, "and gave little attention to the question of his personal safety."[31]

As it happened, Colonel Charles Thorburn had just arrived in Greensboro. Formerly a blockade runner, he had a small boat concealed on the Indian River on the east coast of Florida. He and Wood now hatched a scheme whereby his associates would first get Davis to Florida, and then Thorburn could take him by boat around the Florida peninsula and across the Gulf of Mexico to Galveston if forces in Texas were still in the field, or to Matamoros, Mexico, if escape were necessary.[32] This may have precipitated Breckinridge's approach to Davis now. In any case, henceforward, even as he battled against the president's continuing resistance to peace and capitulation, the secretary of war would take control of the retreat of the government, and make Davis's escape from Yankee hands his own special mission. No one asked him to assume this responsibility, certainly not the president. Breckinridge simply took it.

That meant there was a lot to do first. Davis himself was scarcely involved in preparations for abandoning Greensboro, being often lost in a black mood. "Everything is dark," he wrote to Varina by courier on April 14. Unburdening to her the uncertainty he could never show to his officials and generals, he confessed that his efforts of the last several days had been "to little purpose," and advised her to prepare for "the worst" by lightening her baggage for swift movement, and leaving Charlotte for somewhere farther south, perhaps Abbeville, South Carolina, now well behind the direction of Sherman's advance.[33] Meanwhile Breckinridge gave orders that the archives be unloaded from the boxcars and transferred to a wagon train that his clerk Micajah Clark was to assemble for the overland trip south to Charlotte. Some just could not be accommodated, and virtually all of the Engineer Bureau records were simply left on their rail car, while clerks, overseen by Clark, loaded the more important material into wagons.[34]

Fortunately, the train with most of the treasury and the midshipmen had left Danville for Charlotte on April 9 before the raiders tore up the track, and moved on again the same day as the fateful cabinet meeting. Varina Davis traveled with it, and coincidentally they were all now on their way to Abbeville. With Trenholm still too ill to attend a meeting, let alone conduct the business of his department, Davis himself directed that $39,000 be taken from the coin being carried with the government and turned over to Beauregard for paying his soldiers. He then assigned Micajah Clark the duty of overseeing personally the balance of the funds that would travel with them, still some $288,000.[35]

By the afternoon of April 15 they were ready to leave, though Mallory feared that preparations were so rushed they were moving "with plans unformed," far too dependent on the result of the Johnston and Sherman meeting. In fact, however, everything was well in hand. Concerned for the government's safety, General Johnston had ordered the depleted cavalry division of about thirteen hundred troopers commanded by General George G. Dibrell to join them at Greensboro as escort, and they arrived in the early predawn hours of April 14. Dibrell reported immediately to Breckinridge, who was still awake making arrangements. His arrival made a reunion of sorts for Breckinridge, for in this command, in addition to a Tennessee brigade, there rode a small brigade of Kentuckians commanded by the secretary's cousin Colonel William C. P. Breckinridge. Late that night the secretary of war and the two cavalrymen sat up late to plan their line of march for the days ahead, including where their advance scouts should be, where they would stop at night, and how to protect their camps. One of the cavalrymen suggested to the secretary that they were heading in the wrong direction. Johnston's pending negotiations must inevitably lead to some kind of surrender, he thought, and however that turned out, it eliminated any hope for the cause in the east. Instead of tying themselves with the impedimenta of cabinet and clerks and archives, Breckinridge, Davis, and a picked escort of horsemen ought to ride out immediately to the west and try to reach General Nathan Bedford Forrest's cavalry corps still in the field in Alabama. Then they could cross the Mississippi with Forrest and have a good chance of joining Kirby Smith to continue the fight. There was good logic to the plan but for two conflicting facts. Davis would certainly not agree. For he knew there would be no surrender and was simply playing for time, which meant he had to be in the vicinity to continue directing the war, while Breckinridge simply did not want to continue the war anywhere.[36]

During the day that followed, they saw all around them again, though this time in daylight, the depressing signs of civil disintegration. The local post quartermaster had large stores of supplies in his warehouses, and after the government train loaded what they could take for their own needs, he began to disburse what remained to the townspeople, who soon wearied of an orderly distribution. Even before Davis and his retinue were gone, a mob formed and stormed the warehouses, looting them at will, and quite a number of returned soldiers were among their number. That alone told Mallory their plight. "The plundering disposition thus displayed was painfully significant of the futility of all further effort in behalf of the Confederacy," he lamented, "for it arose from the conviction of the soldiers that further fighting was useless." And as at Richmond and Danville, once the looting began, it soon became not a search for food and useful equipment, but a sheer grab for anything, whether practical or not, with people fighting each other over possession of even meaningless articles. It showed how even Confederates could now sink quickly to the lowest ebb of human behavior. Many of them got drunk on plundered brandy and only retreated from the storehouses when fired on by guards.

Despite their often voiced anxiety to see the backs of Davis and the rest, the looters even got in the way of Clark and the others as they tried to assemble the wagons and animals necessary to get the government out of town. Only after much exertion did Clark, with carte blanche orders from Beauregard to take whatever he needed, finally complete a wagon train for the archives, baggage, and provisions needed for the trip, even as the number of those seeking to come along steadily increased. Meanwhile, Davis had actually forgotten to notify the War Department of the evacuation of Danville, with the result that Kean and the department archives arrived late at Greensborough. Now the bureau chief was hard-pressed to transfer his boxes to wagons to form a train with his own archives and those of the Senate and a few other offices, with himself in charge, which would not leave until the following day.[37]

It was a disheartening spectacle that saw them off. Trenholm could hardly move on his own accord, let alone ride with the others, so they got him an ambulance, and his host, John Morehead, provided a mattress atop some straw for him to lie on.[38] Benjamin, hardly one to rough it, decided at the last minute that he did not care to go on horseback and informed Harrison that he would not mount a horse until forced to do so. Accordingly the aide found him a seat in an ambulance pulled by broken down, fly-bitten old horses, mounted with a harness that looked as if it could break at any moment. Still, for the rotund Benjamin, that was better than riding, though he had to share his seat with Cooper, who grumbled even more about his reduced seating, especially considering whom he had to sit with.[39] George Davis joined them, while most of the remaining bureau officials occupied other ambulances. Davis and Breckinridge mounted and took their place at the head of the column. Mallory, who had helped Davis's aides to assemble the rolling stock, would ride behind, as did Reagan, Johnston, Lubbock, and Wood. The position of the secretary of war beside the president suggested not only who was in charge of the procession but also where the Kentuckian now stood in the cabinet pecking order. Yet Reagan, at least, fully believed that Davis did not confide his true hopes or expectations even to Breckinridge, knowing that they were fundamentally opposed in their views. Certainly Davis told no one else of his plans.[40]

One of the Kentuckian's last acts before leaving was to issue a general directive that any soldiers from Lee's army in the department, whether stragglers or escapees from Appomattox, could join the companies of their choice in their arms of the service in Johnston's Army of Tennessee. All others who chose not to make such a choice were to be organized into informal companies and battalions under whatever officers were available, and then attached to the first corps of Johnston's command they should encounter.[41] His motive was twofold. Seeing what these unattached soldiers were doing in Greensboro, it was important to get them back into organized units under discipline. At the same time, expecting a surrender soon, he wanted them to be under Johnston's command at the time so as to be covered by its terms and presumed general parole. Otherwise, men in uniform and still under arms but without commands ran the risk of being regarded as partisans or irregulars and treated roughly as a consequence if captured. He had told the senators back in Richmond that they needed to think first of the soldiers in the days ahead, and he did not forget his own words.

They galloped south out of town in yet another gloomy rain, joined at the last minute by the newly arrived Captain Given Campbell and his company of the Ninth Kentucky Cavalry, whom Breckinridge assigned as scouts and personal bodyguard for Davis.[42] Looking on was James Morgan, recently of the navy, and as the head of the column passed, he remarked on Breckinridge. "He made a great impression on me with his superb figure mounted on a large and fat charger," he observed.[43] Within the column, Mallory noticed something about the other man in front. Davis appeared moody, visibly showing his depression. "This was the first day on which I had noticed in him any evidence of an abandonment of hope," the navy secretary recalled.[44] The clerk Swallow, who would follow the next day with a number of other bureaucrats and the archives wagons, rode to the edge of town with the cavalcade and then watched them pass on until out of sight. Seeing the departure of the Confederate government, reduced to a few riders and ambulances, he thought that the cavalcade "on the whole presented an appearance little calculated to produce enthusiastic admiration."[45] A resident of the town stood nearby to witness this history leaving Greensboro. As Breckinridge and Davis rode past, he gazed on "the graceful forms and dignified countenances of the two horsemen riding side by side." Years later he confessed that at that moment "I wept for them and my country."[46]

They progressed slowly, the red clay mud here as sticky and unyielding as it had been at Danville. The riders at the front soon got ahead of the wagons behind, and Benjamin's became so mired that frequently it had to turn off the road into an adjacent field where the ground was less churned up. Benjamin himself had to get out on occasion and use fence rails as levers against the axles to prise the ambulance forward. By dark almost the entire column had passed him by until Burton Harrison came up with the rear to find the vehicle completely stuck in the middle of the road, its front wheels and the rear legs of the horses fully two feet deep in a hole. Benjamin loudly berated the driver for ineptitude, the poor horses gasped for wind as they strained against the mire, and old Cooper groused that he would not be in this predicament if some upstart brigadier general had not taken his seat on one of the other wagons. Harrison sat his horse amid the confusion and laughed out loud until conscience prompted his offer to find help. He rode and ahead and found a camp of artillerymen who agreed to go back and get the wagon going. A few minutes later, before he moved to the head of the column, Harrison looked back in the darkness and could just make out the glow from Benjamin's cigar, while his ears told him that Cooper and the driver had stopped their complaining. Nothing was to be heard but Benjamin, in his best oratory voice, reciting for them verse after verse of Tennyson's ode on the death of the Duke of Wellington.

They made only ten miles that first afternoon, stopping for the night at Jamestown, where a local doctor took in the president and the cabinet, including many of the staff, and there they had their first good hot meal since leaving Danville. There was something of a scramble to find space for everyone, but their host insisted that all sleep indoors, and after working out the arrangements, the doctor sent his house servant to lead Davis to the best bed in the house. Unfortunately, the hapless slave mistook General Cooper for Davis and led him with much pomp to the bed chamber. No one disabused him of the error, for they sympathized with the sufferings of Cooper who, at nearly sixty-seven, was far and away the oldest of the party. Davis and Trenholm took the other remaining beds, while the rest found places on the floor around the fireplace.

They were off early the next morning, Breckinridge and Davis sharing a breakfast of soldiers' fare on the ground with the enlisted men in Campbell's company.[47] Their generous host provided a fresh team for Benjamin and Cooper's wagon, and a new mount for Davis, but still they made slow progress, passing through High Point and coming to a halt about nine o'clock that evening a few miles outside Lexington, where they camped in a pine grove. A local woman took the Trenholms into her home, while Davis and most of the rest of the cabinet found beds in another house.[48] Otherwise the rest met with much the same cool reception as in Greensboro. Nevertheless, though he started out in a dark mood again, Davis's spirits seemed to return to him during the ride. He always took cheer when out of doors on horseback. Even in earlier dark days of the war, as when Richmond was seriously threatened with capture in the spring of 1862, he became a changed man when he left his office and rode out to the army. Never destined to be an executive or a bureaucrat, he was always at heart a man of action, and once he was out in the open and on the move, his companions saw the difference. "He seemed to have had a great load taken from his mind, to feel relieved of responsibilities," said Harrison. The moodiness disappeared, and in its place, Davis was once more cheerful, unusually so. His conversation turned on literature, Lord Byron and Walter Scott, to his favorite themes of horses and dogs he had owned and loved, even horticulture and wildlife. "His familiarity with, and correct taste in, the English literature of the last generation, his varied experiences in life, his habits of close observation, and his extraordinary memory, made him a charming companion when disposed to talk," said Harrison, and now he felt so disposed. Others like Mallory caught the mood, and that evening the wit and conviviality flowed almost as if they were not on their way to a funeral. Indeed, the elevation of Davis's spirits no doubt stemmed from his own conviction that he was leading them not to the end but only a new beginning.[49]

Of course that depended in large part on the progress made by Johnston. A telegram from the general awaited them when they reached Lexington. Johnston wired it from Greensboro, to which he had returned after their departure, and significantly he addressed it not to the president, but to Breckinridge. "Your im-

mediate presence is necessary, in order that I should be able to
confer with you," was all it said, nothing more. Johnston already
had a long history of communicating as little as possible with
Davis, one of the reasons he was relieved of command at Atlanta
the year before. Knowing that he and Breckinridge were of like
mind, he sought his counsel now, and by not stating explicitly
what for, he could hope that Davis would not interfere. Indeed,
Johnston's terseness suggested at least the possibility that he
and the secretary of war, even before they left Greensboro, had
discussed the idea of Breckinridge joining him in the Sherman
meeting, thus leaving no need for explanation now. Certainly
Breckinridge was ready. A train had been held for him at Lexington since the previous day, and now before midnight, he left
for the short trip north as far as Jamestown, where the Yankees
had broken the line, meanwhile wiring ahead to Beauregard at
Greensboro to send a train from there down to the break to take
him the rest of the way.[50]

Before he left, Breckinridge went to Davis, of course, though
if this trip to Johnston came about by any prearrangement, he
would have kept that news to himself. Yet it was evident enough
that the general wanted some counsel in his negotiations with
Sherman. The United States did not recognize the existence of
the Confederate government, thus Sherman could hardly treat
with Davis or any other civil officials, but Breckinridge was in
the unique position of being both a cabinet member and a general officer. In what was supposed to be a military negotiation,
there could be no objection to the Kentuckian attending in that
capacity. Johnston said nothing about this, either, in his telegram, suggesting once again that he and Breckinridge may have

worked out beforehand the gambit of Johnston's suggesting Breckinridge's inclusion in the talks. Davis made no objection to his going. He did not trust Johnston and could at least expect that the secretary of war would prevent the general from going beyond his authority, while at the same time, if Breckinridge saw for himself Sherman's anticipated rejection of any discussion beyond unconditional surrender, then that might subdue what the president surely recognized as the central power in his cabinet's recent rebellion. Win Breckinridge over to his belief in the futility of seeking terms and in continued resistance being their only alternative, and the weaker elements would likely follow.

The president did insist on one thing, however. He wanted Reagan to go along. Since he had initiated in that April 13 cabinet meeting the list of terms as a basis for negotiation, Reagan could be useful in representing them in case Johnston needed reminding. Davis fully believed, indeed hoped, that negotiations would fall down on those very terms authored by Reagan. Because the cabinet had approved them as the only basis for discussion, any variation would go beyond Johnston's authority and require at least another cabinet airing and executive decision to be binding. The postmaster's presence would be Davis's guarantee that no substantial variation or compromise would come about. Without realizing it, Reagan was being sent as Davis's concealed weapon to kill a peace.[51]

Breckinridge and Reagan traveled slowly through the night to Jamestown, found a train waiting for them on the opposite side of the burned bridge, and reached Greensboro again at 9:30 on the morning of April 17, only to find that Johnston had left for Hillsborough, some miles to the east near Durham. All Breckinridge could learn was that Sherman's initial response to Johnston's request for a meeting had been encouraging.[52] Ninety minutes went by, and then Breckinridge received a telegram from Johnston saying that he was about to meet Sherman to commence their discussion. He would know in a few hours if Breckinridge's presence was needed.[53] There was nothing for the secretary to do but wait. Meanwhile he met with Governor Vance, who had come to town hoping to meet with Davis but arrived too late. Now, probably for the first time, Breckinridge learned the full details of Vance's own peace initiatives.

In fact, Vance had been involved for some days in a secret scheme to pull his state out of the Confederacy and back into the Union. Where he had hesitated some weeks before, the change in circumstances now put him on the same side as Breckinridge and others. Vance initially agreed on April 9 to call the legislature as a first step to opening negotiations, and then to hold a conference at Raleigh three days later with William Graham and former Governor David Swaim to plan their course. That same day, he wrote a letter to Sherman proposing a truce in order to proceed to negotiating a peace, and sent it by Graham and Swaim to the Yankee commander. He said nothing of this to Davis, of course, and when Sherman met with the envoys, he told them to assure Vance that he would cooperate and gave them a letter inviting the governor to meet with him. Meanwhile Davis inadvertently got word of the plan and immediately ordered the arrest of Graham and Swaim, but too late. Vance protested to the president that he had done nothing untoward and would have made no agreement "subversive of your prerogative," but that of course technically meant nothing, since even Davis asserted that the states were sovereign and free to act for themselves. In short, his "prerogatives" did not include

North Carolina's own choice as to its destiny. In the end, Vance decided not to go meet with Sherman immediately, since he wanted to see Davis in Greensboro first and reveal to him his intentions. But Davis's hasty departure put an end to that.[54]

Finally around 5:30 P.M. another wire came. Johnston definitely needed Breckinridge with him and urged him to come on immediately. They must confer before talks with Sherman resumed the next morning at nine o'clock.[55] The two cabinet members set out as soon as a locomotive could be fired up to take them, but not before Breckinridge sent a private note to Governor Vance, inviting him to come along.[56] It could be useful to have Vance with them, for though Sherman might not recognize civil officers of a government that he regarded as illegitimate, there was no denying that Vance was the lawfully elected governor of North Carolina, and Sherman had already evidenced his willingness to meet with him. Indeed, Breckinridge thought Vance ought to be included in their deliberations. The year before, Sherman had been anxious to meet with Georgia's governor to discuss a separate peace. If he and Vance could come to a similar arrangement now, that coupled with Johnston's surrender on any terms would surely end it all.

It was not an easy trip to Hillsborough. The best they could get was a freight car, and thanks to the poor condition of the track, they did not reach Hillsborough until after midnight, where Johnston and cramped quarters in General Wade Hampton's headquarters at the Alexander Dickson house awaited them. There were already rumors that distinguished guests were coming, though some thought Davis would be with Breckinridge.[57] Perhaps that explained Dickson's neighbor Cadwallader Jones having a twenty-five-pound turkey and his best china and silver on the table for a late meal that the ministers and generals enjoyed heartily.[58] The conviviality soon turned sour, however, when Hampton challenged Vance. This was one general who had no intention of making peace with the enemy, and he as much as accused the governor of being a traitor. It was up to Johnston, as Hampton's superior, to upbraid him for his intemperate outburst, but he said nothing, himself perhaps displeased that Vance's freelance efforts were not coordinated with his own and might have prejudiced Davis against his efforts. Instead, Johnston asked the governor to leave him alone with Breckinridge and Reagan so that they might discuss the next day's meeting.[59]

Ordinarily there would be no reason for a governor not to be included in the meeting that followed, but Johnston had extraordinary news that had to be kept as confidential as possible for the moment. That day, Sherman had informed him that three nights earlier an assassin had murdered Abraham Lincoln in Washington while another attempted to kill Secretary of State William Seward. Breckinridge would have been stunned by the news. He had been friends with both men before the war. Lincoln's wife, Mary, came from a Lexington, Kentucky, family, and she claimed some distant kinship to Breckinridge. Even after the election of 1860, when Lincoln took office, Breckinridge was a frequent guest at the White House. Lincoln spoke of Breckinridge during the war, recalling that "I was fond of John, and regret that he sided with the South."[60] With an irony that could not have escaped him, Breckinridge later learned that after being shot in Ford's Theater, Lincoln actually died across the street in the same boarding house—perhaps even the same room—that Breckinridge occupied when he served in Congress.

However shocking the news, Johnston told them that he and Sherman had thought it best to keep it quiet, for if it became generally known just then, it might produce an uncontrollable reaction in the Union army that would make their efforts fruitless, since the soldiers in the ranks would likely assume the murder to be the work of Confederate agents sent by Davis. Then the general went over that day's first meeting with Sherman. The Federal commander initially just offered the same terms that Grant gave Lee at Appomattox, saying nothing about any more far-reaching aim. When Johnston pointed out that his message initiating the meeting had spoken of trying to bring about negotiations between their governments, Sherman countered with the objection that Davis had expected. But then Johnston persisted, saying that if their meeting could not lead to civilian talks, then the two of them could still discuss the surrender of not just his own army but all remaining Southern land forces. Military talks came within the purview of both, and though Johnston could not negotiate—as Lee could have—as general-in-chief on behalf of all Confederate armies, as senior officer still remaining in the field, he might still claim some de facto power to do so.

Johnston told Breckinridge and Reagan that Sherman gave him the impression that once agreement was reached to end the rebellion and acknowledge the authority of the Union, everything else but emancipation might be on the table for negotiation. Sherman was skeptical that Johnston could get sanction for any such agreement they might make, but then the Confederate asserted that he believed he could get Davis's approval and told Sherman that Breckinridge would be with him late that evening. He asked for a continuation of their discussion the next day, to give him time to meet with the secretary of war, clearly implying that Breckinridge was the key to Davis.[61]

For some time the Confederates discussed their approach for the coming meeting, Johnston making it clear that he hoped what he called "the confidential relations of the Secretary of War with Mr. Davis might enable him to remove the only obstacle to an adjustment."[62] Breckinridge told him that he would assume authority for granting Johnston the power to surrender all Confederate forces still in the field. Encouraged by the impression that Sherman was open to liberal terms, they determined not to be deterred by the Federal's initial insistence on discussing only the surrender of armed forces. The murder of Lincoln changed the equation, and the sooner all Confederates were covered by the parole and general amnesty, the safer everyone would be. At the same time, they could all see how existing forces in the field continued to dwindle. What such stragglers and deserters did at Danville, Greensboro, and elsewhere raised the awful possibility that their own men might pose a greater hazard than Yankee armies to the persons and remaining property of their citizens. Their chances for favorable terms were lessening with every passing day. It was worth an effort now to push Sherman toward something more, toward that "Confederate reconstruction" that Breckinridge and others had foreseen since before leaving Richmond. Moreover, from the moment Sherman agreed to talks with Johnston, both sides imposed a cease-fire agreement not to move their forces during the period of the discussions. The longer they could keep those talks going, the

more difficult it would be to start the armies again. In order not
to cripple them on a technicality, Johnston also suggested that
any proposals they made should not have reference of any kind
to the president, or to what role he should have to play in executing a peace agreement. Sherman would likely balk at any
such inclusion regarding an officer of the government that the
Union did not recognize, while making Davis personally a stip-
ulated party to an agreement only gave him the opportunity to
kill it by declining to play his specified part.[63]

In spite of Sherman's demurrer, Reagan agreed to prepare in
writing a draft of the terms they hoped to receive, it being
largely a reiteration of the suggestions he outlined in cabinet a
few days before. Then they retired for a few hours to try to sleep
before arising to leave for the noon appointment. It was scarcely
dawn when they ate a hasty breakfast and Reagan began his
writing, but before he could finish, Johnston and Breckinridge
prepared to leave for the several mile ride, and Reagan agreed
to send the document on as soon as he finished.[64] Breckinridge
meanwhile took Vance aside, perhaps to soothe his feelings over
the slight from Hampton the night before, and in the process
confided to him the news of Lincoln's murder, as well as informing him that Johnston thought it best if he remained here
to meet them on their return that evening. That done, the general and the secretary of war left for Durham Station. Already rumors ran through Johnston's army of what was up, one captain
writing in his diary that day that "'tis supposed that they are negotiating with Sherman for the surrender of this army."[65]

When they arrived shortly before noon, the Confederates and
their escort stopped a few hundred yards away from the farmhouse where the meeting was to take place, and Johnston rode

ahead alone. He did not want his staff and escort mixing with the Yankee soldiers gathered all around the building, no doubt for fear that they would hear of Lincoln's death, and then the news would sweep through his army and the state before he and Davis were ready to deal with it. For his part, Breckinridge waited with the escort and saw Johnston and Sherman greet each other, then go inside the farmhouse. Johnston told Sherman that he now had the power to treat fully with regard to all armies, and then immediately pushed for some guarantee of his soldiers' rights as citizens after the surrender. Sherman had but to refer to the recent paroles given to Lee's army, and to Lincoln's long-standing amnesty proclamation of 1863, to show that no enlisted man or officer from colonel on down need have any fear of indictments or prosecution. Johnston was not entirely satisfied with that, however, and continued talking on the point awhile, probably stalling for time for Reagan's draft to reach them.[66]

At last Johnston told Sherman that Breckinridge was waiting back with his escort and asked that he be allowed to join them, since he was, in fact, the authority that would allow them to settle on a general capitulation. Predictably Sherman refused, as he had to, because the Kentuckian was an official of the unrecognized rebel government, but Johnston countered that he was also a general officer. On that basis Sherman agreed and was no doubt encouraged that Breckinridge would be involved. When Breckinridge approached the house, he had to pass through a crowd of Union officers, several of whom gave him an icy glare. A Cincinnati journalist looked on in awe as the "tall, commanding figure" of the secretary of war met every glance with "defiance" in his own cold, blue-gray eyes. He might have wanted this moment for a long time, finding some personal victory in

Confederate defeat, but he was not about to hang his head low before the victors.

When Breckinridge entered the little house, it was his first meeting with the general whose name had become so feared in the South. Sherman may have offered both of the generals a drink of whiskey from the bottle he carried in his saddlebag, but then they continued the discussion and Breckinridge seconded Johnston's plea for some explicit protection of the rights of their soldiers.[67] From there the conversation wandered—or was led—on to other matters, including slavery, both Breckinridge and Johnston agreeing that the institution was dead.[68] Indeed, Johnston actually joked that the Confederacy itself had driven a few nails into slavery's coffin by its recent legislation to enlist slaves as soldiers in return for emancipation, and Breckinridge knew better than anyone else what it had taken to see that come to pass. After half an hour a messenger brought to the door a parcel that he handed to one of the Confederates. Inside were Reagan's draft for terms, and for a few minutes Breckinridge and Johnston conferred privately as they read the document.

It began with a preamble asserting that "wisdom and sound policy alike require that a common government should rest on the consent and be supported by the affections of all the people who compose it," and suggested the terms that followed as a means of securing that consent and affection. First, all Confederate military forces would "disband," a term that did not necessarily imply outright surrender. At the same time it provided for "the recognition of the Constitution and authority of the Government of the United States" but did not say who should do the recognizing, the disbanding armies, the Confederate people at large, or their government. In return, existing Southern state governments were to be continued in power, and their citizens were to continue to enjoy all rights of person and property recognized by the Constitution, with an indemnity against any future prosecution or penalty for their part in the war. Reagan acknowledged in a postscript that the terms avoided much in the way of detail and ignored the required ratification of the states, and they did not include any reference to Davis's necessary role in securing the cooperation of the states.[69]

Having agreed that Reagan's document reflected the sense of their conclusions the night before, Breckinridge and Johnston returned to the table, and the latter read the document aloud. Sherman's immediate response was that it was far too unspecific, as indeed it was, and purposely. The fewer specifics, the fewer initial stumbling blocks there would be to getting the discussion going. But now Breckinridge took the floor for several minutes and spoke earnestly in advocacy of the general principles they advanced.[70] Perhaps first and most important, he reiterated that Johnston would have the ability to carry out an agreement encompassing these propositions, and by confirming this, Breckinridge was in effect telling Sherman that he—in his unacknowledged capacity as secretary of war—could make certain of that.[71] While Reagan's paper spoke of property rights, Breckinridge wasted no time on slavery, the species of property that lay behind the war in the first place. Instead, he devoted most of his words to his "Confederate reconstruction" plan, the restoration and preservation of the civic rights of Southern citizens, and the maintenance of the existing state governments. He argued it as a means of achieving the quickest and most painless transition from disunion to reunion, one that promised to leave the fewest scars, while easing the pain of those that must inevitably remain.

The best way to restore government under the Constitution to the whole Union was to recognize and protect the rights that charter guaranteed to all citizens. Sherman himself had told Johnston that he thought the Northern people felt no real desire for vengeance against the Southern *people*, only toward their leaders, and thus what Breckinridge advocated could seem eminently practical, since they were leaving Davis and his officials entirely out of the discussion, it being commonly assumed that no agreement for amnesty could cover them.[72]

Some discussion ensued as Sherman raised issues and Breckinridge frequently spoke in reply and rebuttal, in one instance making the point that if Confederate armies were allowed to disband with their arms and return home to hand them over to their state authorities, then those states would be able to field the necessary militia to maintain civil order during the transitional period, whereas if all surrendering soldiers had to hand over their weapons, the states would be defenseless. Unspoken, no doubt, was the fact that doing this would also obviate the need or justification for stationing occupying Union military forces in those states to keep order, a fate that no Confederate would welcome, and one that must inevitably lead to confrontation and turmoil.[73] No doubt Breckinridge also returned to his "let it not terminate in a farce" entreaty by advocating that Confederate soldiers go home as cohesive units rather than simply being paroled and discharged where they stood, a suggestion that Beauregard had reinforced in a telegram to Johnston that very day. That would discourage their breaking up into roving bands of guerrillas preying alike on Union outposts and Confederate civilians, a concern shared by Johnston, and they had already seen how quickly that could happen. Sherman himself said that all Confederates not on the rolls of regular units would be regarded as outlaws and hunted down, the very eventuality Breckinridge anticipated when he ordered stragglers in Johnston's department to attach themselves immediately to a unit and be enrolled.[74] Breckinridge impressed upon Sherman that Davis himself did not have the constitutional power to enforce all of the provisions they discussed, some requiring state action.[75]

As to slavery, while Breckinridge, like Johnston, admitted that practically it was extinct, he still convinced Sherman not to insist on a specific acceptance of the Emancipation Proclamation or the new Thirteenth Amendment in any proposed terms. Each of the Southern states, he argued, in applying for readmission to full rights, would have to act on the amendment independently, just like the Northern states, and so they should leave the matter to be settled at that future time. By the very terms of the Constitution they were about to reinstate in the South, that was the only lawful means of imposing emancipation. Sherman's own attitude was that this was not a proper topic for a military "convention," apparently failing to appreciate that neither was most of the rest of their discussion. Sherman felt, or was persuaded, that if the South simply stated that slavery was over, it would be. "Our simple declaration of a Result, will be accepted as good Law everywhere," he would tell Johnston.[76] He quailed from introducing into any cartel a subject that had kept the country in a turmoil for half a century. Very likely at Breckinridge's or Johnston's insistence, he also left it out in order to remove what would surely be a major impediment to getting approval from Davis. Sherman simply did not see the trap Breckinridge set for him. If no requirement to admit the end of slavery were a part of the surrender, and if the Southern states were to be free to reassume their full sovereignty merely by taking oaths of allegiance, then their legislatures would also be free to vote on the Thirteenth Amendment as they saw fit. The eleven returning Confederate states would be more than enough on their readmission to kill the amendment by denying it the necessary ratification of three-fourths of all the states. In effect, the Confederates could threaten to use the United States Constitution to defeat the one great social change the war had wrought, the fear of which in turn had helped bring about the war itself.

Furthermore, by keeping any mention of slavery out of their cartel, Breckinridge avoided making any definitive statement that would have Confederates specifically acknowledging or endorsing its end. That could be very important, indeed. He well knew that Lincoln had implied at Hampton Roads that emancipation might not have to be perpetual following the end of the war, a hint that Lincoln repeated in his talks with Campbell in Richmond. The Emancipation Proclamation, too, could be defeated. Both were tissue-thin scenarios that Breckinridge and Johnston alike surely regarded as highly unlikely, but that did not mean there was nothing to gain. Southern votes to ratify the amendment might just be used as leverage to pry some financial reparation out of Washington in return for the loss of their enormous capital investment in blacks. Lincoln had more than once proposed the idea of such compensation as a lure during the conflict. Given the financial devastation of the South after four years of war, restitution even at pennies on the dollar could save them from a prostration that might last for decades.[77]

Sherman asked for a few minutes in which to draft a proposal of his own, and while he wrote, Johnston and Breckinridge stepped outside until he called them back in, saying, "Gentle-men, this is the best I can do." Sherman's best, in fact, probably amazed both of them. It left Johnston mistakenly supposing that Sherman may have had such terms in mind all along, while Breckinridge believed that his brief address had more than its desired effect, for Sherman had given them everything Breck-inridge asked for, and more.[78] Indeed, when the details of Sherman's terms became known to Northern friends of the sec-retary's, some, like fellow Kentuckian James Speed, Lincoln's attorney general, declared that Sherman "had been seduced by Breckinridge."[79]

Sherman proposed that Confederate armies would disband rather than surrender, and then the individual state regiments would go home with their arms to their several capitals and turn their weapons and other accoutrements over to their state arse-nals. Every man would give his parole not to take up arms again, and acknowledge the authority of the state and national gov-ernments. Better yet, so soon as a Southern governor and legis-lature affirmed their recognition of the Constitution and the supremacy of the Union, it was to be recognized as legitimate and not interfered with, except in cases like Kentucky and Mis-souri, in which there were rival Union and Confederate legisla-tures. The Supreme Court should decide which was to hold office in those instances. Federal courts were to be reestablished in all the Confederate states, and the people would be guaran-teed all of their defined rights under the state and federal con-stitutions, free from molestation by Washington in retaliation for the war, so long as they maintained the peace. Finally, Sherman proposed that his document constitute "in general terms" an end to the war, invoking a general amnesty if all of the above conditions were met by the Confederates. Acknowledging that neither he nor Johnston had vested in them the power to enforce his terms, he provided that each should pledge to obtain that authority.[80]

To his delight, and probably amazement, Breckinridge saw that Sherman went far beyond Reagan's opening proposal, and instead offered virtually everything that he had been working for in his own reconstruction plan. Indeed, the terms were practically identical to what Campbell had proposed independently to Lincoln, suggesting the common origin of both proposals in the discussions Breckinridge and Campbell held back in February and March, and that the secretary of war had pressed them hard on Sherman now. When it came to recognizing the existing state governments, Sherman did at least have before him the example of what had been started in Virginia, not knowing that Lincoln and Campbell's plan there would soon collapse, but on most of the other concessions there was no precedent.[81] Sherman even omitted any mention of emancipation. Perhaps Breckinridge in fact did seduce Sherman to some degree, and years later Sherman himself recalled how "those fellows hustled me so that day."[82] Now the proposal of universal amnesty made no exceptions for Davis and his leaders, which the day before, Sherman told Johnston was impossible. Undoubtedly Breckinridge and Johnston appealed to Sherman's vanity in their discussions by portraying him as potentially a great peacemaker, for within hours, when he wired his terms to Grant for approval, Sherman almost boasted that his cartel constituted an absolute submission. "The terms are all on our side," he wrote his wife that afternoon. "I can hardly realize it." His work that day would "produce Peace from the Potomac to the Rio Grande."[83]

Once the three stood agreed on the terms, Sherman and Johnston signed it and Sherman called for copies to be made for their two governments.[84] Then he spoke to the two Confederates of Lincoln's assassination. Johnston confided to Sherman his horror at the deed, fearing it would be blamed on the Confederates, and that Lincoln might have been their greatest ally in reconstruction.[85] Stepping outside to their now mingled escorts, they found the news generally known, as Sherman introduced the two of them to his staff, and Breckinridge and Reagan discussed it with some of their followers. The postmaster said he hoped no connection between the murdered and their cause would be found or it should go hard for them, while Breckinridge said Lincoln's death at this time and in this manner must precipitate great calamity for them. "Gentlemen," he told them, "the South has lost its best friend." At once he wrote a message to be taken by courier to Davis, announcing the assassination and what he called the "dastardly attempt" on Seward. As soon as he got back to Goldsboro and the telegraph, he would send a wire with more details.[86]

Sherman also took Breckinridge aside privately and advised him that despite the provision for universal amnesty in their agreement, he doubted that the North would allow it to apply to the civil leaders. If they could, they had all better leave the country, especially Davis. Noting that there was particular hostility toward Breckinridge since, as one-time vice president, he was the highest ranking living civilian to go over to the rebellion, he advised the Kentuckian to be sure to get away. Breckinridge replied that he would give the Yankees no more trouble on his own account, and that he would attempt to get Davis and himself and the rest out of the country as soon as possible.[87]

Indeed, Sherman left under the impression that Davis and Breckinridge would fly at once, and that they would be killed rather than suffer capture.[88] It was implicit in Sherman's warning to the secretary of war that he was not eager to have to take him alive or dead. Lincoln himself had said months before that he would prefer that Davis and the others simply leave the country. Now with the military cease-fire in effect and movement of the armies halted pending the outcome of their agreement that day, Davis and his cabinet would have time to get away and Sherman would not interfere with them. As for Breckinridge, circumstances had changed since his declaration in Richmond that he would stay and take his chances with the soldiers. He and Johnston had helped secure here all that he wanted to protect Southern soldiers, indeed more than he expected. If the two governments accepted the cartel, there was nothing further to be gained by his remaining. His sole aim hereafter must be to persuade the president to approve the document, and then get him to safety. Breckinridge had helped to beat Sherman, so it seemed. Now he had to beat Davis.

Chapter Six

"WE ARE FALLING TO PIECES"

Returning to Hillsborough, Breckinridge sent a wire through Beauregard's headquarters in Greensboro to be forwarded to Davis wherever it should find him on the road to Charlotte, informing him of the day's result. Then he joined Johnston and Reagan for a late dinner, also wiring ahead to Beauregard to have a train waiting in Greensboro to take him south the next morning. The negotiators had expected Vance to join them here to go over the agreement, but through a confusion, the governor was not at the depot at the appointed hour, and they either did not or could not get a message to him before Breckinridge and Reagan boarded their train for Greensboro.[1]

They arrived in the early hours of April 19, an angry Vance coming on a train behind them. With Raleigh now in Yankee hands, he had made Greensboro his temporary capital, only to find on arrival that Johnston's demoralized troops were threatening to plunder the warehouses and boxcars holding North Carolina's archives and treasury funds. He actually proposed that he be allowed to return it all to Raleigh under the current cease-fire, preferring the protection of the Federals, but Breckinridge directed that it remain where it was until they knew if Washington would accept Sherman's terms.[2] It took a little time to smooth the governor's pique, as well as Breckinridge's—for there was no train waiting for him in Greensboro, and no immediate prospect of one. At the moment when he most needed to get to Davis to act quickly on the cartel, the terrible condition of the rail line, made worse by breaks due to recent Yankee raids, had him all but cut off. At least the telegraph was working, for his wire of the night before had gotten through, finding Davis at Concord, and now Breckinridge received a response directing him to join the president at Charlotte, which the government ought to reach that same day. While he scrambled to find some conveyance to get him there, Breckinridge sent another telegram south to meet Davis at Charlotte. Now that he was in Greensboro, it was safer to trust the wires with the news of Lincoln's assassination and the attack on Seward. Davis must know of that immediately. It could not wait on a courier, or on Breckinridge's own luck with the locomotives.[3]

His telegram made the trip to Charlotte a lot faster than the president's party. After Breckinridge and Reagan left them at Lexington on April 16, the government moved on late the following day, delayed by Trenholm being too ill to travel. On the road they found that a bridge over the Yadkin River had been destroyed, and some of the cavalry escort actually had to carry Trenholm's ambulance across the stream. As a result, they only reached Salisbury well after dark, and when they rode onto its principal street, the rail depot still smoldered from fire, evidence of a swift raid through there just the day before by Yankee cavalry.[4] Not surprisingly, having had one bout with the Federals, the locals felt skittish about hospitality to the party. Still, a clergyman offered Davis a room in the Episcopal rectory, and the president sat up over tea with his host and staff well into the night. Davis's mood was lifting, and he felt talkative, joining his host and his aides on the porch as they discussed Lee's surrender. Still, Davis was preoccupied. Throughout the evening he kept a cigar in his mouth but never remembered to light it. All the while, knowing that the enemy was prowling the vicinity, Harrison insisted on staying out on the front porch as guard.[5]

It was a late start again the following day, as they did not get off until the afternoon, riding until just outside Concord when they got a report that enemy cavalry was believed to be operating in the vicinity of Charlotte itself. That made staying out in the open extremely dangerous, and they delayed only a few hours for rest at the Concord home of most genial hosts, where Davis got Breckinridge's first telegram notifying him of the basic agreement with Sherman. Leaving well before dawn, they pushed on toward Charlotte in the hope of evading enemy patrols.[6] The party halted a few miles outside the town, and Harrison sent a messenger ahead, both to see if the road was clear of Yankees and to notify Varina Davis that her husband was near. Word came back that the road was open but that the president's wife had moved on south a few days earlier. Worse, even though advance news had been sent that the government was coming, and several officers and citizens offered hospitality to the cabinet members and staff, only one house in town volunteered to accept the president. The Yankee cavalry passing through the area shortly before, knowing that Davis was on the road somewhere, actually made threats of retaliation against anyone who took him in. The one man willing to open his door to Davis was Lewis Bates, a Yankee by birth and a bachelor known to like a drink and to entertain friends of similar taste. Harrison thought such a man's home altogether "not at all a seemly place for Mr. Davis," but there seemed no alternative.[7]

Accompanied by his escort, Davis rode to the Bates house, on the corner of Tryon and Fourth Streets, to find a small crowd of citizens and officers of the local garrison awaiting him. Despite the unwillingness of all but Bates to grant him their hospitality, they gave him a welcome, at least courteous if not enthusiastic.[8] The Kentucky cavalry brigade of Brigadier General Basil W. Duke had arrived in town the day before, joining Brigadier General Samuel W. Ferguson's brigade of Alabama and Mississippi troopers, and now Duke and his men rode up the street and halted in a cloud of dust, cheering the president and waving their regimental banners. They wanted a speech from Davis. As the cheering continued, it took some minutes for the government party to dismount from their horses and wagons. A leading citizen, William Johnston, whom Vance defeated for the governorship in 1862, greeted Davis and led him to the door of the Bates house, but they found it locked. Bates was not there, having mistakenly gone to the railroad depot to meet the president. An officer walked around to the back of the house to enter by a rear entrance and unlock the front door from the inside. But that would take a minute or two, and in that time more and more people gathered. The crowd meanwhile looked expectant, so Davis stepped onto the threshold to speak.

He said very little. He would have expected a cordial welcome if he came bearing good tidings on the wave of a great victory. Since he came in the wake of disaster and as a refugee from their fallen capital, he said he appreciated their reception all the more, keeping to himself his humiliation that none but Bates would welcome him. "This has been a war of the people for the people," he continued in an unintentional echo of Lincoln at Gettysburg, "and I have been simply their executive." If they were ready to continue the fight, so was he. "Only show by your determination and fortitude that you are willing to suffer yet longer and we may still hope for success." He granted that he had made many mistakes during the war, yet still he could say that through it all his sole purpose had been their welfare and the preservation of those constitutional principles that impelled them to leave the Union. "I have nothing to abate or take back," he concluded. If those principles were right in 1861, then they were right today, "and no misfortune to our arms can change right into wrong."[9]

Perhaps even as Davis was dismounting, the wires began to sing in the local telegraph office, bringing in Breckinridge's announcement of Lincoln's death. The telegrapher John C. Courtney and his wife had been looking forward to seeing Davis when he arrived. "We knew when he came we would welcome him with aching hearts," recalled Mary Courtney, but her husband had to be in the office instead of out on Tryon Street, and thus he heard the news first as it came off the line. As soon as he wrote out the message, he left the office and raced for the Bates house, arriving just as Davis concluded his brief remarks.[10] Courtney pushed through the crowd and handed the telegram to the president. Coincidentally, the courier to whom Breckinridge had entrusted his written copy of the same information had just then ridden into town and dismounted, intending to hand the message over to Davis's aide William Preston Johnston when the president finished his address.[11]

Davis was just pleading fatigue and about to excuse himself from saying anything more when he opened the envelope with Courtney's telegram and read it, then folded it, put it back in the envelope, and handed it to townsman William Johnston, who stood next to him in the doorway. "This contains very astounding intelligence," said the president. Johnston absorbed the telegram while Davis finished his speech, but the crowd had heard his remark to Johnston and called out for the telegram to be read. Davis gave the nod, and Johnston read the telegram aloud. Neither he nor Davis made any public comment, and most in the crowd who heard Johnston's voice simply received the news in silence. A few of the soldiers on the street cheered until a look of reproof from Davis silenced them. He then simply shook hands with a few of those in front of him, and when the door behind him finally opened, he immediately stepped inside without further comment.[12]

Inside the Bates house, Davis quickly showed the telegram to the others of his party, and an excited discussion ensued. Davis himself was not inclined to credit it at first, an impression that his face had even communicated to some in the crowd outside.[13] Now when Mallory expressed his own disbelief, the president replied that frankly he thought it probably a canard, but in times such as theirs, anything was possible. Mallory went on to say that if it were true, Lincoln's moderate views and essential justice would be missed in the days ahead. Worse, he feared that the Confederacy would be blamed for the crime. "I certainly have no special regard for Mr. Lincoln," Davis replied, "but there are a great many men of whose end I would much rather [hear] than his." Davis regretted the act, he went on. "I fear it will be disastrous to our people."[14]

There had been suggestions during the war of plans by Confederates to kill or kidnap Lincoln as a legitimate war target, but Davis routinely dismissed them all. He may not have liked Lincoln, but he paid him the respect of regarding him as, like Davis himself, "a western man" and "a man of courage," one who would die fighting before being taken alive, thus making kidnapping impossible. As for assassination, he felt it would do their cause no good, because Lincoln was only the president, not the Northern cause itself.[15] Moreover, Lincoln's death would make his vice president, Andrew Johnson, his successor. Davis knew and detested Johnson, a Tennesseean who had remained loyal to the Union. That made him a renegade in Davis's eyes. Too, Davis entertained the disdain that most men of his class felt for poor whites like Johnson, who started life as an illiterate tailor, and Johnson vocally proclaimed his detestation for the Southern aristocracy in return. They had tangled in the 1840s when both were in the House of Representatives, and bad blood had existed between them ever since. Davis had every reason to believe that Johnson would be far worse to deal with than Lincoln, having neither the intelligence nor the character of the incumbent.

Nevertheless, the moment Lincoln died, there were many Northerners and even Southerners who suddenly "remembered" new words in some of Davis's early war speeches in which supposedly he had boasted that Southern armies would march all the way to Philadelphia and beyond if the Yankees did not give them their independence. Now they recalled him threatening to burn and destroy Northern cities and assassinate Lincoln and the whole Washington Congress.[16] Within a few weeks Davis's host Bates, who was not even present until after the fact, added to the fiction. A Massachusetts native stuck in the South at the commencement of the war, he may well have had his own special motive for giving false testimony in the wake of having offered Davis hospitality despite Yankee warnings of retribution. He would claim in May that after reading the telegram, the president reacted with a quotation from *Macbeth*: "If it were to be done, it were better it were well done," meaning Davis approved the act and that Johnson, Seward, and others should have been killed as well.[17]

The Confederates were still dealing with the surprise of the news when they scattered to their temporary lodgings, the president commenting to his aide William Preston Johnston that Lincoln would have been much more lenient and easy to deal with than Johnson on any terms, such as those Sherman was now sending north for approval.[18] Of course, if Johnson was even less likely than Lincoln to accept those terms, that played into Davis's expectation of rejection and worked to his purpose of continuing the war. On the other hand, the more vindictive Johnson would be less likely to admit defeat and ultimately allow what he had himself called the "illegitimate, swaggering, bastard, scrub aristocracy" of the South to have its independence.[19]

Davis and his three aides Lubbock, Johnston, and Wood stayed at the Bates house, while Harrison and Benjamin went to the home of Abram Weill, a local Jewish merchant. The Trenholms were taken in by another family, who found the secretary of the treasury now completely bedridden.[20] For the balance of

the day there was little for them to do but settle in while awaiting Breckinridge's arrival with more details of the cartel, and
meanwhile Lincoln's death commanded the attention of citizens
and officials alike. The next morning Davis, Harrison, General
Cooper, and several of the cabinet attended St. Peter's Episcopal Church, only to hear the Rev. George Everhart offer a vigorous condemnation of the assassination as a "blot on American
civilization," the "tapping of a fountain of blood, which, un-
checked, will burst forth and flow onward through the South as
well as the North." Referring to the looting and robbery already
starting in Confederate cities in the face of the collapse, he
warned of rampant anarchy everywhere, in a commentary on the
sad condition of the Confederacy in this dark hour. Lincoln's murder only made the outrages all around them the more heinous and
the more dangerous for their immortal souls.[21] The service ended,
and as the officials walked out of church, Davis turned to Harrison and Preston Johnston, with a smile, and commented, "I think
the preacher directed his remarks at me; and I believe he fancies
I had something to do with the assassination."[22]

At least the people of Charlotte relaxed more in their hospitality in the ensuing days. Bates, whatever his motives, set a lav-
ish table and enlisted Courtney's wife and some of her friends
to act as hostesses for his guests. "It was an honor and pleasure
never to be forgotten," Mary Courtney declared.[23] Preston Johnston found that they lived splendidly while there, with "all good
things to eat and drink."[24] Davis's mood continued to be cheerful, and as his spirits rose, so did his optimism. His most immediate concern was Varina and their children, from whom he had
heard nothing. Wood established an office for him in the second-
floor directors' room offered by the Bank of North Carolina, and

there Davis and his cabinet prepared to do what little business they could, though their archives remained for the most part packed away in the wagons.[25]

In fact, there was virtually nothing for any of them to do now, Mallory being without a navy, Reagan's post offices still functioning in a creaky fashion without the need of high supervision, and Benjamin and George Davis having been all but supernumerary for some time. With Breckinridge still absent and War Department functions in abeyance during the cease-fire, only the Treasury could really conduct any real work with the specie traveling with them or in the wagons under the midshipmen's care farther south. But Trenholm could do nothing at all, being entirely bedridden.[26] The government was at a virtual standstill, and what time Davis spent in his makeshift office, he passed either in monitoring the continuing deterioration of forces in the field, or on inconsequential affairs, such as trying to find saddles for some of Duke's troopers and handling a dispute over rent due from the government for warehouse space in Salisbury.[27] If Davis felt optimistic, those around him did not share his hope. "Disintegration is setting in rapidly," Wood noted. "Everything is falling to pieces."[28]

The secretary of war saw evidence enough of that just in his frustrating efforts to catch up to the government. When finally an engine appeared to take Breckinridge and Reagan south on April 19, it got only as far as Jamestown by 10 P.M. Despite orders to get the bridge damaged by the Yankees back in service, it was still out. Worse, crowds of paroled men from Lee's army and stragglers from Johnston's now jammed the roads, and Breckinridge found that no one would exercise authority over them, and they were no longer answerable to him. As a result, he could not get across the bridge until the next day.[29] It only got worse. A train was to meet them at Salisbury but it did not come, and Breckinridge feared rightly that it had been taken by the parolees and stragglers, who forced it to take them back to Charlotte. In a fury, Breckinridge sent an order to Charlotte for the ringleaders to be arrested and "severely punished," then ordered another engine to be sent north immediately. Davis himself took care of getting the engine on its way. The next morning Reagan and Breckinridge were still waiting for the train, however, getting reports that stragglers were seizing trains throughout the region, and even that some had burned a bridge in order to prevent Confederate authorities from pursuing them. It was the farce he had feared and no mistake. Urgently he wired to Johnston to impose some organization on all the parolees in the department and to concentrate them in order to feed them and arrange transportation to their homes, since those were the principal concerns now making the men lawless. Johnston agreed, urging also that some of the Treasury be paid out to the men as another mollifier before sending them home. Finally an engine arrived, and early on the morning of April 22, Breckinridge and Reagan at last pulled into Charlotte.[30]

Word that Breckinridge was on an incoming train got out among some of the Kentuckians that morning. Many of them were his friends or had served under him earlier in the war, and a number went to the depot to meet him. Upon stepping onto the platform, he said he had not time then to talk with them but must go straight to the president. On the way Breckinridge walked past Benjamin enjoying a warm spring morning and a cigar, and smiling as ever. Benjamin waved greeting and asked if the story of the assassination were true. Without stopping, the

Kentuckian simply acknowledged that it was and hurried on to the Bates' house, where he found Davis also taking the sun, sitting on a chair in the open doorway. They shook hands quickly, and then Davis asked about Lincoln. Breckinridge confirmed the story and told the president how much he personally deplored the tragedy and believed that at this particular moment it would be most unfortunate for the people of the South. For his part, Davis agreed, referring specifically to Andrew Johnson and how much harder he was likely to be on any Confederates who came under his control.[31]

At once they went inside, where Breckinridge handed Davis a copy of the Sherman–Johnston agreement, and now the confirmation of Lincoln's death paled against the shock of what he read. For the sake of security, Breckinridge's initial telegram conveyed no real details. Davis, of course, had been counting on Sherman's refusal to negotiate for anything other than Johnston's surrender, hoping it would act like the Hampton Roads failure to renew resistance spirit and put down the now overwhelming sentiment in his cabinet against continuing the war. Instead, he was being given almost everything he could have asked for save independence, though he would still complain to Varina that these terms were "hard enough." While naturally there was a great deal of room in the document for the Yankees to squirm around to impose a more harsh reconstruction, when Breckinridge gave the president his own oral report of the last day's meeting with Sherman, he no doubt reinforced Johnston's conviction that the Federal had negotiated in good faith, emphasizing Sherman's own belief that the terms he was granting reflected the wishes of the late Lincoln and the Northern people.

While Davis and Breckinridge conferred, they heard calls from a crowd gathered outside in street, wanting Breckinridge to come out. Before the war he had been one of the most popular and spellbinding orators in the nation, and Kentuckians especially always delighted in hearing him speak, including many of those here under Campbell and Duke. Now they wanted to hear something, anything, from him. He stepped out while Davis pondered the agreement, but only to excuse himself from speaking just then. They could tell from the gravity of his manner that something important was at hand.[32] Davis immediately called a cabinet meeting for ten o'clock that evening, at the bank building. When they gathered, there was but one topic of discussion. Davis presented them with the terms of the cartel, gave each a copy, and then asked for their views. Should he ratify the terms, he wanted to know, and if he did, what was their best course to pursue?[33] Significantly, he did not invite discussion but asked for their reactions in writing, to be presented at another meeting at ten the following morning, this to be held in Trenholm's second-floor sickroom at the William Pfifer house, in order that the invalid might participate.[34] Davis kept his motive to himself for wanting written opinions. It was a momentous decision. Perhaps he simply wanted there to be no future mistake. Perhaps, too, he hoped that being forced to commit themselves on paper, those arrayed for submission would lose heart. And by getting their opinions before any general discussion took place in cabinet, he could at least hope to prevent Breckinridge and perhaps Mallory from influencing the others in open discussion. Certainly giving them twelve hours to reflect on the terms, albeit overnight, would allow all of them some time for reflection before committing themselves.

That night Benjamin, Reagan, Mallory, and George Davis all began composing their responses. Trenholm was too ill to write, and Breckinridge was too busy to get started until well after midnight, when he got to the room he shared with his sons Clifton and Cabell, and Micajah Clark.[35] Reagan produced a lengthy essay, understandable considering his intimate association with the terms offered, while Mallory and Benjamin were wordy, though only half as long as the postmaster. George Davis, who appropriately was concise in a lawyerly fashion, went directly to the central issues. Several of them may still have been writing the following morning—as Breckinridge was—until just before the appointed hour.[36]

The president also held a pen in his hand that morning before the meeting. He wrote a long, heartfelt letter to Varina, his "Dear Winnie," and he did not attempt to conceal from her the anguish that he masked in front of his ministers. Uncertain as yet of her whereabouts, he assumed she was in or on her way to Abbeville, and would send the letter there in care of Harrison, whom he was dispatching south as soon as he finished. There was still the old lack of realism. If only Lee had been able to hold together, he still believed they might have made the junction with Johnston "and would have been today on the high road to independence." Even after Lee surrendered, if only the men who had straggled from his army before Appomattox had rallied, they might have repaired the damage. If ever a man thrived on wishful thinking it was President Jefferson Davis. But now, with stragglers actually attacking Confederate trains, throwing away their arms, drifting home in large numbers, and Johnston and Beauregard confessedly unable to hold them in the ranks, what was to be done? Bitterly he complained that the generals' only idea was to retreat. So many men had discarded their weapons that even now if a sudden bolt of spirit should shoot through the dispersing men in uniform, they would not be able to arm them adequately.

He did not like Sherman's terms. The best he could say was that they did not impose "wanton humiliation" on the Confederacy. At least they recognized the state governments and the rights of the people under state and national constitutions. He implied that he knew Breckinridge played a significant role in formulating the terms, and Reagan too, which meant he could anticipate how they were going to respond when the cabinet convened at ten o'clock. "The issue is one which it is very painful for me to meet," he told her. "On the one hand is the long night of oppression which will follow the return of our people to the 'Union'; on the other, the suffering of the women and children, and carnage among the few brave patriots who would still oppose the invader." To choose between two equally unacceptable evils was a torment. Davis rightly assumed that reconstruction, even under Sherman's terms, would not be painless, and to this proud Confederate, convinced that he and his cause were just from the outset, any imposition or restriction would be intolerable. Yet as clear as his vision could be in some affairs, in others he could be hopelessly blind. "I think my judgment is undisturbed by any pride of opinion," he said, a notion with which few who knew or worked with him would agree. He had sacrificed much for the cause, and was ready to sacrifice everything else except his family. At least he was aware that a point could be reached when to continue would be to spill good blood over bad, but if he thought he could emotionally separate himself from the cause and make the decision that enough was enough when the time came, he yet knew himself too little. Never had he admitted either error or defeat, and now having recognized the possibility of the issue being motivated by his pride, he immediately closed the subject without actually asking the question of himself.

He hoped that patriotic cavalry like Duke's and Ferguson's and others would stand by and rally to him, and ride west across the Mississippi to join Smith. "If nothing can be done there which it will be proper to do," he said, "then I can go to Mexico, and have the world from which to choose." He apologized for the anguish their circumstances must bring her. "This is not the fate to which I invited [you] when the future was rose colored to us both," he pleaded. Indeed, he could not bring himself to close, but over and over again expressed his love and the hope that "there may be better things in store for us." That done he wrote an introduction for Harrison to his friend Armistead Burt, of Abbeville, with whom he expected Varina would be staying, and sent his secretary on his way. In his note to Burt, Davis warned that Harrison would bring him up to date on affairs, "and I am sorry that he will have little to tell which it will be pleasant for you to hear."[37] As Harrison left, the president told him what he had confided to Varina, that he would probably set out for the Trans-Mississippi Department and Kirby Smith's army as soon as he got the results he expected from the Johnston-Sherman meeting.[38] One thing that determination seemed to make clear was that even if the Sherman-Johnston cartel were agreed upon, he was not going to regard it as binding on the army west of the Mississippi, or else he expected to be able to reawaken the spirit of independence among Texans, who had actually been their own independent nation just twenty years before. With them perhaps he could create a new western Confederacy, or at least one free state as a rallying point for some future resurgence of Southern rights sentiment. However much he spoke of all the sacrifice and cost, and regardless of the result of this morning's cabinet meeting, it is clear that Jefferson Davis was not about to abandon his dreams for independence, but merely to change their shape. As Harrison left, Davis said almost defiantly, "I *cannot* feel like a beaten man."[39]

When the ministers gathered in Trenholm's room at Pfifer's, the president heard and read a remarkable unanimity of opinion, even though Mallory swore that they had not discussed their answers among themselves beforehand. Benjamin stated the problem succinctly, and now, at last, he finally came over to the majority. Was there any reason to expect that if they continued to resist, they could either secure their independence or garner terms any better than those offered? He answered no to both. North Carolina was ready to make a separate peace, and that must isolate Virginia, even if people in the Old Dominion were prepared to continue resistance. Too few men felt willing to go on, and not enough arms were available even for them. "The Confederacy is, in a word, unable to continue the war by armies in the field, and the struggle can no longer be maintained in any other manner than by a guerrilla or partisan warfare," he said, and that form of war was neither desirable nor likely to be productive. "We have been vanquished in the war," he concluded, and they ought to accept. As for Davis's responsibility, constitutionally he had not the political power to surrender the cause, but in his role as commander-in-chief, he could accept and ratify the military convention at hand and order the disbanding of the armies. "He can end hostilities," said Benjamin, though only the states themselves could dissolve the Confederacy and by their sovereign action reenter the Union.

Reagan, Davis, and Mallory said substantially the same, though some painted an even bleaker portrait of the current state of the Confederacy. "The Government of the Confederate States is no longer potent for good," the attorney general observed. "It is already virtually destroyed." They had but to look at their current circumstances to see the worth of his words. They were on the run, dependent on the hospitality of communities that, if not hostile, still were not overfriendly, meeting in a cramped bank office while the substance of their government sat outside in wagons and railroad cars. The only power left to the president was to disband the armies, resign his office, and call on the people of the several states to meet in convention to act on the terms. For Mallory the very fact of their having this meeting was an admission that the cause was dead, and he hurried to preempt any suggestion of guerrilla war by arguing that it would be more damaging to their own people than to the enemy, and in the end stood no chance of shaking the Yankee hold on the country. "The Confederacy is conquered," he said, "its days are numbered." Reagan did suggest asking for an additional stipulation that Federal forces be withdrawn from the Southern states, except for the garrisons necessary for the permanent coastal fortifications in national defense, as he feared that a long period of occupation would aggravate bitterness. Somewhat incredibly, he also wanted the massive war debt of the Confederacy to be absorbed into the Union war debt, since in their view—conveniently ignoring their own armed seizure of Federal arsenals and forts and the firing on Fort Sumter—the Southern states only went to war when it was forced upon them.

Besides, in a reunited nation, Southern taxpayers would be expected to contribute to retiring the North's indebtedness, so it was naturally equitable that Northerners reciprocate. He even noted that the terms made no mention of slavery, and actually suggested that as a result they could hope that the institution might remain untouched in spite of the Emancipation Proclamation and the pending Thirteenth Amendment. In short, he was arguing that the North and South could act simply as if no war had taken place at all and nothing had changed. Reagan was coming perilously close to asking that the North apologize for beating the South, and of all of them, he alone argued that if Washington rejected Sherman's terms recognizing the right of local state government, or of the personal and property rights of Confederates, and if it did not agree to a full amnesty, then they should continue the fight, even to devastation and death.

Interestingly, none of the others even mentioned slavery, including Breckinridge in his shortest and most pointed response of all, less than a fourth the length of Reagan's. In a single paragraph he covered the collapse of their armies, Johnston's inability to campaign further, the closure of their ports, the lack of arms, and the occupation of most of their major cities and large swathes of the countryside. With North Carolina especially in mind, he anticipated that several states would soon make their dependent peace with the Union. Then he addressed the fear he first expressed back in Richmond almost two months before. "Ineffective hostilities may be prosecuted, while the war, wherever waged, will probably degenerate into that irregular and secondary stage, out of which greater evils will flow to the South than to the enemy." Guerrilla warfare would be a disaster, he warned. If they rejected the cartel and tried to continue in that fashion, their contest "will be likely to lose entirely the dignity of regular warfare."

"In any view of the case," Breckinridge concluded, "grave responsibilities must be met and assumed," and granting the need for peace, he said they must act. Davis was the only person who could take appropriate action. He should immediately disband all Confederate forces and recommend by proclamation to the states that they take the action required of them in the agreement. That done, Davis ought to resign an office that brought with it a trust he was no longer able to defend. "Whatever course you pursue opinions will be divided," he said. "I think the better judgment will be that you can have no higher title to the gratitude of your countrymen and the respect of mankind than will spring from the wisdom to see the path of duty at this time, and the courage to follow it regardless alike of praise or blame."[40]

When called upon, Trenholm simply offered his oral agreement, and having heard their unanimous opinion, Davis probably ventured his own belief that, bleak as their affairs appeared, they were perhaps not yet entirely this desperate, and his expectation that Washington would reject Sherman's terms in any case. During the discussion, Governor Vance arrived in Charlotte, at Davis's summons, and came straight to their room. Knowing little of Vance's recent peace efforts, and recalling the governor's onetime defiance in the face of defeatism, Davis sought an ally. When the governor asked the president's recommendation on what course he should follow, Davis asserted again, as he suggested that morning to Harrison and Varina, that even if they accepted the cartel it did not necessarily mean the end of the war and the cause. "Mr. Davis appeared still full of hope," thought Vance, as the president spoke of Kirby Smith and the Trans-Mississippi. If Vance would come with him and encourage remaining North Carolina troops to follow, then the chance of reviving their hopes was good.

Davis's response stunned Vance, who could not answer at first, while others in the room, having just spent hours essentially arranging the last obsequies for the Confederacy, were openmouthed that the president was suddenly trying yet again to resurrect the corpse. More surprising still, old habits returned among at least a couple of the cabinet, no doubt including Benjamin, who suggested that such a plan might in fact work. In his whole political career, Davis had never been as successful as a politician as he had been these last few weeks in staving off peace, and now he seemed about to win again. Then, in an effort to bring them back to reality, Breckinridge spoke up. With what Vance called "the courage of sincerity," the secretary of war said that Davis and his supporters were not being honest with the governor. The hope of accomplishing what the president proposed was so remote that he, for one, refused to advise the governor to ignore his duty to his state by following the fortunes of a government in flight. North Carolina needed Vance in this hour, and it was his duty to remain here as governor and do the best he could for his people and share their fate. Breckinridge's words brought an enormous relief to Vance. "I shall never forget either the language or the manner of that splendid Kentuckian," he said later, and in the moment, he forgot entirely his miffed feelings at being left behind at Hillsborough. The secretary of war was not about to abandon him to Davis's obsession to keep fighting. The president sighed deeply and admitted defeat, at least for the moment. "Well, perhaps, General, you are right," he said to Breckinridge. Then when Vance

spoke, it was to confirm that his views matched the Kentuckian's, putting an end to any idea of North Carolina continuing
the war. Davis shook Vance's hand, wished him well, and saw
the governor off.[41] Ever to Davis's credit, he offered not a word
of censure for any of those leaders who disagreed with him and
thought the cause lost.[42]

Davis still determined to delay. He simply could not bring
himself to say the words authorizing Johnston to go ahead, while
he continued to hope that Washington would reject Sherman's
terms before he had to make the humiliating concession. Breckinridge, meanwhile, finally found time to go out to the camps of
the cavalry brigades, where he discovered that an active rumor
mill had most of them already aware that terms had been negotiated. He made a brief speech or two to the troopers, compli-
menting them on being among the most staunch in remaining
at their posts and in their saddles when so many others had
simply deserted. To Duke's and Colonel Breckinridge's commands, his fellow Kentuckians, he showed special solicitation,
and met them with his old cheer unabated as they gave him a
warm reception.[43] Duke heard him make "one of those brief, fe-
licitous speeches which were easier to him than to any one I
have ever known." He told them that the terms were not perhaps the best they could hope for, but were better than expected. That done, Breckinridge sat down at the foot of a tree
and simply spoke with the men for an hour or more, taking their
questions and trying to meet their concerns by explaining the
specifics of the terms frankly. Just then one young cavalryman
rode up on a mule, took off his hat and saluted, and asked if rumors of the surrender were true.

"It is true," replied the general, "and I think the terms such as they all should accept."

"Do you really think, General, that *any* terms of surrender are honorable or should be accepted?" Entirely disregarding the enlisted man's impertinence, Breckinridge replied, "I do, or I certainly should not have assented to them."

"Well, I shall not accept or be bound by them," said the soldier, with all the self-importance of callow youth.

"I regret that, and your comrades here, who are all true soldiers, do not agree with you," said the secretary of war.

"I can't help that," the trooper shot back. "They can do as they please; but the sun shines as bright and the air is as pure on the far side of the Rio Grande as here, and I'll go there rather than give up to the Yankees." Even as the boy turned and rode off on his mule, quite full of himself, everyone including Breckinridge laughed good-naturedly. Duke thought it "the strangest combination of the ludicrous and the heroic I ever witnessed."[44]

While he laughed, Breckinridge knew the boy had touched on a subject that he must address again. Just now he received a telegram from Johnston advising that Sherman expected his government's response the next day, April 24.[45] With the end imminent, a number of men declared they simply could not accept Yankee rule again and the best alternative seemed to be to cross the Rio Grande to Mexico, where they would be free from prosecution. There, if they chose, they could take service either with the French-backed imperialist forces led by Archduke Ferdinand of Austria, or the rebels backing Benito Juarez. Earlier that same morning, Davis had written to Varina of possibly going to Mexico if he must.

Having seen the negotiations result favorably, and Davis apparently yielding at last to the consensus of his cabinet, the secretary of war regarded the safety of the president as now his first priority. He and Reagan had discussed the matter during their long trip to Charlotte, as they had previously, but did not yet broach the subject to him. Breckinridge also came armed with a tacit suggestion from Sherman that he would not interfere with any effort to get Davis out of the country, so long as it came soon. As soon as they got confirmation that Washington was ratifying the cartel, he and Reagan would approach Davis again and argue more strenuously for him to flee, while some of those soldiers determined to go to Mexico could perhaps provide sufficient escort once they fixed an escape route.[46]

Johnston's telegram that day was not just informational. It also reminded the general that he had not heard whether the president would ratify the terms, and significantly Johnston wired not Davis but Breckinridge to make certain that he got action. The secretary of war went to the president the next morning, and a few hours later Davis finally acted, though the strain on him told in his terseness.[47] "Your action is approved," he wired Johnston. If Sherman notified the general that Washington also agreed, then they were to proceed with arrangements, though Davis still reserved his prerogative to give "further instructions...as to the details of negotiation and the methods of executing the terms of agreement." Davis could still either delay or even kill the cartel by quibbling over specifics, and was holding the door open for himself to do so. He need not have bothered. Within hours of Breckinridge's notifying Johnston that Davis's acceptance was on the way, Johnston sent another telegram that evening to Charlotte. It was all for nothing. Washington rejected Sherman's agreement and ordered him to treat only for the surrender of Johnston's army on the same terms as those given Lee. He had forty-eight hours to agree before the cease-fire ended. Once again the Yankees gave Davis what he wanted. As before, Johnston notified Breckinridge, not the president, and asked him for instructions, adding that they had better disband his army now or risk devastation to the country when the Yankees resumed active operations.[48]

While informing Davis at once of Washington's response, Breckinridge met with Reagan, whom he seemed to trust most among the cabinet as a man of action. It was time to try to put into effect their plan of getting Davis out of the country. The Kentuckian immediately wired back to Johnston to ask if he could disband just the infantry and artillery but manage to get his cavalry and any soldiers who could be mounted on wagon horses away with a few light field pieces. Joining the escort now with them, this would form a force sufficient to push aside anything in its way on a march to the Mississippi, and once across, they should easily get the president to safety in Mexico. Johnston quickly replied that he thought the idea impractical, as it only addressed saving the president and perhaps his cabinet while still leaving the soldiers in the greatly enlarged escort liable to fighting and death, and the countryside subject to further invasion and devastation as Sherman would have no choice but to pursue. At the same time, Breckinridge and Reagan went to Davis with the plan, and with Sherman's suggestion for a speedy escape. Predictably, Davis rejected both plans, declaring that he would never leave the country while a single Southern regiment remained ready to fight, as well as repudiating entirely the idea that he should make himself beholden in any way to Sherman or his government.[49]

What hardened his resolve was the fact that just two days earlier the hotheaded General Hampton wrote to Davis, announcing that he would refuse to surrender and would go to Mexico
himself, if need be. However, if Davis should try to get to the
Mississippi and continue the cause in Texas, he promised that
he and most of his cavalry command would gladly get him there.
Here was at least one general ready to fight on, and one was all
the president needed for encouragement. Moreover, for the past
few days a number of small parties of soldiers had been filtering
into Charlotte, themselves wanting to escape any surrender, and
they brought with them talk of going west of the great river to
keep fighting. When they saw Davis on the street, they cheered
him, and this, added to the apparent steadfastness of the men in
Duke's, Dibrell's, and Ferguson's brigades, only renewed Davis's
hopes. "It was evident that he was greatly affected by the con-
stancy & spirit of these men," observed Mallory, "& that he became indifferent to his own safety thinking only of gathering
together a body of troops to make head against the foe & to
arouse the people to arms." In spite of Johnston's objections,
Davis directed Breckinridge to allow Hampton to leave, taking
with him as many men from the infantry and artillery as wanted
to go and could find horses. The cause was still alive.[50]

Davis wanted Johnston to get his whole army away if he
could, though by the terms of the cease-fire, neither he nor they
could move before noon on April 26. Dutifully Johnston gave orders for his corps to be ready to march an hour before the dead-
line, but he had no intention of putting them on the road again,
for on the morning of April 25, he sent a proposal to Sherman to
negotiate the surrender of his army. His commanders assured
him that most of their men would not fight if confronted by the

Yankees, and he had long since passed the point of taking Davis's instructions seriously. His morning muster totaled no more than twenty thousand of all ranks present, and that included thousands not fit for duty. Sherman outnumbered him by more than three to one. If the president would not think of the lives of his men, the general would. He told Davis nothing of his plans but wired Breckinridge of his proposal to Sherman. By his own admission he was going to disobey instructions and surrender all except Hampton. The secretary of war sent back no order to forbid him, nor any word at all even acknowledging that he had received Johnston's notification. Instead, for the next twenty-four hours, Breckinridge remained strangely silent, and the absence of anything from Davis to Johnston forbidding surrender suggests strongly that the secretary of war simply chose not to tell the president what the general was about to do.[51]

Regardless of his ignorance of Johnston's intentions, Davis immediately realized that Washington's rejection meant the government would be a target again within hours and would have to move again. Disintegration was all around them. Fearing that the enemy might come swooping down on the city at any moment, the Bank of North Carolina officers decided to take all their remaining specie, about $250,000, and spirit it out of the vault. By candlelight they loaded the money into a wagon, and then the bank president, teller, and cashier, together with two drivers, drove several miles out of town to a dense wood, where they buried it and prepared to camp for several days until any danger passed.[52] Tench Tilghman of Maryland was in town with one of the Confederate wagon trains and remarked that "the government is completely disorganized, and can support neither its soldiers nor paroled officers."[53]

The previous evening a deputation representing the Virginia officers, most of them detached from commands that had surrendered with Lee, called on Breckinridge. They were following a government on the run that seemed to have nothing for them to do, and were only getting farther from their homes at every move. They asked him where their duty lay now. Breckinridge replied that there was nothing they could do for the Confederacy. The situation was hopeless, and they should go home to share the destiny of their state. He added that he would do the same and return to Kentucky but for the position that he held, and added further that he advised Governors Vance and Smith both to stay with their states. Immediately he gave Cooper an order authorizing them to return to Virginia, but before the deputation left, Breckinridge impressed upon them what one thought "a perfect conviction that he considered the military situation as utterly hopeless."[54] A disheartened Preston Johnston wrote to his wife, "I fear the spirit of the people is broken," and John Taylor Wood frankly confessed, "we are falling to pieces."[55] And yet, with no sense of the ridiculous, some of the inexorable grind of bureaucracy continued. Cooper actually ordered Gorgas and two others to sit that evening as an examining board for an infantry cadet being considered for a lieutenant's commission. They met at sundown in the upper floor of a warehouse and with all solemnity went through the pointless exercise, examining the boy in history and geography, mathematics, and even English grammar. The youth passed and won his commission, for all the good it would do him, and yet somehow the incongruity of the event in the midst of what was happening attracted notice even among Hampton's men just coming into town.[56]

Just after dawn on April 26, Johnston broke the silence to telegraph Breckinridge that he was leaving to meet Sherman. After that the wires went silent again, but soon everyone but Davis seemed to know what was happening, and Gorgas warned War Department staff.[57] Davis called an early cabinet council in Trenholm's sickroom, and though the Pfifer family could not hear what was said, the sight of the cabinet arriving in a group with bowed heads and serious expressions told them eloquently enough that a crisis loomed.[58] Regardless of their differences on the future of the Confederacy, if it had one, they could all at least agree that they had to move, and immediately, rather than risk capture. They would go south through South Carolina and Georgia, and on westward to the Mississippi, the only route that could keep Sherman behind them, while trying to evade other substantial Federal forces in north Georgia and Alabama. Attorney General Davis spoke up then, saying his family concerns did not allow him to go on with them. He would have to stay in North Carolina and take his chances with the Federals. The president accepted his resignation without protest or condemnation. The Justice Department existed only on paper now, anyhow, a post with nothing to do, and Jefferson Davis himself had said he would sacrifice everything but his family, so he could hardly judge ill of another who served the same priority. General Cooper also said he would have to remain behind, his age and infirmity making it impossible for him to face the sort of pace the rest would have to follow.

Hampton and Major General Joseph Wheeler had arrived the night before, and Davis sent them back north to try to rally as many of their cavalrymen as possible, with orders then to ride south to join him somewhere along his route.[59] Meanwhile there had been some disagreement among the several brigadier generals commanding their brigades as to who was senior and should therefore assume overall leadership of the escort. Breckinridge cut the knotty problem by taking the command himself, since, as a major general, he outranked them all. So now, in addition to acting as secretary of war and taking charge of planning for their flight, he would also take over active field command of around three thousand cavalry.[60] They would leave town that afternoon, their future itinerary left subject to conditions as they found them, though they would make initially for Abbeville. They planned to leave by noon, the very moment that the cease-fire expired. Rigidly true to his word at times, Davis would not countenance leaving a minute before the expiration of the armistice.[61]

Once again there was much to do. The War Department never actually went into operation in Charlotte, and the bulk of the archives only arrived the evening before, still packed in their wagon train. Breckinridge had originally ordered them to be shipped on south, but a damaged bridge prevented the train from leaving, and now the secretary gave Kean strict instructions to store them in safety here in town, where they would be secure until the Yankees moved in. He wanted the papers turned over to the enemy intact, and as a safeguard, Breckinridge gave exactly the same orders to General Cooper. The archives, he said, were "essential to the history of the struggle." The only things Breckinridge wanted kept apart were the responses from his bureau chiefs to his first request for a statement of their resources and ability to continue back on February 7. These were the basis on which he had founded his campaign, since taking office, to bring an end to the war and the Confederacy, and he charged

Kean with keeping them in his personal possession. If nothing else survived and Breckinridge himself should perish, those documents at least would tell posterity that he had tried.[62] As soon as Breckinridge saw to his archives, Kean took the reports and joined the party of Virginia officers just leaving for home.[63]

By the appointed hour, the party was ready to leave in several wagons and ambulances, one carrying the Trenholms, with Davis booted and spurred on horseback, along with the remaining cabinet. Duke, Dibrell, Ferguson, W. C. P. Breckinridge, and General John Vaughn and his brigade made up the escort, along with Captain Campbell's scouts. Just before leaving, Davis met Gorgas, who was taking another road, and told him that they were heading for the country west of the Mississippi. Gorgas thought to himself that before Davis ever got there, "events will have shaped themselves."[64] Johnston was even then trying to get word of his completed surrender negotiations to Breckinridge, making no attempt at all to inform Davis, but by the time his telegram reached Charlotte, the government was gone. Nevertheless, they had a hint. Just before they left the city, a telegram to Johnston's wife came through the Charlotte office, advising her that he would be seeing her in a few days. To Davis and Breckinridge that could only mean that Johnston himself was leaving his command temporarily, or that there was nothing more to command.[65]

It had been an eventful week in Charlotte, and a number of the townspeople gathered in the streets to watch as the column left. The Courtneys stood in their yard, waving as the ranks galloped past their house, Breckinridge and Davis mounted in the lead. Mary Courtney sensed that grief and despair were moving in to fill the place of those riders, "for hope with her brighter joys left with them."[66] Others felt the same atmosphere of portent. Some thought Davis himself looked downcast. "Poor President, he is unwilling to see what all around him see," thought one watching soldier. "He cannot bring himself to believe that after four years of glorious struggle we are to be crushed."[67] The postal clerk Stuart thought the president looked like a man who "felt himself unseated but not unthroned."[68]

That remained to be seen, but as the column disappeared to the south, the cloud of dust raised in the afternoon heat by thousands of hooves cast a pall over those, like Mary Courtney, who watched them gallop out of sight. "The sun shone as if in eclipse," she remembered, "and the shadows turned so deep and heavy."[69]

Chapter Seven

"ALL IS LOST
BUT OUR HONOR"

The fugitives rode slowly and, Mallory thought, "not at all like men escaping from the country."[1] Davis set their pace by staying at the head of the column with Breckinridge, and others noticed that he seemed in no hurry. Duke thought their advance positively leisurely, and to cavalrymen accustomed to moving fast, this sloth was almost demoralizing; troopers in the ranks soon interpreted their halting progress as evidence that Davis either did not know where he was going or else had no firm purpose in mind. Scouts reported a column of Yankee cavalry about fifteen miles west of them, riding parallel and at the same pace, obviously shadowing their movements, which only further troubled the men.[2] They made less than twenty miles that day, to Fort Mills, a few miles above the Catawba River. With nightfall coming on, they passed the home of Colonel A. B. Springs, whose daughters somehow heard in advance who was coming and were waiting at the front gate with flowers to throw before the president's horse. Colonel Springs insisted that Davis spend the night in his home, and Davis accepted, sharing quarters with some of the cabinet, while Trenholm and others went to William White's nearby home.[3]

The ambulance ride so aggravated Trenholm's misery that this evening he told Davis he simply could go no farther and must resign. Davis called a meeting of the rest of the cabinet and proposed appointing Reagan in Trenholm's place, and they concurred. Only Reagan objected, pointing out that he was already postmaster general and had also taken over supervision of the telegraph lines, but Davis mollified him by suggesting, perhaps wryly, that there would not be much for the secretary of the Treasury to do. Reagan reluctantly agreed and, later that evening, met with Trenholm, who gave him a sketchy and incomplete briefing on the hard money and the several hundred thousand dollars in now worthless Confederate notes they had with them, as well as the treasure from the Treasury and the Virginia banks still south of them with Parker and the midshipmen. Never before in America had a single officer held two cabinet posts simultaneously, and it was possibly unconstitutional, but that hardly mattered under the circumstances. Reagan was healthy and active, and there was still a Treasury to oversee.[4] That same evening Trenholm wrote his resignation and gave it to the president. Davis of course accepted it, with a grace and expression of confidence and thanks that could endear him to the few men he chose to let see that side of his personality.[5] That done, they sat outside and watched their host's two sons, Eli and John, play marbles in the yard until someone suggested that the men should join the boys. At once the president, the secretary of war, secretary of state, and the postmaster–treasurer were on their knees, marbles in hand, spending an hour at a spirited contest amid peals of laughter, while Mallory watched and saw good evidence of many hours' employment in their own boyhoods, as they revealed a sure grasp of the rules of the game.[6]

The next morning they held a conference on the lawn of the Springs's home to decide on their route. In the end they concluded that they should move southwesterly toward Lieutenant General Richard Taylor's army, last known to be near Mobile. Breckinridge assigned the duty of picketing and scouting to Dibrell's two brigades, they being better armed and equipped than the other units and, at the moment, generally under better discipline.[7] That done, they crossed the Catawba on a pontoon used as a ferry. It took several trips to get the whole party of wagons and men across, while the cavalry mostly swam. Tench Tilghman, with the wagons, watched as the leaders crossed first and rode into South Carolina. "What a sight to see Jeff Davis and Breckinridge and the Cabinet standing on the pontoon," he wrote that evening. They reminded him of King Robert the Bruce withdrawing into the mountains of Scotland with the faithful, to bide the time for their return. But Tilghman did not expect a return. "The cause has gone up," he concluded. "God only knows what will be the end of all this."[8]

All that day they continued their slow pace, and perhaps sensing the increasingly sullen mood among the cavalrymen, Davis, Breckinridge, and the rest began to mingle with them at every opportunity, often riding among the troopers rather than at their head. "The effect was excellent," thought Duke, "largely counteracting the feeling of uneasiness induced by our lack of activity." He found that the president, Breckinridge, and Benjamin particularly influenced the men. Benjamin, now on horseback, often rode among the troopers, always cheerful and smiling, talkative, and fascinating.[9] Looking on, Micajah Clark found the president especially impressive at such a moment. "To me he appeared incomparably grander in the nobleness of his great heart and head, than when he reviewed victorious armies returning from well-won fields," he thought. While some in the party occasionally gave vent to frustration and sorrow at their current fate, and indignation at their shabby treatment in North Carolina, Davis did not complain. Instead, Clark saw him presenting an almost serene face, "beguiling the tedium of the weary miles with cheerful conversation, reminiscences, and anecdotes—as a gracious host entertaining his guests." Everyone knew that this proudest of men must be suffering within, but what he felt he kept to himself. Mallory frequently observed him at rest stops, when Davis stretched out on a blanket, his head resting on his saddle, or sat leaning against a tree, cigar in mouth, and regaled his associates with reminiscences. "He was always more at ease, & pleasantly talkative in the woods, than under a roof," said Mallory, "and he decidedly preferred the bivouac to the bed room." Nor did many miss Davis's little acts of kindness along the way when he stopped for rest or a meal. Paroled and deserting soldiers had stolen from citizens as they had passed through, including horses and mules to speed their journeys home, and many a robbery victim appealed to the president when he passed through. When he could, he actually redressed the crime by handing over a government animal in recompense. Neighborhood children soon found their way onto his lap, bringing him flowers while he told anecdotes to cheer the men, talked about his favorite cures for ailments in horses, and compared notes with the cavalrymen on the best way to cross rivers.[10]

When not talking with the leaders, the troopers talked among themselves in their idle time, speculating on the chances Davis and others had of getting away from the Yankees. So far that enemy column west of them showed no inclination to attack, and almost certainly did not know yet just who they were shadowing. But when the time came they might move swiftly. The men concluded that Davis could get away if he chose, chiefly because they would make it their settled determination to see that he did. For Breckinridge they felt no worry; he would get away if he wanted to, unless duty forced him to stay with Davis in the moment of capture. They knew the old frontier ranger Reagan would escape. But when it came to Benjamin, almost universal opinion was that he would fall into enemy hands in a chase. Somehow no one expected this roly-poly little fellow whose skin and manner gave evidence of not a day's physical exertion in his life, could possibly escape should the time come.[11] As for themselves, their morale was still holding. When some of his Tennessee troopers spoke of leaving the ranks and returning to their state, General Dibrell told them imperiously that "we are not going home."[12]

They spent the night of April 27 in private homes at Yorkville, due west of the Catawba crossing, visiting with Hampton's wife briefly, then late the next morning set out for the Broad River crossing at Scales' Ferry.[13] Davis and Reagan rode in advance of the column a little way and stopped at a house to ask

for a drink of water. The lady of the house asked Davis if he was
the president, and on his answering, she held up her infant, saying, "He is named for you." Davis reached into his pocket and
took out a gold piece, giving it to her to keep for the child. As
they rode off again, he confided to Reagan that it was the last
coin he had.[14] That evening, worried about the attention such a
large column attracted to itself, Breckinridge ordered Dibrell
and the cavalry brigades to ride on separately and meet them in
Cokesbury in a couple of days, choosing Campbell's company
to remain with Davis and the cabinet.[15] As they got deeper into
the interior, they pulled up at a house just a mile short of the
river. It was a beautiful night, and the whole party spent several
hours out of doors. Breckinridge sent what would be his last orders back to Greensboro, telling Hampton that if the instructions authorizing him to detach himself and some men from
Johnston's army were received before the surrender had been
agreed, then he was free to do so, but otherwise he would have
to surrender as well.[16] Whatever their straits, they must not dishonor the rules of war. Breckinridge then joined Davis in conversation on their host Dr. James Bratton's porch, while Mallory
and Reagan lightheartedly pitched silver half-dollars out in the
garden for five-cent bets.[17]

Perhaps it was the sight of the two cabinet members playing
with coins, and the recollection of Davis's gift earlier that day,
that later gave rise to a conversation among them all on the
porch. One by one each speculated on his current financial
worth as a result of the war. Benjamin had been a planter in
Louisiana, and his house and slaves were gone. Mallory added
that his own Florida property had been mostly destroyed by the
Yankees. Reagan offered that he had lost up to fifty thousand

dollars in the last four years. George Davis was no longer with them, but they knew that his North Carolina holdings were now in Yankee hands, and even Trenholm, who had been the richest man in the South before the war, was probably broke now. Breckinridge never owned plantations, though he had a little property in Wisconsin that he transferred to other hands before adopting the Confederacy, as he had his house in Lexington, Kentucky. His principal residence, a new home he had built within blocks of the capitol in Washington, had been taken over by the enemy and used as a soldier hospital during the war. He could not know it, but within a few weeks it would be fitted out as a home for General Grant. Davis spoke last. He had twenty-eight thousand dollars on deposit in the Bank of Virginia at Richmond, but when he tried to draw it out in Danville from that bank's funds traveling with the Treasury, its teller refused to cash his check without authority from his employers, who were back in the fallen capital. His plantation in Mississippi had been overrun by the Yankees, and the only money he had was in Confederate notes in his pocketbook and whatever Varina had with her. Almost with pride, the president said it gratified him that no one could ever accuse them of profiting personally from the war.[18]

In the morning they left at dawn to cross the Broad—Davis and the baggage wagons crossing first, and the four cabinet officers on the next crossing.[19] Breckinridge sent a rider ahead several miles to the inappropriately named Unionville to arrange a place for lunch, and when the column arrived about 11 A.M., Davis was shown to the home of General William H. Wallace on east Main Street. His hosts took Davis to a bedroom to rest for an hour or so, and then he and the cabinet were treated to a sumptuous luncheon of dishes sent by several of the neighbors.

Mallory could not get over how "wherever Mr Davis went he found the people of towns & hamlets at their doors or outside their gates, ready to greet him, & to offer flowers & strawberries, and prayers & kind wishes; for the straggling soldiers, passing him every day regularly heralded his progress."[20] The meal done, they remounted and rode on to Rose Hill, still making very slow progress. They arrived early in the evening, Breckinridge riding ahead to the home of Jane Giles, the widow of a Confederate captain, to ask if the president and his escort could stay the night.

"General Breckinridge was one of the handsomest men I ever saw," the hostess recalled, but just down the street he could see others less pleased by his arrival. Just before the secretary appeared, a small body of men that Major General Wheeler had sent south arrived, saying they were part of Davis's escort, and indeed their general had originally arranged with Davis to rendezvous with the president somewhere in this vicinity.[21] At least they identified themselves as Wheeler's men, but as soon as they realized that it was Breckinridge who had arrived, they rode out of town in a rush. Wheeler himself probably was not with them, but he had always been a notorious liability to the Confederacy, indifferent to orders, unreliable, and maintaining woeful discipline in his command. Now, confronted with the choice between dangerous service with the arriving government and a last chance for a bit of plunder, they chose the latter, stealing one of the hostess's mules as they left town. Davis was appalled when he arrived, not so much by the theft of the animal as that the men pretended to be a part of his escort.

Mrs. Giles was so thrilled to have the president in her home that the next morning, April 30, she went to her back garden and dug up the china she had buried to save it from the Yankees. She served Davis and the cabinet newly picked strawberries on her best. They were the first berries of the season, but there were not enough for everyone, and Tilghman at least looked on enviously as the president and cabinet enjoyed what appeared to him to be "an elegant breakfast." The party then rode on toward Cokesbury, through country almost untouched by the war, with the young daughters of the homes they passed standing on their porches to wave handkerchiefs and throw small bouquets to the riders.[22] By midday they rode into the village of Cross Keys to take lunch at the Warren Davis home. Mrs. Davis and several of her family entertained them, but as evidence that his spirits were back up again, the president playfully did not introduce himself. Apparently no one else told the Davises just who the dignitaries were, either. Only in leaving did he finally say, "Mrs. Davis, I thank you for your hospitality, we have the same name." Identifying himself, he walked out, mounted, and the party rode off, leaving a somewhat bewildered woman who did not actually realize just who he was until he was out of sight.[23] Jefferson Davis never had much of a sense of humor, and when he did try to make a joke, it was usually at the expense of someone else. Now amid collapse and ruin, his fooling this Mrs. Davis was about the only victory he could achieve.

They reached Cokesbury the evening of May 1, where Davis had originally expected to meet Wheeler. Instead he found another. From Yorkville Davis had sent Preston Johnston off on a locomotive south to Chester to meet General Braxton Bragg and bring him to join them. Riding hard across country, Johnston and Bragg were waiting in Cokesbury when the column arrived. Bragg had always been Davis's most dependable sycophant, never arguing, never contradicting, ever faithful even to the point of fabricating evidence if necessary, as he had done in his feud with Breckinridge over defeats when Bragg was in command at Stones River and Chattanooga. Davis wanted Bragg's opinion of their military prospects, no doubt expecting that at least this old friend would not gainsay his optimism. It was something of a scene when they all met. Bragg took off his hat as he stood after Davis asked his views. The president must have felt crestfallen when the general said not what he wanted to hear but that he agreed entirely with the cabinet and felt that any further fighting was pointless.[24] That said, Bragg quietly walked over beside Breckinridge and stood there silently, hat in hand. Captain Campbell was present. Like all Kentuckians, he despised Bragg, largely for his attempt to blame his own failures on Breckinridge, and now he looked on with grim satisfaction as Bragg stood humbly beside the same man he once tried to disgrace.[25]

If what Bragg said surprised Davis, he had little time to indulge his disappointment. News from his wife finally caught up to the president here. His friend Henry Leovy of Abbeville came into town with a letter written by Varina just three days before, announcing that she and the children were safe and well and leaving the morning of April 28 for Washington, Georgia, and would probably go on to Atlanta from there until she heard from him. She had gotten his anguished letter delivered by Harrison, and agreed that what lay before them was not the fate she expected when they wed, "but you must remember that you did not invite me to a great Hero's home, but to that of a plain farmer." She had shared all of his triumphs, she went on. "Now I am but claiming the privilege for the first time of being all to you now these pleasures have past for me." She implored him to not on her account turn aside for a moment from his intended route to safety and continuing the cause. She would go on to Florida, from there to Bermuda or the Bahamas, and on to England to put the children in school. Then she would make her way to Texas "once more to suffer with you if need be."

She felt nothing but contempt for those who quailed from continuing the fight: "They cannot bear the tug of War." She hardly saw a single soldier pass her in recent days who had any heart left. Believing that no determined stand could be made east of the Mississippi, she urged him not to try but to hasten to Kirby Smith. "The spirit is there," she urged him, but he must be wary passing through a Georgia ruled by his old enemy Governor Brown, who was rumored to be on the verge of rebelling against the Confederacy and seizing all government arms and property. She all but spat as she spoke of the defeatist, spineless people east of the Mississippi now. "They are a set of wretches together," she said, "and I wish you were safe out of their land." And she said one thing more. "You have now tried the 'strict construction' fallacy," she said, referring to his observance of the constitutional limitations on his authority, though his critics for years had accused him of overriding that document and assuming almost dictatorial powers. Henceforward he must *be* a dictator if necessary. Their constitution, if it was to survive at all, "must be much stretched during our hours of ou[t]side pressure if it covers us at all."[26] As he read, the president likely mused that here was a woman worthy of an emperor. If the soldiers in his armies only had her spirit and determination the Confederacy would by now be independent.

Breckinridge had been sending scouts out frequently along the way to feel for enemy cavalry, and now one came in reporting the Yankees not ten miles away. Anticipating that this might happen, Davis had already sent word back to Wheeler that he should try for Washington, Georgia, instead.[27] Faced with imminent danger, the party decided to remain just a few hours to rest. The mother of General Martin Gary gave the president and cabinet the hospitality of her home, but they only stayed until 2 A.M. on May 2, when another scout brought intelligence that elements of Federal General George Stoneman's cavalry were on their way and would be in Cokesbury within two or three hours. Breckinridge took over rousing Campbell's little company and preparing them for what would surely be a hopeless fight if they were attacked, but still with a hope that they might hold out until the arrival of Dibrell, who was due any hour. The secretary assigned the men to their positions to meet and delay an enemy advance, but by dawn neither the enemy nor Dibrell had appeared, and as soon as it was light enough, they all mounted and this time pressed hard toward the southwest, leaving word for Dibrell to meet them in Abbeville.[28]

In fact, Yankee cavalry under the immediate command of Colonel William Palmer had gotten word of just who were in this column of Confederates and had been following them for some time until he captured some stragglers from the cavalry escort who freely told him that Davis was heading for Abbeville. As Mallory himself lamented, despite all precautions, Davis and his escort "travelled through the country from Charlotte with greater publicity than Dan Rice's Caravan engaged & the enemy knew every foot of its progress."[29] Learning that, Palmer decided not to try to catch up to the fleeing government along the way but rather to concentrate his forces somewhere west of Abbeville expecting that then Davis would simply ride into his arms.[30] Palmer's relaxing the pursuit meant the danger that seemed so imminent now passed for a time, though hereafter the Confederates would be looking over their shoulders all the same.

Breckinridge thought he might have to shave down the escort to even fewer men, equipped with the best horses, to ride all the faster to get Davis safely to the west. "I want you to keep close to me," he told W. H. Swallow, who had been with him on and off since leaving Richmond. The reports coming in indicated that north Georgia and southern Alabama teemed with Yankee cavalry, meaning that it might be impossible to get to Taylor's army. In fact, though Breckinridge did not yet know it, Taylor was in a cease-fire pending negotiations to surrender his army and was too cut off from the government to attempt to communicate his actions or seek guidance. "We shall move forward to Washington, Georgia," Breckinridge told Swallow, and once they were there they would have to decide what next. "From this time forward nearly every man thought of little save the best and surest way to get out of the reach of the common enemy," said Swallow. "Delays were not now thought of," remarked Charles Stuart, and as they rode through the early morning daylight, Mallory could see that the tiny mounted band held every weapon at the ready, expecting at any moment to see the bluecoats coming after them.[31]

After twelve nervous miles, at around 10 A.M., the weary party galloped into Abbeville at last. No community in the South had been more enthusiastic for secession in 1860, thanks largely to Armistead Burt, and spirit still ran high. There would be no shunning of the officials here as in North Carolina. Davis immediately went to the home of his old friend Burt, which Varina

and the children had left only three days earlier, while Breckinridge and the cabinet found hospitality at the home of T. C. Perrin, nearby, and many other houses opened to members of the
fleeing party.[32] Awaiting them as they rode into town, the government found another reunion, for there were Captain William
Parker and his midshipmen, with the treasure train that they
had not seen since Danville.

Parker had gone first to Greensboro, and then on to Charlotte,
where he unloaded his treasure and placed it in the local mint
vault as ordered, amid rumors of a Federal company of raiders
intending to sweep into town to capture the money. It was nothing but a rumor, but everyone spent a nervous night nevertheless.[33] When no raid materialized, Parker thought at first that
this would be an end of his term guarding money. But then new
reports of Stoneman's cavalry prowling in the area forced him to
act without waiting for the government to take charge of the
money once again. So he ordered it all loaded back onto a train,
and finding Varina Davis and her children in town, he insisted
that they accompany him and the midshipmen to safety. Parker
had to practically take at gunpoint stores and supplies from the
local naval warehouse, since the man in charge at first refused to
release anything without an order from Mallory, who at that moment could not be reached. Parker had a large party with him,
including Charles Iverson Graves, nominally in charge on behalf
of the Treasury Department, and several clerks and their families. To be on the safe side, once he got into the storehouse,
by his own admission, Parker had his midshipmen take enough
supplies to last them "several months." That way he would have
no further confrontations with bureaucrats.[34]

Their train took them to Chester, South Carolina, and there they transferred all of the specie and notes to wagons. Parker armed all of the midshipmen, as well as a naval company who had joined them in Charlotte, making a band of about 150, and declared that all civilians and treasury officials traveling with him henceforward would be under martial law. It was going to be next to impossible to keep secret the passage of hundreds of thousands of dollars through the countryside, not to mention the family of the president, and he had already seen sufficient signs of disintegration in civilian morale and soldier discipline to expect he might have to defend his charge against Southern looters as well as Yankee raiders. That first night they stopped at a wayside church, Varina Davis sleeping on the pews, while Parker himself dozed in the pulpit. Lieutenant Edward C. Means of the navy, now off duty at home, took the rest of the ladies to his house, where his family treated them to what Mrs. Graves described as "lovely meals, glorious baths, and downy beds."[35] When they left the next morning, everyone except the women walked, and in two days they covered forty-five miles. Along the way wonderful hospitality met them, and to everyone's delight, a train for which Parker had sent ahead was waiting in Newberry when they arrived on April 15. Once more they transferred their precious cargo to the cars for the forty-five-mile ride to Abbeville, arriving late that night.[36]

While Varina Davis left the cavalcade here and went to Burt's home, the rest of the party spent that night on the train. The next day, they transferred the treasure to wagons to start for Washington, Georgia, on April 17. It took them two days to cover the forty miles, and more and more they heard reports of disaster behind them. First came rumors of Lee's surrender, and then the swift-moving stories that Johnston was meeting Sherman. Urged on by this and the even more disturbing intelligence of Stoneman's cavalry, the wagon train left in its wake a continual trail of debris as they lightened the wagons to make better time. A drenching rain further dampened their spirits as they discarded blank departmental stationery, then books, and in the end even Confederate paper money, until they rolled into Washington, Georgia, around 10 A.M. on April 19.[37] Uncertain just where he should go next, Parker shifted the treasure to a house in town and placed a heavy guard around it, while the women in the party, including Parker's wife, who had come with him from Richmond, went to the local hotel, only to find the rooms stripped of furniture and everything else, forcing them to sleep on the floor. Parker and Graves, meanwhile, called on Judge Garnett Andrews to seek his advice on how best to protect the treasure. In the end they decided that it would be safer in a vault in Augusta, and in the morning Parker had it reloaded on another train and set off to the southeast, leaving the wives and some of their baggage behind.[38] It was on reaching Augusta that evening that definitive news of Lee's surrender reached them. "I fear all is lost but our honor," lamented Midshipman R. H. Fleming. Indeed, Parker feared he might even lose the treasure here, for the city appeared to be a stronghold of Unionism. Officers in town told him openly that the war was over, arguing that he should pay the money out to them, or even the civilians. The Yankees would get it otherwise, some said, and before long warnings came to him that Confederates, soldiers and citizens, might well attack them and take the treasure. Parker replied that so long as this money had been put in his charge, no one would touch it until he could get definitive orders from Davis himself, and he and his midshipmen would die defending it if they must. At first he kept the cargo under heavy guard on the train cars, but now he immediately transferred it to a local bank vault, much to the relief of the midshipmen. "I am glad we haven't it to guard," Fleming confessed.[39] They were tired of the responsibility of guarding the treasure.

Parker also learned in Augusta of the armistice between Sherman and Johnston, which applied to all forces, military and civilian, and as a result he settled down in Augusta to await developments somewhat nervously. On April 25 word of Washington's rejection of the peace cartel reached Augusta, and with it the announcement that the cease-fire ended at noon the next day. The local commander, Brigadier General Birkett D. Fry, knowing the sentiment of the civilian population, and seeing the evaporating discipline of his own meager soldiery, quietly advised Parker that he would be wise to get the treasury out of town. That same day Navy Paymaster John Wheless told Parker that soldiers at the local arsenal, workers at government shops, and civilians, all of them with no means to buy food now, would almost certainly try to take the money, and urged him to get it out of town.[40] After some deliberation, Parker finally decided that the only way to shed this burden would be to take the money to Davis and turn it over to him. Expecting from reports that the president's itinerary must bring him to the Savannah River somewhere between Abbeville and Washington, he decided to try to meet him, and so the midshipmen loaded their boxcars once more.

Just after noon on April 26, when the armistice expired, they set out, Fleming observing with some exasperation, "Here we go back to Washington again." Once there, Graves went to the ladies' hotel room where he found them sitting in what his wife called "an ominous silence," as if they knew bad news was coming, and he then informed them of Lee's surrender and the death of Lincoln. Now the party decided to break up. Graves left the treasury to Parker and took his wife and family back to Augusta.[41] Parker allowed furloughs to all the midshipmen who asked, after they transferred their load to wagons. At the same time he sent to Judge Andrews's home for storage and safekeeping several boxes of records and a number of useless nautical instruments brought from Richmond.[42] Then on the morning of April 29, with only six midshipmen remaining along with the company of navy men, he set out on April 29 for Abbeville. "It is hard to part with boys after the many pleasant hours we have spent together," Fleming observed sadly as he and the other five said farewell to their comrades.[43] Along the road they met Varina Davis and Burton Harrison, who had left Abbeville that same morning, on their way to Washington, but they could give Parker no definite news as to Davis's whereabouts. By now Parker was so frustrated and sick of the burden of the treasure that when they were crossing the Savannah back into South Carolina, he suggested only half in jest to one of his officers that if the money were his, he would throw it in the river.

Late the next day they rolled into Abbeville again, and once more the treasure had to be unloaded and stored in a small warehouse on the public square, where Parker and the remainder of his command sat guard in the face of frequent threats by paroled soldiers in town that they would take the money if he did not turn it over. The next day, May 1, while his men stood their vigil, Parker went to a party, for the townsfolk were just as hospitable to the treasury guard as they would be to Davis in a few hours. During the evening, a paroled officer back from Lee's army came to Parker and said he had heard of a plan among other paroled soldiers and stragglers to attack the treasure house that night. The captain immediately returned to his small command, doubled the guard, made certain that an engine was waiting with steam up in case he had to load the money on a train quickly to get it out of town, and then went to bed. At 3 A.M. the officer in charge of the guard tapped on his window and quietly said, "Captain, the Yankees are coming." Nothing further developed of the threat from Confederate soldiers in town, but enemy cavalry capturing a couple of men some thirty miles away sparked a rumor that the raiders were on their way to Abbeville next. Not knowing it to be a false alarm, Parker awakened everyone and in the dark ordered them to transfer the treasure to the waiting train. By now the guard must have felt like the mythic King Sisyphus, endlessly pushing his boulder up a hill only to have it roll back on him to be pushed up again. They obeyed nevertheless, and yet again shifted "the things" onto the cars. By dawn everyone was aboard but Parker, who paced the platform lost in thought, not entirely certain whether to leave or not. Then in the distance he saw a column of riders approaching town from the northeast. If it was the Yankees, they should have been coming from the north, but just to make certain, Parker sent two riders out. A few minutes later they galloped back to the station to give him the news that it was not the enemy but the approach of President Davis and his escort. For Parker, who had seen the president in his days of glory in Richmond, it was a sad sight. Riding into the town with a dirty, ragged following of sailors, government clerks, and cavalrymen,

Davis's party reminded him of some pitiful Central American revolutionary junta on the run.[44]

As they entered town, the jaded column first encountered Ferguson's and Duke's brigades camped on the outskirts, having taken a different route from Dibrell. Davis halted briefly at Ferguson's bivouac, where the cavalrymen had just finished their breakfast. They spoke only briefly but not before one of Ferguson's staff noted the simplicity of the president's clothing and his gentlemanly demeanor. Only later did he find out that it was Davis. "I was struck with the coolness and calm deportment of the great man," F. E. Richardson recalled. "It did really appear to me that Mr. Davis wanted to remain with his troops, and share their fate whatever it might be." The staff officer observed further that the president "did not act to me as a man that had the least fear of what was ahead."[45] Ferguson joined Davis and Breckinridge to ride over to Duke's bivouac, and there Breckinridge briefly heard from them what news of the enemy there was in the area, and told them of the reports of Yankee cavalry in their rear. He ordered Ferguson to take his command back to Cokesbury to meet and support Dibrell if necessary, should the Yankees materialize.[46]

As soon as the party reached the center of town, Davis went immediately to Burt's house, where his old friend gave him a room in which to rest from the road. Breckinridge, Mallory, and Reagan meanwhile surveyed what remained for them to do for the moment. The secretary of the navy, in fact, had almost nothing on his plate, his authority now extending no farther than the midshipmen at the depot. The cabinet officers met first with a very relieved Captain Parker, who asked Mallory to take his burden from him. His little command, besides being exhausted, were simply not sufficient to continue guarding the treasure in the face of constantly increasing threats of attack. Mallory obliged with an order to turn the treasure over to Reagan, and the Texan in turn asked Breckinridge for a detail from the cavalry to assume guard duty. Breckinridge knew Duke and his men better than any of the others present, and at once ordered Duke to assume charge of the train, which he did simply by riding up to the cars and, without written orders, telling Parker that he was relieved. That done, Mallory immediately discharged Parker and his remaining midshipmen, as well as the naval company from Charlotte. The captain issued them several days' rations from the seemingly inexhaustible supply he had taken at Charlotte, and then the young men, done at last with rolling their heavy stone up an endless hill, left, singly and in small groups, for home.[47]

After giving Duke his orders, Breckinridge learned that Dibrell was coming, and he ordered Ferguson to bring his command back and make camp just west of town on the road to the pontoon bridge they would have to use to cross the Savannah to Washington. That road needed to be kept open if they were to continue to the southwest, while Dibrell's arriving men could bivouac north and east of town to delay any pursuing Yankees, should they come.[48] Then the secretary of war took stock of the men in the camps. At the beginning of the war, a cavalry brigade could have numbered twenty-five hundred or more. Now the five brigades around Abbeville scarcely mustered a total of four thousand, after the straggling of the past two weeks. Moreover, their morale had sunk even lower during the desultory and, to them, seemingly pointless movement from Charlotte. "These men belonged to the raiding cavalry of the west," said Duke.

They were accustomed to speed and decision. "Sauntering along at the rate of ten or twelve miles a day," he grumbled, "induced them to suspect incapacity or irresolution." The seeming inability of the cabinet to go any faster sapped the confidence of the troopers in their civilian leaders. Even worse was being slowed by what Duke called "the most useless and impedimental procession of ambulances and dressing cases on wheels, that I ever witnessed."[49] Unremitting reports of disaster and dissolution had sapped their determination. Many were evidently only staying with the column because there were ample supplies of rations, while others had actually sold or simply discarded their weapons, evidence enough that they did not intend to fight again.[50] A few may even have kept on simply in the hope of getting a crack at the treasure train if they met it again, and now they had. Vaughn's command seemed to be the worst, but the infection ran throughout all the brigades to some degree, and Breckinridge could see more than enough to realize that, at least as organized commands, these outfits could not be depended upon much longer, though there were still many dependable and determined men scattered throughout, especially among Duke's and Colonel Breckinridge's Kentuckians.

While Breckinridge and Bragg looked over the troopers and their dispositions protecting the town, Captain Parker left the depot and the burdensome treasure behind to go to Burt's house to call on Davis. Several generals without commands had attached themselves to the brigades along the way, and as Parker walked across town he saw the seemingly endless train of baggage wagons belonging to these officers as they rolled into Abbeville, making him suspect that more brigadiers and would-be brigadiers than ever actually served in the army were clinging to the president. Davis greeted him warmly enough, and welcomed what Parker could tell him of Varina and the children. "I never saw the President appear to better advantage," Parker thought. Davis seemed quiet and dignified, giving no sign of despondence or lack of resolution. When Parker told him that Mallory had discharged his train guard, Davis appeared visibly chagrined, and only afterward did the captain suspect that it was because the president, too, had taken the measure of the cavalry brigades and lamented losing any command, however small, that still seemed ready to take orders. Parker also told him of the previous night's planned raid on the treasure. Even though that one did not materialize, inevitably another would, and soon. Moreover, he said, Davis was in imminent danger of capture himself if he did not leave—and not just Abbeville but the country. The president declared yet again that he would never leave Southern soil in inglorious flight.

"The mere idea that he might be looked upon as fleeing, seemed to arouse him," thought Parker, and there the captain saw to the heart of the matter. Wholly apart from his rigid sense of duty, which itself ought long since to have yielded to the reality of his situation, Davis's own towering pride drove him now. Contrary to what he had written Varina just a few days before, unconsciously he was willing more soldiers to fight and even die, not just to keep alive a cause that all objective men knew was dead but to spare him the personal humiliation of defeat or flight. Davis even rose from his chair and began pacing the floor, saying over and over again that he would never flee while his people needed him. Parker bravely persisted, during the course of an hour, repeatedly stressing the unreliability of the escort and how demoralizing it would be to the South to see its leader taken prisoner, but Davis would not be persuaded. When the captain left the room, he found Mallory and Benjamin outside waiting to enter. The navy secretary said frankly that if they remained here for long, they must certainly be captured, while Benjamin's customary aplomb had deserted him entirely and he could not conceal his nervous anxiety to be off again.

The baggage wagons still rolled through the streets when Parker left the Burt house and went to his lodgings. Behind him, Davis was not to be moved. He knew how his remaining cabinet felt, Mallory and the edgy Benjamin probably reiterating Parker's entreaties even then. As for Breckinridge and Reagan, he did not need to ask to know their views. Parker had seen how much Mallory and Benjamin still stood in awe of the president's force of will, but even they had sided against him in Charlotte. Davis never intimidated Breckinridge, and Reagan was standing up to him now, too.[51] Those two had already proposed more than once that Davis leave the country, and likely would only do so again, and they had all told him that there was no further hope for their cause. To him, however, that meant only that there was no further purpose in consulting them as a cabinet. To that extent, Breckinridge and the others had won a battle in their campaign to keep Davis from prolonging the war, because after that last cabinet meeting in Charlotte, the president never again appealed to his constitutional council to condone what was now his personal will to continue. At least this denied him anything like the sanction of government or his administration.

That left only the generals. What Parker said and what the president saw for himself that morning should have shaken Davis's confidence in the cavalry, if only a little, but he ever believed what he chose to be true rather than what his eyes told him, and so it was now. Davis believed that there was still one other constituency to which he could appeal, and now they were all reunited here, as the sound of wagons still passing in the street testified. Sometime that afternoon Davis decided to consult the brigade commanders, and he asked Breckinridge to summon them to the Burt house at 4:30.

In fact, the generals spent that morning and afternoon surveying their commands themselves, probably at Breckinridge's instruction, and concluded much the same as Parker. Duke found his men anxious, chafing at the uncertainty of where they were going next and for what purpose, their mounts all but broken down, though the spirit of the men seemed good. The desultory pace of their ride south had affected everyone, Colonel Breckinridge derisively referring to it as "a junketing."[52] On one thing they agreed, however, and that was that their war was over. The best they could hope to do was see Davis safely out of the country, and if they had to fight to protect him, they would do so. But once he was safe, they intended to seek terms, give their paroles, and go home.[53] Ferguson called his regimental commanders together as soon as he made camp west of Abbeville, and they told him unequivocally that their regiments were demoralized, as were they themselves—so much so that Ferguson gave them a stern lecture, in the hope of reviving their spirits.[54] At least his men still looked good and were well mounted. They were South Carolinians, now close to their hearths and reluctant to go farther. Indeed, Colonel Breckinridge had good-naturedly teased Ferguson that his command only came along on the ride in order to have company as they went home. As for Breckinridge's brigade, he thought them in excellent condition, though he could not deny that they all regarded the war as over, and already there were stories that a few from his command had straggled and committed robberies along the way. Some of the men in the brigade that Dibrell led now seemed in superb condition, yet others looked unreliable, and Vaughn's small command of Tennesseeans had not only bad horses and poor arms but very shaky discipline as well.[55] Dibrell himself confessed that, in the last day or so, demoralization had begun to set in both in his own and Breckinridge's brigades.[56] In short, the generals were not hearing from their men what Davis wanted to hear from his generals.

At the Burt house meeting they all reported first to Breckinridge, at his order, since Davis had probably briefed him on the purpose of the meeting, and now the secretary wanted to give them some warning to prepare themselves. Entering the parlor, they saw only Davis and Bragg and Breckinridge. Reagan, Mallory, Benjamin, had not been invited. But for Breckinridge's position as overall commander of the escort and overseer of the daily planning of the cavalcade, as well as being the senior general present except for Bragg, Davis might have excluded him as well. He received the generals with all the respect that he might otherwise have accorded to foreign heads of state, then immediately tried to put them at ease. "The union of dignity, graceful affability, and decision which made his manner usually so striking, was very marked in his reception of us," Duke observed. Davis almost jocularly referred to them as a council of war, and as usual engaged in conversation on general subjects for a few minutes before getting to the point, leaving Duke marveling that "I had never seen Mr. Davis look better or show to better advantage." Then the president came to his purpose.[57]

"It is time that we adopt some definite plan upon which the

further prosecution of our struggle shall be conducted," he began. "I have summoned you for consultation. I feel that I ought to do nothing now without the advice of my military chiefs." Davis actually smiled when he called them that, and some of them found it rather a glib remark applied to five well-worn brigadiers commanding no more than a couple of thousand men, coming from one who once addressed chieftains like Lee, Johnston, and Beauregard. A crisis was at hand, he said; they must decide what to do, and he needed to hear from them a statement of their arms and equipment and animals. Davis conducted the interrogation himself, starting with Dibrell. What was the condition of the troopers? How dispirited were they by all the paroled men and stragglers they had passed in recent days, evidencing just how many men had lost their fight? Could they be depended on if attacked? Dibrell affirmed that his men were not demoralized, though unhappy to have seen Bragg disband a couple of South Carolina units that were now close to home. That brought Bragg to his feet to make a hasty explanation.[58]

Each of the others followed, but in replying, they apparently did not go beyond his request to give him any detail on the morale of their men. Davis then went on at some length to tell them the cause was not lost. He reminded them of the darkest moments in their grandfathers' Revolution, and how determination and patriotism had won independence in 1783 just as they still could win it now. "Even if the troops now with me be all that I can for the present rely on," he said, "three thousand brave men are enough for a nucleus around which the whole people will rally when the panic which now afflicts them has passed away." That said, he wanted to hear their views on the future conduct of the war.

Five stunned brigade commanders stood looking at each other, and to Breckinridge and Bragg, who had remained silent thus far, for some sign of what to do. The secretary of war, at least, realized that it was important now for Davis to hear the worst directly from the only alternative voices available to him and thus made no effort to speak for them. "We hardly knew how we should give expression to views so diametrically opposed to those he uttered," said Duke. They knew they had to contradict him, yet he was still their president, and they all felt a high degree of reverence—Duke said "veneration"—for him. As senior officer by date of his commission, Dibrell spoke first and told Davis that it was no longer feasible for him to try to take his command to the Mississippi and beyond to go on fighting, nor did he feel it likely that they could make a junction with Forrest, while rumors had reached him that Taylor was no longer actively in the field.[59]

One after another the others spoke, Duke and Colonel Breckinridge coming last, and they all seconded Dibrell. None of them believed there was any point or hope in continuing. The country was broken down by the rigors and cost of the war, and any attempt to prosecute it further would be "a cruel injustice" to their people. Ferguson reduced the question to two points: were they strong enough to cut their way through the forces they would encounter if they headed for the Mississippi; and if so, could they count on their commands remaining intact in the face of the temptations to break away as men, like his Alabamians and Mississippians, came near their homes. His answer to both was no. They were too small to fight the foe they would meet, and too large to move swiftly enough to evade detection.[60] They would have to fight as guerrillas and partisans, living off a countryside already denuded of sustenance, and to continue would be to invite being branded as outlaws, destroying any hope of returning to their homes, and making themselves liable for treatment much more harsh than that given to Lee's and Johnston's men. They could not know it, but Lee's last report to Davis, written April 20 and probably still on its way to the president by courier, said virtually the same thing. In words Lee should have used weeks before when they would have added real weight to the peace movement, he advised now that the war could not be sustained east of the Mississippi. "A partisan war may be continued, and hostilities protracted, causing individual suffering and the devastation of the country," said the great general, but it would be pointless. "To save useless effusion of blood, I would recommend measures be taken for suspension of hostilities and the restoration of peace."[61]

His composure already starting to slip, Davis asked them why they and their commands were still in the field, and all responded that they felt their honor bound up in guaranteeing Davis's safety and escape. Neither they nor their people wanted to see their president a prisoner, put on display before the world in a humiliating trial for treason, perhaps even condemned to the gallows. To avoid that, the generals would risk their lives and ask their men to do so as well, but not for any hopeless dream of going on with the war. Ferguson even expressed doubt that his men would go on much longer to protect the president, though that very morning when he made a speech to his brigade, the men shouted that they would follow him to preserve Davis's safety. He feared that the sight of a now constant stream of paroled and deserted soldiers on their way home must inevitably demoralize the remaining men.[62] Colonel

Breckinridge believed that he and the other generals engaged in "a free interchange of views," and Dibrell thought the discussion "full and free," but Davis had brought them there to agree with him, not to dissent.[63] He quickly and peremptorily told them that he would not listen to any suggestions of his leaving the country.[64] He had heard enough of that already from Breckinridge and Reagan and others. Instead, regaining his composure, he tried again to win them over. They might only be three thousand strong, as he told Parker that morning, or twenty-five hundred, as he said now, or even the nearly four thousand that in fact were probably still there. But they were enough. Summoning all of the eloquence he could muster, he appealed to their patriotism as Southerners, their pride as soldiers, their dignity as men. They must agree with him. Colonel Breckinridge believed it was the most striking scene he could remember, and he credited Davis with views that were "noble, disinterested, and lofty," but he knew that not one other man in that parlor shared them.[65] Duke gave the president credit for unselfish motives, still the brigadier later confessed, "I am compelled to say that I do not think he at all realized the situation."[66]

They went quiet again. "We were silent," said Duke, "for we could not agree with him, and respected him too much to reply."[67] Moreover, some feared that to continue to disagree with the president might take the discussion too far because, said Duke, "The painful point had been reached, when to speak again in opposition to all that he urged would have approached altercation." Instead, the silence continued—some thought for several minutes—as Davis fought some inner battle with his refusal to give up. Never in his heart did he accept that a few trusty regiments standing by him could not outlast the demoralization in the South and provide a focal point for new resistance to grow and eventually win their independence. "Continued war was not the greatest of evils," he believed then and later. He was so constituted that he could believe nothing else. "The very ardor of his resolution prevented him from properly estimating the resources at his command," concluded Duke, and he was right.[68] In the light of that, the response of these officers, his last apparent hope, so hurt him that years later he claimed to have no recollection at all of this conference, and when he wrote his memoirs he pretended that the meeting never occurred. He chose simply to erase it from his consciousness. Forced in the end to acknowledge that he did meet with these officers, he ever afterward insisted that it was not a council of war at all.[69]

They had been there nearly two hours, and when Davis could take the silence no more, he tried to stand.[70] The color drained from his face, and for the first time, he gave way to bitterness and recrimination. If these officers and their men would not stand by him, he said, if it was true that "all the friends of the South were prepared to consent to her degradation," then truly all was indeed lost. Men had often noticed that Davis invested so much of himself in the cause that when another appeared less committed it "seemed to arouse his indignation," as Duke remarked.[71] The blame he suddenly cast on them now was unworthy of him, uncharitable after all they had endured in standing by him this long, and wholly undeserved, but in that final instant of realization, the iron willpower and determination that had sustained him imperturbably for so long suddenly shattered. The emotional strain all but enfeebled him. Colonel

Breckinridge thought he saw the president actually manifesting "physical suffering," while Duke saw the same, and as he turned without any word of dismissal and started to walk out of the room, Davis was actually indignant. Then he almost collapsed before Breckinridge rushed forward to take his arm and lead him out. "It was a sad sight to men who felt toward him as we did," Duke lamented.[72]

When Breckinridge returned to the parlor, he thanked the officers for their candor, telling them that he agreed that the president's views were "wholly erroneous."[73] Bragg seconded him, and then both explained that they had remained silent during the painful meeting because they did not intimately know the troops at Abbeville, and Davis would not have accepted their opinions as authoritative. Now that the brigade commanders had apparently overcome Davis's last reserves of stubborn optimism, Breckinridge promised to continue to press on him the necessity of leaving the country at once. In fact, from this moment onward, it was apparent that these officers were going to take orders from the secretary of war and no one else, and that included Davis and the rest of the remaining cabinet. "With the exception of Breckinridge," said Duke, "none of them knew what was going on, what was going to be done, or what ought to be done."[74] Ferguson, Colonel Breckinridge, and Duke expressed their determination to go on as long as necessary, the last two volunteering to take their brigades and follow General Breckinridge to Texas, or even Mexico if need be, either to convey the president or to act as a decoy to distract the pursuing Federals. Alternatively, Colonel Breckinridge offered to take command of Davis's escort and see to spiriting him from the country personally, but the secretary told him that his first duty now was to the men in his own brigade. Dibrell and Vaughn, in the end, confessed that their men had gone as far as they would go, unless positively ordered to do so. It was decided that they would accompany the column to the Savannah River and then remain to surrender and give their paroles whenever the Yankees should arrive.[75]

After some discussion, Breckinridge determined that they should leave Abbeville that night at eleven, and he would personally assume command of the escort again. Their initial destination would be Washington, Georgia, where they hoped to find the president's family. From there they must be guided by circumstances but would aim toward Florida and the original plan of getting Davis out of the country by boat. The secretary announced that he would detail Campbell's company to continue as personal escort to the president, sending that party on ahead of the main column to Washington, since Breckinridge and the balance of the cavalry would be necessarily slowed by the treasure and baggage wagons. As to his own course, he indicated that he might lead the bulk of the remaining cavalry in some diversionary direction to allow Davis and the small escort to move quickly to the coast. Before he adjourned the conference and sent them all back to their brigades, Breckinridge told them to announce to their men that any who wanted a discharge or furlough should have it at once, and any officers wishing to tender resignations would have them accepted. He was not going to order anyone to continue, either as escort to Davis or with the cavalry that he would command, for that way no man who did not wish to go could be considered guilty of disobedience.[76] He would take with him only those men willing to volunteer for further danger in the cause of the president's escape. There was also some discussion of paying something to such departing troops from the Treasury funds that had been traveling with the column since Danville. Equally to the point, in authorizing now what would surely be the discharge of much, if not most, of the command, he would put a final end to any possibility of Davis hoping to use it as a rallying point for continuing the struggle. There in Burt's Abbeville parlor, after three months of battle with the president, Breckinridge finally won by burying any further practical hope of renewing the cause.

The officers read the mood of their men well. When Ferguson got back to his brigade, he discovered that while he was in the meeting a part of one of his regiments had deserted and another company forcibly charged the supply wagons and took ammunition against orders. Ferguson confessed to himself that conditions now were such that he had no power to punish the offenders, as even their own officers had not tried to stop them. Discipline sat at a standstill, and all he could do was make a speech appealing to the men to honor their oaths and stand by the president a little longer.[77] As the evening wore on, more than half the cavalrymen around Abbeville decided to go no farther but to take their furloughs and discharges, most of them Vaughn's men and the Tennesseeans whom Dibrell had told just the week before, no one would be abandoning the president.

It was nearly 7 P.M. by the time the commanders returned to their camps. In the meantime others began to make arrangements for the departure. After allowing the president to rest for an hour, Breckinridge met with him again and found his resistance much reduced, though his composure had largely returned. Breckinridge pressed on him the necessity that henceforth he should waste no more time dallying on the road but must leave that night with the reduced escort, collect his family at Washington or wherever they were to be found on the road, and make haste for Florida.[78] The Kentuckian could not now guarantee that anyone other than Campbell's small company would go with him.[79] Indeed, Breckinridge may have presented the case to Davis in the form of an order, for hereafter the president made little effort to give instructions to anyone for a while, suggesting that his resistance had finally collapsed. In either case, he apparently agreed—or as Mallory suspected, he simply stopped voicing his objections and kept silent—for Breckinridge was sufficiently satisfied of the president's cooperation that he notified the brigade commanders that Davis had given in.[80] Of course, Davis may have been simply yielding to current circumstances. If these men would not go west with him to keep fighting, there was still Wheeler out there on his way to Washington. If the admittedly unreliable Alabamian came through with a few hundred men, there might still be a glimmer of hope. The west was on Breckinridge's mind, too, though with a different purpose, for now he sent an order to his old nemesis General Bragg, who, though senior in military rank, was subordinate to Breckinridge as secretary of war. Bragg was to use the portion of the Treasury that the escort had brought with it from Charlotte and disburse some of it to the troops remaining behind, then take the rest with him and try to reach the Trans-Mississippi. Neither ever disclosed Bragg's mission, but it was likely to act as Breckinridge's emissary in directing Kirby Smith to surrender, if he had not already.[81]

Parker saw all of the cabinet but Reagan that evening, the

naval officer thinking that "General Breckinridge presented his usual bold cavalier manner," while Mallory and Benjamin appeared depressed. Perhaps it was because in the rush, Breckinridge had forgotten to tell Benjamin, at least, that they were leaving. Meanwhile, Mallory had decided that he could not go much farther. His family was somewhere in Georgia without means of support and needed him. "The hour has approached when I can no longer be useful," he concluded. Calling at Burt's, he told Davis that he could neither leave the country with him nor go to the Trans-Mississippi and therefore had decided to resign. He added, though, that if Davis did try to escape through Florida, he would remain with him longer and could at least help him on the way, since he knew his home state well. The president said nothing decisive as to his plans, despite his assurances to Breckinridge, and as a result, while Mallory wrote his resignation that evening, he did not yet present it to Davis.[82] Soon afterward the navy secretary had a farewell cup of tea with Parker, and Benjamin joined them, imploring the captain to see Davis again and get him to agree to depart at once. Parker walked over to Burt's house and found that Davis was up, though still keeping to himself, but after some brief discussion, the captain gathered that the president had finally taken in and accepted the afternoon's verdict. As Parker left, Davis sent for Mallory, Reagan, and Benjamin, no doubt finally to inform them officially of the decision to leave in just a couple of hours.[83] At the same time, Davis dashed off a hasty note to Harrison that he sent ahead by courier. Giving vent to his feelings after the afternoon conference, he confessed, "I have the bitterest disappointment in regard to the feeling of our troops."[84]

An hour before they were set to depart, Breckinridge summoned Duke to his temporary headquarters and ordered him to have his guard transfer the treasure from its cars to a wagon train. The sum was considerable, though the secretary did not know exactly how much was there, but he directed Duke to superintend the loading personally, with a guard of fifty armed men on hand all the time. Duke protested, understandably enough, that if he did not know exactly how much was there when he took it off the train, it would leave him open to suspicion later on if an actual accounting showed there to be less in the wagons than supposed. Certainly he would have no time to make a count now. Disinclined as ever to allow paperwork to impede expedition, the secretary of war waved him away and told him to get to work. Duke did as he was told but was appalled to find the specie packed in all manner of shot pouches, kegs and crates, even iron chests, some of them in terrible condition, and much of it among boxes of documents and books. Moreover, Walter Philbrook, chief teller of the Treasury, had several special money belts made while in Abbeville, so that Davis and each of his leaders could carry a few thousand dollars in gold on their persons for their needs in their flight. But the president refused to take a dollar, as did most if not all of the others. As a result, Duke now had these stuffed money belts on his hands as well.[85] Stationing guards at the doors of the boxcars, he personally inspected the interiors by candlelight, assisted by the remaining Treasury clerks, and directed the removal of everything that appeared to contain money, including a chest with a false bottom that held the jewelry brought out of Richmond. Even then, Duke missed a pine box with another two thousand dollars or more in gold, which one of his officers later retrieved. As soon as he had the wagons loaded, Duke set off under heavy guard to meet the rest of the escort and party about to depart.[86]

Meanwhile in town, all his preparations done, Breckinridge sat on the steps of a hotel opposite the Abbeville County Courthouse to rest a few minutes before the column assembled to leave. The signs of hurried departure were all around. Breckinridge had ordered that the enormous train of seventy-five or more vehicles be reduced to just three ambulances and one additional wagon, and so back at Perrin's, Benjamin was burning in the family's fireplace some remaining State Department papers that he could not carry, while Johnston, Wood, and Clark opened boxes of Davis's papers that Harrison had carefully husbanded all the way from Richmond, and destroyed what they could not carry or safely leave at the home of a friend. A small trunk of Harrison's, into which Davis's aides had put a last-minute grab of papers from the president's Richmond office, Micajah Clark managed to get onto a wagon to save it from the flames.[87] There was still much to decide, not least what to do with the treasure now that their force would be too small to protect it against a determined attack. Treasury clerk Robert Gilliam found Breckinridge sitting on the steps and spoke with the secretary for a few minutes. He asked if he ought to join Duke's command, which he presumed to be bound for the Trans-Mississippi. "My young friend," said Breckinridge, "I advise you to return to your home in Richmond by the nearest available route." Once the handover of the treasure to Duke's care was complete, that is exactly what Gilliam and several remaining Treasury employees did, leaving immediately for the long walk to Augusta and transportation north.[88]

Shortly before it was time to leave, Breckinridge received a scout's report that a party of Yankees were believed to be heading for the pontoon bridge over the Savannah River that he intended to use both for Davis and the cavalry.[89] Hurrying now, Breckinridge sent a man to fetch Davis, finding the president sufficiently recovered in spirits that he was actually talking with a number of ladies from the town who had called to pay their respects. It was a moment of the ridiculous. Earlier, while Davis and Breckinridge spoke, a few of the brigade commanders returned to report, and while they were there, a message came in that the women wished to pay their respects. Davis initially told them that he could not see them, but the matrons of Abbeville society were not to be denied. One of them came around to the window of the room in which he was speaking with Dibrell and others, raised the sash, and called in to the president that if he did not come out, she and her friends would raid the room. Davis had already lost one battle to his generals and his secretary of war that afternoon; he could not face another with the fair set. Excusing himself, he left the conference to spend the balance of the evening in what was, after all, much less difficult and more pleasant company.[90] Once Davis came out and was mounted on his horse, Captain Campbell and his company gathered around him, Reagan, Mallory, and Benjamin. They set off almost exactly at 11 P.M. As they rode out, Reagan could see the old story of Danville and Charlotte and elsewhere start to unfold, as citizens began breaking into and looting the remaining military storehouses. "I was forced to the thought," he lamented, "that the line between barbarism and civilization is at times very narrow."[91]

Breckinridge rode at the front with Davis for a time, still defending the brigadiers for speaking honestly that afternoon, and at the same time reiterating that they would do no further active service other than to protect him. Earlier that day, two of the Kentucky troopers had come to Breckinridge, in great condition and mounted on fresh horses. Knowing them, Breckinridge asked if they were game for special service, and they agreed. He confided that Davis would be trying to escape to the Trans-Mississippi or Mexico, and asked if they would accompany him. It was the secretary's idea now that Davis should strike out on his own with only a couple of guards, and perhaps one aide, to ride as fast as possible to Florida, ship from there to Cuba, and thence by vessel for the Rio Grande. The soldiers offered their own variation on the plan later that afternoon, but then Breckinridge was still at work persuading Davis to accept the idea of any kind of escape. In all the rush he was not able to raise it again until now. Reagan joined them for a time, and the two cabinet ministers urged that henceforward Davis should disguise himself as a common soldier and make speed south with the two Kentuckians, while the cabinet officers took the remaining escort as a diversion across north Georgia to strike for the Mississippi. Even though Breckinridge and the rest wanted Davis to go to England or some foreign nation beyond the clutches of the Union, the secretary would not have argued at this point if Davis said he wanted to get to the Trans-Mississippi, which he could do by boat from Florida. The important thing was getting him out of the eastern states. If ever Davis did reach Kirby Smith, it would certainly be too late in any case, since the wave of capitulation must inevitably sweep beyond the Mississippi before the president got there. But now Davis felt better and stronger, as he always did when in the saddle, his aide Lubbock finding him once again calm and unflustered by the afternoon's tor-

Some of the devastation left behind in Richmond as the government
abandoned the capital and began its flight.
U.S. Army Military History Institute, Carlisle, Pennsylvania

General Robert E. Lee, who tried to help Breckinridge overcome the president's refusal to admit defeat, photographed by Mathew Brady in Richmond in April 1865. *Library of Congress*

The Executive Mansion on East Clay Street in Richmond. President Davis's office was on the second floor. He left it for the final time through this front door. *Library of Congress*

General John C. Breckinridge of Kentucky, secretary of war, and Davis's chief opponent in the struggle to end the war, as he appeared in 1864. *William C. Davis*

Jefferson Davis and First Lady Varina Davis, in the late 1860s.
No photographs taken of them during the war have survived.
Museum of the Confederacy, Richmond, Virginia

General Joseph E. Johnston, never an effective army commander, stood up to Davis at the end in trying to achieve a general cartel with William T. Sherman and later surrendered his own army without authorization.
Valentine Museum, Richmond, Virginia

General P. G. T. Beauregard, whom Davis distrusted and disliked, joined with Breckinridge and Johnston in trying to persuade the president to give up and accept the inevitable.
Library of Congress

Secretary of State Judah P. Benjamin, Davis's closest confidant in the government, kept his attention fixed upon his own safety above all. No one expected him to escape. *Museum of the Confederacy, Richmond, Virginia*

Postmaster General —and, at the end, treasury secretary— John H. Reagan of Texas joined Breckinridge in making the president's escape his own priority, but was instead captured with him. *Library of Congress*

Secretary of the Treasury George A. Trenholm was simply too ill during the retreat of the government to do anything more than bend to the majority until he finally resigned.
Library of Congress

Secretary of the Navy Stephen R. Mallory stayed with Davis until almost the end, since he still had some part of his responsibility to exercise with the naval cadets and officers accompanying the government.
Southern Historical Collection, University of North Carolina

Attorney General George Davis had virtually nothing to do and left the government when it passed close to his home. However, this was just the beginning of his flight which turned out to be the longest escape odyssey of all. *Museum of the Confederacy, Richmond, Virginia*

English artist Frank Vizetelly accompanied the fleeing government through the Carolinas and caught the scene as Davis rode at the head of the column (second from left) with Benjamin (fourth from left) and Reagan (sixth from left) behind him. *Illustrated London News*

Davis's aide Colonel William Preston Johnston, the son of his closest friend, stayed with him to the end, even when he might have escaped. *Museum of the Confederacy, Richmond, Virginia*

Colonel Francis Lubbock, one-time governor of Texas, served on Davis's staff throughout the flight and actually threatened to retaliate against the Yankee cavalrymen who plundered the Davis baggage at their capture. *Museum of the Confederacy, Richmond, Virginia*

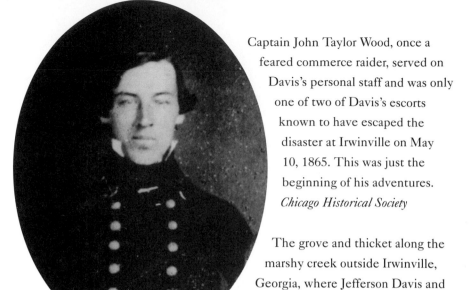

Captain John Taylor Wood, once a feared commerce raider, served on Davis's personal staff and was only one of two of Davis's escorts known to have escaped the disaster at Irwinville on May 10, 1865. This was just the beginning of his adventures. *Chicago Historical Society*

The grove and thicket along the marshy creek outside Irwinville, Georgia, where Jefferson Davis and his party camped on the night of May 9, 1865. Before dawn the next morning they were surprised and captured here, all except Wood and Captain Barnwell, both of whom successfully hid in the swampy brush. *Tulane University, New Orleans, Louisiana*

Micajah Clarke, last treasurer of the Confederate government, disbursed
the treasury and oversaw its remnants down to the last dollar.
Museum of the Confederacy, Richmond, Virginia

The scene on the street in Macon, Georgia, on May 13, 1865, when Davis and the other prisoners arrived at General Wilson's headquarters. The ambulance that carried the president and his wife is at left, their baggage wagon to the right, both surrounded by mounted troopers curiously looking in them. Davis is probably already inside the hotel at right meeting with Wilson. *Library of Congress*

Breckinridge in Havana in June 1865, his moustache still cut short, and his face showing the ravages of the ordeal through which he had just passed. At last, however, his own struggle to end the war and the Confederacy was over.

Sallie Breckinridge Johnson Scrapbook, courtesy of Peter Ten Eyck

Colonel James Wilson, Breckinridge's friend and adjutant, shared all of the dangers and hardships of Breckinridge's escape, photographed in Havana on their arrival. *Private Collection*

Sergeant J. O'Toole who proved to be brave and resourceful during Breckinridge's flight through Florida, photographed in Havana in June 1865. *Private Collection*

Thomas Ferguson had been with Breckinridge throughout the war on a score of battlefields and stayed with him on the escape even though he was not Breckinridge's slave. He could have run away to nearby Federal lines a number of times. *Private Collection*

Jefferson Davis, 1867, wearing the clothes he had on when he was captured. He was not wearing the hat, however, and there is no sign of the raglan or shawl that gave rise to the "hoopskirt" myth.
T.C. DeLeon: Belles, Beaux, and Brains of the Confederacy

One who did not try to get away. Vice President Alexander H. Stevens chose to stay at home in Georgia (much as he had when he should have been in Richmond at his post), simply waiting for the Yankees to come to him.
Library of Congress

ment.[92] He began wavering in his resolve, the recent shocks all but shattering his ability to make a clear decision. Once more he started to raise objections to the idea of flight.[93]

When Breckinridge became concerned that it was taking too long for the bulk of the cavalry to come up behind them, and he turned his horse to ride back to Abbeville, Davis finally assured him that he consented now to being spirited out of the country, whatever the destination.[94] With that relieving his mind, an exhausted secretary of war went back to Abbeville, where he found that inevitably it had taken more time for the several cavalry commands to get themselves and their wagons in motion, along with the treasure train. It was almost 2 A.M. on May 3 when Ferguson, acting as rearguard, finally moved out. At the moment concerned as much about what might be behind them as in front, and aware as well that of the three brigades, these South Carolinians were the shakiest despite volunteering to go on, Breckinridge rode beside Ferguson, where he could supervise personally as they set off in the nighttime blackness for the Savannah River bridge and Georgia.[95]

Chapter Eight

"THE CONFEDERATE GOVERNMENT IS DISSOLVED"

They rode through a night intensely dark, made worse by a drizzle, yet they made good time, only losing an hour at a crossroads where it took some time to determine the right way to the bridge. Mallory and Johnston rode in advance with a guide most of the way, but then Johnston and the guide rode ahead. By himself on the road now, Mallory shortly came to a small house from which the dim light of a fireplace or lamp cast a faint glow to the road. He actually rode up to and close enough to touch a mounted horseman before he saw him facing him in the road. In the dim illumination he could make out no features, only the reflection of light on the gold lace of a military cap. Duke had a similar hat, and at first Mallory thought somehow the Kentucky cavalryman had gotten ahead of them by some other route.

"What troops are these coming up?" barked the horseman. "What party is this?" Only then did Mallory realize he was a Yankee officer. Immediately fearing that the enemy had beaten them to the bridge and cut off their route, Mallory thought of pulling his pistol and taking the man prisoner but then decided to lie instead. There were plenty of groups of paroled men from Johnston's and Lee's armies met everywhere on the roads these days, and the Yankee could easily assume this was just another, though traveling at night should have seemed suspicious. He accepted whatever evasion Mallory gave him, and simply moved his horse to the side of the road to watch as, unbeknownst to him, the most wanted man in America rode past him.[1] Just the day before, Union authorities had posted a hundred-thousand-dollar reward for Davis.

The president saw the waters of the Savannah just as the sun began to rise over his left shoulder, and found to his relief that the military pontoon bridge was still in place, undisturbed by the rumored Yankee raiders. Quickly he and his party went across, and then, weary from an all-night ride in the dark, they halted at a farmhouse a mile or so on, to eat breakfast and rest their horses and themselves.[2] At the same time, he sent a rider ahead to see if it would be safe for them to go on to Washington. The Savannah was more Rubicon than rest stop for Judah Benjamin, however. Forced to leave his ambulance behind, he had ridden horseback with the rest, but as luck would have it, he drew an unusually tall animal, which only made his stubby legs look the more incongruous as he bounced along in the saddle. Perhaps he was uncertain that the president was going to honor his promise to get out of the country, and simply could not face the prospect of his ample posterior being bruised by a saddle all the way to the Mississippi and beyond. Whatever the reason, this was as far as he was going to go with Davis. Besides burning some of his more sensitive official papers the evening before, he had also taken from his ambulance a trunk with more of his possessions and had left it in the care of his friend Leovy, at the same time making arrangements with Leovy to meet him on the road with his carriage once Benjamin had safely crossed the Savannah.[3]

Now Benjamin went to Davis at the farmhouse and told him that he was going to leave and take his own route by more comfortable means. He did not resign his cabinet post, however, but announced that he would escape by way of Florida, Cuba, or the Bahamas. That being the case, Davis asked him to look into diplomatic funds there, with a view to arranging further credit with foreign suppliers for Kirby Smith, and then to rejoin him in the Trans-Mississippi.[4] Significantly, Davis's authority among his remaining adherents was now so diminished that his secretary of state could simply announce that he was leaving without resigning, as George Davis and Trenholm had done. Both Benjamin and Davis later claimed that he asked permission to leave, but the fact of his having all his preparations laid out in advance, including arrangements to be met here by Leovy, put the lie to that.[5] Benjamin was going to go whether Davis wanted him to or not, and while the president may have expected Benjamin to appear later in Texas, the pragmatic secretary of state almost certainly never had any intention of returning to the South once gone. He said his farewells to the president, searched out Micajah Clark and bade him good-bye, and shook Reagan's hand a final time. Asked by Reagan where he was going, Benjamin gave him a much more honest answer than what he told the president. "To the farthest place from the United States," Benjamin replied, "if it takes me to the middle of China."[6] Then as Leovy arrived in his buggy, Benjamin tossed in his small remaining portmanteau, got in himself, and no doubt with a parting smile disappeared in a whiff of cigar smoke on a road leading due south toward Florida.[7]

About the time Benjamin left, Davis received another and sharper reminder that his moral authority was all but gone. Not long after they dismounted, one more of the seemingly endless reports of nearby Yankee cavalry came in, this suggesting that the enemy might be about to move into Washington ahead of them to take some quartermaster supplies. At once the president sent an order back to Vaughn, directing that he come forward as quickly as possible. But when Vaughn received the note, he only passed it on to Dibrell, and both decided that they would not ask the men still with them to take any more risks, since they had been promised by Breckinridge that they need go no farther than the Savannah, there to be discharged.[8] That was the second refusal in as many days, for the previous afternoon, before his conference with the generals, Davis had called on some of the discharged midshipmen to return to their posts to defend the treasure when a report suggested that a band of stragglers intended to attack. The response was blunt to rudeness. "Our lives are as precious to us as yours is to you," one boy said. "The war is over and we are going home!" At least one midshipman believed that the man so abruptly rebuffed was Jefferson Davis himself.[9]

Benjamin was just leaving, and Davis had just gotten the disheartening word that Vaughn and Dibrell would not be coming farther, when finally the only good news of the morning arrived.

The rider he sent ahead to Washington appeared once more, accompanied by a teenage boy bearing a message. Dressed in simple farmer's clothes in order not to give any hint of who might be behind him, the scout had reached Washington around 11 A.M. Happily he attracted no notice as he entered the village, but seeing a gathering of people deep in conversation on the front porch of the branch office of the Bank of the State of Georgia, he rode toward them, and on getting closer saw that two of the men wore Confederate uniforms. From habit the scout saluted, which all but gave him away, and then asked if there were any soldiers in town.

"What soldiers do you mean?" asked one of the men on the porch.

"Why, any kind of soldiers—soldiers are soldiers, ain't they?" he replied.

"Ah, my friend," said Major General Arnold Elzey, one of those in uniform. "You are no ignorant countryman; you betrayed yourself by that military salute, and we strongly suspect your being one of the President's party. Tell us of him. Is he safe? Where is he?"

Seeing himself found out, the scout brought his horse almost onto the porch itself in order to whisper another question. "Are you Confederates? Are you all friends?" he asked with some naïveté. If they were not friends, it was a little late to be asking now. Told that they were, he asked if there were any Yankee soldiers in town, and was relieved to learn that there were none. "I have just left Mr. Davis," he added, "and he is not an hour's ride from here." At once the group on the porch began making plans to receive the president's party, when Mrs. M. E. Robertson, wife of bank cashier J. J. Robertson, spoke up and said she would entertain Davis in their home in the bank building, where she had accommodated Burton Harrison only a few days before when he and Varina Davis and their party passed through. When the gentlemen approved, her husband and Elzey wrote a hasty invitation to Davis and entrusted it to her son Willie, whom they sent back with the courier.[10]

Dispirited and weary and tired of delay, Davis decided to act on the news and Willie Robertson's invitation and ride on to Washington without waiting for Breckinridge and the rest to catch up to him. It was as well that he did, for he was entirely unaware of yet another drama unfolding behind him. Not long after dawn the head of the main column reached the Savannah, several miles and a few hours behind the president. Breckinridge kept them together during the night march only with considerable difficulty. Even then some men just disappeared into the darkness, while hundreds of others discarded their weapons, not only to lighten their load but as a gesture that they would not fight again under any circumstances. Crossing the state line into Georgia seemed somehow symbolic to some, as to Benjamin. Many of the South Carolinians under Ferguson had gone as far as they were willing, and the bulk of Vaughn's and Dibrell's men wanted to stop. Being almost the last to cross the river, as he satisfied himself there was no immediate danger of pursuit, Breckinridge posted a guard at the bridge, with orders to destroy it in the event of enemy approach from the other side, and then rode forward, to find the command halted. From grumbling among groups to protests to their company and regimental officers, and finally through Vaughn and Dibrell themselves, Breckinridge found that of perhaps twenty-five hundred men present, only a few hundred were willing to continue. The rest were going to stop here, and they wanted money.

By 9:30 Breckinridge knew that he had trouble. He sent word ahead to Davis that the cavalry was "by no means satisfactory," and that "they cannot be relied on as a permanent military force." Breckinridge had apparently suggested distributing some of the specie among them when talking with Davis the previous evening, but the president declined to act.[11] Now it might be too late. The officers told him that their men complained they were risking their lives to guard a train of money that would only in the end go to the Yankees, probably. They might never even get to Washington, and the paper money that had already been paid out to some of them by Bragg the day before was notoriously worthless. "Discipline was gone," complained Quartermaster Joseph Broun with the wagon train, adding that this was "one time it was not pleasant or safe to be a quartermaster." The cavalrymen of Vaughn's and Dibrell's commands, with some of Ferguson's and perhaps even a few of Duke's and Colonel Breckinridge's brigades, had become what Broun called "a mob."

Breckinridge at once fell back on a weapon he had used many times before, not just in war but in peace—his eloquence. Wearing the old Kentucky hunting jacket that he preferred to a uniform, on the road, he took a position surrounded by hundreds of demoralized and resentful soldiers, many of them still armed, and began to play on their consciences by appealing to their honor as soldiers not to disgrace themselves and their cause in its last hours. They were "Southern gentlemen and Confederate soldiers," Broun recalled him saying. "They must not be-

come highway robbers." Having shown on many a battlefield
that they could die bravely, it would all be for nothing now if
they did not live honorably. "Breckinridge in his native manhood was equal to the occasion," said Broun. The soldiers answered him with apparent candor, saying they did not want to
violate their oaths, and some avowed they would continue to
guard the train against any threat, Union or Confederate, but all
affirmed they felt that, after months of serving with no pay and
having stood by the government's leaders longer than any others, they were entitled to being paid something. When Breckinridge responded that Davis and Reagan were in Washington
and only they had authority to approve disbursement, the leaders of the crowd declared they were not going a step farther—
and since they might not be able to reach Washington, anyhow,
if reports of Yankee cavalry were true, they ought to be paid
there and then.

There was an undeniable logic to their argument. More to the
point, if Breckinridge did not quell the incipient mutiny here,
even at the cost of some of the Treasury, he well risked losing
all of it, anyway, not to mention adding one more scene to that
"farce" he was still hoping to forestall. Very well, he told them.
If they wanted him to make good right now his promise to see
them paid, he would do it. He immediately ordered Duke's
guard to bring the treasure wagons to a nearby house belonging
to David Moss, there to start unloading the money, while at the
same time he directed the brigade commanders to have their
staffs begin preparing payrolls of all those present. Broun believed that Breckinridge thereby completely silenced and contented the crowd, but the secretary was not going to take any
chances.[12] At the same time, knowing the potential in any mob

for sudden shifts of mood and action, he went to Duke and ordered him to quadruple the guard from fifty men to two hundred and to take personal charge of the wagons. Duke agreed and revealed his own appreciation of the situation by further suggesting that he pick the guard detail evenly from among each of the five commands. That would prevent any one brigade being resentful or jealous of the trust placed in another. More subtle than that, however, such a move would make it more difficult for members of the guard from any one brigade to organize and mount a threat themselves, since they would constitute only one fifth of the complement. At the same time, should an attack come from any one of the brigades themselves, four-fifths of the guard would not face the problem of being called on to repel their own compatriots, perhaps at rifle point. Breckinridge agreed. Tragically, after four years of heroic sacrifice, what remained of the Confederacy had to be protected from its own people, and Breckinridge and Duke were clearly willing to fight if necessary.[13]

As soon as he could, the secretary of war sent word forward to Davis of his situation and asked for authorization to do what, in fact, he was already preparing to do.[14] It was just after 3 P.M. when a disgusted Davis, angered by the refusal of Vaughn and Dibrell to answer his summons to Washington, received Breckinridge's entreaty and sent back authorization through Reagan. It would not reach the Kentuckian until eight that evening, however, and by then it did nothing more than ratify a process already well under way.[15] Breckinridge could count on it taking most of the rest of the day to make the payrolls, as well as for quartermasters to count the money for disbursement, but the promise of being paid diffused the more threatening talk. He directed his adjutant, Major W. J. Davis, whom Breckinridge considered "a superior man, of real merit," to requisition all of the silver coin from the wagons, amounting to $108,322.90.[16] If he had to dig into the gold as well, he would do so.

While the Moss family looked on, Duke's troopers began bringing the boxes of coin into their house, eventually taking over all of the downstairs except the bedrooms.[17] Then began the work of counting the money, and knowing what was going on inside the house, crowds of soldiers soon gathered around the building, their eager faces filling every window as they peered in to watch the quartermasters at their tallying. Most of them had not been paid in genuine hard cash for years, and the sight of all that silver, from dollars to dimes, entranced them. The counting went on well after nightfall, and still they watched. "The sight of so much money seemed to banish sleep," said Duke, while Breckinridge continued to worry that the sight might induce other ideas.[18]

Though close to collapse from weariness, he continued to watch over the situation closely, convinced that if he had attempted to move the treasure train on that morning, it would have been stopped and plundered. Indeed, at 8 P.M. someone reported to him some renewed threats from the crowd to seize the whole treasury, but with all of it inside the Moss house, and Duke's two-hundred-man guard, he hoped it would be safe enough. He still intended to hold back the remaining $180,000, and planned to turn it over to Reagan when they got the train to Washington the following morning. Just then Davis's authorization to pay the troops reached him, but all Breckinridge could do was to send back word of what he was already doing. The demoralization and collapse of discipline induced him to warn Davis that thereafter no more than a few hundred men could be counted on, mostly Duke's and Colonel Breckinridge's Kentuckians, who would serve on not only out of loyalty to Davis and because any westward march would get them closer to home but also because of a singular devotion all Kentucky Confederates felt for Breckinridge himself. As Duke and Colonel Breckinridge had told him the day before in Abbeville, their men would go where they led them, and the two commanders would follow General Breckinridge anywhere. For his part, he still intended to lead them west as a decoy, as agreed with Davis, but now in the face of the collapse of most of the command, that decoy would be smaller and necessarily less effective as a result, and so he earnestly renewed urging the president to follow through on the plan to ride for Florida without delay. Should Davis make any change in his plans, Breckinridge needed to know at once, for he did not expect he could himself reach Washington before morning on May 4.[19]

The counting out of the silver took so long because of the great variety of coinage in the boxes and kegs and sacks. When the job was done, well after dark, it was impractical to attempt to disburse it then, so Breckinridge gave orders that the payments commence at dawn. Meanwhile, it was important to get the remaining command to Washington as soon as possible. Finding Ferguson and many of his men still reliable, Breckinridge sent him off on the road at 7 A.M., promising to hold in reserve the pay for those troops until he joined them in Washington.[20] Then the rest of the disbursement began, each soldier and officer to be paid an equal $26.25. Somehow the ranks swelled as word spread that there was a payroll about to be made. The paymaster handed the pay for each unit out through a window of the Moss house as the payrolls were presented and approved, and by the time they finished, some forty-one hundred men had been given their mite, Breckinridge taking the same as the rest. That done, he put Duke and Colonel Breckinridge's commands on the road after Ferguson. Still concerned and anxious that no man lose his share, he ordered Broun and others to surreptitiously load into their handkerchiefs enough coin to pay Ferguson's men and Davis's escort, and carry it with them to Washington so that if anything happened to the wagon train before it got there, those men would still be paid.[21]

Meanwhile the staff officers and Duke's guard cleared the mess they had made of the Moss house and began reloading the remaining specie and bullion. The empty boxes and sacks made a considerable pile, and somehow they overlooked an unopened wooden box at the bottom of the heap. They may have left it behind because it only appeared to contain receipts and business documents from the Treasury Department that hardly mattered now, but when the Moss family found the box a few hours later, they discovered that beneath the documents a layer of tissue covered something else. There beneath the paper lay the jewelry contributed by Richmond's ladies for the war effort and carried about with the treasure train ever since. Gold, diamonds, table silver, and more, all gleamed in the bottom of the box. Elated at their find, yet afraid to do anything with it, they kept the box a secret, or so they thought, burying it in their garden and telling only their Baptist minister. But a few days later a Union officer with a squad of soldiers appeared at their door and demanded the jewelry, and after that it either went into the pockets of the Yankee soldiers or disappeared into the even then labyrinthine corridors of the United States Treasury.[22]

When it was all done, Vaughn and Dibrell called on Breckinridge at the Moss house to say their farewells. They and their
men were going to stay where they were bivouacked and wait
until some Federal party came along to whom they could surrender and give their paroles. Then they would go home. Whatever he may have felt, Breckinridge had no recrimination for
them or for their commands, wished them a safe and speedy return to their families, and added that he hoped the time was not
too far distant when he might return to Kentucky himself.[23]
Then he mounted and rode off for Washington to rejoin the
president.

It was noon the day before, one of the loveliest May days residents could remember, when Davis rode into Washington in
advance of his escort. The village had swarmed with rumors
about him for days, ever since Varina Davis passed through and
the citizens assumed her husband could not be far behind. One
story even said that the president had already passed through
secretly on April 29, hidden in a wooden box marked "specie."
Varina told people there that she did not know where he was or
where he was going, while Harrison had simply stayed quiet,
though the wiser sort did not expect that the two would reveal
his intentions even if they knew. News of Johnston's surrender
had arrived on May 1, the day the first rioting broke out, and
after Varina and Harrison left the next day, people expected the
president to appear any moment.[24]

When Davis appeared at the head of his small column, the
townspeople turned out to give him an enthusiastic welcome
made ironic because Washington's most noted citizen was Davis's
most implacable enemy Robert Toombs, who was in town even
now but would make no effort to see the president. Surrounded

as he was by Campbell's Kentuckians, Davis encountered even more, for the remnants of Breckinridge's very first command in 1861, the First Kentucky "Orphan" Brigade, were there, covered by Johnston's surrender and now simply waiting for some Yankees to come take their parole. As Davis entered town, many of the "Orphans" stood in the street watching, some of them, like many citizens all along the long road from Richmond, feeling tears well in their eyes at the sad sight of their president in flight.[25] As the president rode up, clad in his usual gray suit, with the trousers stuffed into high-top cavalry boots, what most struck one of the Kentuckians was the president's wide-brimmed felt hat, turned down in front to shade his eyes. Around the crown he wore a wide strip of black mourning crepe. None had ever seen him so dressed before. The crepe could have been for any of hundreds of thousands now gone, or for all of them. Almost everyone but Davis himself would have felt it signified the demise of the cause itself.[26]

The president rode to the bank on the public square, where Robertson, Elzey, and several others awaited. They took off their hats as he dismounted, one of them holding his horse as the weary president stepped down, and Robertson immediately repeated the offer of quarters in his home in the bank building itself. Here, at last, Davis got irrefutable confirmation that Johnston had actually surrendered, though by now he probably expected it. Townspeople swarmed around the arriving celebrity, but Davis, exhausted after the overnight ride, went immediately to the room awaiting him, while Elzey's wife acted as protector to keep the curious and well-wishing from disturbing his sleep. A few minutes later Reagan, Mallory, Micajah Clark, and several of the other civilians with Davis came into town, looking "half-starved," as one girl of the town thought, after their long ride without a stop for food. "The party are all worn out and half-dead for sleep," observed Eliza Andrews. Thorburn, too, ignored the offer of food and went straight to a bed, from which he would not arise for fourteen hours, in the Andrews house.

At almost the same moment, more reports arrived that Yankees were moving toward Washington, and at once the people scrambled to assemble a meal of milk and bread and some other bits. Even while Mallory and others ate, Campbell's cavalry escort rode in, accompanied by the welcome news that the rumors of advancing Federals were false. Now everyone could relax, and the townspeople went to work to produce a feast for all the ravenous men in case they had to leave again quickly.[27] They soon found themselves seated in some of the finest dining rooms in the village, diving into a bounty of fowl and ham, neither of which had often been on their diet during the war.[28]

As Davis slept on through the afternoon, with a company of the Fifty-Sixth Alabama Cavalry stationed around the bank as a guard, his escort settled themselves to rest in and around town.[29] All about them, even here in Washington, which had been largely untouched by the war, they could see the signs of disintegration. Just two days earlier the Eighth Texas cavalry began to riot around the local commissary warehouse, soon joined by other soldiers and some citizens, and before they were done they had looted the warehouse of food and then turned on the quartermaster store, taking even nonsensical things. Men who could neither read nor write took pens and reams of paper, only to give it away on the streets or simply throw it about on the ground in purposeless rampage. All the while the provost guard refused to fire on fellow soldiers, but simply watched.

"Nobody seemed to care much," Eliza Andrews wrote in her diary, "as we all know the Yankees will get it in the end, any way, if our men don't." The rioting lasted into May 2, as every passing group of paroled soldiers from the armies caught the fever. Men who had surrendered their weapons to the Yankees even plundered the ordnance warehouse, taking shells and powder that they clearly could no longer use. "Everybody is demoralized and reckless and nobody seems to care about anything any more," complained Andrews. "The props that held society up are broken."[30]

Davis surely learned of all this when he was awakened from his sleep that afternoon, if he did not actually see evidence of it when he rode into town. Further and wrenching signs of the demoralization came around 3 P.M. with Breckinridge's first message regarding the soldiers at the Savannah and the treasure. Davis sent authorization to pay the silver coin to them, but Breckinridge's second message, received late that evening, was no more encouraging. The numbers of paroled and deserted soldiers on the road along his ride that day certainly did nothing to enhance Davis's optimism, and now once he roused himself and met with some of the townsfolk and the local officers like Elzey, he heard nothing but gloom. As if to emphasize the disintegration, Mallory actually handed Davis his resignation at around four o'clock, and the president had no choice but to accept. The secretary of the navy told Davis in a brief meeting that he was still willing to accompany him if he would make his escape through Florida, but the president, despite his assurances to Breckinridge, now said he was undecided. That being the case, Mallory announced that he would be leaving the next day for Atlanta to join his wife and children and take his chances with the Federals.[31] All Davis could do in return was take a few moments to pen a brief note of thanks and tribute for the secretary's loyalty for the four years past. At least one man riding with Davis, however, complained that "Mr. Mallory deserted us," added evidence that the hour of "every man for himself" lay not far distant.[32]

Coincidentally, Davis's old political foe Louis T. Wigfall was in Washington, on his way to the Trans-Mississippi, or Mexico if necessary, and Mallory decided to join him for the trip by train to Atlanta.[33] Indeed, there seemed to be several of his enemies clustering around now, chief among them being Toombs. Postmaster General John H. Reagan went to Toombs's house and was invited to stay the night. More than that, his host offered him money if he needed any. Surprisingly, Toombs even offered to extend money and his carriage to Davis, though it was surely more from concern over the Confederacy being humiliated by the capture and prosecution of its president than from any concern for Davis the man. But that was as far as he would go, and it was only official courtesy due to the office. He adamantly refused to invite Davis into his home or even to see him. Reagan, and later Breckinridge, would have the hospitality of his house now, but not the president.[34]

Davis must have been even more distressed when, shortly after Mallory left him, General Elzey and other prominent men in town had a discussion with the president in which they all pressed hard to make him realize the personal danger he faced. The increasingly frequent reports of Yankee cavalry made it evident that the enemy was on his trail and closing in. Earnestly they implored him to travel hereafter with more speed and less publicity.[35] This admonition, at least, Davis took to heart, but most immediately his concern was for his family. Shortly before he met Mallory, Davis got word that Harrison and Varina and his children were only about twenty miles distant along the rail line out of Washington, and at first he thought he would take an engine down to see them briefly, then return by the same train to continue his own journey.[36] It had been more than a month since he had last seen them, and for this most devoted of husbands and fathers, the separation was proving unendurable, especially amidst all his other disappointments. Yet he knew for certain that he could not afford to remain with his family, for fear that the Federal manhunt after him might bring them into danger. "I think all their efforts are directed for my capture and that my family is safest when farthest from me," he had said in a message sent by courier to Harrison the previous evening. What he had seen of Confederate soldiers in recent days, punctuated by the near mutiny back at the Savannah, left him so bitter about his own men that he could not trust Varina's safety even to their protection should he go to his family and bring the Yankees down upon them. He "would not have any one I love dependant upon their resistance against an equal force," he declared sadly.

In the end, having admonished Harrison not to take any risks with Varina and the children just for the sake of gratifying his desire to see them, Davis finally decided to heed his own advice and not attempt the overnight visit.[37] Instead, he had met briefly with Mallory and Reagan and a few others to discuss what lay ahead, but this was no council of war, or cabinet meeting, either. Having been abandoned by everyone, it seemed, hereafter the president would take only his own counsel.[38] That done, there was a late dinner at the Robertsons' table, and his hostess outdid herself with soup, fresh vegetables, a roast turkey, a large ham, chicken, eggs and salad, even lobster and salmon, and real coffee, the sort of meal that most in the Confederacy had not seen in years. Ironically, the president seated with his staff before this bounty had little taste for food other than corn bread and buttermilk.[39]

Davis likely found only fitful sleep in his room in the bank that night. When he arose the next morning, May 4, he had finally made a decision. There had been no word from Breckinridge since his message of the previous evening saying that he was paying out the specie with him and that he could do nothing further with Vaughn's and Dibrell's men. Not knowing whether those troops might have mutinied, anyhow, or been cut off or attacked by Federal cavalry, Davis realized that he could delay here no longer, especially as a fresh report of enemy cavalry moving toward Washington reached his ears early that morning. He sent a message back to Breckinridge that he would have to leave.[40] He would listen to Elzey and the others.

First Davis called Reagan and Mallory to another meeting, along with Generals Lawton, Bragg, and Duke who had just arrived, as well as his aides Lubbock, Wood, and Johnston, and Colonel Thorburn. Curiously, also present in the room was a man Breckinridge might have arrested had he been present.[41] Back in October 1864 Felix Robertson of Texas, one of Major General Wheeler's subordinates who had proved just as unreliable as Wheeler himself, commanded a small cavalry brigade with an unconfirmed appointment as brigadier general. He led it at the Battle of Saltville, in Breckinridge's old department in southwest Virginia. The day after the fight, Robertson's men combed the battlefield for wounded black soldiers of the Fifth

United States Colored Cavalry and murdered every one they found, Robertson himself joining in the act of villainy as the death toll of blacks rose to one hundred or more. Breckinridge was away fighting under General Jubal Early in the Shenandoah Valley, but when he returned he immediately filed charges against Robertson, who had left the department.

The general collapse of Confederate civil and military affairs allowed Robertson to evade prosecution, though not without Breckinridge making a fresh attempt to secure justice after he took over the War Department. Either several orders for him to appear before a court miscarried or Robertson simply ignored them, and by then it was too late and there were too many more pressing affairs to engage Breckinridge by that time. At least Breckinridge's influence was felt when his housemate, Henry Burnett of Kentucky, sitting on the Senate's Military Affairs Committee, convinced the committee to refuse to consent to Davis's nomination of Robertson as a brigadier. The Senate itself rejected the nomination on February 22, the same day that General John Echols, Breckinridge's successor in southwest Virginia, issued a fresh call for Robertson to appear before a court of inquiry, most likely at Breckinridge's request.[42] Robertson had been one of Bragg's favorites, supplying the contentious general with perjured testimony in his 1863 attempt to blame the loss of the Battle of Stones River on Breckinridge. Just days earlier Robertson had been in Macon, still calling himself a general but in fact holding no confirmed rank higher than lieutenant. Captured on April 20 when Macon fell, he was almost immediately paroled, and came to Washington to join some of his old troopers from the Eighth Texas Cavalry, fellow participants in the Saltville atrocity, most of them having deserted from Wheeler and now on their way home. It was those same Texans who began the plundering and riot on May 1, continuing as ringleaders the following day, though Robertson may not have been involved. They were now stealing horses from every farmer in the county to provide themselves with mounts for the long ride home.[43] The fickle hand of irony brought Robertson here to meet his old patron Bragg once more, and to narrowly miss justice from Breckinridge.

Even had the secretary of war been here, he might have foregone making any attempt against Robertson as futile in the circumstances. Besides, United States authorities knew about the Saltville massacre and had launched their own hunt for culprits, though they did not know about Robertson's personal involvement as yet. But those War Department records that Breckinridge so anxiously guarded and preserved held the story. If the Kentuckian could not bring the man to justice for his crime, at least he was leaving behind ample evidence for the Yankees to do it someday if they chose. That a man only a small step short of being a wanted criminal could now be sitting here in what would be the last official meeting Jefferson Davis would ever hold as president spoke eloquently of just how deep ran the overall collapse, civil and military.

Everyone present, even his hosts, the Robertsons, understood that Davis called this meeting not as a council.[44] He was through listening to advice. Rather, it was merely an informal discussion, but just in case, he cut off any suggestions of surrender by reasserting his belief that he did not have the constitutional authority to dissolve the government. However, since further resistance this side of the Mississippi was obviously futile, he had decided to disband the government temporarily, to reassemble in the Trans-Mississippi if and when they all succeeded in escaping the Yankees. For himself, he announced that he would not take the route through Florida after all. Instead, he would move south and then west, trying to slip below known Union forces, to join Richard Taylor's army in Alabama, unaware that Taylor was even then in the act of surrendering. Then with Taylor he would press on to join Kirby Smith and fight on in the far west. He believed that he could assemble sixty thousand to eighty thousand men, virtually all of them cavalry, and subsist them and their mounts on Texas cattle and grass. Reagan seemed to think that the president hoped thereby to simply hold out for better terms than unconditional surrender, as with Johnston and Lee, but Davis himself still had grander visions.[45]

Before learning of Johnston's disobedience of orders by surrendering, Davis had clung to hopes that such of the Army of Tennessee that could escape Sherman, joined with the five cavalry brigades that had been at Abbeville, would be enough to defeat any forces between them and the Mississippi. Augmented by Taylor's army and Forrest's cavalry, this new army would then inspire the demoralized and the dispirited to renewed patriotism and determination, and when they crossed the river to join with Kirby Smith, they would continue the war until the Yankees became too weary of continued resistance. Years later Davis claimed that his object was to bring the enemy to a "quasi-treaty" that guaranteed constitutional rights of person and property in return for reunion, in effect achieving all of the Confederacy's original goals except independence. Yet it is clear that at that time, he really still envisioned a resurrected army in the Trans-Mississippi as a means to "continue to uphold our cause."[46] Just as the loss of a capital was not the end, so even the loss of everything east of the great river did not mean defeat

if enough men had the stomach to hold out in the Texan vast-
ness, where space, geography, and distance from the North all
worked in their favor. There was no consultation, no exchange
of opinion. Davis assembled them simply to tell them what he
was going to do, then dismissed them. As he left the meeting,
General Lawton said sadly to a bystander that "it is all over; the
Confederate Government is dissolved."[47]

Chapter Nine

"THIS, I SUPPOSE, IS THE END OF THE CONFEDERACY"

Either during the meeting or shortly before, Reagan spoke privately with Davis. His position as postmaster was pointless, while his having charge of the Treasury was equally meaningless since they could not take the money train with them on their flight to the Trans-Mississippi. Determined as he was to safeguard the president and accompany him on the journey—as Breckinridge intended to do when he arrived—Reagan could not stay behind to administer the money. Instead he suggested that Davis appoint Micajah Clark acting treasurer with full authority to oversee the funds in Reagan's absence. The president agreed and while his aide Johnston went to find Clark to order him to report to Reagan, Davis and the postmaster discussed what was to be done with the treasure.

When Clark called on Reagan, the Texan handed him his written appointment from the president, and then gave him his instructions. Clark was to go back along the road to find the treasure train, now only a few miles outside town, and then oversee any further payments to the remaining troops out of the thirty-five thousand dollars in silver specie still on the wagons, dispose of some other immediate debts, then divide the rest of the coin among several men for transmission to the Trans-Mississippi. There was still eighty-six thousand dollars or more in gold coin and bullion, and Reagan wanted it turned over to two naval officers who were to keep it hidden until Davis was gone and the pursuing Federals had passed, then spirit it out of the country to Bermuda and eventually to their agents in England. Deposited in British banks, it could fund their efforts once more when they reached the Trans-Mississippi. Reagan also told Clark to take the nearly forty thousand dollars in silver bullion, far too heavy and bulky to be transported or hidden as effectively as the gold, and hand it over to an officer for storage in a local warehouse. As for the six hundred thousand dollars or more in worthless Confederate Treasury notes, that should be burned. He was also to send money forward to Washington to pay the men of Davis's immediate escort, as well as an additional five thousand dollars in specie for a special purpose. The president concurred fully in the dispositions.[1]

That special purpose was his future escort's pay. He called Captain Campbell to him and said he intended to greatly reduce their number. As it was, the journalist–postal clerk Charles Stuart thought the sixty-odd cavalrymen with Davis were "only enough to make a respectable raiding party."[2] Davis told Campbell to pick just ten men from the escort to continue the journey. With his three aides and one or two others, this would make Davis's party small enough to move faster, and less likely to attract attention. To aid in preparations, he gave Campbell the specie to buy fresh mounts and provisions and, at the same time, handed him a new pair of pistols he had brought from Richmond.[3]

There were a few other preparations to make that morning, including storing the president's remaining trunk of valuable papers with the Robertsons.[4] Still, somehow, Davis could not avoid the civilities. While Campbell made his preparations, several callers came to the bank to pay their respects, even one or two prominent local Unionists, and they all thought the president calm and collected. Indeed, he found himself having to be strong for their sakes, for most were in tears. To the Robertsons and others he spoke calmly and hopefully of uniting Kirby Smith with other fragments to continue fighting with a reorganized army west of the Mississippi. "This seemed to be a fixed hope in the mind of Mr. Davis," Mrs. Robertson believed, so firmly planted that he could not see beyond it to his own imminent danger.[5] General Elzey had to turn away and pretend that he had dust in his eyes when the tears came, and his wife sobbed openly, her nose and eyes red from almost continual weeping since the night before. Meanwhile, others in Washington showered Davis with edible delicacies for the journey, so much that he had to give some of it to others.[6] He also gave away some of his personal items to lighten his load, a mess chest to one, some china to General Lafayette McLaws, some books, brandy, tea, and coffee to Mrs. Robertson. He also gave his hostess an inkwell and his portable dressing case, neglecting to remove its contents, including, for some reason, his certificate as an honorary member of the Mobile Cadets. Most treasured of all to her, however, would be her own parlor table, around which Davis and his ministers and generals had sat during their last meetings, and upon which he had written Clark's appointment as acting treasurer, the last document he signed as president of the Confederacy before dissolving its government.[7]

By 10 A.M. Davis was ready to leave.[8] Dressed as usual in a suit of gray, he made his farewells, walked out of the bank building, and stood briefly on the sidewalk beside his saddled horse. He had the bridle in his hand and was about to mount when the Rev. H. A. Tupper, the town's Baptist minister, walked up to him and offered some prayerful words of comfort and encouragement. The president took Tupper's hand in his own and thanked him. "Though He slay me, yet will I trust in Him," said Davis. Seeing many of his escort standing near, those he would not be taking with him, he accepted their tearful good wishes and urged them all to make haste in seeking their own safety. Frank Vizetelly, a reporter for the *Illustrated London News* who was traveling with the fleeing government, saw tears in Davis's eyes, too.[9] Then he mounted, joined Campbell and the reduced escort, now totaling no more than twenty men, two ambulances, and a single baggage wagon, and rode out of town while hundreds of citizens turned out to watch him go.[10] The veterans left behind looked sorrowfully on the departing party until it passed out of sight, while the civilians quietly wept alone, or whispered in little groups. "There was for the moment the stillness of a benediction," recalled a Kentucky cavalryman, "and there was a look of despair on every face as if suddenly had been severed the cord that bound them to the distant past of happiness and hope." None, however, had a word of recrimination for Davis.[11]

When the president rode past Acting Treasurer Clark, just getting his baggage train ready to move into town, he stopped for a few moments to say farewell to the trusted clerk.[12] Eliza Andrews was sitting under a cedar tree beside the front gate of her home as Davis passed by. Elzey's wife had already told her of the sorrowful meeting of the night before, and her father had called at the Robertson home that morning, so she no doubt knew of the last meeting, its result no secret. "This, I suppose, is the end of the Confederacy," she mused.[13]

Not long after Davis left, others began to arrive. Brigadier General Edward Porter Alexander, until recently in charge of the artillery of one of Lee's corps, arrived on the afternoon train, disappointed to have missed Davis. He had spoken with Lee following Appomattox, hearing from the general's own mouth the conviction that the only proper course for all Confederates now was to submit and try to rebuild the South. Naively, Alexander thought that if he could have met with Davis, he might have persuaded him to surrender rather than continue his flight and resistance, though years later Varina would tell Alexander that no power on earth could have persuaded her husband to give up the cause.[14] Meanwhile a seemingly endless column of cavalrymen rode and walked through town that afternoon, many of them men from Vaughn's and Dibrell's commands, now on their way home after being paid. Many led extra horses they had taken from farmers along the way. It almost made some like Eliza Andrews wish that the irascible Bragg, a noted disciplinarian if nothing else, still had some influence. "He looks like an old porcupine," she said on seeing Bragg that day, and then confessed that even his rigid discipline probably would be useless now

on "men without a leader, without a country, without a hope."
They were all demoralized now, soldier and citizen alike, and
nothing was going to stop the plunder of farmers and government buildings. "It has gotten to be pretty much a game of grab
with us all," Andrews lamented that evening, "every man for
himself." Disconsolately she complained that "there seems to
be nobody responsible for anything any longer."[15] When Mallory left with Wigfall at 4 P.M. it only punctuated the gloom, and
then to add more painful coincidence, Major General Wheeler
and the remnant of his command finally pulled into town, missing Davis by twelve hours. He had never been a dependable officer. Being late and ignoring orders were his habit, and now,
though still under Davis's earlier instructions to join him for the
move westward, Wheeler simply contented himself to learn that
the president had already gone, apparently did not even bother
to report to the busy secretary of war, and then decided to disperse his men. "Bent chiefly now on escape," he later confessed,
"I did not linger long near Washington."[16]

Breckinridge arrived at the head of Ferguson's brigade at 1 P.M.,
with the remaining reliable men under Ferguson and Colonel
Breckinridge to augment Duke's brigade, and he stepped once
more into the vacuum and assumed responsibility. Eliza Andrews
was still sitting under her cedar tree when he rode into town.
"Breckinridge is called the handsomest man in the Confederate
army," she mused, and did not disagree.[17] He took Davis's recently vacated room at the bank with the Robertsons, and before
long went to Duke's camp about a mile out of town on the
Abbeville road.[18] The treasure train had arrived there not long
after Davis's departure, and as soon as Clark learned of its com-

ing, he rode to Duke's camp along with Bragg, Colonel Hypolite Oladowski of Bragg's staff, and John Wheless, the naval paymaster.[19] There Clark presented his appointment, taking over responsibility for the remaining funds from a much relieved Duke.[20] By the time Breckinridge appeared, Clark had set up an informal office beneath an elm tree.[21] His was going to be a time-consuming task, yet with the imminent threat of Yankee cavalry in the vicinity, Clark had to finish that day. Reagan stayed behind to help him, and Breckinridge lent assistance as well, along with Quartermaster General Lawton, while Breckinridge gave Clark his own personal wagon and driver to use for the numerous trips back and forth to town during that afternoon and evening.

First there had to be that inevitable paperwork. Breckinridge gave them a full account of the disbursements he had made back at the Savannah. Davis had approved the action, though only after Breckinridge was already in fact doing it, but now they decided that the proper documentation must be drafted to make the action formally correct, even amid dissolution. Lawton wrote a retroactive requisition for the $108,322.90 paid out the day before. Breckinridge approved it and handed it to Reagan, who immediately gave Clark an order to turn over the funds that had already been spent, and then Lawton gave his receipt. The niceties of bookkeeping complete, they turned to the remaining treasure's disbursement.

They found coin and bullion totaling $179,700 left in the wagons after the Savannah payments, not including the Virginia bank funds traveling with the Treasury. At Reagan's direction, Clark now turned the Virginia money over to cashiers and tellers from the Richmond banks who accompanied the train. Since the Confederate Treasury was to be dispersed here, and the government was dissolved, there was no one to guard those funds any longer, and the Virginians would have to take care of it themselves. They immediately placed it, some $450,000 in specie, in the vault of Robertson's bank for temporary safekeeping. Meanwhile, from the shade of the elm, Breckinridge, Reagan and Lawton, began writing requisitions and handing them to Clark. First they paid most of the silver coin to the remaining soldiers, each one getting $26, a few of whom would keep some or all of the much needed coin for years as souvenirs.[22] Then Clark issued $1,454 to pay those of Davis's escort whom the president had left behind in Washington, another $5,000 for the post quartermaster in town, who would now have to supply these troops until they surrendered, and an additional $4,000 to one of Breckinridge's staff to support the body of troopers he intended to keep under his command for a few days more.[23]

Meanwhile, Paymaster Wheless spoke up. For many days prior, he had been asking one of the cashiers with the Treasury train to issue a few thousand dollars to pay the midshipmen for their gallant and exhausting services in guarding the train. Trenholm had been too ill, and with his successor, Reagan, in advance of the train most of the time, no one would take the responsibility of issuing an order. Finally on the morning of May 3, Wheless suggested to Parker that he catch up with the fleeing government at Washington and try to secure an order from Reagan to pay the young men, and Parker sent him on. He arrived that evening, found Davis and Reagan and others in the parlor, and Reagan gave him a requisition for $1,500. Now he offered Reagan's order to Clark, and Duke, who was also helping out, handed him the money, which he promptly took back to Abbeville to pay the cadets.[24]

At the same time, Clark paid Wheless's companion Bragg another $2,000 in gold, which he was to take to the Trans-Mississippi if possible, there to turn it over to Davis, and another $1,000 to Breckinridge for the same purpose. Then Clark started paying the remaining officers and some of the civilians of the Treasury and Post Office Departments still present.[25] Among them was the colorful Colonel Oladowski. Much to the chagrin of Duke and the rest, Davis had given his old favorite Bragg an order providing that the general and his staff should be paid a month's salary in gold, even though most of the rest of the officers, including Breckinridge, only got the same $26 as the soldiers. Oladowski had never been popular, like many of Bragg's staff, especially given the officious manner and air of superiority that the protection of his general afforded, not to mention his being a foreigner. Now he presented himself for his pay, and while Clark was counting out the gold for him, Oladowski looked at the glinting metal contemptuously. He profanely damned "de filthy stuff" as a corrupting influence. "I wish it had never been digged out of de bowels of de earth," he spat. "It tempt a men to every evil. It make him false to his friend, to his brudder, to his fadder. It make him do all mean and bad acts. I hate de sight of it." Nevertheless, when Clark pushed $150 across the table to him, Duke watched as Oladowski made a quick count, then spoke again. "Fifteen dollar more, eef you blease, Misser Clarke," he said. "My pay is $165 per month."[26]

It was sunset when the payments finished. Clark said farewell to Duke and took two wagons with the remaining bullion and coin, along with a safe with more gold now placed in Breckin-ridge's wagon, back to Washington. Duke provided a guard from his command, and along the way Clark heard the cheerful sound of the silver dollars jingling in the pockets and saddlebags of the cavalrymen as they trotted beside his wagons. Just outside town he met Major R. J. Moses of the commissary department, to whom Davis had earlier given an order for $40,000 to be used for feeding paroled and straggling soldiers from Johnston's army as they passed through Washington on their way to homes in Georgia, Alabama, Mississippi, Louisiana, and elsewhere, hop-ing thus to prevent their plundering already impoverished civil-ians for subsistence. Clark was expecting this, having been ordered by Reagan to relinquish the bullion. Lawton and Isaac St. John earlier promised to give him the proper requisitions, but as yet had not. Nevertheless, Clark shifted all of the re-maining gold coin and bullion to his ambulance and gave Moses the other two wagons containing twenty boxes of silver bullion worth approximately $35,000 to $40,000, though not without noting on Moses's receipt the irregularity of the transfer, having no proper requisitions. Confederate paperwork, it seemed, was destined to outlive the Confederacy itself.

On reaching Washington after dark, Clark completed his task by handing over to James A. Semple of the navy some $86,000 in gold to be taken abroad if possible, as Reagan and Davis had instructed. That done, all he had was about $36,000 remaining from funds that the presidential party took from the Treasury at Greensboro to cover the expenses of their journey south, and this Clark kept under guard on the ambulance Breckinridge had given him. That evening he performed his final duty by taking the several hundred thousand in Confederate notes to Reagan's hotel room, where he burned it in the fireplace while Breckinridge and Reagan watched.[27] Bragg had already distributed the $1,454 for the remaining escort in town, and thus the dispersal of the Treasury was done. At 11 P.M. an exhausted Clark remounted his ambulance and set off after the president.[28]

Meanwhile Breckinridge had been busy on his own, when not with Clark and Reagan. Acting on word from Reagan of Davis's disbanding of the government, Breckinridge sent an order to each of the heads of the War Department bureaus still with him. "In the present condition of the Government," he said, they were to use their own discretion by remaining or leaving, whichever might best serve them in continuing to perform their duties, now chiefly just looking after paroled and straggling soldiers trying to get home. That done, he ordered them to make their way to the west, to rejoin and reconstitute the War Department if and when he called on them, no doubt that they might perform the same services for the men beyond the Mississippi. As for the public property in their keeping, he directed them to dispose of it in whatever manner was best for the service, meaning in the main to turn it over to the soldiers, or else hand it over to the Federals to be used to aid the men in the ranks.[29] The secretary of war personally discharged some of the men in Washington, and there was no small irony in the fact that one of his last acts was to accept the resignation of Lieutenant James B. Clay, Jr., whose grandfather Henry Clay had devoted much of his life to averting the very sectional tragedy now in its last moments.[30]

Breckinridge also conferred with Reagan late that evening about the remaining troops in and around Washington. They had all been paid now, and gave conflicting signals as to their intentions. Many of Duke's and Colonel Breckinridge's Kentuckians assured him during the day that they were prepared to follow him farther, even west of the Mississippi, if he would lead them. Apparently when Breckinridge broached the subject to Ferguson, he said that he, too, would follow where the Kentuckian led.[31] Breckinridge until this time had expected to catch up with Davis and continue to direct his flight, still hoping to persuade him to leave the country by boat from Florida. But now it occurred to him that if enough troopers would follow, he might do better by leading them west as a decoy to lure pursuing Yankees away from Davis. Along the way he might be able to facilitate the surrender of other remaining bodies, such as Richard Taylor's small army, which Breckinridge had no way of knowing had already surrendered. Should both he and Davis actually make it to the Trans-Mississippi, then he would be present to counteract any attempt by Davis to keep the war going.

Reagan argued otherwise, saying that he had himself spoken with a number of the soldiers that day and found them all determined that the war was over and they were going home. He doubted that the general could get any more than a loyal bodyguard to follow him west. Breckinridge felt more optimistic, and was still hopeful when they shook hands and said good-bye at eleven o'clock. Agreeing that the postmaster should leave with Clark to rejoin the president at once, Breckinridge insisted on sending along a dozen of Duke's troopers as an escort.[32] He could not know that events even then were putting the lie to his optimism.

When Breckinridge and Ferguson had arrived that afternoon, Breckinridge ordered the cavalryman to take his men a mile or two out of town to the southwest to watch the approaches from that direction while Duke guarded the road into town from the east. Once in position there, Ferguson disbursed to his men the pay he had drawn for them on the Savannah. Late in the day Breckinridge moved his headquarters from the bank to a house on the Madison road about five miles beyond Ferguson's camp, and in passing gave him an order to bring his brigade up. But now discipline even in Ferguson's command broke down. One of the men found a Savannah newspaper with the definitive word that Johnston had surrendered all of his army, and they considered themselves as included. Now, after all their loyalty, even after Vaughn and Dibrell fell by the road, one of Ferguson's regimental officers simply refused to obey, and quickly spread the infection to others. They wanted to go to Augusta or some other convenient point and take their parole, they said. When word reached Ferguson, he first ordered the officer arrested, but then the others refused to answer any order at all until the offender's release. A frustrated Ferguson ordered the brigade to form ranks on either side of the road, even though it was close to midnight, and angrily asked what their behavior meant. He did not care if Johnston had surrendered, for he and his men reported to Johnston's superior, Breckinridge, now. That said, he made a moving appeal to stand by their duty a little longer, explaining that Breckinridge wanted them to go on west of the great river, to protect the president. Still they remained adamant. In some disgust, Ferguson then announced, "Seeing I have no command, and am determined not to surrender, [I] will go on, and those who desire to follow me can go." Those who had not lost all sense of duty should follow him in executing Breckinridge's order to move a few miles farther out on the road. "Everything seemed to be in perfect confusion," thought

F. E. Richardson of Ferguson's staff. "The men did not know what to do." When the general and his eight staff rode off into the night, only one of his regimental commanders and seventy-nine of his men followed. On what seemed a prearranged signal, a bugler sounded the call to mount, and the rest simply left on the road south that led toward Macon and surrender.[33]

Breckinridge learned of the incident about dawn on May 5, when he sent orders for Ferguson to join Colonel Breckinridge's brigade in advancing onward to the southwest, toward Madison, Georgia. Ferguson galloped to headquarters and told the secretary the sad tale of the night before. The little band of eighty-eight were resolved to go to the Mississippi, even to Mexico, if need be, to protect the president, but none of the rest would follow. Breckinridge offered no recriminations for either the general or his men but spoke to him kindly of his belief that Ferguson had done all he could. The men willing to stay with him were too few to be of use, and too many not to be an encumbrance to the swift movement needed now. Ferguson himself offered to continue with the secretary, but Breckinridge declined and sent him back to his little band with orders to discharge them and send them home with his compliments for their bravery and loyalty. When Ferguson did so, with tears in his eyes, he shook the hand of every man who had remained, gave them their discharges, and placed an officer in command to lead them toward their Alabama and Mississippi homes. That afternoon they left, heading west, and rode no more than a mile or two before they encountered Union cavalry heading for Washington. Acknowledging that Johnston's surrender covered the Confederates, the Yankees merely told them to leave their arms behind, and then let them pass on homeward.[34]

The loss of the majority of Ferguson's brigade effectively
ended Breckinridge's plan of leading a substantial command
west, and so now he abandoned the idea. In fact, he may have
given it up even before Ferguson's discouraging news, for in
sending the general back to his command, Breckinridge told him
that he had decided to proceed henceforward with only his sons,
his servant Tom Ferguson, and a handful of loyal followers. Now
that he had disbanded his department, he would also leave Generals Lawton, St. John, and Gilmer in Washington, each to decide his course for himself.[35] Instead, he now designed simply
to use men he could depend upon, to create brief diversions in
the hope of throwing the Federals off the fleeing president's
path.

He asked his cousin Colonel William Breckinridge to call for
volunteers to accompany him personally, and about fifty stepped
forward, the rest being ordered discharged and sent on their way
back to Kentucky. Duke and 350 of his men would also join the
effort. Breckinridge's plan was for the two bodies to move by
different roads toward Woodstock, about twelve miles west of
Washington, the hope being that each group might decoy Yankees in the opposite direction from Davis's route south. Duke
left early that morning, but Breckinridge was delayed by last-minute business and did not get away until some time after
sunup.[36] Among other things, Ferguson discovered that he still
had six thousand dollars in gold on his hands, even after paying
his men. He informed Breckinridge, who ordered it immediately sent back to Washington. There being no longer any representative of the Treasury in town, and with the remaining
members of his War Department already leaving for their homes,
to surrender, Breckinridge decided, without asking him, to leave

the gold with Toombs, who himself intended to escape to Europe and could presumably take it with him to add to what Semple took. In fact, Toombs later claimed that Breckinridge simply threw the bag of gold over the fence of his yard as the Kentuckian rode out of town. Had Breckinridge actually asked Toombs about accepting the gold, the Georgian would have refused, and within hours he simply turned it over to the Federals when they entered Washington, getting their promise to use it to buy provisions for homebound Confederates.[37]

Finally Breckinridge was ready to leave. Outside his headquarters he unpacked a valise, all that remained of his own baggage wagon, and lightened his load by giving away to men staying behind some of his shirts, tobacco, and other nonessentials. What was left he stuffed back inside or tied to his saddlebags. A few hundred yards away he could see Ferguson's loyal remnant cresting a hill on their way to surrender and to their homes. As they looked back, they saw him mount and disappear into the woods to join Colonel Breckinridge.[38]

The people in Washington never even knew that Breckinridge had departed. He simply disappeared, his last act being to send an order for the discharge of the remaining balance of Duke's brigade, with instructions that they should surrender.[39] His stratagem to misdirect the Yankees was already common knowledge among the citizens, however, but that may have been Breckinridge's own doing, for rumor also erroneously said his purpose was to buy him time to destroy some papers and give the enemy the slip but said nothing about covering the flight of the president. Such misinformation would surely get to the enemy when they came into town, and might instead buy Davis a little more time. Yet some also thought it entirely unnecessary. Eliza Andrews heard common speculation that the Yankees wanted Davis and Breckinridge both to escape, as well as the rest of the government officials, and would have let them get away openly. There was a general belief that Grant and Sherman, acting on the orders of the dead Lincoln, did not want to have to try and hang rebel leaders.[40]

In fact, the Yankees came into Washington that same evening but showed no haste in pursuing. They were still there the next day when the several hundred remaining Kentuckians of the Orphan Brigade came into town, under arms and with flags flying, to surrender. There, too, were the remnants of Colonel Breckinridge's men, waiting here to give their parole. Perhaps it was the sudden presence of such a substantial Southern command that held up Yankee pursuit of General Breckinridge, his old friends from his very first and very last military commands thus doing him one last service, albeit unknowingly. Eliza Andrews thought that the Kentuckians would have an armed collision with the Yankees, and soon isolated individual fistfights broke out between men in blue and gray. There may even have been a brief skirmish between some of the Kentucky cavalrymen and the Union provost guard. Miss Andrews actually hoped for a battle, wanting to see the Rebels whip the foe just one more time before it was all over.[41] But it was not to be. All that evening the Federals prepared parole papers, and the next day, May 6, it would be done and the Kentuckians on their way home.[42] Many of them wept openly in the streets.

That delay allowed Breckinridge to take his time. While Duke and his command reached Woodstock by the early afternoon of May 5, Breckinridge and his cousin's small company moved only a few miles beyond his headquarters, and at what

Colonel Breckinridge himself confessed to be an intentionally leisurely pace.[43] The general wanted to be sure the Yankees got their scent and followed. In fact, he soon dismounted the command and took quarters briefly in a farmhouse, bivouacking his cousin's company in a nearby orchard, while he sent young Clay, now a volunteer aide, off to Duke with word that he would be late arriving in Woodstock. Clay got no more than a mile or so, however, when he met a battalion of Union horsemen in front of them, barring the road. It was Major Andrew Campbell and about 250 troopers from Colonel William Palmer's brigade of cavalry.

Clay raced back to report, finding the two Breckinridges in conference in the farmhouse. Fortunately Colonel Breckinridge's horses were still saddled, and he suggested that he mount his men and advance to form a skirmish line across the road. The general agreed but told him not to open fire or do anything to precipitate a fight, not wanting any of these brave men to have the unfortunate distinction of being the last to die in a lost war. The two stepped out of the farmhouse, and while the colonel rejoined his men, the general mounted his own horse in order to be ready to move on the instant. Within a few minutes the Confederates were moving and soon came up to the cautiously advancing Yankees, who knew they had been spotted. Colonel Breckinridge halted his command, raised a white truce flag, and sent it forward with young Clay Stacker, who just the year before had been a cadet at the Virginia Military Institute, fighting under General Breckinridge in the Battle of New Market. The colonel demanded to know Campbell's intentions, saying that for his own part he only wanted to be allowed to pass in peace. Breckinridge himself would confess that "it was a delicate and dangerous five minutes" before the Federal agreed to a parley.

At first, citing Johnston's recent capitulation, Campbell simply demanded their surrender or that they stand aside and leave the road back to Washington open, adding the threat that he had reinforcements on the way. Breckinridge stalled by pretending not to believe the news of Johnston, which he already knew to be true. Instead, he said they were on their way to Atlanta, and if when they got there they found it was true, then they would surrender. Campbell could see from Breckinridge's uniform that he was a colonel, and knew that he had commanded a brigade that might outnumber his battalion several times over. Breckinridge had also posted his company just on the brow of a hill, concealing the size of his force. Thus Campbell concluded that Breckinridge had his entire command with him, an impression that Breckinridge later admitted "I took no pains to remove." As a result, the Federal was not willing to risk a fight when Breckinridge went on to threaten that he would himself order a charge unless Campbell agreed to terms. In the end, Breckinridge's bluff bested Campbell's, and the major agreed to keep his battalion on one side of the road and not go farther until Breckinridge consented, while Breckinridge himself and any other Confederate parties that he designated were to be allowed to pass unmolested toward Woodstock.

Meanwhile General Breckinridge anxiously awaited the outcome, at the same time readying his sons and a few others standing with them. When his cousin sent back word that the Federals had agreed to terms and that the company would be allowed to proceed toward Woodstock, Breckinridge knew it was time for him to leave. With Yankees in unknown numbers in their immediate front, any further movement under arms only risked a bloody clash to no purpose. The diversion had failed before fairly begun, but if he remained with either Breckinridge or Duke now, he knew that it only increased the chances of a fight. Uninterested as the enemy might be in an isolated company of Confederate cavalry riding home, he had every reason to expect that the Yankees would be far more aggressive if they knew the Confederate secretary of war was with them, a man under indictment in the North and with a price on his head. His cousin was buying him at least enough time to get away with his small escort. Before leaving, however, he told the colonel that he was convinced that by now both Richard Taylor and Bedford Forrest would have surrendered. Even if they got all the way to the Mississippi, they would likely just find Kirby Smith, too, about to give up. He told his cousin to tell Duke that he wanted them all to surrender at once, for it was foolish even to think of holding out longer, and criminal to risk the lives of their men to no purpose. Forbidding them even to contemplate helping him in his own journey, he said, "I will not have one of these young men to encounter one hazard more for my sake." He told them all to go home to Kentucky, to their homes and families. That said, he mounted and, with his party around him, and a local citizen as a guide, turned off the road toward the south and disappeared into the woods.

Even then his cousin kept his company at the ready for several hours, to give the general a good start, before finally he advised Campbell that he was ready to proceed to Woodstock and that there would be no other Confederates following him. Campbell pulled his men away from the road, and the Kentucky Confederates trotted past, the men in blue and gray actually cheering each other as they passed. "You rebs had better go home and stop this nonsense," shouted one of the Federal troopers. "We don't want to hurt each other!"

The Confederates reached Woodstock and Duke soon afterward, to find that Duke himself had been facing a substantial Federal cavalry force across his path to the west of the village and had been parleying for some time, neither commander wishing to precipitate a skirmish. Duke, too, stalled for time, delaying until Colonel Breckinridge arrived in the early evening. Then the two of them formed their commands. Breckinridge spoke first and told them all what General Breckinridge had said: Their war was over. Duke followed, speaking with unconcealed emotion. After expressing their appreciation for what their gallant followers had done, the commanders disbanded them at last.[44]

Chapter Ten

"THIS MAZE
OF ENEMIES"

A s Jefferson Davis rode out of Washington, he could still recall the words of Varina's letter of May 1, which found him just after he reached Washington. She held nothing back in condemning Johnston's "treacherous" surrender, and having heard from her husband of the unreliability of his cavalry, declared that she thought him safer without it. He was surrounded, she feared, in "this maze of enemies." She advised him to cut loose entirely from any escort, and strike out alone or with only one or two companions. She and Harrison planned to move straight south through Georgia, and then turn west to Pensacola to get a ship abroad. "Do not try to meet me," she had concluded. "I dread the Yankees getting news of you so much, you are the country's only hope."[1]

Davis did take some precautions. He and his party rode out of Washington eastward on the road toward Abbeville, presumably to mislead townspeople as to his intended route, though certainly he had discussed it with Breckinridge and Reagan, both of whom he expected to join him. When a mile or two out of town, he turned right and struck south for Sandersville, along the route Harrison and Varina advised they would travel. He probably continued to ride sometimes at the head of his party, or at the rear, or in the middle, to decrease the chances that he might be taken if they were surprised. Reagan had previously urged him to disguise himself as a simple soldier, which the president refused to do, but hereafter he presented himself to those they met along the road as a congressman from Texas bound for home.[2]

Davis covered more than twenty miles on May 4, stopping for the night near the north bank of the Ogeechee River, though already he felt concern that they did not travel faster. Campbell frankly told him that their wagons were a dangerous encumbrance that might prove fatal.[3] That was disturbing, since Davis himself still appeared hopeful for the future and told his escort at a stop during the day that if they could only reach Kirby Smith, they might "carry on the war forever."[4] Thus he was anxious to make better time the next morning, but they were just rising at dawn when Reagan and Clark arrived, having ridden all through the night in their wagon. Along the way Reagan sent the escort back to Washington, arguing that they were not strong enough to provide real protection and that everyone would be safer if they returned. Intent on following their orders, the soldiers demanded a written order, but incredibly, after spending all of May 4 in paperwork, Reagan had neither pencil nor paper left. Only on his repeated entreaties did they finally leave him and Clark to complete their journey on their own.[5]

As Reagan and Clark greeted the president's party, they found that it consisted of Davis and his aides, the ten men of their escort under Campbell, a few others attaching themselves, and the small baggage train that Clark sent ahead the day before. Their numbers were small enough, but still too many to move quickly, especially encumbered by the wagons. The addition of Breckinridge's ambulance with Clark and the remaining gold was no help. Though they rode hard all of May 5, still they covered only about thirty miles, halting for the night a few miles above Sandersville.[6] Davis was already distressed, not only from their slow progress but from the belief that most of the cavalry escort had abandoned him and the cause on the Savannah, being unaware that in fact a number of men from Duke's, Ferguson's, and Colonel Breckinridge's commands had wanted to follow him. That he would not discover until thirteen years later, and then he would declare that had he known it at the time, he would have adopted a much different course, most likely continuing his armed westward march rather than turning south.[7]

Now even worse news came into camp. That evening, young Preston Johnston and others rode to the ferry over the Oconee River and, from locals there, heard a report of wagons some miles east of them, believed to be a Confederate quartermaster or commissary train, and, further, that paroled Confederate soldiers in the neighborhood intended to take and rob it, by force if necessary. The description of the wagon train matched that of Harrison and Varina's party to an alarming degree, and Johnston hurried back to Davis, only to find that the president had heard a similar report and had come to the same conclusion. During the night Davis made a decision—when they rose in the morning, he would leave the encumbering wagons behind with Clark and ride ahead accompanied only by Reagan, his aides, and Campbell's party.

Late that night, or in the early hours before dawn, Clark made a decision, too. He fully expected that his slow-moving train of wagons would be easy prey for Federal cavalry, which meant the loss of the $36,000 in gold he carried. He called Davis's aides Wood, Johnston, and Lubbock, as well as Thorburn, to ask what funds they had. Lubbock carried a little coin, but the others, as well as Davis himself, had nothing but worthless Confederate notes. Clark told them his remaining treasure must surely be captured, while they would need money on their journey, especially if they reached the Florida coast and had to buy a boat. With Reagan's approval, he gave each of the four of them $1,510 in gold. Clark also handed $300 to Campbell as a last payment for himself and his men. Then as Davis and his party mounted, preparing to leave, Clark took a sack holding $3,500 to Reagan and asked him to take it along just in case. Reagan was already weighted down with $2,000 of his own that he'd brought with him from Richmond, wearing it around his waist in a cumbersome money belt, but he yielded to Clark's entreaties and put the additional gold in his saddlebags.[8] That done, Davis said farewell to Clark and his assistants. "This move will probably cause me to be captured or killed," he declared. He gave his aides and Campbell the option of stopping here. "I do not feel that you are bound to go with me," he said, "but I must protect my family." None would abandon him.[9] While Clark prepared to continue south with his wagons and about $26,000 in remaining gold,

Davis left him four men as a guard to be commanded by the president's distant kinsman Captain Watson Van Benthuysen. Then Davis struck out by the back roads, to find Varina.

They rode south all morning. That afternoon Reagan's horse threw a shoe, and while they stopped at a smithy to have another one fitted, Davis learned that a party of discharged soldiers had passed through on foot sometime earlier, announcing their intent to fall on and capture a small train of wagons with good horses and mules reported to be near Dublin, just below the Oconee, and perhaps half a day's ride away.[10] The description sounded like Varina and Harrison well enough. Thus alarmed, Davis and his escort rode on, frustrated at being unable to tell which of the several roads they passed might have been taken by the wagons. They pressed on until well after dark, and it was midnight or later when they came upon some men who said they were discharged from the Thirty-Sixth Alabama. Without identifying himself, Davis asked if they had seen a wagon train with women and children in the vicinity, and learned that such a party was only a few miles ahead on this same road. Davis strongly suspected that these were the men intending to attack his wife's train, just waiting for a late enough hour that everyone would be asleep, but seeing himself and his mounted men well armed, the would-be plunderers abandoned their design. The president anxiously rode on. Soon Campbell told him that some of his men's horses were exhausted and would have to be rested until morning. Davis decided to ride ahead on his own with his staff, trying first one path then another as he sought his family, even peering in the bright moonlight to see evidence of wagon tracks.[11]

Davis was just outside Dublin when the moonlight revealed

some wagons in the distance parked beside the road, and as he approached he saw the commotion caused by the sounds of his party's horses on the road. Men rose and ran around the camp waking others, and then an armed man stepped into the road some distance in advance, clearly intent on placing himself between the riders and the wagons. From the dimness came a shouted command to halt. Instantly Davis and his men reined their animals. "Who comes there," said the voice again, one that Davis thought familiar. "Friends," he called in reply, and out of the gloom stepped Burton Harrison.[12] Within moments Davis and his family were in each other's arms for the first time in more than a month.

Varina and Harrison had stayed two nights and a day in Washington, Harrison spending all of May 1 putting together a train of four army wagons with mule teams, and securing drivers and others to help, promising them the wagons and mules when their journey was done. He prudently parked them in the woods outside town, where they escaped the depredations and plunder that broke out in Washington that day. On the morning of May 2, he and his party loaded the wagons with tents and camping supplies, the presidential family's baggage, and some rifles and ammunition. By 10 A.M. they were ready to go, intending to head west to Atlanta first, but just then they got news of Johnston's surrender, and word that Major General James H. Wilson's Yankee cavalry would now be forming a cordon to close all roads leading west. That forced them to change their plans, the only safe route appearing to be due south through Sandersville and then on to southern or southwestern Florida.[13]

That afternoon when they finally pulled out of town, heading first for Madison, the wagons carried Harrison in charge, Varina and her sister Margaret Howell, the four Davis children, two servants, and two army officers. In addition, Breckinridge's Kentucky friend Leeland Hathaway had turned up again, accompanied by his fellow cavalrymen Winder Monroe and Jack Messick, all of them without a command. In Abbeville, Leovy had asked them to accompany Varina, since he felt some doubts about Harrison's ability to cope with the responsibility, and they were still with them. Hathaway had found the president's secretary ill and somewhat demoralized, "a more forlorn & hopelessly helpless creature in mans estate I had never seen," he recalled rather hyperbolically.[14] Nevertheless, there was no doubt that Harrison was in charge, whatever Hathaway thought of him, and Harrison had given them all explicit instructions to be quiet about who they were and where they were bound. To anyone who inquired, Varina was "Mrs. Jones," and the men driving the horses were so uncommunicative with the curious as to be almost suspicious. Asked by those they passed where they had come from, the men would only reply, "Up the road." Asked where they were going, the reply was an equally laconic, "Down the road a bit."

Harrison and Varina had no better idea of where her husband was going. Shortly after they rode out of Washington, a courier came up to them with Davis's letter, written late on May 2 from Abbeville, venting bitter disappointment in his generals' refusing to agree to continue to the Trans-Mississippi. All he could say of his future course was that he would be in Washington in a day, but after that his route must be decided by events as they unfolded.[15] That afternoon, Harrison had fallen ill with severe diarrhea and had had to drop back from the train to rest, only catching up with them that evening, still nearly too weak to climb into a wagon to sleep. The next day, as the president rode into Washington, they were continuing south and heard the first rumor that there might be an attempt to steal their wagons and teams. One of the officers with them actually parleyed with the intended marauders and got them to call it off when they discovered that it was the president's family. Further, their leader was a Freemason as was Harrison's emissary, which enlisted the obligations of fraternity for the party's protection. Indeed, the leader of the soldiers offered his services to the fugitives, and even gave Harrison a "pass" to get them past other intended marauders farther down the road.[16]

In the face of this evident danger, Hathaway and the other Kentuckians, accustomed to the speed of cavalry travel, protested that they moved too slowly, unnecessarily endangering the caravan. They wanted to leave all the baggage behind and press on with only the family and their essential clothing, moving day and night until well past danger. Varina and Harrison refused, however, the secretary only further earning the Kentuckians' contempt. "He had never been a soldier & knew nothing of a soldiers duties or methods," protested Hathaway. Before long the Kentuckians openly showed their contempt for him, enough so that in his later recollections of the journey, Harrison all but wrote them out of the story. Inevitably the discussion turned adversarial.

"Mrs Davis don't you know that the yankees know that you are traveling this course & that you are burdened with all this stuff," asked Hathaway.

"Not necessarily so," Harrison responded in her place.

"You certainly underrate your enemy then which is always dangerous," replied the Kentuckian. "If a regiment of Morgans old command were in the neighborhood of such a train as this it would know to a dot every thing about it—just what route taken—numbers—rate of travel & all about it."

"They cant overtake us," insisted an adamant Harrison.

"They will travel as far in 24 hours as we are doing in 3 days & nights if they have a leader worthy of the name," Hathaway shot back, but to no avail.

In the end, unable to influence Varina or Harrison, the Kentuckians decided to do the best they could and enjoy the trip, taking special pleasure in the company of the Davis children. Often little ten-month-old Varina Anne, called "Winnie" by her family, was hoisted onto the saddle of one of the riders, one officer or another sometimes singing to her as they rode.[17]

Thus they continued. By day they passed over grassy savannas dotted with blooming magnolia and scuppernong, and through the shade of dense pine woods, while their evenings seemed almost like camping parties, with ample food and plenty of brandy from a cask Varina brought from Richmond, had it not been for the ever-present sense of danger. Indeed, almost every day they heard fresh rumors of an attack on their train, and each night they mounted a guard to be ready in case, until May 6 when another small band of plunderers actually followed them close enough to capture a teamster temporarily riding one of the Kentuckians' horses, robbing him of the animal and giving away their intent to attack the wagon train itself that night. Fortunately the teamster was released and managed to run a couple of miles to catch up with Harrison and give the warning. Thus he had the wagons off the road and circled on high ground that evening, the horses corralled inside and sentinels on duty around the camp. Harrison had been standing guard when he heard Davis's voice in the night.[18]

At first Varina felt alarm when she saw her husband, for she had imagined him to be some distance away, on the road to the west and safety. He explained his coming and his concern, but happy as she was to see him, she complained that he should not have come. Reunited now, however, the president was not about to leave her again with the danger of marauders still present. During the night Campbell's men scouted the road west to the Oconee ferry. Finding it clear, the next morning, May 7, the enlarged party moved off southwest through Dublin, Davis riding most of the time with Varina in her ambulance. By that evening they had covered only about thirty miles, stopping not far from Abbeville, Georgia, on the Ocmulgee. Again the soldiers protested. Hathaway complained that they were leaving a trail behind them as easy to follow as that of an army corps. When they should have been covering fifty or sixty miles a day, they were going at half that pace. He had reasoned, warned, and almost quarreled, but no one listened.[19] Johnston spoke with Davis about the size of their train as well, and now Campbell added his voice, begging the president and Reagan and the staff to ride ahead while the captain left four of his troopers to protect Varina and the wagons. Davis would not have it, even when scouts brought back news that Yankees in the vicinity were known to have heard of the wagon train and its important passengers.[20]

Only after breakfast the next morning did the entreaties of Varina and the rest persuade the president to ride ahead again with his own party. Heavy rain and getting lost on an unfamiliar road so slowed him that by evening he only reached Abbeville, where he found shelter from the furious storm in a deserted house. Harrison and the wagon train almost caught up, having taken the right road, and now made camp barely a mile away on the west bank of the river, near Campbell's small bivouac. There was to be no repeat of the family reunion here, however, for Campbell had brought in a report that Federal cavalry were seen just twenty-five miles upriver. That put the danger only a few hours away. At once Davis sent word to Harrison that he must get the wagons going again and keep them going through the night. The storm had worsened, and amid booming thunder and flashes of lightning, the little wagon train started out in the darkness. As it rolled through Abbeville, Harrison dismounted briefly and went into the old house, where he found the president lying on the floor, wrapped in a blanket and trying to rest. He told Harrison that his own group's mounts were so jaded that they had to risk giving the animals a few hours' rest, but he would leave before dawn and hoped to catch up to them in the morning.[21]

That night trip provided a stark contrast with the almost idyllic evenings the wagon party had passed only a few days earlier. The road south led through a dense forest, while the storm obliterated the moonlight that could have illuminated their path. Instead, they found themselves running into trees downed by the storm, losing the road and sinking into the sandy soil, dependent on the lightning flashes to show them their path. They were still picking their way in the tempest a few hours later when Davis and the rest came up again. After dawn they all stopped for a hasty breakfast, but then immediately Davis pushed them on again, rolling all day. He had announced that he intended to separate from the wagons once more that day, but found himself too weary and unwell, and instead rode in Varina's ambulance until 5 P.M., when they stopped just a mile outside Irwinville, having covered something over thirty miles.[22]

People and animals alike were exhausted, and could go no farther without rest. By now the reported enemy cavalry should be more than fifty miles in their rear, and they felt some relief from the most immediate danger. Moreover, they had not met a single traveler all day in the thinly settled countryside, which meant that no one would be able to tell inquisitive Yankees of their passing. Nevertheless, Johnston rode on into Irwinville while the rest made camp and collapsed in their blankets.

The near miss in Abbeville had still thrown a scare into them, and now Harrison, Wood, Thorburn, and Lubbock all begged Davis not to tarry but to leave the wagon party behind. Johnston told him the day before that he did not believe they could make it to Texas cross-country, and that their only hope of reaching the Trans-Mississippi was via boat from Florida. Thorburn still had that boat waiting on the coast to take Davis to Texas via the Gulf of Mexico, and he and Wood urged the president to take the opportunity, while the others argued that no matter what route he chose, a voyage across the gulf or a hard ride overland to the Mississippi, he must leave at once. Finally they prevailed. "It is true," said Davis, "every negro in Mississippi knows me." Even should they get through Georgia and Alabama, he could hardly expect to go unrecognized across his home state, now overrun with Yankees. At last Davis promised that he would leave with his mounted party and ride at least another ten miles toward safety that evening just as soon as they could cook and eat their dinner.[23]

As he drank tea and dined with his family and followers, however, he decided it best to keep his plans to himself. He neither committed himself to Thorburn's scheme nor to any other suggestion, resolving on his own to ride due west, cross

the Chattahoochee into Alabama, find and unite Taylor and Forrest, and then either wait for other loyal men to rally to them, or
lead the army west of the Mississippi. He felt now that maintaining secrecy, even from his family, would be for their protection as much as his own. He could not yet know that Taylor had
completed his surrender three days earlier, nor that this very day
Forrest was disbanding his cavalry. Also this same day, in faraway
Shreveport, Louisiana, Kirby Smith's headquarters, a rumor arrived that Davis and the Confederate treasure were on their way
there with the Yankee cavalry in hot pursuit. "If Mr. Davis gets
into this Dept., he will make a last effort to sustain himself but
his efforts will all be in vain," complained one citizen. "The soldiers are disheartened, & disgusted, and determined not [to]
sacrifice their lives to gratify anyboddys ambition."[24] Even had
Davis known the feeling of the people in the west, however,
nothing in his behavior to date suggests that it would have
changed his resolution to keep fighting.

When he finished eating, Davis had his horse saddled and
was about to mount, when Johnston returned from Irwinville,
where he had bought some eggs for their breakfast. While there,
he learned that yet another band of marauders, this time reported to be more than one hundred, intended to plunder the
wagon party that night. Assuming that such men would be discharged or paroled Confederate soldiers and that he might still
have at least some influence with men who once followed his
banners, Davis decided to postpone his departure in order to
appeal to them not to rob his family should they approach. Expecting to continue his journey during the night as soon as he
dispersed the threat, he left his horse saddled and hitched near
the road for a speedy departure, his pistols in the saddle hol-

sters. There being nothing to do until the marauders appeared, he went into the tent erected for Varina and lay down in his clothes, where he fell immediately into a deep sleep. Beside them another tent held the children and their nurse. A few yards away the exhausted Johnston slept on the ground beneath a pine tree, while Wood and Lubbock rested under another pine a hundred feet away. There Reagan and the rest sat up late listening to Lubbock grouse about their being slowed by the wagons, until they, too, turned in. Young Harrison, too exhausted to eat, simply collapsed in sleep on the open ground near the tents, where another officer soon stretched a tent fly over him and immediately fell down asleep beside him. Campbell and his men rode ahead to reconnoiter a river crossing about four miles to the west. By midnight virtually the entire presidential party lay asleep, and without a guard.

An hour later Lieutenant Colonel Benjamin D. Pritchard and 150 troopers of the Fourth Michigan Cavalry quietly rode into Irwinville, learned from residents where the Confederate party was camped, and silently moved down the road to within a few hundred yards of the wagons, settling down to wait for dawn. Scarcely a mile away to the north, the First Wisconsin Cavalry rode up on the Abbeville road, having learned who was camped ahead of them, and they, too, made a hasty bivouac to await daylight.[25]

They were all still sleeping, and Campbell had not yet returned, when Davis's servant James Jones was awakened by the sound of carbine fire scarcely a hundred yards outside the camp. Advancing through a drizzle in the predawn half-light, the two Yankee commands accidentally collided and opened fire on each other. Jones rushed to wake Harrison and Johnston, and the latter sent him on to Davis's tent. Harrison stood just in time to see

Pritchard and his men galloping up the road toward him. He pulled his pistol and took aim for a moment but saw that it was pointless and dropped his arm. Within seconds the Michigan men were upon them. Preston Johnston ran for his saddle and his pistol, but three Yankees were on him in an instant, and he gave up without a shot. Ordering Johnston to go under guard to a smoldering campfire, his captors went next for Wood and Lubbock.[26] Wood, who was sleeping near the horses, had a Yankee uniform blouse and put it on, saying to Lubbock, "I will walk through these fellows," and suggested that he accompany him, but Lubbock decided to remain. Wood tried to mount, but a Federal instantly appeared and grabbed the animal's head, and Wood let go in order to get away, heading toward the Davis tent. Then two Yankees leaped on Lubbock, who also tried to mount but could not gain the saddle. Instead a comic tug-of-war ensued, the Yankees threatening to shoot him if he did not yield his horse and saddlebags, and he telling them to "shoot and be damned" before he'd let them rob him. Reagan watched the struggle, his pistol in his hand in case shooting should start, when a Federal major rode up beside him and asked for his arms. Seeing resistance to be hopeless, the rough old Texan handed over his pistol.[27]

Pritchard himself first encountered Harrison. He did not yet know that the outbreak of shooting was between his men and the Wisconsin regiment, and demanded to know if the firing still sporadically heard in the distance meant there were Confederate soldiers with the party. Supposing that it was the wagon teamsters who had opened the skirmish, Harrison said that of course it was Confederates shooting, whereupon Pritchard galloped off to investigate, while some of his troopers remained in the camp to disarm the rest of the party and begin plundering. Not a shot had been fired in the camp itself. Neither, Harrison noted as he was left alone for a few minutes, had Davis been seen as yet. Indeed, at first the tents and their occupants were not molested, but Harrison did observe one Yankee leisurely walking his horse toward the Davis tent, still some distance away.[28]

When the commotion first began, Davis thought it was the anticipated raid by the rumored Confederate marauders. As he rose from his blanket, he told Varina who it must be. "Those people have attacked us at last," he said. "I will go and see if I can stop the firing; surely I will have some authority with Confederates yet." But when he stepped briefly outside the tent flap, he could see the attackers some distance away and recognized them as Yankees. Immediately stepping back into the tent, he told Varina, "It is the Federal cavalry, and they are on us."[29] Within moments Wood ran to the tent, unobserved by the Yankees, who were still engaged in capturing the other staff and teamsters and distracted by the worrying fire in the distance. He met Varina standing outside, where she had stepped to get a look for herself. Pointing out that the cavalrymen had as yet shown no interest in the occupants of the two family tents and were in fact mostly on the road, preoccupied with the firing off to the north, he pointed toward a wooded creek bottom just a hundred yards in the opposite direction. In the dim light and commotion, the president could still escape if he hurried. She agreed, asking Wood to distract the trooper moving toward their tent, long enough for her husband to slip out. At the same time, seeing the lone Yankee still approaching the tent, she boldly spoke to him, Corporal George Munger, and persuaded him to return to the road, presumably telling him there were no men in this tent. At that moment Harrison walked over and actually strolled back to the road with Munger to keep him distracted.[30]

Stepping back inside, Varina urgently implored Davis to go at once. His cabinet had always complained of his unwillingness to make quick decisions, and he hesitated now, a prisoner to his instinct not to run from a fight, also out of concern for his family. It was only a few seconds before he yielded, but they were precious moments. His saddled horse and his pistols were still near the road, all but surrounded by the Yankees, so he could not ride away. He would have to go on foot. Since it was still drizzling and he would need some protection from the elements if he got away, he reached for his overcoat but, in the half-light, grabbed Varina's dark gray raglan cloak instead. Draping it over his shoulders, he stepped outside the tent and started to walk at a calm pace toward the woods. Varina looked after him and at once feared that his face was still so recognizable that someone would spot him. She rushed out after him and threw her own black shawl over his head and shoulders, then thought to have her children's mulatto nurse, Helen, grab a bucket and run to Davis's side to walk with him as if they were simply going to the creek for water.[31]

Corporal Munger happened to look back and made out someone leaving the tent. He turned to go back. As he approached the tent and called to the two figures to stop, saying that there seemed to be some firing in the direction of the creek, too, and they could be in danger, Varina emerged. Munger asked what she and the other two were doing. "We are going to the brook to get water to perform our toilet," said Varina, adding that they were not afraid of bullets. Meanwhile Davis and the woman, now about forty paces away, changed their path as if heeding the trooper, but kept walking. Then two more troopers rode to the tent, where Varina tried to distract them, too, becoming increasingly excited as they kept looking at the two receding figures. Finally, Munger made out Davis's distinctly unfeminine cavalry boots and spurs.

"Who is that?" he demanded as he pointed to Davis.

"That is my mother," said Varina.

"What is your mother doing with boots on?" Munger replied, and yelled for Davis to halt. When the walkers kept on, he repeated it several times and then moved his animal toward the figures, lifted his carbine from the pommel of his saddle, drew back the hammer, and aimed it at Davis. Varina lost her remaining self-command, and while the other two soldiers began to speak somewhat abusively to her, she screamed in fear for her husband's life and moved toward him at the same time that the children emerged from their tent and began crying for their father.

It was too much for Davis to bear. He stopped and turned around, just as the cries attracted more troopers to the scene. Rapidly the president walked back toward the tent, operating purely on the instinct to protect his family. He first encountered Munger. When the Yankee ordered him to surrender, Davis threw off the shawl and cloak, and defiantly shot back that he would never surrender to thieves and plunderers. Instead, he advanced on the man, thinking perhaps to employ an old trick he had learned in the war with Mexico whereby he could unseat the horseman by grabbing his boot heel out of its stirrup and flipping the man over the other side to the ground. He might then have been able to jump into the saddle himself and still get away, seeing that the only danger now was to himself and not his family. Uncertain what to do, the trooper held his fire as

Davis advanced, but he kept his carbine aimed at him. Just then Varina reached them, and seeing the gun still leveled at her husband, she ran up to him and threw her arms around his neck to shield him, crying out, "Don't shoot!"

Hers was a daring and selfless act, but it held Davis back for an instant; meanwhile other cavalrymen hastened to the scene. The whole episode happened in just seconds, and then the moment of opportunity was lost. It was too late now to run, and some of the troopers had recognized him. There was nothing he could do but give up. Munger ordered him to go back to the tents. "God's will be done," Davis muttered. Saying nothing more, he simply took Varina's arm and walked with her back to their tent, surrounded now by the cavalrymen with their carbines. Getting her safely inside, he stepped to the other side, where a campfire from the night before still smoldered, and sat down on a fallen tree to try to warm himself against the morning chill. There he struggled against the profound mental and emotional upheaval of the past few minutes in order to regain his wonted iron self-control, even as at last he was forced to come to grips with the now inevitable fact that his dreams of continuing the cause were dying before his eyes like the fading embers at his feet.[32]

Shortly the women were allowed to come out and begin to cook breakfast for the captives, while the cavalry commenced relieving everyone of their money, watches, jewelry, and even rifled through the clothing in their baggage, all while Davis resentfully looked on. Johnston lost his father's horse and saddle, and all of the others saw their mounts appropriated, some of the Yankees even quarrelling among themselves over who should have which booty. Only Lubbock, by pure stubbornness and combativeness, managed to hang on to most of the money Clark had given him a few days earlier. All the party got in return were promises that what was taken would be returned later, though it never was. At least Harrison took advantage of the commotion to empty onto the fire some personal letters and official papers still in his haversack.[33]

Witnessing all this, Johnston walked over to Davis. "This is a bad business, sir," he said. He could hear Varina sobbing inside the tent.

Bitterly the president looked up, still lost in reflection on the moment of his capture, and replied, "I would have heaved the scoundrel off his horse, but *she* caught me around the arms."

"It would have been useless," said Johnston, but that was no cheer to Davis now. He complained of the damp chill, noting that he had dropped the raglan before his capture, and Johnston gave him his own. There was still firing off in the distance, for the Federals had not yet determined conclusively that they were shooting at each other, and Johnston walked over to an officer and tried to convince him that there were no armed Confederates with the party and that everyone was now a prisoner. The officer rode off to investigate just as Pritchard returned to the camp, and Lubbock told him the same thing. Meanwhile, another officer, compiling a tally of the prisoners, approached Davis and demanded his name. The angry president told the fellow to find it out for himself, but before tempers could rise in response Varina gave the man what he wanted. Then Pritchard and another officer approached Davis, the other man addressing him rather contemptuously as "Jeff."

"Who commands these troops?" Davis demanded to know. Pritchard acknowledged that he was their commander.

"I suppose you consider it bravery to charge a train of defenseless women & children but it is *Theft*—it is *Vandalism*," he declared with what Pritchard thought was almost regal dignity. "You command a set of thieves and robbers," Davis went on in heat. "They rob women and children." Such men were not gentlemen and soldiers, but ruffians.

"Who may I call you?" an unruffled Pritchard calmly asked, not yet entirely sure of his identity.

"You may call me whom you are a mind to," Davis responded petulantly.

At that Pritchard felt sure of his man. "Well then," he responded, "I will call you Davis."

"I thought your government was more magnanimous than to be chasing women and children around over the country," said the president, sticking to his theme.[34]

"Mr. Davis," he said, "you should remember that you are a prisoner," and then remarked that such bravado was easy for a man who well knew that his captors could not harm him no matter what he said. The suggestion of cowardice only made Davis bristle the more.

"I am fully conscious of that," he shot back. "It would be bad enough to be the prisoner of soldiers and gentlemen; I am still lawful game, and would rather be dead than your prisoner." Hearing this, Lubbock spoke up in high temper and demanded that the officers in charge protect the president from such personal insults, threatening rather pointlessly that he would himself kill the offenders if he got the chance. Then Reagan added his voice, turning what Hathaway called "the edge of his Texas tongue" on the officers, even when one of the guard threatened to shoot if he did not keep still. The Yankees exchanged no more words with the agitated captive but rode off to consolidate their spoils, while Johnston vainly tried to calm the excited president and get him to reconcile himself to his condition.[35] Before long they ate what breakfast they could get down, Hathaway and his two comrades actually inviting a few Federal officers to dine with them, though when one of them became offensive, Hathaway gave him "a piece of my mind, which I did with a lot of soldier trimmings." Still in the main, even while plundering their belongings, the cavalrymen treated the captives themselves with courtesy.

Pritchard and his men did not yet know that, in fact, they had not taken the entire party. Campbell and his half dozen men were still out scouting when the attack came, and on approaching the camp and finding it in Yankee hands, they simply rode away. Earlier Thorburn had left some hours before the attack, intent on reaching Florida to ready his boat and expecting that Davis would come, even though the president himself adamantly denied that he ever committed himself to that route. In the darkness Thorburn had actually run into Pritchard's advancing troopers in Irwinville, and one or two fired at him. He returned their fire, but he easily outdistanced them on his horse, then rode hard for Florida. Some days later he reached the Indian River, to find his boat waiting. He had it made ready while he rode to Madison, Florida, where he had proposed all along that Davis should meet him. He would still be there waiting when news of the president's capture put a final end to his plans, and he destroyed the boat.[36]

Wood proved even more daring, as befit a bold sea raider. Captured shortly after he warned Varina Davis, he found himself under guard by the same German-born trooper who had grabbed his horse and saddle. Once Davis's attempt to get away failed, Wood joined him and Johnston at the breakfast fire, and in whispered conversation with the president confided that he thought he could get away. Davis told him to try if he could, and one or the other of them then advised young Johnston to join in the attempt, but he declined, thinking he would be condemned by his friends for thus abandoning Davis.[37] Wood then calmly and, as he hoped, unobtrusively strolled about the camp while the cavalrymen continued their ransacking of the wagons and baggage, until he encountered his former guard. He still had two twenty-dollar gold pieces in his pocket, and taking out one, he showed it to the trooper, who spoke little English. By words and signs, Wood indicated that he would give the coin to him if the fellow would take him into the woods by the creek. The trooper agreed, probably thinking the Confederate only wanted privacy to heed a call of nature. But once they reached the cover of the trees, Wood signaled for the man to leave him and return to the camp. The cavalryman shook his head in refusal, still holding his carbine pointed at Wood, who then took out the other gold piece, as he did so, turning his pockets out to show that there were no more. The soldier took the coin, weighed the situation for a moment, then lowered his carbine and walked back into the camp.

Wood immediately dropped down into the high sawgrass and alder brush, and crawled some distance into the swampy area along the creek where he would be out of sight. There he huddled for the next couple of hours until he heard the Yankees and their captors leave the camp and take the road for Macon. Not long after their departure, he saw a figure leading two horses out of the camp toward the creek, suddenly recognizing Captain

Stephen Barnwell, a South Carolina artilleryman and nephew of one of Davis's few close friends in the Confederate Congress, Senator Robert W. Barnwell. The twenty-three-year-old artilleryman was wounded and in the hospital at Greensboro when the government stopped there, and being a favorite of the president's, he attached himself to the party and had remained through Washington and beyond. Varina Davis affectionately spoke of him as "that gallant young soldier whom I shall never forget."[38] Wood came out of hiding to greet Barnwell, who had himself darted into the brush when the Federals first appeared, and together they led the horses into the cover of the woods, then went back later to scavenge what they could from the abandoned camp. They managed to assemble two makeshift saddles and bridles from remnants they found, including a small derringer pistol that Davis had given to Johnston a day or two earlier.[39] Of food there was only a little, and that they gave to a local man in return for directions to a house some ten miles south, where they would be well fed. By the end of that disastrous day, they, too, had disappeared south on the road to Florida.[40]

Meanwhile, the prisoners and their captors were off on the road for the four-day ride to Macon and General Wilson's headquarters, mounted again on their own horses, returned to them temporarily by the Federals for the journey. Davis they placed in the ambulance with Varina and the children. On their second day out they met with some of the rest of Pritchard's brigade, who showed them a broadside offering a one-hundred-thousand-dollar reward for Davis and other Confederate leaders believed to have had some part in plotting the murder of Lincoln. Pritchard handed a copy to Davis, who read it calmly. Already he and his family had heard the cavalrymen singing verses of the popular tune "We'll Hang Jeff Davis from a Sour Apple Tree." Now one trooper mounted the broadside on a flagpole and carried it along the column right before the eyes of his wife and children, planting in them fresh seeds of terror. "The miserable scoundrel who issued that proclamation knew better than these men that it was false," he told Varina. "Of course, such an accusation must fail at once; it may, however, render these people willing to assassinate me here." He believed the charge of complicity in the Lincoln conspiracy to be the work of his old enemy Andrew Johnson, now president. As a result, Davis had difficulty calming his family, especially when he spoke thus of his own possible murder, but even more so when thereafter along the way they heard repeated threats of retaliation. Some soldiers pointedly insulted him and spoke profanely in the hearing of his family.[41]

When they reached the outskirts of Macon on May 13, Pritchard stopped the column and drew his men up on either side of the road while he went into town to report to Wilson. He soon came back with another brigade to escort them the rest of the way. The Davis family in their ambulance endured a gauntlet of insults and profane oaths from the troopers as they rolled along between the lines. Finally they halted at the hotel where Wilson made his headquarters, as a considerable crowd gathered at the news of the celebrity prisoners and a local photographer set up his camera on a balcony opposite the hotel to capture the moment Davis stepped out of the ambulance onto the sidewalk, where a strong guard of soldiers stood in front of the entrance. As he approached, they stepped aside to allow him to pass through the door. Then, in what was probably an unthinking spontaneous act, they brought their carbines to the "present arms" position, a standard acknowledgment to a dignitary. It would be the last formal salute Davis would ever receive as president of the Confederacy, ironically given him by his enemy.[42]

That afternoon Davis had a somewhat cordial dinner with General Wilson, who showed considerable solicitude for him and his family, and then that evening they were put aboard a train for Savannah, to take a ship north to Fort Monroe, in Virginia, and prison. For Jefferson Davis, one war had ended, with another one just beginning, but the battle ahead would find him just as ready to fight as ever. Meanwhile, word of his capture spread rapidly, shocking the South but hardly coming as a surprise to many who had been with him on the journey from Richmond. When he heard of the episode, Duke spoke for many of the cavalrymen who had followed Davis as far as Washington, saying he believed that the president never really intended to escape but deliberately dawdled and actually wanted to be captured rather than outlive a cause he knew to be doomed. Though he was mistaken in that notion, there could be no denying that Davis probably could have gotten away had he made a concerted effort.[43]

Even his closest associates and friends blamed the president himself for his capture. A. Y. P. Garrett, who had been with the party until it left Greensboro, complained about the president's slow progress to that point, and the ever-loyal William Preston Johnston, himself now a prisoner, claimed the president's obsession with not leaving the Atlantic states while any organized Confederate troops remained had been a fatal mistake.[44] Virtually all of the final party—Varina, Campbell, Reagan, the aides, even Harrison—had repeatedly urged him to make greater haste, even if it meant leaving his family, yet as so often before he hesitated to be decisive. "Had Mr. Davis continued his journey without reference to us," Harrison believed, "there is every reason to suppose that he and his party would have escaped."[45] But Jefferson Davis felt two all-consuming commitments, the one to his cause and the other to his family, and in the final hours when the two came in conflict, he could not choose a higher loyalty.

Chapter Eleven

"THE LAST HOPE
IS GONE"

For all of those who had been left behind on the road from Richmond, Davis and Reagan were the first high officials captured, but that tally soon began to grow. The very next day after the surprise at Irwinville, Federal troopers rode up the drive of Vice President Alexander H. Stephens's home "Liberty Hall," at Crawfordville, just twenty miles south of Washington. Disenchanted with Davis early in the war, the vice president had all but divorced himself from the government after 1863, devoting most of his public energies to supporting the dissident antiadministration faction, while privately sulking that the president did not run the war and the government as the Georgian would have him do. When the collapse came, he made no effort to get away, adopting the fatalistic attitude that characterized him for much of his life. Robert Toombs, his closest friend in the world, left Washington on the afternoon of May 4, shortly after being given the sack of gold, and drove over in his carriage to spend a day or two with Stephens. Toombs announced that he had no intention of submitting to arrest should it come, for though he had not been a member of the government since he resigned as secretary of state in July 1861, still as an ardent secessionist and one of the founders of the Confederacy, he expected the Yankees would want him. But his friend "Little Aleck" would not run. He told Toombs that he intended to stay at home, gather his family around him, and await the inevitable, and so he did. Toombs soon returned to Washington by a circuitous route, concealing himself in a wagon part of the trip, while on May 11 Stephens calmly took the news that Federal cavalry had come to a halt outside his house. In fact, he already had a bag packed, and after very politely entertaining the Union commander in his library for a few minutes, he went with them to the depot in Crawfordville to board a train for Atlanta.[1]

The only good news was that Toombs was to have been arrested that same day but got away. After he returned to Washington, Toombs boldly remained in his home near the town square, even while the community teamed with Yankees, his effort to elude capture on the return from Liberty Hall appearing unnecessary, since the Federals seemed to show no interest. He even turned over to the garrison commander the six thousand dollars sent him by Breckinridge, wanting it used to supply homeward bound Confederates. But finally, only hours after Stephens's arrest, Toombs saw cavalry coming to his front door and correctly assumed that they wanted him. He simply walked out his back door and into a field, where a servant brought him a horse. That started him on six months of hiding, mostly in more remote northern counties, spending much of it fishing and hunting, and combating boredom more than danger.[2]

Nor was Toombs the only founding father on the run. Robert Barnwell Rhett, of South Carolina, most outspoken of all the secession "fire-eaters" and cousin of Captain Stephen Barnwell, fled from his home near Charleston when that city fell, in February 1865, and was now in hiding in a small farm outside Eufaula, Alabama, a place he aptly called "Castle Dismal." Wigfall was on his way back to Texas, if he could make it, and not a few Congressmen from Richmond sought hiding, not to mention even some generals. Most had no real need for concern, except those who had been former cabinet officials or prominent secessionists. Even Lee and Johnston had been paroled and allowed to go unmolested to their homes, and it soon became apparent that the Yankees were really only interested in the high civil officials and any others, like Clement Clay, whom they thought might have been involved in the Lincoln conspiracy. Even then, they were capricious. Former cabinet members James A. Seddon and R. M. T. Hunter went behind bars soon after the fall of Richmond, yet Union authorities made no effort to apprehend either Leroy P. Walker, the first secretary of war, nor Christopher G. Memminger, for three years secretary of the Treasury, both of whom remained undisturbed at their homes. Onetime Attorney General Thomas Watts, of Alabama, was governor of his state when he was arrested a few days before Davis, yet his immediate cabinet predecessor, Thomas Bragg, stayed at home in North Carolina without incident. On the other hand, most of the Confederate governors and even some former governors were apprehended, and before long Governors Brown, Vance, and others shared cells in Washington, D.C. Gustavus W.

Smith, secretary of war for only three days in 1862, found himself, too, sent to a Northern prison.

With Davis, Stephens, and Reagan in custody now, however, Federal interest would concentrate on their remaining executive compatriots, Breckinridge, Benjamin, Trenholm, Mallory, and George Davis. The attorney general, first to leave the party, went to hide at his brother's home in Camden, South Carolina, and so far had successfully eluded detection, though he was never a high Yankee priority. If he could, he hoped to get to the coast somewhere and take a ship abroad. The ailing Trenholm was simply too ill to run, and after he left the cabinet at Fort Mill, South Carolina, he got no farther than his home near Columbia. As for Mallory, he also decided not to flee. Upon leaving Washington on May 4, he went to Atlanta, and then on by rail to LaGrange, where he joined his family, but that was as far as he would go. He was tired of running. If the Federals wanted them, they could have them any time they chose.

That left Benjamin and Breckinridge, both equally wanted, and certainly there is no doubt that the secretary of state intended to get away. When he left Davis on the Savannah in Leovy's carriage, he took with him something over one thousand dollars in gold and a small trunk with his belongings. Unfortunately his initials "J. P. B." appeared on its top, and Reagan warned that they might betray his identity, but Benjamin was ready for that eventuality. "There is a Frenchman traveling in the Southern States who has the same initials," he told the postmaster, "and I can speak broken English like a Frenchman." Out of that same trunk he pulled a pair of goggles to cover his eyes, a large cloak to hide his rotundity, and something like an old farmer's hat that he jammed onto his head, the brim pulled well down over his face.

He may have appeared an oddity to any who passed them, especially with Leovy pretending to be his interpreter, but no one was likely to mistake him for the Confederate secretary of state. For the immediate future he became Monsieur Bonfals.[3]

For the next week Benjamin moved almost straight south on the road toward Madison, Florida. He traveled slowly in his carriage, making no more than twenty-five miles a day, yet still always a day ahead of Davis and his party coming behind him on the same road. Along the way he left nine hundred dollars with a friend to take to his sisters in LaGrange, and passed through Irwinville probably no more than a dozen hours before the ill-fated Davis party arrived. By the afternoon of May 11 the carriage and its occupants were about twenty miles below Irwinville when two riders overtook them. It was Wood and Barnwell, with the shocking news of Davis's capture. If Benjamin had been nervous during the flight from Richmond, he had even more cause now, learning that the Federal cavalry was less than a day behind him. Perhaps all that saved him from capture up to this point had been the fact that a single carriage attracted much less attention than the president's small cavalcade. Certainly his disguise helped, and his face was not anywhere as well known in the South as Davis's. Then, too, he had stopped shaving, and more than a week's growth of full beard rapidly covered the pudgy face that most men knew only to wear trimmed chin whiskers. Even Wood admitted that Benjamin was hard to recognize. Benjamin's horses being in far better condition, he could travel faster than Wood and Barnwell on their jaded mounts, and he declared in some anxiety that he intended to go on as fast as possible for Madison, which they believed to be clear of Yankees. Benjamin promised to wait for them there, where they could find a network of friends who would help them get somehow to safety. When they reunited they could make final plans on their best course for escape.[4]

For the next several days the two parties traveled independently, both keeping to back roads in the sparsely settled countryside. Benjamin covered more than thirty miles a day, sleeping at night in log huts by the road and subsisting on whatever he and Leovy could find on the way to eat, and yet he remained unfailingly cheerful and confident. His companion found him noble under adversity. "With all his plans shattered and without definite hope for the future, his superb confidence and courage raised him above all," said Leovy.[5] On May 13 they crossed the line into Florida, stopping at Monticello, not far from Madison, and sent word of Benjamin's arrival to the home of Brigadier General Joseph Finegan, Confederate commander in the area, himself now paroled. But then Benjamin learned from a local that Federal cavalry were actually in Madison. He had expected to meet Wood, and thought they might move toward Jacksonville, from there following the St. John's River down to the Indian River. It was much the same route advocated for Davis by Thorburn, and Benjamin may well have hoped to use the boat that Thorburn had ready for the president. But the presence of Yankees in Madison seemed to block his path in that direction. Moreover, Finegan or someone else told him that now there was no boat available on that eastern shore that could get him safely to Mexico or the Texas coast in the Trans-Mississippi. Finegan also gave him news of the reward for Davis and others. "Satisfied," said Benjamin, "of the savage cruelty with which the hostile government would treat any Confederate leader who might happen to fall into their hands," he decided to change his plans. Fearing that his pose as a Frenchman might work against him now, since no European was likely to be traveling in this backwater and Leovy had to return home and could not maintain the guise of interpreter, Benjamin changed his identify yet again. Now he would be a farmer from South Carolina, traveling on behalf of friends at home who wanted to buy land and resettle. Using some of the money still with him, he bought a rough saddle and outfit for the horse Leovy left with him, mounted his steed, and set off around Madison to the south, heading into the thinly settled counties of the Gulf coast, determined thereafter to avoid every village and keep to the most little-used roads.[6]

Hampered by their weak horses, whose backs were in such poor shape that most of the time they could not be ridden, Wood and Barnwell made much slower progress than Benjamin, passing themselves off along the way as paroled soldiers going home. Indeed, sometimes they had to drive the animals in front of them, only keeping the beasts in the hope that they might sell or trade them for food or money. After a day or two, however, they simply abandoned the horses, which were actually slowing them. On foot the two finally approached Valdosta on May 13, having walked most of the sixty miles from Irwinville. Barnwell's uncle Major Thomas Osborn Barnwell lived there, a refugee from South Carolina, and in his rude home they took refuge to rest for a couple of days, Wood even chancing a walk into Valdosta to buy some clothing since all his baggage had been looted or left behind. He found the hospitality of the Barnwell home delightful, not least of all because of his host's four teenaged daughters. Stephen Barnwell decided to remain at his uncle's when Wood left on May 15 for the expected rendezvous with Benjamin. Mounted on a better animal, he reached Madison that evening, and sent word to Finegan that he had arrived. The next morning Wood received a message summoning him to the general's home, and when he got there, he found a familiar face awaiting him, but not Benjamin's. It was Breckinridge.[7]

His adventures to date rivaled Wood's own. Upon riding into the woods on May 5, while his cousin's troopers faced the Yankee cavalry on the Woodstock road, Breckinridge and his companions struck out for the south, aiming first for Sandersville to pick up the president's trail. The general had been unwell recently, and that slowed him somewhat, but still he covered a good distance. Also, he was debating whether to press on to Florida when he caught up to Davis or still try to ride west as a decoy and perhaps get to Texas overland after all. The president's much smaller party now had at least a hope of traveling quickly and without attracting attention, and Breckinridge did not know that Davis was about to slow himself by staying with Varina's wagon train.[8]

During the night he came to two decisions. First, he resolved to head for Florida, either assuming that Davis would have no choice but to seek the same route, or else realizing in the face of his experience near Woodstock that the Federals were simply too numerous and widely spread for his hopes of misdirecting them away from Davis to work. The Yankees had more than enough resources to follow as many trails as they wished, meaning he could expect them to come after him the moment they got the scent. That influenced his second decision. His son Clifton was still with him, probably his favorite of his three boys, and so was James Clay. He could expect little but danger and hardship hereafter, and he decided not to subject them. Over their protests, he sent them to Fort Valley, near Macon, some fifty miles or more southwest, to his friend Robert M. Thompson. He wanted them to stay there for a month, perhaps, until things settled down, after which they should be able to get home to Kentucky. "I would gladly have died for you," said his son, but the general insisted. Before they separated, he gave Clifton a treasured saber that his brigade commanders had presented to him the year before, and with it a letter to Thompson in which, after asking him to look after the boys, the general passed his own judgment on his efforts to bring about an end to the war. "Should my friends ever know my part in the occurrences of the last three months," he said, "I venture to think it will give me an increased claim on their confidence and regard."[9]

Not long after the boys departed, their place in the file was filled partially when the clerk W. H. Swallow caught up with the general's party, having left Washington before the Yankees arrived. Now, in addition to Swallow, their company numbered Breckinridge, his oldest son Cabell, the servant Tom Ferguson, the general's friend and former adjutant Lieutenant Colonel James Wilson, and Major Oscar Dawson, also formerly of Breckinridge's staff.[10] They rode on that morning until the general's horse threw a shoe just outside Sparta. Leading the animal into town, Breckinridge stopped at the commodious home of a local doctor named Whitten and stepped up onto a wide porch where a number of paroled Confederate soldiers had stopped to ask for water and bread on their walk homeward. Apparently none knew the general to recognize him as he asked who lived there. "My horse has cast a shoe, and I wish to learn where I can have it replaced," he said. One of the soldiers said there was a man resting on a sofa in the hall who might be able to help him, and Breckinridge stepped through the door. Much to his amazement he saw Sutton S. Scott, commissioner of the Bureau of Indian Affairs in his own War Department, who had left Richmond on leave back in March in order to get his wife safely out of Columbus, Georgia, as Wilson's cavalry swept through.

"What are you doing here?" Breckinridge asked in surprise.

Scott could see a number of the lounging soldiers peering through the door, and was more than enough aware of recent events to know that Davis and the cabinet were somewhere in the vicinity. Seeing Breckinridge now could mean that the president was nearby, yet so were Federals, and it would not pay to give away the general's identity.

"Come in, Captain Thompson!" he said, then pointedly repeated the impromptu alias a few times for the benefit of the listeners at the door. "What am I doing here? Well, I suppose I am, like many others, just seeking a quiet place to rest." That said, he took Breckinridge into the parlor away from curious eyes, actually walking past his host without speaking or introducing the visitor. While the general sat down, Scott went back in the hall to tell his host that the visitor needed to get a horse shod, and probably some food for himself and his party. Feeling rather abused in his hospitality, the doctor at first mumbled something in disgust, then signaled his refusal with a grunt.

"Who is Captain Thompson, anyway," he barked, "and why didn't you introduce him to me?"

Only then did Scott realize that in his concern to get the general out of sight, he had forgotten the basic civilities. "Ah, yes," he replied. "You will understand—come with me now."

The two stepped back into the parlor, Scott closed the door behind them, and then said, "Dr. Whitten, permit me to present to you—General Breckinridge!"

Quite coincidentally, Whitten had been a political admirer of the Kentuckian for years, without ever meeting him, and thought more highly of him than of any of the other Confederate leaders. Now when Breckinridge gracefully extended his hand, Whitten was so surprised and caught up by the moment that he threw his arms around the general instead. Needless to say, there was no problem about getting the horse shod, and while they waited, Whitten, Scott, and Breckinridge enjoyed a hearty luncheon at Whitten's table, augmented by the last two bottles of prewar champagne left in his cellar. They stood and drank the final glass in silence, conviviality inevitably sobered by the sadness of the hour, and then after a handshake at last, Breckinridge rode off to rejoin his companions.[11]

The episode of Scott's hasty alias awakened Breckinridge to the need to disguise himself somewhat, if he had not thought of it already. His portrait in lithographs and engravings and even photographs had been widely reproduced and distributed all across the South during his political and military careers. Indeed, in many places his face would be better known than the president's. Consequently he cut off most of the long flowing moustaches that had been unique among Confederate high commanders. He had long before traded his uniform coat for the Kentucky hunting jacket he had been wearing for some time now, so there was nothing to indicate his rank, or even that he was a military man other than, perhaps, his riding boots. While he appreciated Scott's impromptu Thompson alias, he decided to choose one for himself, and settled on his own middle name. Henceforward on the journey, he would be Colonel Cabell.[12]

Breckinridge stopped that night some miles below Sparta, in Granite Hill, the home of Colonel A. J. Lane of the Forty-Ninth Georgia Infantry, where he met Lane's nephew Lieutenant Draughton S. Haynes, recently home after being paroled. Breckinridge probably knew Lane thanks to the prewar interest of both in horses, back in Kentucky, and now Lane sent young Haynes along with the general, as a guide through the unfamiliar countryside. The next morning Haynes led them south toward Sandersville. Along the way now, like the other fugitives, Breckinridge was husbanding his gold, instead leaving his belongings in return for favors or kindnesses, as with the French field binoculars he gave that morning to Mrs. Edgeworth Bird, a friend of Haynes's. By noon they reached the hamlet of Warthen, ten miles north of Sandersville, and while the rest made camp, Haynes took Breckinridge to the door of Colonel Richard Warthen's home in hopes of finding dinner. They tied their horses behind the house, out of sight of anyone who might pass on the road, and then, introducing Breckinridge as Colonel Cabell, Haynes and his companion ate well. During the meal the lieutenant asked Warthen to recommend a safe place to spend the night near Dublin, almost fifty miles south. Given a few names of friendly families, Haynes and Breckinridge excused themselves, pleading that they had a long way to go and must get started. Only after they left did another at the table, who recognized the Kentuckian, tell Warthen the real identity of his guest.[13]

They did not make it to Dublin that day in spite of hard riding, and the next day, May 8, the same heavy storm that delayed

Davis and his party also slowed their progress. Only that evening did they reach the bank of the Oconee, a mile or two from Dublin, unaware that the president was then just a good day's ride, about forty-five miles, south of them at Abbeville. Given the rate at which Davis was traveling with his family and the wagons, Breckinridge could catch up to him in another two days, and if he needed any inducement to make haste it came that night. One of their party went into Dublin after dark to buy a few provisions and came back without, he thought, exciting any suspicion. They made camp just a hundred yards off the roadside, and about midnight a squad of Yankee cavalry rode past their camp, close enough that the general could make out their uniforms in the lightning flashes. Breckinridge could not know if it was coincidence or if someone in Dublin had given them away, though most likely it was just one of the several elements closing in on Davis farther south. But the Kentuckian could not afford to tarry, regardless. He decided to try to leave before daylight and cover at least sixty miles the next day, crossing the Ocmulgee at Hawkinsville if possible.[14]

Despite their early start on May 9, they found that the heavy recent rains turned the rude country roads into mires that made their progress frustratingly slow. They rode until sometime after midnight before they finally halted, hungry, exhausted, some suffering chills and fever, and their animals worn out. They made camp in a thicket a mile or two short of the river and spent a bad night in the cold and damp. In the morning they awoke in much the same condition, and only took comfort in the belief that, for the moment at least, they were safe from Yankee pursuit. It would have shocked them rudely to know that the day before, Clifton Breckinridge and James Clay were taken prisoner near

Macon and that even as they awoke this morning, the president and his party were being surprised and captured. Seeing the need for all of them to recuperate a bit, Breckinridge decided they would stop for a rest at the first house they came to that day, where they could beg or buy a hot meal and give themselves and their mounts a rest. It was noon before they came upon a prosperous-looking farmhouse, and when they identified themselves, the occupants gladly offered them hospitality. While the horses ate, the men slept where they could; Breckinridge and the feverish Swallow were given beds in the house.

Isolated as their hosts' house appeared to be, it was not long before word somehow spread that important-looking guests were at the farm, and others in the neighborhood soon came to call. Their hosts told the visitors that the party were officers from Lee's army, heading home, but when the general rose from his nap and mingled with the callers in the parlor, Wilson feared that at least the older women did not entirely believe their story. More than once he caught a couple of them carefully looking at Breckinridge and then comparing him to a woodcut of Davis hanging on the wall. One woman wanted to hear a detailed description of each member of the cabinet, and as Wilson gave it, she kept staring at the general. Breckinridge, freshly washed and shaved, and changed into a broadcloth suit that he carried in his saddlebags, remained completely unperturbed and entertained the guests as if he were the host himself. Nevertheless, he may have found in the penetrating stare of those women a renewed impulse to keep moving. Instead of staying the night, Breckinridge announced to his party that they would leave that afternoon. Swallow, however, was too ill to go on, and would have to remain, promising that after a good night's sleep he would catch up. The general thanked his hosts, then rode off toward the Ocmulgee, leaving behind some suspicious old women and a young lady who told Swallow that she thought Breckinridge "a very pert gentleman."[15]

Breckinridge intended to cross the river on the Hawkinsville ferry, but before getting there Haynes spoke to an old planter, and then summoned Breckinridge for a whispered conversation that resulted in their leaving the road at a gallop. He was told that Yankees had been in town the day before—Pritchard's regiment—and clearly it was unsafe to venture there. The planter told Haynes of a boat tied on the bank a safe distance downriver from town, and following his directions, Haynes got them there, where they dismounted in a thicket only to find no boat. While Haynes set off to find it, the rest unsaddled and spread out on the ground, since it was still light. Ferguson brought a blanket for the general to lie on, and Breckinridge pulled from his saddlebag the copy of Plutarch's *Rise and Fall of Athens* given to him, ironically, when he passed through Sparta. Wilson looked on amazed. "What a subject to be read by such a man, so circumstanced, and at such a time?" he marveled.

Several hours passed before Haynes returned with the boat, and only then could they begin crossing the swollen stream. Wilson and Dawson did the paddling, first ferrying over the saddles and saddlebags. Then they had to cross each horse separately, making it swim almost three hundred yards alongside the boat, then climb a steep bank on the west shore. Finally, after more hours had passed, they rowed Cabell and Ferguson over, and only Wilson, Dawson, Haynes, and the general remained. The sun was setting now, and time for a safe crossing was short, but when Wilson went to get the general, he found him staring distractedly across the river. Wilson had to call him three times before Breckinridge acknowledged that he had heard, then he raised his hand for them to pause a moment. To complete what Wilson already thought an incredible moment, the Kentuckian stood in the twilight on the bank of the Ocmulgee and recited from memory A. B. Meek's popular poem "O, Come to the South," with its stanzas about a land of flowers, bright skies, and shimmering waters, of a region where "winter shall never intrusively come," and where life would "pass away like some delicate dream." It well depicted the scene before their eyes, but it must have struck them all that the South of the poem was all but gone behind them. A cruel winter had come out of the North after all, and it was Meek's South, their South, that was now passing away. "We remained almost spellbound by the grandeur of the occasion," said Wilson. None of them spoke during the final trip across the river until they reached the other side, when Breckinridge simply told them to mount and ride on.

The several hour delay at the river probably saved them from sharing Davis's fate. Soon after they made the road and started riding down the west bank, they met someone who told them that several hundred Yankee cavalry had passed that way just hours before them—the rest of Pritchard's regiment on its way to catch up with its commander and his captives. Meanwhile more Federal horsemen had arrived behind them at Hawkinsville. By sheer chance, the general's party hit the road in the stretch between the two bodies of the enemy, yet no more than a few miles from either.[16] As yet they would not have heard of Davis's capture that morning, but the news of the enemy was probably enough to impel them to ride well into the night to escape discovery. They would have heard the next morning, May 11, news spreading through the country that Davis had crossed the Ocmulgee at Abbeville two days earlier, with a host of Federal cavalry on his trail. Given their own narrow escape from Pritchard's men, they could easily credit such news, which had to have made them both more cautious themselves and anxious for the president. Their most direct route south was the road along the Ocmulgee, and they still found homes happy to feed them and their animals. A good day's ride on May 11 saw them through Abbeville, and hard riding the next brought them to the Alapaha River and Berrien County. That night or the next day, May 13, they reached Milltown, no more than a good day's distance from Madison.

So long as he could do so safely, Breckinridge intended to await Davis in Milltown, which the president would have to pass through on the way to Florida, and since there was no word of the Davis party having come as yet, he could assume that they were somewhere behind him after taking a more circuitous route from Abbeville to evade pursuit. On May 11 Breckinridge had sent Haynes back to get Swallow, whom he'd told to meet him here, and the two actually met on the road that same afternoon. The next morning, however, Swallow again felt too ill to continue. He sent Haynes back to Breckinridge with more news about the Yankee vise closing in on the president, urging the general to press on to Florida without delay. The lieutenant reached Milltown sometime late on May 13 or early the next day to deliver his news, and within hours the general learned even more. Yankees were patrolling in Berrien County, perhaps no more than fifteen miles behind him. And at last he learned somehow of Davis's capture.[17]

It had to be a shock, though probably not entirely unex-
pected. If the general felt any relief that at least he no longer
must fight the president over continuing the war west of the
Mississippi, he quickly realized that this was only half the
dreaded "farce" forestalled. Now, instead, there was the equally
humiliating and divisive probability of a public spectacle, a treason trial for Davis, Stephens, Reagan, and any others captured.
Such an event could only inflame sectional animosities, further
postpone the reconciliation he longed for, and lead to the quite
tangible possibility of hanging, guaranteeing that the "magnificent epic" would not end with dignity but in bitterness, hatred,
and more blood. Breckinridge probably learned now that
Stephens, too, had been taken. He already knew that Trenholm
would be captured and that Mallory did not intend to flee. No
one expected Benjamin to get away, and Attorney General
Davis, like his predecessors, was little better than a cipher in office, virtually unknown to the Confederate soldiers and people
alike. Even if not already captured himself, he could exert little
authority or leadership. This meant that soon Breckinridge
would likely be—if he was not already—the sole remaining
official of the government still at large and free to act and with
power to command remaining Confederate funds and agents
abroad. Moreover, as secretary of war, he was even now the
supreme authority over remaining armies in the field. Thus he
had two duties: the one to settle honorably as many Confederate debts as possible and bring any leftover financial resources
to bear to secure Davis and the others the best legal counsel
should they go to trial, and the other to command and oversee
the surrender of remaining forces in the field. Both responsibilities required that he, of all the cabinet, must not be taken.

Henceforward, the general realized, his sole immediate aim must be to get himself out of the country and across the Gulf to the Trans-Mississippi, realizing also that Yankee efforts must inevitably concentrate on him hereafter. Haynes had done good service as a guide, but now the general sent him off to his home, and Major Dawson with him, to reduce the party even more.[18] Accompanied only by Cabell, Wilson, and Tom Ferguson, Breckinridge left immediately for Madison, arriving a few miles outside town late that night at the home of Judge Benjamin Wardlaw, where several other Confederates were already enjoying the judge's hospitality. Haynes or someone else had advised him that Wardlaw's was a safe house.

Breckinridge had had a letter from a South Carolina friend introducing him to Daniel Livingston in Madison and saying that he begged Livingston to give the general all assistance, so the next morning Breckinridge risked going into Madison with Sampson Butler, another of Wardlaw's guests, to see the man. Livingston spoke with him about a good route to the Indian River and gave him a letter that would secure cooperation from Lewis Moseley, operator of a ferry on the Suwannee River some twenty miles southwest. He also traded a fast and fresh mare for the general's worn-out mount, and Breckinridge almost needed her speed after he left Livingston to visit some stores in town to secure fresh supplies for the trip, including a wide-brimmed straw sombrero to shield his face from the exposure he could expect ahead. Federal authorities had stationed a company of soldiers there to keep the peace, but in his civilian clothes, his moustaches gone, and perhaps already hidden beneath the sombrero, Breckinridge seemingly felt little fear of being recognized. However, a Yankee lieutenant immediately saw from the general's bearing or manner that he was not some ordinary north Florida Cracker. Not having seen him in town before, the officer could also assume that he was newly arrived, and just then anyone passing through attracted some suspicion. As a result, without actually recognizing Breckinridge, the lieutenant began to follow him about the town, finally confronting him and demanding to know who he was and what was his business. The general turned, stood erect to his full six feet, said not a word, and just stared the fellow full in the eyes. "The effect was magical," said Butler. "The man turned and went away, and we did not see him again."[19]

Wardlaw got word to General Finegan that Breckinridge was near, and that evening Finegan sent a message for Breckinridge to come to him. Intimately familiar with the country between there and the Indian River, as well as with friends who could be trusted, Finegan helped Breckinridge plan his route of escape and gave him more letters of introduction and safe passage. He also told him that Benjamin had passed through the vicinity a few days before, so at least Breckinridge knew that the secretary of state was still at large. Then came more heartening news when, probably while they were conferring, the word arrived that Wood had reached the vicinity.[20] At least someone escaped from the president's party, though the Yankees were anxious that no one else get away. That same day the New York *Herald* ran a report of Davis's capture, commenting that "such disposition of the national cavalry has been made as is believed will completely cut off the escape of Breckinridge himself, as well as of Judah P. Benjamin with the other Cabinet officers and fellow criminals."[21]

The next morning Wood and Breckinridge met at Finegan's and agreed to travel together, though they differed as to their route. Wood argued to head for Indian River, according to the old plan, and find a boat that they could sail to the Bahamas. Breckinridge needed to get to the Trans-Mississippi as quickly as possible and wanted to go to the Gulf coast instead. From there, if a boat could be had, the trip to Texas would be much faster than the voyage from the Bahamas down the Atlantic, around Florida, and across the Gulf. In either case, the first leg of their trip would have to be the same, through Gainesville, where Colonel J. J. Dickison would be able to help them and offer information that would likely settle their course. Wood and Wilson set off at once for Moscley's ferry, Breckinridge promising to join them on the road. Before he left, however, he reduced the party one more time. His son Cabell's health had already suffered somewhat after spending several months in a Union prison camp following his capture on Missionary Ridge in November 1863. As it happened, he was also seriously allergic to insect bites. Knowing what to expect in the swamps and along the rivers they would have to travel, Breckinridge decided not to risk his son on the journey and said farewell to him now, sending him on his way back to Kentucky. Then the general and Ferguson set off south along a swamp for the Suwannee.[22]

Moseley's son-in-law had served during the war under Breckinridge, and so the ferryman was delighted to accommodate the travelers in his home for the night, informing them as well that Benjamin had passed through there just two days earlier, meaning there was some hope of catching up to the secretary of state and including him in their party. The next morning they crossed the river and rode hard toward Gainesville on the old St. Augustine road, a little-used path through a pine wilderness in which during one twenty-mile stretch there was not a single source of drinkable water. They stopped for the night at a home in the tiny hamlet of Collins Post Office—the first time anyone charged them for hospitality—and the next evening, May 18, reached Gainesville after a ride of thirty-five miles.[23] They had hoped to stay at the home of James B. Dawkins, whom Breckinridge knew by reputation as a former Confederate congressman, but found the Dawkins home already crammed with visitors and had to settle for sleeping on the floor at a filthy tavern.

That same evening Breckinridge sent word of his arrival to Dickison and asked him to come immediately to consult with them, prudently signing the message only "Confederate officer." Dickison had no way of knowing who "officer" was, but well aware that prominent officials were reported on their way to and through Florida, he could easily assume that it was someone important enough to warrant his immediate departure. He traveled ten miles through the night and found Breckinridge the next morning at the Dawkins house, where now there was room for him. The general—who had actually appointed Dickison to his colonelcy just a month before, when at Greensboro—outlined his desire to get to the Gulf coast, barely sixty miles west, with which Gainesville had a direct connection via the Florida Rail Road, in order to reach Kirby Smith. Dickison soon persuaded him otherwise. He knew of no available boat fit for the open sea and doubted they could reach the Gulf coast, anyhow. Even then Yankees were preparing to parole Dickison's command a few miles north at Waldo, and more Federals were expected in Gainesville at any time. He did have a lifeboat he had taken when he captured the Yankee steamer *Columbine* a year earlier, however. The colonel had good men at his command who could get it ready for them and accompany them at least as far as the coast. He kept it hidden on the St. John's River, at Fort Butler, about sixty miles southwest. That would commit them to the Atlantic coast route, but it was the only alternative, and Breckinridge gratefully agreed.[24]

Dickison immediately left to begin making the arrangements. Wood agreed to meet them all the next day some distance south at a plantation, then rode off to the home of Breckinridge's old friend Senator David Yulee, thinking that Benjamin, and perhaps Thorburn, would have gone there for refuge after crossing the Suwannee. He found none of them there, not even Yulee, who returned during the night with the news that President Davis and the other captives were last heard of on the Georgia coast, going north by boat to an unknown destination. Yulee himself was so discouraged that he advised Wood to surrender and seek parole, but the sailor had been through too much already to think of giving up and the next day rode several hours to Orange Lake, some twenty-four miles south of Gainesville, where he rendezvoused with Breckinridge and the others at the luxurious plantation home of the wealthy Colonel Samuel Owens. Breckinridge's party found most hospitable entertainment there the night before, making up for the hard tavern floor, and spent May 20 resting and awaiting Wood, while back in La-Grange, Georgia, Mallory was being arrested at last and sent on his way to a Northern prison.

The next morning they were met by Dickison, with Lieutenant William McCardell and two soldiers, Sergeant Joseph O'Toole and Corporal Richard Russell, from Dickison's Second

Florida Cavalry. All of them gave their parole the day before at Waldo with the rest of the regiment, and in assisting Breckinridge now, they risked violating that parole, putting themselves in some danger. Nevertheless all were anxious to help. McCardell would act as their guide to the St. John's, while the two soldiers went ahead immediately to retrieve the boat from hiding and make it ready for a long voyage.[25] Dickison himself could go no farther, but he gave Wood his pistol when it was agreed that Wood and McCardell would ride ahead to check the safety of the road, skirting east of Ocala, and on some thirty miles south to Colonel A. G. Summer's plantation, Wauchula. There Breckinridge was to meet them in a couple of days.

Later that day the general continued the journey, deeply impressed with the hospitality being shown them almost everywhere. At each night's stop—now and hereafter—hosts refused to accept payment and sent them on to known safe houses from one night to another. "All through Florida we received nothing but kindness," the general remarked, and Wood found that no matter how the war may have impoverished some, they managed to send the travelers on their way with everything they needed for each day's journey.[26] They were still traveling as "Colonel Cabell" and his party of paroled soldiers, but Wood was sure several of their hosts had recognized Breckinridge, though he felt confident their secret was safe so far. They all might have felt even safer for the moment had they known that this same day off Cape Sable, the southernmost tip of the Florida mainland, Federal pickets captured a boat, bound for Cuba, with seven white men aboard, and the authorities believed the names these men gave were fictitious, reporting they suspected Breckinridge and perhaps Mallory were among them.

They were not, of course, but the names were false all the same, one of the men being Confederate Congressman Thomas A. Harris, of Missouri.[27]

On May 22 the general reached Wauchula and stayed that night and the next as Summer's guest, awaiting Wood. Their host even took Breckinridge and Wilson hunting, and the general killed one deer, which would be useful in filling out their larder for the trip. But he became a meal himself when he sat on a log and scores of chiggers or no-see-ums bored into his ankles, legs, and what he called "other parts of the person." After Wood rejoined them, they left Summers on May 24 and rode only about ten miles to the bank of Lake Weir, perhaps slowed now by Breckinridge, scratching himself raw from the itching of the bites and finding that some of them made sitting his saddle particularly uncomfortable. They bathed that night in the lake, probably the first bath the fugitives had enjoyed in two weeks or more. North of them, in both Florida and Georgia, more sad scenes of the dissolution were enacted.

After separating from Davis, Micajah Clark and the baggage train with the remaining Confederate treasure had continued on the road south, aiming for either Madison or Tallahassee. Clark was accompanied by Van Benthuysen and five Maryland Confederates, including Tench Tilghman, who had been a military engineer in Richmond before the fall. They reached the Ocmulgee on May 11 and continued on south, frequently traveling at night to avoid detection. "What will be our destiny is uncertain," Tilghman confided to his diary, "but we are hopeful." On May 15 they crossed into Florida, finding the trip tiring but pleasant, the passing farmhouses generous with their bread and fish. They soon learned that the northern part of the state was all but overrun with Yankees, however. The next day they got word that Cabell Breckinridge was in Madison without his father, and they feared that meant the general had been captured. But the fact that they heard nothing at all of the general possibly meant he was free and traveling largely undetected.

Clark and his party crossed the Suwannee at Moseley's ferry just a day after Breckinridge and continued on for several days until May 22, when they reached Yulee's home below Gainesville. Their host showed them Northern newspapers that brought the news of Davis's capture and Taylor's surrender, casting a gloom over them all. "Of course the last hope is gone of the Confederacy," Tilghman lamented. He determined that there was nothing left for him to do but surrender and give his parole.[28] Clark faced an even larger decision. The capture of Davis and Reagan left him, as acting treasurer, with the full responsibility for the money he was transporting. He concluded it was his duty to put into safe storage the papers and other materials in their wagons, and then get the money to England as quickly as possible, there to be used along with the money entrusted to Semple, either to fund continued operations in the Trans-Mississippi or to settle Confederate debts.

Van Benthuysen and his brother, Martin, strongly disagreed, however, Watson arguing that as senior military officer in the party, the decision was his. He said that, since the Confederacy was clearly defunct, there was no point in taking money abroad, and he demanded that they set aside a fourth of the treasure for the immediate support of Varina and the children, then divide the rest among themselves in payment for their services. Moreover, when all of the others agreed with the major, it was clear to Clark such a plan had been in the making for some days, and that alone he was powerless to resist. After the expenses of the journey south from Washington, they had something over $25,000 remaining, and on the day following the deciding argument Van Benthuysen distributed $1,940 to each of the seven members of the party, plus an additional $55 for traveling expenses. Obligingly he also gave Clark one month's pay and distributed another $600 among their cook, guards, and black servants. The balance, $6,790 for the Davis family, Watson Van Benthuysen would hold for delivery to his kinswoman Varina. Rather conveniently, he never got around to delivering it to her, and more than two years later Burton Harrison was still trying to shame Van Benthuysen into honoring his pledge. Finally, in 1867, he grudgingly handed over a fraction, just $1,071. Jefferson Davis would never forget or forgive the betrayal. Once again, it seemed, in the turmoil of the collapse, opportunism and greed proved greater forces than loyalty, honor, and even blood.[29]

Leaving the president's papers and other baggage with Yulee, the party broke up. Tilghman and the soldiers left to give their paroles, while Clark remained for a week, fearful that as a civil official he had more to fear of arrest, since he now held the same position for which Reagan was going to prison. Finally he hid his share of the gold and made his way to Atlanta, where he found Cabell Breckinridge safely on his way home. Clark was still concerned about the safety of executive papers left along the way, like those at Yulee's, thinking they might if captured be somehow used in the prosecution of Davis. He went on to Washington, Georgia, hoping to reclaim those left there in storage, but found it too full of Yankee soldiers to risk trying to secrete archives out of town. Instead he continued to Abbeville, where he went through the papers left with Leovy for several days, and burned those he thought of little consequence, repacked the others, and told Leovy to keep them well hidden. That done, the acting treasurer and indefatigable clerk went north to his Baltimore home without difficulty.[30] Behind him, Yulee went into Gainesville with the Van Benthuysens when they gave their parole. He was soon afterward arrested, and the stored boxes of Davis's effects were found in his keeping. Therein were a host of personal items—clothing, some of it recently worn and un-washed; a pistol; a fancy imported French rifle; razors and combs and the like; cigars; Confederate paper money; and a portrait of General Lee. There was also much private correspondence, some military telegrams, and several reports by Lee and others. Most interesting of all, however, were Davis's copies of the re-ports from his cabinet ministers on the Sherman-Johnston car-tel, offering in detail a glimpse into the last, troubled official days of the Confederate government.[31]

There was worse to come within hours of the breakup of Clark's party in Florida. The next morning, May 24, Richmond bank officials removed the Virginia specie from the vault in Washington, Georgia, and loaded it onto five wagons bound for home. They got as far as Abbeville, where they made camp just across the road from several groups of Vaughn's paroled soldiers going home. During the night some of those Confederates took the train by surprise, bound the guards, and emptied the wag-ons of about $250,000. They took off their trousers, tied knots at the cuffs, and filled the legs with gold, then threw the make-shift saddlebags over their horses' backs and rode off into the night. The next day the bank officials persuaded locals to help them apprehend the looters, and actually captured a few when one raider turned informant in disgruntlement after comrades, who got away with more than he, refused to share with him. The captors recovered $80,000 or more, but the bankers suspected their own posse might be in collusion with the raiders in concealing the rest. The officials went back to Washington and appealed to General E. P. Alexander to come take charge of the captives and bring a guard to return the money to Robertson's vault, which he did. When Alexander took charge of the money and prisoners the situation became so tense, as onlookers became outraged at armed Confederates threatening former soldiers, that a fight almost broke out. Alexander got the money back to Washington, only to see it eventually fall into Yankee hands, while the stolen treasure, except for a few hundred dollars in gold later found hidden in a hollow tree, was never seen again. Locals years hence told of friends who removed to Missouri and California with sudden fortunes, never to return.[32]

Meanwhile, Breckinridge's party then turned east the next morning, May 25, passing between low scrub and spruce pine on one side and a swamp on the other until they crossed the Oklawaha River on a punt so rickety that their horses had to swim over alongside. Breckinridge spent some of his gold that evening to lay in enough provisions to last them two weeks, while their host, Major Thomas Stark, gave McCardell directions on getting through the next day to reach the St. John's. The road all but ended now, and Wood lamented, "Here we bid good bye to civilization & launch out into the wilderness." The mosquitoes and other insects pestered them increasingly as they went farther south, and even staying indoors as they did this night at a plantation house, with thirty hard miles ahead of them on the morrow, they got almost no sleep. Breckinridge would have slept even less, perhaps, had he known that in Washington that afternoon a District of Columbia grand jury had returned an indictment against him for high treason, only adding to other similar indictments against him, Davis, and others. "The Davises, the Benjamins and the Breckinridges should die by the most disgraceful death known to our civilization," crowed the New York *Times*, "death on the Gallows."[33]

With McCardell picking the way through the forest scrub oak and dwarf pines, they walked and rode in the difficult sand for nearly thirty miles the following day, May 26, until, sometime in the afternoon, they came to Fort Butler at last. They found O'Toole and Russell waiting for them with the boat, and also Private P. Murphy of Dickison's regiment, whom the others had picked up along the way. The boat was about eighteen feet long, with a step for erecting a short mast well forward, rigged as a cutter, and four oars for rowing. Thinking it might serve them well enough for going down the river, Breckinridge was no sailor, and he felt less than sanguine about its possibilities for crossing a significant piece of ocean.

By 4 P.M. they had their provisions and belongings loaded and were ready to embark. They gave McCardell their horses—Wood's to keep as a gift and the rest probably to be given to those who had shown them hospitality—and Wood bought from the lieutenant a shotgun. McCardell should have been pleased enough at that, with a new horse and some money for his gun, but Breckinridge wanted to reward him, too.

"I will have but few more hours of authority," he said, "but such services as you have rendered your country deserve reward. You shall be a major; I will make out your commission now."

As the Kentuckian sat down to write the commission on a scrap of paper, McCardell seemed noticeably nonplussed, scratching his head as if he wanted to say something.

"Well, my friend," said Breckinridge.

"Well, you see, gineral, that's a feller in our regiment what hain't done nothin', and he is a major and a quartermaster," volunteered McCardell, "and if its all the same to you, I would just like to rank him for onst."

Breckinridge promptly completed the commission, making McCardell a lieutenant colonel. The irony, not to mention the humor, of the situation could not have escaped him. What likely would be his last official act, and therefore the last official act of the Confederate government itself, was to be a commission given largely in jest to a soldier who had already surrendered and given his parole. Breckinridge had never wanted either secession or the Confederacy, and now he brought both to a close with a joke. The occasion would have struck him all the more if he could have known that just a few hours earlier the bulk of the Trans-Mississippi army east of Texas, the last important Confederate armed force in the field, had surrendered in New Orleans. There was nothing left but some rapidly disintegrating Texas troops west of the Sabine, making his determination to reach the Trans-Mississippi moot.[34]

Once the seven of them were in the boat—for O'Toole, Russell, and Murphy were going along as far as the coast—the craft sank in the water nearly to its gunwales, adding to Breckinridge's concern about taking it to sea. Carefully they got out the oars and began rowing south up the north-flowing St. John's with a fair wind giving them some help in their sail. That evening a torrential thunderstorm soaked all of them, however, and they were forced to anchor in the stream, thankful only that the rain cooled the air and kept the mosquitoes off them temporarily. Cramped and sodden, they passed a wretched night without sleep, and found in the morning that the rain had ruined most of their dry provisions and soaked part of their store of gunpowder.

For the next two days they stayed at the oars in shifts, a good wind helping them along, while those not rowing replenished their food somewhat by tying ersatz flies and catching trout. Still, at night, there was no relief from the mosquitoes along the banks except by anchoring in midstream, which meant they had to sleep as best they could sitting up. Even then they could only stand it for four or five hours, after which they gave up and resumed rowing through the darkness. Breckinridge found the river bewildering. Though generally it flowed due north, it twisted so that the bow of the boat pointed in every direction of his compass as they rowed. Worse, numerous side channels made them lose the main stream more than once, wasting time and energy rowing up tributaries that suddenly came to an end. Wildlife abounded on either side, deer and pelican and cranes, as well as more sinister denizens. Huge alligators sunned themselves on the banks and frequently dove into the water to swim menacingly past their bow. Having witnessed the Confederate ironclad *Arkansas* in action on the Mississippi, Breckinridge likened the giant reptiles to "a gunboat low in the water." With his pistol he shot one that came too close, and they dragged it ashore, but it took three more bullets from his gun to kill it. Ugly as they were, the alligators made excellent eating along with the fresh fish, and when they found an abandoned orange grove, they managed to extract some sour juice and mix it with brown sugar to make a poor imitation of lemonade. By adding a bit from their store of rum, they could have a punch to brace them during the rainy nights.

On May 28 they pulled ashore at Holden's Landing, where the river suddenly widened to several miles to form Lake Monroe. They were nearing the Atlantic and the Indian River, and the next day would reach another widening of the river, called Lake Harney. From there they could reach the Indian River along the coast, if they could find a wagon and team to portage the boat roughly fifteen miles over level ground. O'Toole knew George Sauls and his family, who lived at Saulsville, a one-house community a few miles inland, and now he and Wood left to walk there to engage Sauls and his wagon. They returned in a few hours with word that Sauls would meet them the next day at Cook's Ferry near the mouth of Lake Harney.

Before Murphy left them to go home in the morning, he claimed the lifeboat belonged to him, and Breckinridge— grateful for Murphy's aid—did not argue but gave him a hundred dollars. Then they rowed on the twenty-five miles to Cook's Ferry, and when they arrived that evening, they found Sauls and his wagon waiting. Now more money had to change hands, for Sauls drove a hard bargain for his ox team and himself. Wood guessed him to be a mixture of African, Seminole, and Florida Cracker, a compound of shrewdness, laziness, and good humor, but Breckinridge quickly concluded that he was "very ignorant, but keener and more provident in all parts of a contract than any Yankee I ever saw." After some difficulty, they got the boat loaded—it was not so much a wagon as two independent sets of wheels on axles—and then passed the night with the Cooks, in real beds. Their hosts were old friends of O'Toole's, and Wood observed that the swelling middle of one of the daughters of the house suggested more than a passing familiarity.

At dawn on May 30 they started, the same day that Kirby Smith, now in Houston, came to a bitter decision. When he left his stymied forces in Louisiana to be surrendered, he had ordered Missouri, Arkansas, and some Louisiana troops that could get away, to follow him to Texas, where he expected to combine them with several thousand local cavalry to form a new army, to either compel honorable terms from the Yankees or struggle to the last. "With an army united in purpose, firm in resolve, and battling for the right," he said, "I believed God would yet give us the victory." But the Texans had disbanded themselves, plundered public property, and gone home. "You have made your choice," he said in a petulant proclamation. "You have voluntarily destroyed your organizations, and thrown away all means of resistance." There was nothing else he could do. "I am left a commander without an army—a general without troops." It was his own declaration that finally for him, too, the war was over. Soon he would be a fugitive, crossing the Rio Grande to Mexico.[35] There was not an organized body of Confederate troops left anywhere in the field now except one division of Cherokees and allied tribal troops led by General Stand Watie, who had somehow been overlooked in the earlier surrender negotiations. Like Breckinridge, they did not yet know of the surrender and dissolution of their army, but the news must reach them soon.

Almost at once the fugitives in Florida met trouble. Having provided the oxen, Sauls seemed to feel he had fulfilled his part of the bargain, and thus showed little inclination to help when the animals refused to work as a team. If one tried to pull in one direction, the other pulled in the opposite, and like as not, when they did move in the same direction, they brought the whole concern to an abrupt halt as each tried to pass on either side of a tree. The path was scarcely more than a trail, overgrown with tree roots that caught the wheels, and more than once the front pair of wheels simply pulled away from the rear ones, dropping the boat to the ground with a shattering thump, Sauls all the while hanging in the rear and reluctant to assist. In the end they got his help only by threatening not to feed him. All the way enormous black sand flies attacked men and animals, soon reducing heads and necks to a bloody mess so that whenever they came to a pond, the oxen simply collapsed into it for protection beneath the water, throwing the boat once more off the axles. Then it took enormous exertion to get them to rise and continue. Wood later concluded that, all things considered, it would have been easier for them to tie the oxen, throw them in the boat, and carry it on their own shoulders.[36] Still, by that evening, they reached a small creek no more than a couple of miles from the Indian River. The night was even worse than the day. Their cornmeal had been ruined by the rain, and all their salt dissolved, so there could be no bread, but at least sweet potatoes, bacon, and the last of their eggs, made a cheering dinner until swarms of mosquitoes from the marshy ground nearby settled on them. Out in the open they had no protection at all, other than to build a large fire and spend the night sitting up in its smoke.

Happily it was only an hour or two the next morning before they saw the waters of the Indian ahead and finally stopped at an uninhabited spot known as Carlisle's Landing. They unloaded the boat and gladly said farewell to Sauls, but not before he complained one of his oxen was so injured by the flies that it would surely die, and Breckinridge ought to pay him another five dollars for the loss of the animal. The general disagreed but decided it more prudent to pay the fellow, since he was convinced that Sauls had recognized him, and a little money might keep his mouth shut. He read Sauls well, for after the man got his money, he raised his hands and declared he had no idea who they were or what their business might be. He was simply a poor man hired to do a job and could not be held responsible for the consequences of what they were doing or what might happen to them. Several hundred miles north, in Washington, President Johnson had just issued an amnesty proclamation pardoning most former Confederates, a first step toward reconciliation, but it pointedly excluded all civil officers of the Confederacy as well as several other categories of individuals. Its phrases offered no haven for Breckinridge and Wood, or Benjamin wherever he was, and if Sauls was as mercenary as he appeared, he was cheaply bought at five dollars.

Breckinridge may not have realized until they reached the landing that the Indian was no river at all but an inland arm of the sea, three miles wide in places, separated from the ocean by a sandy strip of land no more than a mile in width, yet running intermittently for fully a hundred miles south along the coast. It had no current but rose and fell with the ocean tides, and now that tide was out and they had to push and pull the boat under a hot sun for nearly a mile across a mudflat, taking care not to step on the stingarees hidden in the ooze. When they finally got the boat afloat in the water, they checked it carefully to see if the rough trip had done any serious damage, but fortunately the leaks were few and easily caulked. That done, they got in, raised sail, and with a fair offshore wind headed south once more, on salt water at last.

Chapter Twelve

"WE ALL FELT PROFOUNDLY GRATEFUL"

"Our beloved *President* is in chains," wailed Clement Clay's wife, Virginia, when she heard the news.[1] During his dinner with General Wilson, Davis discussed freely his expectation that the North would bend every effort to try him as a traitor, and with it his conviction that he and the rest were guilty of no such crime. How could exercising their legal and constitutional right to reassume their sovereignty be treason? Indeed, the president refused to countenance that four years of war and more than three hundred thousand dead might rationally disincline the North to scruple at Davis's legal niceties. In fact, Wilson thought Davis almost mad in his complete unwillingness or inability to see another point of view in the matter, but then that had characterized him all his life. As for the charge of being

behind Lincoln's murder, the Confederate dismissed it contemptuously, adding that he knew without a doubt that at least
one man in the North knew it to be a lie, that man being the
president. "*He* knows that I would a thousand times rather have
Abraham Lincoln to deal with, as President of the United
States, than to have *him*," Davis said bitterly.[2] He may have regarded Lincoln as a usurper and tyrant, but that was far better
than being an ignorant, poor white Southern traitor.

Given his option, Davis chose to make the trip north by ship
rather than overland, and within an hour of the end of his dinner
with Wilson, he was on his way to Augusta, still under guard by
Pritchard and some of his troopers. They boarded a river steamer
that took them to Savannah, and there they transferred to an-
other vessel bound for the major Union naval base at Hilton
Head Island. Already memories closed in on the president, for
now he saw Vice President Stephens for the first time since
February. Estranged as they had been for some time, they
spoke briefly, with no effort to feign good feeling, and thereafter
Stephens kept largely to himself, pleading his perpetual illness.
Here, too, was Clement Clay, recently a Confederate agent in
Toronto and now charged with being involved with a supposed
Confederate Canadian connection to Lincoln's murder. And then
there was Wheeler, late as usual. The general had been captured
a few days after he left Washington, and having been taken on
the run, without a parole, he was arrested and sent north as well.
Hathaway and his Kentucky friends were also aboard, and found
that "grim old Reagan" kept his spirits best of all. At Hilton
Head they all transferred to an ocean steamer that set out on May
16 for an unknown destination to the north. During the voyage
Davis actually went to see Stephens, and for a change their mu-

tual resentment melted as they had a pleasant conversation. Clay desponded, as was his wont, Reagan shared a cabin and some conviviality with Stephens, and Wheeler typically hatched two hare-brained escape plots for Davis, both of which the president dismissed.[3] Three days later they anchored at Hampton Roads, Virginia, there to remain aboard for some time until orders came through for the disposition of the prisoners. The next day a tug took Lubbock, Johnston, and Wheeler to be sent to a Delaware prison. Soon Reagan and Stephens left to take another steamer north to cells in Fort Warren in Massachusetts.

Then, on May 22, another tug came for Davis, but only him, for Varina and the children were to be released immediately. The president then discovered that his was to be the shortest trip of all; the tug took him only from the steamer to Fort Monroe, scarcely a mile away. Walking into the fort, he was led to casemate number 2, which had been prepared as a cell. Inside he found a table and chair, a sofa, an iron cot, and nothing more. It had sparse accommodations for a man who believed he ought to be treated at least as a prisoner of state. Soon it became dramatically worse. On orders of Brigadier General Nelson Miles, his jailer, guards entered the cell the next day and locked leg irons and chains to his ankles, while a light was kept burning in his cell twenty-four hours a day, making sleep all but impossible. That same day Pritchard called on Varina and asked for the raglan that her husband had been wearing when captured. Ten days earlier Wilson heard a soldier rumor, perhaps not even from one of Pritchard's men actually on the scene, that Davis had tried to disguise himself as a woman. In the dim light that morning, with the long skirt of the raglan about his legs and Varina's shawl on his head, Davis might have been mistaken for a woman as he walked away in the drizzle, though such had never been his intent. Varina's trying to convince soldiers that it was only her mother would have added to the impression. Certainly at the time she hoped so.

Stories of the female clothing, filtered through rumor and resentment, and perhaps fueled by echoes of that earlier canard of his leaving Richmond in a dress, quickly became a full-blown accusation that the Confederate president had tried to elude captors in the most unmanly fashion possible. As soon as Washington got Wilson's report of the rumor it hit the Northern press and was already causing a sensation, unbeknownst to Davis himself, when he stepped into his cell. Orders went out to find any evidence in confirmation, those willing to "remember" an event they had not even witnessed were plentiful, and Union authorities prepared to humiliate the fallen president. Unfortunately, they got not a dress or petticoat or hoop skirt, as the exaggerated stories soon proclaimed, but only Varina's raglan, virtually identical to a man's. Pritchard later demanded the shawl, too, but even that was of little value, for men commonly wore shawls, Lincoln himself often covering his shoulders with one in the White House. Rather than put the two garments on display and risk killing the useful press exaggerations, Washington instead put them in a War Department safe, not to see daylight again for decades. Unable to humiliate Davis with evidence, authorities chose to let unbridled press exaggeration do the work in its place, for anything that embarrassed the captured leader might serve to reduce his stature in the eyes of former Confederates and lessen the chance of his becoming a symbolic rallying point for future resistance. Undoubtedly it occurred to some, too, that if they actually executed Davis, then anything that made him less a likely candidate for martyrdom only advanced their purpose. Not even pointed denials from several of Pritchard's men who were undeniable eyewitnesses, including Munger himself, could stop the frenzy, and generations passed before all but the most credulous accepted that the "hoop skirt" stories were false.[4]

By the end of the month, as Breckinridge and Wood embarked on the Indian River, Davis's conditions improved somewhat. Miles removed the irons, and a doctor was allowed to examine the prisoner, but the former president's spirits clearly plummeted in the days following as the magnitude of defeat finally and undeniably confronted him. His sight and hearing began to fail him, he could not remember things, he lost weight and his usually taut frame began to go flaccid. He could not eat, or refused to, and had trouble keeping down what he did swallow. Before long he would be spending entire days sitting in his chair staring through time rather than space. After the enormous emotional and physical concentration of the past two months, he was suffering a physical and nervous breakdown. Even his jailers began to worry for his health.[5]

If Davis was able to think of it during those dark hours in his soul, he might have taken slim comfort from the fact that at least not everyone in his government shared his captivity. Trenholm and George Davis were at large and undisturbed, and Breckinridge and Benjamin were both somewhere in Florida, on the run to be sure, but still free. After leaving Madison behind, Benjamin, too, rode to Moseley's ferry and crossed the Suwannee on February 15, two days ahead of Breckinridge. Thereafter he had little choice but to move along much the same route that Breckinridge and Wood would follow, south past Gainesville and Ocala, no doubt stopping briefly with his cousin Yulee, and then deeper into central Florida, his objective being the myriad inlets and keys above and below Tampa Bay, where surely he could get a boat to Cuba or the Bahamas. Posing now as a Mr. Howard, he rode thirty miles a day, slow for a more seasoned rider perhaps, but necessarily retarded by the need to keep to back roads, riding around every village and keeping to the least inhabited areas he could find.[6]

Even then the jolly "rotundity" did not avoid adventure altogether. More than once he stopped to stare in bewilderment at places where the unmarked road forked in several directions. Once he simply halted, unsaddled, and took a nap in the brush, hoping to see some other traveler pass who might direct him. Instead he was awakened rudely by hearing someone shout, "Hi for Jeff," a cry repeated again and again. Unable at first to see where it originated, he rose and followed the sound until he came to a small flock of birds, with a parrot in the center. Reasoning that any bird cheering for Jefferson Davis must belong to a loyal Confederate, Benjamin concluded that if he could follow it home he might get aid and directions from the owner. It took several pebbles thrown at the bird to herd it homeward, with the less than agile secretary of state running along behind, but finally it brought him to a house and assistance.[7]

It was late in May, about the 25th or 26th, when he met Major John Lesley, of Tampa, who led him westward to Robert Gamble's sugar plantation, on the Manatee River just south of Tampa Bay and only a few miles from the Gulf. Gamble was away from home, and Captain Archibald McNeil, himself hiding there from the Yankees, cordially welcomed Benjamin into the handsome two-story planter's house. There were several other refugees in the area as well, and with the Gulf in enemy hands and the Manatee navigable up to and beyond Gamble's, they kept a constant watch from the second-story gallery for signs of a Yankee gunboat coming upriver. Indeed, a few days after Benjamin's arrival, the Federals arrived unseen, appearing at the front door, and Benjamin and McNeil just had time to slip out the kitchen at the rear and hide in the cane. McNeil's dog loyally followed them, and its fearful master had to hold him tight and keep his muzzle still for fear he would bark and give them away. The soldiers had walked into the brush around them for a time, and the fugitives later claimed that at least one Yankee came within little more than the length of an arm before he passed them by without discovery. Even after the Federals left, Benjamin and McNeil stayed hidden outside until the cover of night allowed them to return to the house.

It isn't surprising that after such a fright, Mr. Howard decided to keep moving. He got McNeil's wife to make him an outfit from farmer's denim, to replace the shawl suit he wore out of Richmond, and engaged a shoemaker to remove the soles from his altogether too fashionable boots and sew them onto uppers made from coarse green fabric taken from his overcoat. The result was a rustic apparition that no one was likely to confuse with the urbane favorite of Davis's cabinet, and as soon as the suit was complete, McNeil took Benjamin across the river to the little community of Manatee, and the home of Captain Frederick Tresca, a French-born blockade runner during the war who knew the keys and inlets as well as anyone. Having himself passed through the patrolling Yankee gunboats many times, he perhaps better than anyone else would know how to slip Mr. Howard through the enemy cordon to Cuba or the

Bahamas. Indeed, on meeting Benjamin, Tresca offered to take him himself but warned that it would take some time to find and ready a suitable boat, lay in the supplies, and choose the right moment for the attempt. Until then, the ever amiable secretary of state settled down in the Tresca home to wait and enjoy the cool Gulf breezes, the sunsets, the fresh oranges and abundant seafood, and all the other hardships of refugee life in one of the most agreeable spots of the now-dead Confederacy.[8]

By this time the other fleeing cabinet member was enduring considerably less comfort on the opposite side of the Florida peninsula, even while erroneous Northern press reports said Breckinridge might already have reached Texas.[9] Once on their way down the brackish Indian, they found the so-called river anywhere from three to six miles wide, giving plenty of room to tack back and forth where necessary to take full advantage of any wind, though they had to row most of their first full day. As a result, they covered perhaps fifty miles on June 1, much of it through increasing rains that should have warned Wood, at least, that somewhere out in the Atlantic a terrible storm was gathering strength. Passing a couple of villages too tiny even to appear on the map Breckinridge had brought with him, and inhabited by folk more destitute than Wood had ever seen before, they stopped to trade some of their tobacco for watermelons, with people whose rags barely covered their bodies, and pulled over at the end of the day near the southern tip of Merritt Island to haul the boat out to caulk and repair more leaks that had appeared.[10] The mosquitoes and other insects let them alone when they were on the water, but as soon as they went ashore they became prey to every flying thing on the island. Breckinridge found their numbers and ferocity indescribable. "They attacked us not two or three at a time, but in swarms incessantly the whole night," he said. That night some of them tried to sleep on land, and the others in the boat, but the sand flies and mosquitoes gave no peace to either group, and the general found that even with both hands swatting them all night, still they bit. Unable to use his hands, a man would be killed in two days of this he feared, and took heart at least that he had sent Cabell home, convinced that the boy could not have survived.

Finally they gave up and, the wind being good, simply sailed on in the night, and the next day pressed on through the heat until a torrential rain that afternoon forced them simply to stop midstream for an hour, unable to see twenty feet in front of them through the downpour, and all hands put to bailing. Now the insects came at them all the time. Wood wrapped his head in a towel and put on buckskin gloves to protect his hands and wrists, while covering every other part of his body except his nostrils and his eyes, and the others did the same, as they could. They ventured ashore only to gather sour oranges and lemons from another abandoned grove, and collect coconuts. Once the heavy rain stopped and they determined just where they were, they realized that Indian River Inlet, an opening connecting the stream with the ocean, lay barely ten miles ahead. Directly opposite the opening lay Fort Capron, and friends along the way had warned them of Yankees posted there to stop any blockade runners from coming in through the inlet, or fleeing Confederates from getting out. The Indian was narrow enough there that they would be spotted easily in daylight, so they decided to wait until night and try to slip past in the dark. They tied towels and shirts to their oars to muffle their sounds, huddled low in the boat, and when satisfied it was dark enough, quietly rowed out into the middle of the stream and approached the inlet. Soon they saw a Federal guard fire on one bank, but thanks to care and the darkness, they managed to glide past undetected. Safely beyond, they landed and attempted to sleep once more, discovering that the only protection from the mosquitoes lay in burying all but their heads in the sand, and then covering their faces with their hats.[11]

June 3 they awoke and pulled on a few miles to an abandoned grove, where they picked limes and dug in the sand for fresh water. The citrus was beginning to become especially important as their provisions dwindled and they were subsisting more and more on their remaining sweet potatoes, coconuts, and the fish they could catch. Wilson even chanced a shot at a deer he saw on shore, but judging from the leisurely way it jumped away, turning from time to time to watch the boat with idle curiosity, he confessed to the amusement of the others that he might have missed. The addition of fresh meat to their stores would have been fortuitous, especially as they intended this to be their last day on the Indian. Breckinridge's map showed two openings to the ocean below them, Gilbert's Bar and, where the river effectively ended, Jupiter Inlet. They would have to pass through one or the other in order to continue down the Atlantic coast to a point from which they could make their bid to reach the Bahamas, the nearest neutral territory.

The voyage to Gilbert's Bar proved fair and easy, the river still wide and straight, but they found the channel to the sea effectively closed by a buildup of sand. With no choice but to press on, they entered the Jupiter Narrows, where suddenly the Indian closed dramatically into little more than a crooked and tangled series of swamps and bayous. They spent half a day trying to find their way through the maze, repeatedly getting lost or coming to dead ends, the water choked by grass and the mangrove, and juniper-laden banks closing in on them to create a jungle too thick to cut through. They had all but abandoned hope of finding their way to Jupiter Inlet when finally, by sheer chance, they emerged from one such tangle to see the ocean ahead of them, just over a low strand of sand not more than a hundred yards wide. In scarcely an hour they had carried their provisions to the beach, dragged the boat through the dunes and reloaded it, and around 5 P.M. pushed out through the surf onto the Atlantic. The old sailor Wood felt enormous relief at being on blue water again, and all of them took heart at leaving behind the snakes and alligators and the millions of mosquitoes.

Still they traded increased risk for their new comfort. From here on they would be exposed to every passing vessel. Just the day before, the press in New York ran an item stating that "the capture of Breckinridge is confidently expected by the authorities," who believed they had reliable information as to his whereabouts and were organizing a pursuit.[12] A reminder of the risk came home to them within an hour or two when they saw a steamer moving south just a mile out to sea. Happily it did not sight them, or took no interest, but out in the open now, even though keeping just far enough out not to be hampered by the surf, they would have no choice but to run ashore and hide in the dunes if spotted. The Yankee blockading fleet still patrolled this coast, so they could expect trouble, and in fact that night, as they continued rowing and sailing after dark, they passed an anchored vessel at Jupiter Inlet that Wood felt convinced was a Federal warship. They did not stop until fifteen miles south of the inlet, then went ashore and walked inland a mile to get fresh water from Lake Worth. Their provisions were dangerously low now, the hard tack exhausted, the sweet potatoes nearly gone, and their main staple, the turtle eggs they could dig daily on the beach. Boiled for ten minutes or more, they at least staved off hunger.

That afternoon, June 4, exhausted from the past several days, much of it passed without sleep, they napped on the beach until 5 P.M., unaware that hundreds of miles up that coast Stephen Mallory was even then walking into his cell in New York's Fort Lafayette. It was to avoid Mallory's fate that, when they woke, they packed the boat with as much fresh water as they could store and as many eggs as they could find, which they boiled. Now Russell and O'Toole announced that this was as far as they had intended to come. They did not engage to leave the country and felt no enthusiasm for an ocean voyage. Their loss would have reduced the complement to just four, hardly enough to work the boat twenty-four hours a day, especially if the voyage proved long. If they encountered other trouble along the way, the loss of two hands would seriously reduce the fugitives' ability to defend themselves, as they were soon to discover. Breckinridge made an earnest entreaty to the two soldiers, and they soon agreed to remain, evidence of the "manly and generous nature" that he saw in both of them.[13] After Wood read a prayer for their safe voyage, they pushed out once more, this time abandoning the shore and setting sail eastward, bound for the Bahamas. Unhappily, they soon found that for the rest of the day the wind came straight out of the east, making headway all but impossible. They never even got out of sight of land, and against such a breeze, there was no hope at all of covering the hundred miles to Grand Bahama Island, the nearest of the islands. With no choice, and no doubt discouraged, they turned back and kept moving south along the coast, hoping for a change in the wind. Then the inevitable happened.

They spotted a United States Navy transport steamer coming down close to shore from the north, and at once put in to the beach and hauled the boat out of the water, leaving one of the soldiers with it while the rest ran inland to the cover of some brush to wait until the vessel passed. When they saw that it was half a mile beyond, they returned to their boat, only to see the steamer come about and bear down toward them until within three hundred yards of the shore, when it lowered a boat full of sailors with pistols and cutlasses. In the instant, Breckinridge thought it was all over for them. They would be taken if they stayed with the boat, or marooned on a desolate coast if the Yankees chose to take or destroy their boat. Wood agreed, fearing starvation if they lost the boat and had to travel through the inland swamps. They chose to risk the latter, however. Breckinridge grabbed his pistols and valise and ran back over a sand dune into the brush with Ferguson and Wilson, even the black preparing to fight, while Wood decided to try to put the Yankees off.[14] With Russell and O'Toole, he pushed out and rowed to meet a boat being sent by the ship.

The officer in the Federal boat demanded to know who they were, and Wood replied that they were just paroled soldiers out fishing, producing O'Toole's and Russell's paroles as proof and lamenting that he had lost his own. As for the others the officer had seen leaving the beach, they were going inland for fresh water and had their paroles with them, if the Yankees wanted to make the long row to shore and back. Wood read the officer well, for the bluff worked. Indeed, the young Yankee was obviously inexperienced as a sailor and entirely ignorant of the coast he was patrolling. He actually asked Wood if there were any Confederate shore batteries in the vicinity—"a battery on a beach where [there] is not a white man within a hundred miles," the captain marveled to himself. Still, the Federals let them go after obligingly trading some tobacco for a few of their turtle eggs, and to complete their pose as ignorant fishermen, as he pulled back to shore Wood yelled back to ask if they wanted to buy any clams.[15]

Greatly relieved, they continued on their way once the steamer passed out of sight, and again sailed as best they could, with the wind now diminishing but still coming out of the east, continuing to make a Bahamas passage impossible. At eight the next morning they saw a few old tents on shore and pulled in to see if they could beg or purchase more provisions. It turned out to be a party of Seminoles after fish and turtle eggs. The only thing they had to offer the travelers were the remnants of the fish they had themselves eaten for breakfast, which Breckinridge, Wood, and the others ate eagerly, and some quantity of a crude bread made from a mashed root that they called *kuntee*, for which they traded some of the precious store of dry gunpowder. When cooked it looked like a thick pancake, though Breckinridge found it "ten times as tough," and Wood remarked that it was about like eating fried wood. Still, if they could keep it down, it would keep them alive.

Several hours later they spotted ahead a sailboat, with three men aboard, coming toward them. At first they felt some brief fear of discovery again, but then saw the boat change course to evade them. Breckinridge and Wood concluded that its occupants were themselves just as afraid, if not more so, and suspected them to be Federal deserters fearful of capture. It was a proper sailboat rather than a clumsy rowboat with a sail, and the two leaders decided at once to overhaul and take it. Laying on their oars, they soon overtook the sloop and fired a pistol shot across its bow. Seeing themselves outnumbered, the deserters hove to, and Wood ran the larger boat up to them. Breckinridge and Wilson, with pistols drawn, leaped into the sailboat, demanding to know who they were and their business. Satisfied that they were indeed Yankee deserters, the general had Wilson disarm them, and then made a bold front to intimidate them. As he later told it, he "put on a bold air and threatened the rascals with all sorts of dreadful things, but finally relented so far as to offer to let them off with an exchange of boats!" Their appearance helped the bluff. Sunbrowned from exposure for several weeks, unshaven, scarred from the insects, and clad in a blue flannel shirt and that straw sombrero so large its brim drooped either side of his head like an elephant's ears, the general looked every bit the pirate, while Wilson's visorless cavalry kepi gave him a distinctly unusual look, not to mention the towel turban on Wood's head. Carefully the occupants switched places, Wood gave the deserters directions to reach their destination at Savannah, and Breckinridge, perhaps embarrassed after all at his venture into piracy, handed them twenty dollars in gold for their boat.[16] Both boats parted company with delighted crews, the deserters at not having been taken prisoner or murdered, and the Confederates for having gotten themselves a proper sailing craft, just as long as their old one but much wider in the beam and thus somewhat more comfortable, with a centerboard for stability, a level deck over half the craft, and a sailing rig that stood a much better chance of breasting the ocean waves.

Wilson, irrepressibly good-humored as always, suggested to the others that at this pace, they might soon trade their way up to an ocean steamer, which would make their voyage much easier—though, on reflection, he regretted they, as pirates, had passed up the opportunity to be true to literature and lore by making the deserters walk the plank.[17]

Now they made an important decision. The prevailing winds were still against their making the Bahamas, but in their new and much more seaworthy craft, Wood was sure they could make the somewhat longer voyage across the Gulf to Cuba in a direction where the easterly wind would allow them to sail straight south on a handsome beam reach. Coincidentally that same day, a first report appeared that Breckinridge and others had made their escape on a boat sailing from the Florida coast.[18] To do that, however, they needed more food and water. They knew of a trading post at old Fort Dallas, in the bay formed by the beginning of the keys at Key Biscayne, and buoyed by Wood's declaration that in this boat they could cross the Atlantic if need be, they sailed on all that day and the next to reach the bay's entrance at the Boca Ratones, well after dark on June 7.[19] They found the opening but encountered so many shallows and reefs on which their boat grounded, and such a heavy ebb tide, that it took all night for them to get into the bay, and all the while their old friends the mosquitoes descended in swarms once again, Wood finding them "as ravenous & bloodthirsty as vampires."

It was dawn when they finally saw the ruins of old Fort Dallas across the bay on the mainland, at the mouth of the Miami River. They would have avoided it if they could have, expecting, for one thing, there might have been a Federal patrol boat in the area. But their meat was all gone and they were living on turtle eggs and *kuntee* now. Every time they went ashore they hunted more eggs and scoured the beach for anything edible, even greedily devouring some onions that somehow washed ashore from a passing vessel.[20] Wood said in some disgust that they were "scratching for a living," but they needed more nourishment than that if they were to attempt a several-day ocean voyage. The traders at Fort Dallas were their only hope now, the last settlement of any kind they could expect to find before heading into the Gulf.

They cautiously steered their boat toward the landing in front of an old barrack that served as the trading post, and soon saw two dozen rough-looking sorts, seemingly of every race and nationality, coming to meet them. It was clear enough from their clothing that many of them were deserters from both armies, a few Cubans, a couple of runaway slaves, and not a few Florida Tories who had fled here to escape service in the South's armies. The fugitives hove to some distance from the wharf, and when one of the men on shore shouted to ask who they were and what they wanted, Wood yelled back that they were coastal salvagers who had left their ship back beyond the reefs and came seeking water and provisions. The men in the boat refused the command to come ashore and prove their identity but said they would send one man in to buy what they needed, if allowed. A canoe came out to get him, but its occupants refused to accept O'Toole, who volunteered to go, and insisted on their commander, presumably Wood, who was doing the talking. Wood refused, even mentioning that they had intended to spend a little gold as a lure, but that failed to change the minds of the men in the canoe, who returned empty-handed.

Wood's unwise mention of gold, however, soon backfired, for as the men in the sailboat pulled out small oars and started to row away in a breeze too light to propel the boat on its own, they saw four or five canoes and bateaux shove off from the wharf with fifteen men or more, clearly bent on pursuit. Abandoning their oars, the fugitives looked to their arms, Wood his shotgun, Breckinridge and Wilson their pistols, Russell and O'Toole with their cavalry carbines, and Ferguson with yet another carbine. Then Breckinridge, having commanded in battles from Louisiana to Maryland, took over. The final land engagement of the war between organized forces had been fought out in Texas three weeks earlier, but with a delicious irony, it would now, on Biscayne Bay, be Breckinridge, the man who had striven for so long to end the war, who would himself direct probably the final hostile shots fired by Confederates anywhere on the continent.

As the lead canoe came within range, Russell tried a shot that broke a paddle or two and hit one of the rowers, the others immediately turning off from the chase. The next boat in line loosed a ragged volley of two or three shots, but the canoe itself was so unsteady in the water that they could not take effective aim. Breckinridge took a carbine and tried a shot next, perhaps the first and only time in his entire life that he fired at someone, and then only after the war was over. He missed, and so did Tom Ferguson. Then the general told them to stop shooting at random, load their weapons, and conserve their fire until the renegades were close enough that they could give them a deadly volley. Soon the range closed. Breckinridge had Russell and Wilson aimed at the man in front of the leading canoe. They fired, and he pitched over, upturning the boat and dunking the others. The two or three remaining boats sent a fruitless volley at them and then turned aside, out of range, for a consultation. The "battle" was over; the victors, a cabinet minister, a staff officer, a naval captain, two cavalrymen, and a slave.

Shortly their pursuers sent one canoe forward to parley, and after more discussion, they finally agreed to allow O'Toole to come ashore and make purchases. Breckinridge gave him fifty dollars in gold, far more than needed, the balance clearly an unspoken payment of tribute to prevent further pursuit, but even then they remained on their guard as O'Toole left them. Nearly three hours passed and O'Toole had not returned. Wary, they pulled their boat farther out into the water, fearing their friend had been killed and another attack on them would be coming. Then at last they saw a canoe put out, and when the sergeant came aboard, he brought twenty pounds of flour, two small casks of rum and water, some bread and fruit, sweet potatoes, and some pork. O'Toole recounted what had, indeed, been a near thing ashore, while the other ravenous fugitives cooked several chunks of pork, put them between pieces of bread to make sandwiches, chased them with toddies of rum and water, and devoured some oranges and bananas as a dessert.[21]

With full bellies, they continued south along the bay side of Key Biscayne to avoid the rough passage back through the Boca Ratones, and also to have the key shield them from detection by any Yankee steamers on the ocean side. That afternoon they tried to get back out to the Atlantic, but once more encountered shoals and reefs and no safe passage. They got out of the boat and waded, hauling the boat over the shallows most of the time, and meanwhile the mosquitoes attacked again, worse than ever before. It was 11 P.M. before they were on the ocean again, but within an hour they were sailing merrily south, leaving the land far behind. Unfortunately, in all the difficulty of getting the boat through the shallows, they lightened it by carrying or discarding much of the baggage, and in the process they again suffered the ruin of most of their flour, leaving them dangerously short on provisions once more. That evening, they landed on the ocean side of Elliott Key and again gathered eggs and coconuts to refill their larder, Breckinridge suggesting a milk punch from the coconuts and their little store of rum. Someone shot a pelican, which they cooked. Breckinridge was the first to eat a bit of the pelican, but he quickly disappeared into the brush for a few minutes to be ill, then returned and simply told Tom to throw out the rest.[22]

They had a fair wind at last, and though with Wilson at the tiller they bumped onto a reef or two in the darkness, the voyage ahead looked peaceful. But during the night the wind came up, driving a heavy squall, and the sea rose, waves breaking dangerously over the boat. Russell and O'Toole lay in the bottom, fighting seasickness, while an exhausted Ferguson slept, and Breckinridge, so weary, was actually close to sleep himself. Wood went forward to take in a reef in the mainsail as a precaution in the high wind, and left Wilson in charge of steering, one hand on the rudder and the other holding the rope or "sheet" that managed the sail. Either he, too, fell asleep momentarily, or he lost his grip on the tiller. The boat suddenly jibed away from the wind, the storm caught the mainmast boom and swung it across the deck and knocked Wood overboard, at the same time that a huge wave washed over them, so filling the boat that it nearly capsized. Startled instantly awake, Breckinridge saw Wood being dragged alongside, holding onto a halyard that happened to be in his hand when he went over, and then, looking astern, he saw "the celebrated Colonel Wilson" in a perfect terror, "holding on like grim death to the rudder." Worse, Wilson's grip on the mainsheet was holding the sail against the wind, pushing their gunwale beneath the waves, swamping the boat. No sailor himself, Breckinridge still knew enough to yell to Wilson to let go of the rope, and when he did, the boat instantly righted itself, while the general grabbed Wood and managed to haul him aboard. Wilson explained afterward that, not knowing anything about sailing, either, he thought it his duty to hold on firmly to everything lest "it might get some advantage of him."

Fortunately the storm abated during the day, the wind calmed, and everyone but Wood had a chance to rest a bit, though hereafter, no more than one of them was to sleep at a time.[23] Especially after his near loss during the night, Wood did most of the boat handling now, and since they were well out of sight of land and embarked across the Gulf Stream, they could only steer by Breckinridge's small pocket compass during the day, and by the stars at night. Fortunately, of course, all they had to do was keep heading generally south and they were bound to hit Cuba. They passed a steamer during the day, but it took no notice of them, but then the seas began to swell again, enough to make most of them nervous, and probably sufficient to warn Wood of what lay ahead. Late that night, June 9, the storm came on again, only with increasing fury, far beyond what they experienced before. By midnight Wood gave up trying to keep the boat on any course as the high waves tossed it to and fro. "A worse sea, I have never seen," he confessed, nor in a career at sea had he ever seen waves as high. Breckinridge knew they were in trouble when he looked at Wood at the helm and could see the worried look on his face. "It seemed to me that she must go under," said

Breckinridge, and Wood wondered "quite how our little boat lived through it." The worst was when two massive waves hit them in quick succession, and as they sank into the trough between them, the men looked up at twenty-foot-high walls of water on either side of their boat. They only stayed afloat by working for hours to keep their bow heading into the waves, for if any one of them had hit them broadside, it would have driven them under.[24]

Finally in the morning, with the coming of light, the storm began to subside, and then Wood confided to five other exhausted and emotionally drained men like himself that had they been in their old rowboat they would certainly have gone down. In his nineteen years at sea, he had never felt so much in fear for his life. But at least the storm drove them most of the way across the Gulf Stream. Now their problem was the sun, hunger, and thirst. They stretched a piece of canvas over part of the deck for some shade and took their remaining soaked hardtack and dried it in the sun. After their previous provision losses, there had been only enough for two biscuits per man each day, and half a pint of rum and water. Breckinridge had taken charge of rationing it to them with a rigid discipline a couple of days before.[25] Now, by dawn of June 10, both had given out, and they faced the palpable threat of death from a combination of exhaustion, thirst, starvation, and exposure. They depended on occasional rain showers that day for fresh water, which they caught in their hats.[26]

Providence came in the form of the threat they had been dodging for days, a Yankee ship. They began to see a number of sails in the distance that morning, but none close enough to have spotted them. Then, when they were almost too weak to work the boat, they saw their path about to converge with an approaching merchant schooner. The breeze being light, they unshipped their oars and rowed as best they could to approach, so desperate for food and water now that they felt no alternative, and in time came almost under the stern of the merchant ship *Neptune,* out of Bangor, Maine. Seeing their approach, the ship's captain prudently had some of his crew armed and ready, and called out for the sailboat to keep its distance. Wood yelled back some story to explain their being there without food or water, and, as Breckinridge thought, rather boldly demanded that the Yankees give them something to keep them alive. After some discussion, and in spite of lingering suspicion, the merchantman tossed over a small keg with five gallons of water, and a bag of a dozen biscuits. "They stared at us very hard," thought Breckinridge, but no questions were asked nor answers given, and the *Neptune* went on its way. Ever after the general believed that this Yankee captain saved their lives.[27]

Soon after passing out the new ration to each man, Breckinridge fell asleep and lay in the sun for several hours, only awakening well into the afternoon feeling severely ill from exposure, and with a pain in one of his ears that held on for weeks afterward. When he awoke, however, Wood gave him the good news that the color of the water was getting lighter, indicating a shallower bottom, and soon they spotted the Double-Headed Shot Keys, a series of islets he knew to be only a few miles off the Cuban coast. Combined with the last-minute blessing of bread and water, the sight so buoyed their spirits that they hoped to make landfall before dark. A few hours after twilight they saw the beacon of a lighthouse in the distance, which only made them the more optimistic, but exhaustion then overcame both

Breckinridge and Wood and they fell asleep, thinking it safe enough now to let Wilson steer them again. "That enterprising officer," Breckinridge said later, proceeded to steer straight for the lighthouse without thinking that it had to be built on some piece of land, and in the darkness, he almost ran them onto the rocks of a key before he woke the others and they made a quick change of course. Even at that they still ran aground on a coral reef, and worn out as they were, they had to get out and laboriously expend what little energy they had left in getting her off. Thereafter they set a course west, fearful to approach an unseen coastline any closer in the darkness. After all they had passed through, it would have been too ironic to kill themselves being caught in the rocks and currents of the very land that meant safety.

Taking shifts in sailing all night, they eagerly peered through the early light and made out a harbor and the houses of Cárdenas little more than ten miles ahead. It was Sunday morning, June 11. They had been on the run through Florida and along its coast for more than two weeks, and for Breckinridge it was thirty-eight days since he had ridden into the woods between Washington and Woodstock to begin his flight. For the past eight days and nights they had scarcely slept, and barely eaten more than that meal at Fort Dallas.[28] They sailed into the harbor, where they could hear the city's church bells ringing, and let down their anchor to wait for a port officer to allow them to come ashore. While they waited, Breckinridge asked Wood to read a prayer of thanksgiving. Already a crowd gathered on the wharf to gawk at the apparitions in the little sloop. They were sunburned to the color of copper, their beards grown, their eyes sunken in their heads from exhaustion and loss of weight, while their clothing showed all the rigor and hardship of their journey. Having had reports of Confederate officials trying to escape the South, some of the Cubans believed that Jefferson Davis must be in the boat.

While a harbor tug went out to tow them in, John Cahill, a Kentucky Confederate living here in exile, came down to the wharf to see the commotion, and as soon as the sloop was tied to the dock, he knew it was not Davis aboard. He watched as Breckinridge and the others stepped out of their boat. "His tall, erect figure, wrapped in a well-worn military cloak, towered above all others on that memorable morning," Cahill recalled. He immediately took it upon himself to be their interpreter. After he explained to the harbor authorities who Breckinridge was and how he had gotten there, the Cubans could not credit that such a boat could have survived the trip through the recent storms, and at first they were disinclined to believe, apparently suspecting that these men were renegades or perhaps pirates who preyed on Cuban coastal boats. Breckinridge did all that he could think to do under the circumstances. He took off the sword belt he wore, the last vestige of his uniform as a major general, and handed it over with his pistols, telling Wood and the others to do the same. That seemed to convince the authorities, but still they could not allow men without passports to go further without permission from the governor in Havana. Happily, the telegraph brought it before long, but still there were innumerable papers to be filled out, one of them a registry for their boat. It required a ship's name, which of course their little sloop did not have. But wasting no time, they soon made out the register for the good ship *No Name*.

Convinced at last of Breckinridge's identity, the harbor master then returned their arms with a small speech paying tribute not only to the general's record in the field but also the heroic journey that all had just completed. Even then they could not yet rest, for they had to be taken to the provincial governor in Cárdenas for a brief audience, and only after that were they shown to rooms at a hotel named appropriately enough for another outcast who made an historic voyage, El Hotel Cristóbal Colón. Still almost too weary to walk, they had coffee and breakfast at a nearby restaurant, and then finally went to their rooms to collapse for hours in the first beds they had seen in weeks. "We all felt profoundly grateful for our deliverance," Breckinridge said later. They might be exiles for the moment, and of course he still expected to rush to Texas as soon as possible, but at least, and at last, they had stopped running.[29]

That still left three other cabinet members at large, but not for long. One never ran at all, and three days after Breckinridge reached Cuba, Federal soldiers simply arrested Trenholm at his home and sent him to a cell at Fort Pulaski outside Savannah. George Davis had spent five weeks at Camden, South Carolina, and then made his way without incident across Georgia and into Florida. Even now he was hiding with friends on a plantation northwest of Gainesville, hesitant to continue his journey with all of the Federal cavalry swarming through the region, and uncertain what route to take. He would not start out again until three days after Breckinridge stepped ashore in Cárdenas.

That left Benjamin-Bonfals-Howard. He remained at Tresca's for three weeks or more waiting for companions and a boat that could take him down the coast and across the Gulf to Cuba or around the peninsula and out to the Bahamas. Two years earlier Captain John Curry had sunk a little sailboat called the *Blonde* in a tributary of the Manatee to hide it from the Yankees, and finally he and others managed to raise her and fit her out for an ocean voyage. Tresca meanwhile persuaded H. A. McLeod to help him sail her, and plans were laid to take her out of nearby Sarasota Bay, Benjamin offering them fifteen hundred dollars to get him safely away. A local minister guided Benjamin from Manatee overland the few miles to the bay, and there he met his boat and crew. On June 23, more than seven weeks since he had left Washington, Georgia, Benjamin was at last ready to leave the country.[30]

They sailed south along the coast uneventfully for the first two days until they came to Charlotte Harbor, just as Tresca spotted a Yankee patrol vessel. When it lowered a boat to chase them, Tresca put the *Blonde* into the harbor through a pass just above Gasparilla Island, and then immediately lowered sail and tried to hide in overhanging trees and brush behind the island. Before long they knew the hunters were near, and at one stage Tresca felt certain he could hear the voices of the Northern sailors, but the *Blonde* escaped detection. Shaken by the near miss, they spent the rest of that night and the following day and night on the island to give the Yankees plenty of time to leave the vicinity before they went back out through the pass and continued on their way once more.

It was not long before they were spotted by another patrol vessel, however, and this time Tresca and McLeod could find no handy way of eluding the boat party sent off to investigate them. Instead, Tresca told Benjamin to smear his face with soot and grease, put on an apron and skullcap, and pretend that he was the ship's cook. When the Federals came aboard, Tresca said they were just fishermen—and they fortunately had enough tackle and netting on the boat to look plausible—while Benjamin seemed convincing enough as a cook, though in leaving, the Yankee officer in charge remarked in amazement that "it's the first time I ever saw a Jew at common labor."

Had the Federal looked closer, he might have seen through the guise, for there was little on the boat for Benjamin to cook. They had not had time to stock the *Blonde* with provisions, and lived in the main on what fish they could catch. A boat hardly needed a cook to prepare the same menu of turtle eggs and coconuts that had subsisted Breckinridge and his party, and the little bacon they brought along was already exhausted. Another day's sail south, they found some bananas to expand their diet, and what they took aboard had to last them for several days as they continued without incident until they passed Cape Sable, fortunately missing the Federal guard that had captured Harris and his companions. Two more days at sea, escaping the kind of storms that almost killed Breckinridge and Wood, brought Benjamin to Knight's Key after a passage of more than ten days.

Tresca knew well enough that the little sixteen-foot *Blonde* was not up to making an open ocean voyage, especially as they determined now to head for the Bahamas, from which Benjamin expected to take passage to England. By now he knew of Davis's capture, had probably had word of Taylor's surrender and that of Kirby Smith's army, and may even have believed the stories that Breckinridge had been taken. There was no point in his attempting to get to Texas, if indeed he ever intended to try. Tresca quickly traded the *Blonde* and no doubt some of Benjamin's gold for a larger and more seaworthy yawl, and on June 7 they set out. They sailed along the keys before they lost sight of land at Indian Key and set a course northeast toward the Bimini Islands, the nearest part of the Bahamian chain.

Their first three days passed uneventfully, with fine weather and no Yankee ships sighting them. As he had during much of the flight from Richmond, Benjamin entertained his companions with droll stories and good cheer, but he turned suddenly very serious on July 9. The day had been intensely hot, and as evening approached they saw the telltale black clouds of squalls lining the horizon ahead of them. Though there was no land in sight as yet, they were close enough to their destination that the bottom was not too deep for them to drop anchor. Doing so, they took down their sail and unstepped the mast in order to ride out the storms without risking the loss of their vital rigging. Immobile now, they could only watch as a series of squalls slowly approached, soon surrounding them. Then about 9 P.M. they saw one approaching cloud suddenly dip down twisting, and as it touched the ocean a giant water spout arose from the surface in the tornado. Then another spout formed, and both came at them. "The furious whirl of the water could be distinctly heard," Benjamin wrote, "as in a long waving column that swayed about in the breeze and extended from the ocean up into the cloud, the spouts advanced." Had they hit the boat, the men would have been lost.

But at that instant the main squall of the group suddenly hit them full force. An immediate blast of wind and rain lashed their faces so severely that they had to turn their backs to keep their eyes open, but as they did so and opened their eyes again, they saw a third water spout forming to come directly at them from another direction. Until now the downward force of the rain and wind actually kept the surface waves low and posing no immediate danger, but then the first two water spouts raced past them no more than a hundred yards distant, and suddenly set the ocean surface furiously whirling and churning with a noise

Benjamin likened to the sound of Niagara Falls. When they could move, they began bailing the rainwater out to prevent swamping and then happily saw the sea go calm again as the squalls wore themselves out and disappeared almost as suddenly as they had come. As the danger passed, Benjamin used his hat to bail, and his good cheer returned. "McLeod," he remarked, "this is not like being Secretary of State." A few weeks later he looked back on the episode as "a scene and picture that has become photographed into my brain, and that I can never forget."[31]

The next day they reached the tiny island of Bimini, and here Benjamin parted company from Tresca and McLeod, their tasks done. After resting for two days he engaged passage on a sloop managed by three black crewmen taking a cargo of sponges to Nassau, where he could get steamer passage to England. They set sail the afternoon of July 13, but only an hour or two after dawn the next morning, they met trouble. The crew had jammed too much sponge into the hold, and it was wet as well. As the sponge dried, it expanded and forced open seams in the hull. Suddenly the overloaded vessel foundered on the Great Bahama Banks, and they just had time to climb aboard a skiff being towed behind, before she went down. Having so nearly met disaster less than a week before, Benjamin now found himself crowded with three blacks on a craft that leaked badly, with no sail and only one oar, and scarcely five inches of gunwale above the surface. Moreover, there had been time to grab only a little cask of water and a pot of rice just cooked. They were thirty miles from land, and certainly well out of sight of it, and they all knew that if any sort of bad

weather hit them, they would go down in an instant. Nevertheless they started off, Benjamin leaving the rowing to the blacks,
and for three hours or more they bobbed about on the sea, making their slow progress.

The weather spared them that morning, and about eleven
they sighted a sail in the distance. For the next six hours they
made for it, while happily the light wind did not itself take the
ship away, and by five o'clock that afternoon they came alongside the brig *Georgina* on an inspection tour of British light-
houses in the islands. Her captain welcomed them aboard and
considerately turned out of his way to return Benjamin to Bimini the next day. There he found Tresca and McLeod still in
port. Done with trusting his life to locals, he chartered the two
once more to take him to Nassau, and they left immediately, but
still his privations were not at an end. They hit so many squalls
and calms and contrary winds, that it took them six days to make
a passage of just one hundred miles, and they did not drop anchor at Nassau until the evening of July 21. On arriving he found
that no ship would leave for England for another month and if
he wanted to be on his way at all, he must take the schooner *Britannia* for Havana the next morning despite his exhaustion.

There was just time to send a few letters to his sister and others to let them know that he had safely reached neutral territory.
"I can as yet give you no idea of my plans or purposes," he confessed. "I can't tell what my condition is. I may be penniless."
He hoped to have some assets still in England, but if not, then
he would try to earn a living by writing for the British press. The
jolly "rotundity" who had so often entertained his companions
in flight, and whom none had expected to escape, remained

unruffled and pragmatic through it all. "I am contented and cheerful under all reverses," he wrote before boarding the *Britannia*. Three days later he reached Havana, where the same sympathizers who had recently welcomed Breckinridge showed him every hospitality. Kirby Smith was also there, having come from Mexico, and thus Benjamin surely knew now that there were no armies left, and no cause. He also heard of Davis being chained at Fort Monroe, and suspected that the Yankees intended to save themselves the trouble and possible embarrassment of a trial by simply mistreating the captive until he died of what Benjamin called "moral assassination."[32]

On August 6 he took ship again, on a steamer for St. Thomas, in the Virgin Islands, and once there, boarded an oceangoing ship for the voyage to England. His adventures were not quite over yet. He left St. Thomas on the afternoon of August 13, but just five hours later, when they were thirty miles out to sea, someone discovered a fire in the forward hold. The captain sounded the alarm, and all the passengers were called on deck, to the lifeboats. It must have seemed a routine drill for Benjamin by now. While he and the others waited for an order to abandon ship, the crew loaded provisions into the boats, and the captain meanwhile tried to get the vessel back to St. Thomas as other crewmen fought the fire. Happily, though they could not extinguish the blaze, they kept it from burning through the upper deck, which would have forced everyone to abandon ship. By 3 A.M., smoke pouring from her ports, and with seven feet of water in her hold, thanks to the fire pumps, she made St. Thomas again, where other vessels quickly helped put out the blaze. "If the fire had been discovered only one hour later,"

Benjamin mused, "I would have been cast adrift on the ocean for the third time in a little open boat." Two days later, repaired and refitted, the steamer left again, this time without misadventure, and he reached Southampton at last.[33] One of his first acts on arriving on August 20 was to write to a friend back in Delaware cheerfully confessing that through all his trials he remained in perfectly good health and spirits and was, he said, "rather pleasantly exalted by the feeling of triumph in disappointing the malice of my enemies."[34]

That left only George Davis, the often forgotten attorney general, who had seemingly been forgotten by the Yankees, too. He spent ten days near Gainesville, guarding his identity so closely that even the husband of a kinswoman with whom he stayed briefly was not told the true name of his guest. Davis moved on toward Ocala, where he stopped for nearly a week before going on south. This progress of brief journeys to change his hideout, followed by going to ground for several days, continued for the next three months until September, when he decided things had calmed enough that he could risk making a bid for escape. Then he went east to the coast at New Smyrna, where he found a sailboat bound for Nassau. With his money exhausted, he offered to work on the boat in return for his passage, but then his heart sank when he saw the vessel itself, a twenty-foot open craft with leaks in the hull and sails rotting from neglect. But it was a chance all the same. "I wouldn't be left behind," Davis recalled, and hoped that if he could survive six days in her, they would reach the Bahamas.

Those six days turned into thirty-three, for they hit the same strong easterly winds that had prevented Breckinridge from sailing for Nassau. Instead they simply spent day after day beating up and down the coast, trying to find favorable breezes. Meanwhile the owner was not much of a coastal sailor himself, or he would have noticed their general progress southward. They entered the Indian River and followed Breckinridge and Wood's route for several days, then crossed an inlet to the ocean again and kept on south until they reached the Keys, the attorney general maintaining his guise as a simple deckhand all the way and working as hard as any other. Continuing to yield to the wind, they sailed along the series of islands until finally, on October 18, they came to Key West, the southernmost tip of Florida. By now he had been a fugitive for almost six months since he had resigned from the cabinet, and he learned that much had happened while he was in hiding. The first of several amnesty proclamations had been issued, and after several months in prison, Stephens, Reagan, and Trenholm had actually been released, though Davis still languished at Fort Monroe, and Mallory remained behind bars. Yet everything suggested that if he gave himself up now, he would face nothing more than a few months of incarceration and then be allowed to return to his home, a far preferable alternative to an ocean voyage in this dreadful sailboat that would end in exile.

He decided to take the first available steamer north to surrender, but before he could do so, Federal naval officers arrested him. It was well into November before they sent him north on the ship *Memphis,* just days after the commerce raider *Shenandoah,* which had not learned of the surrenders until October, turned herself in at Liverpool, England, on November 6 and brought down the last flying Confederate flag. A day or two later, after months in hiding in north Georgia, Robert Toombs finally arrived in Havana on a steamer from New Orleans. "I have no idea what my destination will be—probably Fort LaFayette and solitary confinement," George Davis wrote on November 14 while aboard ship. "Even that will be preferable to the life I have been leading."[35] At last the running was over.

Aftermath

"WHEN ALL THESE WOUNDS ARE HEALED"

The United States govern-
ment, having captured all of
the high officials of the Confederacy but two, had no idea what
to do with them. With striking speed, the vindictiveness over
the war and Lincoln's assassination collapsed under the weight
of the relief that the long ordeal was done. Though feelings
remained high against the Southern leaders, sheer exhaustion
seemingly sapped Northerners of the energy to prosecute them.
While many continued to call for trials and executions, or else
lengthy prison terms, more reasonable elements prevailed. For
one thing, none of the captured leaders, not even Davis, had
been among those who brought about secession. Stephens, of
course, actually opposed it in Georgia, and of the rest not one
had even served as a founding father in the Montgomery convention that framed the Confederacy.

Moreover, there was the problem presented by treason trials themselves. The Constitution failed specifically to define what they had done as treason. They had not attempted to overthrow the United States government, nor had any of them been leaders in the separatist movement that resulted from secession. Rather, Davis and Stephens had been elected without seeking office, and the rest were simply appointees. On top of it all, as Reconstruction policies began to be implemented and Washington sought to engineer the referenda in the former Confederate states that would formally readmit them into the Union, it took little perception to realize that trying and punishing some of the most prominent citizens of those states would do nothing for reconciliation. Once the government's attempt to link leading Confederates with the Lincoln murder broke down, the final impulse for trials died. Indeed, Stephens, Reagan, and Trenholm were all released by the end of the summer, and George Davis spent only a few weeks in prison before being released on January 1, 1866. All of the arrested governors and former cabinet members were also soon freed, and only Mallory was held longer. Being secretary of the navy made him ultimately responsible—except for Jefferson Davis—for the privateering activities of Confederate vessels like the *Alabama* and Wood's *Tallahassee*, not to mention the *Shenandoah*, and another ten weeks passed after the attorney general's release before Mallory walked free. All of them left with some political disabilities until and unless they took an oath of allegiance and applied for pardon and the return of full rights of citizenship, but they were free.

That left only Jefferson Davis. Ironically, his initial harsh treatment worked in his favor, as even some Northern public opinion recoiled at his being manacled and mistreated. Indeed, his conditions rapidly improved during the summer of 1865, and so did his health and mental and emotional state. Influential Union editors called for leniency, especially when authorities failed to link him to the Lincoln assassination, even after employing perjured witnesses. The longer Davis stayed in his cell without trial, the more difficult it became to decide what to do with him, proof positive of Lincoln's and Sherman's wisdom in hoping that the president and his ministers might have simply gotten away. Grasping this, the longer he remained in Fort Monroe, the more Davis himself came to look forward to a trial. Convinced as ever of his infallibility, he actually believed he could prove himself, and therefore his cause, to have been in the right, and secession itself to have been a defense of constitutional rights rather than an act of disloyalty. Meanwhile legal and jurisdictional delays kept any sort of trial postponed for months. Finally on May 13, 1867, two years and three days after his capture, he was released on bail, posted largely by prominent Northerners. Another year and a half passed with no action, and finally, on December 5, 1868, the chief justice of the United States dismissed the treason indictments, declaring that since Davis had already lost the right to hold any state or federal office, thanks to the passage of the Fourteenth Amendment, he had therefore already been punished, and any further trial would be a violation of the ex post facto statute. Three weeks later the Universal Amnesty that President Johnson issued on Christmas punctuated the decision to put the war behind them. Even Jefferson Davis, if he so chose, was now eligible to apply for pardon.

It was that same amnesty that finally brought back home the man who had striven so hard against Davis in order to end the war in a manner that could pave the way for just this sort of relatively lenient peace to follow. As soon as Breckinridge and Wood and their party were rested, a sympathizer furnished them a special train car for their trip to Havana, but not before they sold their gallant little *No Name*. Five years later she would be washed out to sea in a hurricane, but then rescued and purchased by the same admirer who now gave them his rail car.[1] In Havana admirers furnished them free accommodations at the Hotel Cubano, and again they found themselves the center of much attention. Breckinridge, Wood, Wilson, and the others all spoke with reporters and gave repeated accounts of their recent adventure, but other than that, the general stayed quiet on public affairs in the Union, only repeating his remark that Lincoln's murder had cost the South her best friend in this dark hour.[2]

One reason for his reticence was Breckinridge's nearly shattered health. Along with Russell, O'Toole, and Tom Ferguson, he visited the Havana studio of the New York photographer Charles Fredericks, where they all sat for their portraits. Breckinridge's showed just what the last weeks had taken out of him. They all gave copies to their hostess at the hotel, but when Breckinridge sent a print to his wife, Mary, now safely returned to Kentucky from Richmond, along with a letter notifying her of his safe arrival, she recoiled in shock. It showed a man older than his forty-four years, worn, unwell, and with the palpable look of a deep sadness in his soul.[3] Others saw that same look here in Havana. They often found him lost in thought or distracted. Friends of long standing thought him greatly changed from the man they knew before the war. Known for his liveliness and charming manner in conversation or drawing room, he was moody and reticent, speaking much of the time only to those who had made the voyage with him.[4]

It was not just the hardship of his escape, though that would have been enough. Breckinridge, like the bleeding nation he had left behind, was exhausted from the emotional turmoil of fighting a war he despised, on behalf of a cause he never wanted, and, more recently, by the constant struggle during the months he held the War portfolio, sometimes standing almost alone against the president's will to fight on forever. The release of all that tension and energy on his arrival seemingly took with it every other sense and emotion for a few days, even relief at his own safety. Added to that was the realization that for an indefinite future he would be an exile. He continued to decline to speak on affairs in the United States for almost two weeks as he struggled to regain his former composure, not least because the news of Davis's sufferings in prison made it unwise to make any public statement that might be misconstrued and used to excuse further outrages against the president.[5]

It must have been within just hours of arriving in Cuba that Southerners in Cárdenas told the general of the surrender of Taylor and most of Kirby Smith's army, and the disbanding of the rest. That meant that at least there was no longer any purpose in his going to Texas. Instead, he would have to get to London to take over management of the remaining financial assets of the Confederacy, pay what outstanding accounts he could, and set aside money to engage counsel to defend Jefferson Davis and the others if a trial should come. But there was still one more thing he could do as secretary of war and now the highest-ranking member of the government at large and able to speak out. On June 23, coincidentally the same day that Stand Watie surrendered his little Indian division, the last remaining armed Confederates in the field, Breckinridge gave an interview to Havana correspondents from Washington and New York papers. Through them he called on all remaining Confederates to accept the verdict of the war, cease resisting, and ask for pardon.[6] It was the last address to the people of the dead Confederacy from a member of its government, a call that the general had wanted the president or the congress or the governors to make more than three months before.

That call was all he could do here in Cuba, other than close affairs with the Confederate consul in Havana and direct that remaining funds in his hands be held for Davis's defense. It was time to move on. Russell and O'Toole were ready go home. Fearful that they might be arrested for being a party to his escape, he gave them a letter addressed to their former commander Dickison in which he made it clear—whether truthful or not—that they had not wanted to leave Florida and only did so in response to his own earnest entreaties. At the same time, he reassured Dickison that he should be in no danger for his own role, since at the time of their meeting, Breckinridge had, in his own words, "ceased to be a belligerent."[7] In fact, the general had formed a considerable fondness for the two soldiers. When he offered to pay them for their aid, they refused, and so instead he gave them his half of the money he and Wood had received for the *No Name*, money that rightfully should have been entirely his since he had paid for both that boat and the one traded for her. Now he also arranged the soldiers' passage to Mobile, and before they left gave his map of Florida to Russell as a souvenir of what he called "our adventures, which may be termed both singular and perilous."[8] Even then Russell, at least, never spoke of his part in the escape, perhaps because he could not help attracting unfortunate attention to himself otherwise.

For years afterward, through six marriages, thirteen children, two divorces, one charge of bigamy and another for abandonment, and near-lynching for his shooting of a black marshal in Ocala, his family always assumed his voyage to Cuba was to escape from prosecution for the shooting, which actually happened years afterward.[9]

Tom Ferguson wanted to go home, too. He had never been Breckinridge's slave, his family belonging to the general's Kentucky friend Jilson Johnson, who had loaned Ferguson to the general during the war. But Tom was not yet legally free, for the Emancipation Proclamation did not affect Kentucky, which had remained in the Union. Even though Congress passed the Thirteenth Amendment in February and the states were in the act of ratifying, it would be December before enough of the re-entering Southern state legislatures added their votes to achieve adoption. Thus technically he was subject to arrest if any authority so chose, though with universal abolition soon inevitable, it would have been pointless. Nevertheless, the resentment in some of the slave states against emancipation, and thus against blacks themselves, was sufficient that Breckinridge thought it best to give Ferguson his own testimonial and letter of safe conduct. "On many occasions of peril and hardship he has proved himself courageous and faithfull," wrote the general on July 7. "He deserves and I hope he will receive such protection and advice as he may need on his journey." Shown such a letter from Breckinridge, no Southerner would interfere with the twenty-one-year-old Ferguson as he, too, went home.[10]

That letter for Tom and the purchase of his passage back to Mobile were the general's last acts in Havana, for that same day, he, too, boarded a steamer to begin his crossing of the Atlantic.

Wood had already gone off to Nova Scotia to spend the rest of his life an exile. So had Wilson, his goal Canada and the growing colony of Confederate expatriates in Toronto, as well as matrimony to a young woman whose name he confessed that at the moment he had forgotten. Now Ferguson, Russell, and O'Toole all accompanied Breckinridge to the wharf as he boarded the steamer *Conway* for his voyage. Even then his recent adventure was still the talk of the salons and editorials, the Havana correspondent of the New York *Herald* speculating that "the manner of his escape from the coast of Florida savors of the romantic, and may yet form the groundwork of an exciting novel or thrilling drama."[11]

Perhaps it would. Certainly Wilson felt the melodramatic lure of their epic, though he complained that he would have to wait until Breckinridge and Wood and all the others were dead before he could publish the story the way he wanted to tell it. "But for the living witnesses who would accuse me, what Munchausen stories I would invent," he told the general. Given his preference, he would have them murdering one old man who crossed them along the way, forcing the deserters whose boat they took to walk a plank to their deaths in the Atlantic, and but for the problem of finding some way to save their lives, would have the *No Name* going to the bottom of the Gulf. "Indeed," the irrepressible colonel confessed, "I have at times felt some mortification that we were not totally wrecked."[12]

On reaching England Breckinridge attempted to settle remaining Confederate affairs, finding them so heavily in debt that little was left to aid Davis's defense, and moreover discovering that one agent who did still have substantial funds, Jacob Thompson, refused to turn over the money. When Benjamin reached England he and Breckinridge both tried to get Thompson to cooperate, but in the end had no choice but to accept a small remittance, while Thompson kept more than one hundred thousand dollars for himself. That same "game of grab" that Eliza Andrews condemned as "every man for himself" could be played by diplomats as well as demoralized soldiers.[13] Months after the fighting was done, there could still be elements of the "farce" in the closing of Confederate affairs. The best Benjamin and Breckinridge could do was keep it quiet.

"My own future is quite uncertain," the general told a friend that fall, "but I trust we shall meet when all these wounds are healed over."[14] In fact, few of them ever met again. Mallory went back to the law in Florida after his release, but never reentered politics before his death, in 1873, the first of them to die. Trenholm finally recovered his health, though his wealth was lost, yet within three years he had a second fortune on the way. He served briefly in the South Carolina legislature before he died in 1876. Stephens, too, reentered politics, only with much more gusto, winning seats in the House and Senate before being elected governor of Georgia, in 1882. He died the next year, shortly after taking office. Benjamin never looked back, nor did he ever return to the South. Instead, he read law for a time, became a barrister and eventually a Queens Counsel and a confirmed Englishman, dying in Paris in 1884. One who visited with him in 1875 noted that Benjamin "did not live in the past."[15] George Davis also returned to the law in Wilmington, North Carolina, and died there in 1896. Reagan returned to politics and Congress, and lived until 1905, the last survivor of the cabinet.

Breckinridge's own future would be tragically brief, for all but Mallory outlived him. He spent the next three and a half years in exile in England and Canada, in the end moving to Niagara-on-the-Lake in Ontario so he could look across the Niagara River to see the Stars and Stripes flying over Fort Niagara, New York. There he waited until Johnson's Christmas amnesty in 1868. Of course, he could have gone home long before then, as friends urged him to do, for the experience of the other cabinet ministers made clear that he had nothing to fear. Yet he saw a matter of principle in play, for even after earlier amnesty proclamations, several categories of former Confederates lived either under indictments or other civil disabilities, and there were thousands of others living in voluntary or forced exile throughout the world. Thus he determined that he would not go home until everyone could. In the end the numerous influential friends working on Johnson on his behalf helped persuade the president to take care of all of them with his Universal Amnesty.

Immediately after that, the general went back to Kentucky, the lion of the hour. Parties on all sides urged him to seek office again, the Senate or the governorship, but he refused. The war had taken something out of him that he never regained. "Politically I am an extinct volcano," he told his friends, yet still he exerted some influence. He spoke out constantly for patience and forbearance between the sections, for reconciliation. He condemned as villains all extremists, including the new Ku Klux Klan, and championed the extension of rights for blacks in Kentucky, including their right to testify in court in cases against white defendants. He encouraged rebuilding, and the economic and industrial development of the South, and he helped construct a railroad to open up backward eastern Kentucky. Through it all, he refused to engage in the increasingly bitter public quarrels between old Confederates over who was responsible for losing this or that battle, or worse, the war. While Jefferson Davis pursued heated feuds with Joseph E. Johnston, Beauregard, and several others, and as the generals squabbled unbecomingly among themselves, he kept out of the fray and advised them to do the same, ever mindful that even years after the war some high-ranking Confederates were themselves tarnishing the memory of their magnificent epic.

As 1876 approached, the nation planned to celebrate its Centennial in Philadelphia. The organizers had frequently consulted Breckinridge in the preceding years regarding plans and arrangements, and by 1875 he had become such a symbol of reconciliation that people North and South called for him to be the occasion's opening ceremony orator the following year, on July 4. He might have done it if invited, but the opportunity never came. His health had been failing for months, the combination of a wartime injury and the wear of his years of campaigning, compounded no doubt by the extreme rigors of his escape. He was only fifty-four, but his once robust constitution had been ravaged. After several days of illness and an operation on his lungs, complications settled into pneumonia, and on the afternoon of May 17, 1875, he died peacefully at his home in Lexington, surrounded by friends and family, ten years to the day after he crossed the Suwannee on the beginning of his flight through Florida. Kentucky mourned for days.[16]

His great opponent, his friendly antagonist in those last days of the Confederacy, outlived him by many years. After his release from Fort Monroe, Jefferson Davis also went abroad, but not to exile. He continued to hope, in fact, that he would someday get his trial, even after the chief justice quashed the indictments against him. Meanwhile, he sought to rebuild his life. He settled in Memphis for a time and tried to prosper in the insurance business, but that failed, and years of litigation postponed his hopes of regaining his cotton plantation and renewing the life he best loved as a planter. Finally, in 1877, he moved to Biloxi, Mississippi, where a friend allowed him to live without rent in a pleasant house on the Gulf coast, and there he embarked on a memoir in the hope that he could make enough to support his family. Typical of the man, it was no memoir at all, but an apologia, a defense of himself, a prosecution of his enemies—Union and Confederate—and a justification for the South in seceding and for the Confederacy in seeking independence.

It was the argument he never got to make in court, and his response to the mendacious memoirs already being published by Johnston and others as they sought to lay their failures at his door. Blinkered, frequently bigoted, and thoroughly contentious throughout, it was typical of the worst in the man. What he did not wish to admit, he simply wrote out of his history. Inconvenient facts he ignored, and embarrassing incidents he expunged. His failures were really those of others; his only mistakes had been putting faith in subordinates who then let him down. In the rush to publish he did not even allow time to write all of it himself, and engaged two writers, one for each volume, while he gathered papers and recollections from old friends and faithful subordinates to serve as material for their pens. At the end, when he read the final text in print, he was more than once surprised to see what they had written on his behalf. In a gesture that said so much of the man, he insisted that the publishers include at the conclusion of *Rise and Fall of the Confederate Government*, when it appeared in 1881, a statement absolving him of responsibility for any changes the publisher had made in his spelling.

Jefferson Davis was never loved by his people during the war the way Northerners revered Lincoln, nor did former Confederates treat him with the sort of veneration they felt for Robert E. Lee, who outlived Appomattox by a mere five years. That lay largely in the nature of the man, for not knowing how to inspire popularity, he never courted it, instead disdaining such pandering to the masses as beneath his dignity. Yet in spite of himself over the years, he gradually won respect, even admiration, from former Confederates, based not on his human qualities—which he rarely let them see—but on what he had suffered on their behalf. During his imprisonment Jefferson Davis became a martyr for them all, a role he was quite ready to play and play well. Southerners saw in his imprisonment and the manacles and the other indignities a Christ-like figure suffering for their sins, and in the long years after his release, Davis's struggle to regain his personal and financial fortunes mirrored those of all. Again almost in spite of himself, by the time he died in New Orleans in 1889, he had acquired an enormous popularity in the South, not for the man he was but for the symbol he had become.[17]

In October 1870, when Lee died, Breckinridge broke his resolution not to speak in public again by delivering a eulogy during memorial services in Louisville. Unintentionally his words bound Davis and himself together, the two leaders who had met in entirely civil combat to determine not the fate of their cause but rather how their cause should meet that fate. "He failed," the Kentuckian said of Lee. "The result is in the future. It may be for better or for worse. We hope for the better." But failure alone did not define a man, or for that matter a cause. Lesser men often met with great worldly success, "but it is disaster alone that reveals the qualities of true greatness." While the world applauded those who erected material monuments to their achievements, he thought there was another kind of triumph that went beyond the material and transient triumphs of men. "Is not that man successful also who by his valor, moderation and courage, with all their associate virtues, presents to the world such a specimen of true manhood as his children and his children's children will be proud to imitate?" he asked. "In this sense he was not a failure."[18]

And in that sense neither were Davis and Breckinridge. If the Confederate president never accepted defeat gracefully, and even if he fell into the bitter postwar squabbles that helped to make so many Southerners look foolish and spiteful, still he always rose above the mendacity and rank falsehoods to which the others repeatedly sank. If he never inspired his people with love, still by his conduct as a prisoner and for twenty years afterward, he gave an example of unbending pride and refusal either to supplicate or apologize. Rather than leave the country and start anew elsewhere as did thousands of others, even Benjamin, he remained in the South and shared the hardships of his people. Jefferson Davis could never provide an enviable case of executive or inspirational leadership for the generations of the future. It was simply not in his character. But he could and would offer something else perhaps just as important for later generations in the South. No one would ever doubt his commitment, his all-encompassing dedication to his cause, and his willingness to sacrifice almost everything he valued for what he believed.

A narrow divide separates heroic commitment from sheer fanaticism. His old foe Rhett had been a fanatic and was soon forgotten, but Davis never crossed that line. If at the end his refusal to face the situation evidenced a departure from reality, it was scarcely out of the ordinary for any national leader facing total defeat. If he had actually reached Texas before the last surrenders, would he have led his people on all the way to Armageddon if they would follow? No one can say. Certainly he would have tried, given the chance. Just as certainly more would have died pointlessly in continuing a lost fight, their lives the currency spent by his unwavering determination.

But then perhaps not, for Davis would have been waging another fight at the same time, a struggle begun in February 1865 with an opponent in gray. For had Davis reached the Trans-Mississippi and found men to command, then another would have followed him there, one dedicated not to continuing, but to ending. There would be no Congress, no cabinet out there, just the president and his secretary of war, two powerful and determined men, each bent on conflicting ends. How long their contest over closing the Confederate epic might have lasted is profitless speculation, just as is the issue of which would have won. But if the events in Virginia and the Carolinas where they last vied are any measure, it is Breckinridge who would have prevailed. Only he ever stood up to Davis successfully. Only he engineered the combinations of other men of influence necessary to counter the president's unrealistic hopes. Only he understood his leader well enough to know how to lead him to countenance defeat, if not to accept it in his heart.

Lee surrendered honorably rather than sending his men to the hills as guerillas as Davis would have wished, and though Breckinridge took no known part in that, still it was the natural end of discussions he and Lee had been having for two months before, the two being entirely in unison on how the Confederacy should die. Johnston accepted the same terms, this time with definite participation and support from Breckinridge, who almost succeeded with him in securing an even more dramatic and favorable end for all Confederates in spite of Davis's opposition. With the secretary of war's advice and encouragement, the cavalry brigadiers in South Carolina delivered a last mortal blow to Davis's hopes of making their men go on, forcing him in the end to accept the inevitability that no one from the East would follow him to the far West. If Davis did not admit defeat until Irwinville, neither did Breckinridge, battering and eroding at every possible opportunity the president's hopes for victory. The actual behavior of the ranks after taking their paroles demonstrated that if the Confederate armies had fragmented into myriad roving bands of partisans, they would have preyed on Southern civilians to subsist, even while sniping ineffectually at the Yankees, a course that could only bring down more misery and repression on the South without changing the result. That such an eventuality did not come to pass owed nothing to Jefferson Davis, and much to John C. Breckinridge.

Theirs was really the last battle of the Civil War, a fight not for Southern victory, which had long before ceased to be a possibility if it ever was, but for Confederate posterity. Who won and who lost? Davis kept fighting until the day he died, head on, the only way he knew how. When Breckinridge told Russell and O'Toole on the Florida coast that he was no longer a belligerent, he meant it. He had accepted the inevitability of defeat long before he became secretary of war, but from February 1865 onward he saw that the one victory he could win was for the memory and example that the Confederate epic might provide for later generations, for "their children, and their children's children." In preserving its archives for future historians, he helped to guarantee that they would be remembered. By thwarting at every opportunity the president's increasingly irrational determination to keep fighting no matter the cost in lives or destruction, the general further ensured that their posterity would want to remember them, and with pride, even in their last days of defeat.

That done, the Kentuckian put down his arms at once, and through the postwar years refused to take them up again either to defend himself or to strike out at his enemies. For he realized that his own story both during the war and after was itself a part of the "magnificent epic," and he refused to taint it, too, with farce. The manner of the Confederacy's death inevitably had to have as much influence as its brief life in determining what it must endure in the years after defeat. In the battle for honor and dignity and reason over desperation, despoliation, and further tragedy in the war's outcome, and in the fight for moderation and reconciliation over bitterness and recrimination in the years that were to follow, John C. Breckinridge would have been the first to declare that in the end the real winner was not a man, but America.

NOTES

Chapter One

1. New York, *Citizen,* May 4, 1867.

2. Robert E. Lee to John C. Breckinridge, March 9, 1865, in Clifford Dowdey and Louis A. Manarin, eds., *The Wartime Papers of R. E. Lee,* pp. 912–913.

3. Fannie Walker Miller, "The Fall of Richmond," p. 305.

4. *Op. cit.,* p. 913.

5. Robert Toombs to Alexander H. Stephens, March 23, 1865, in Ulrich B. Phillips, ed., *The Correspondence of Robert Toombs, Alexander H. Stephens, and Howell Cobb,* p. 661; Robert Barnwell Rhett Memoir, Aiken Rhett Collection, Charleston Museum.

6. Varina Davis, *Jefferson Davis, Ex-President of the Confederate States of America,* vol. II, pp. 12, 163.

7. E. A. Pollard, *The Lost Cause,* p. 685; Myrta Lockett Avary, ed. *Recollections of Alexander H. Stephens,* p. 241.

8. William C. Davis, *Jefferson Davis, the Man and His Hour*, p. 235; Lynda Lasswell Crist and Mary Seaton Dix, eds., *The Papers of Jefferson Davis, Volume 5, 1853–1855*, p. 155.

9. Washington, *Evening Star*, March 14, 1861.

10. Robert Barnwell Rhett Memoir, Aiken Rhett Collection, Charleston Museum.

11. New York, *Citizen*, August 17, 1867.

12. Stephen R. Mallory to S. R. Mallory, December 8, 1865, Stephen R. Mallory Papers, Southern Historical Collection.

13. William J. Bromwell, Memorandum, January 28, 1865, Causten-Pickett Papers, Library of Congress.

14. William C. Davis, *Jefferson Davis*, pp. 582–585.

15. Jefferson Davis to William Preston Johnston, September 20, 1864, in Dunbar Rowland, ed., *Jefferson Davis, Constitutionalist*, vol. VI, p. 340.

16. For full background on Breckinridge, see William C. Davis, *Breckinridge: Statesman, Soldier, Symbol*.

17. Henry W. Cleveland, "Robert Toombs," p. 457.

18. Gustavus W. Smith to Breckinridge, April 14, 1865, Joseph Rubinfine *C.S.A. List No. 69*, n.d., item 84.

19. Sallie B. Putnam, *In Richmond during the Confederacy*, p. 356; William Preston to Louis T. Wigfall, January 19, 1860, Louis T. Wigfall Papers, Library of Congress.

20. C. Vann Woodward, ed., *Mary Chesnut's Civil War*, p. 706.

21. Edward Younger, ed., *Inside the Confederate Government*, pp. 199–200; Sarah Woolfolk Wiggins, ed., *The Journals of Josiah Gorgas, 1857–1878*, p. 152.

22. John B. Jones, *A Rebel War Clerk's Diary*, vol. II, pp. 410, 435.

23. General William Preston, in the Louisville, KY, *Courier-Journal*, June 18, 1875.

24. New York, *Citizen*, August 24, 1867.

25. Breckinridge to Isaac M. St. John, May 16, 1871, in Dunbar Rowland, ed., *Jefferson Davis, Constitutionalist*, vol. VII, pp. 356–357.

26. Breckinridge to J. Stoddard Johnston, February 23, 1865, John C. Breckinridge Papers, Filson Club.

27. William C. Davis, *Breckinridge: Statesman, Soldier, Symbol*, p. 489.

28. Bromwell Memorandum, January 28, 1865, Causten–Pickett Papers, Library of Congress.

29. John A. Campbell to B. R. Curtis, July 20, 1865, "Open Letters," p. 952.

30. Mallory to S. R. Mallory, December 8, 1865, Stephen R. Mallory Papers, Southern Historical Collection.

31. John A. Campbell to James Speed, August 31, 1865, "Papers of John A. Campbell," p. 71.

32. Campbell to Curtis, July 20, 1865, "Open Letters," pp. 952–953.

33. Campbell to Speed, August 31, 1865, "Papers of John A. Campbell," pp. 69, 71.

34. Edward Younger, *Inside the Confederate Government*, p. 199.

35. United States War Department, *War of the Rebellion: Official Records of the Union and Confederate Armies*, ser. I, vol. 46, pt. 2, pp. 1211–1214.

36. John B. Jones, *A Rebel War Clerk's Diary*, vol. II, p. 423; United States War Department, *War of the Rebellion: Official Records of the Union and Confederate Armies*, ser. I, vol. 46, pt. 2, pp. 1242–1245; Lee to Breckinridge, February 21, 1865, chap. IX, vol. 31, Secretary of War, Register of Letters Received, February 1864–April 1865; Breckinridge to Lee, February 24–25, 1865, chap. VIII, vol. 232; Misc. Register of Letters and Telegrams Received, Army of Northern Virginia 1862–1865, record group 109, National Archives.

37. United States War Department, *War of the Rebellion: Official Records of the Union and Confederate Armies*, ser. I, vol. 46, pt. 2, pp. 1252–1253.

38. Ibid., pp. 1257, 1264–1265.

39. Breckinridge to Johnston, February 23, 1865, Breckinridge Papers, Filson Club.

40. James Longstreet, *From Manassas to Appomattox*, p. 584; William C. Davis, *Jefferson Davis*, p. 592.

41. John B. Jones, *A Rebel War Clerk's Diary*, vol. II, p. 442.

42. Ibid., p. 440.

43. Ibid., p. 426.

Chapter Two

1. R. M. T. Hunter to William Jones, n.d. [November 1877], in Dunbar Rowland, ed., *Jefferson Davis, Constitutionalist*, vol. VII, pp. 576–577.

2. John B. Jones, *A Rebel War Clerk's Diary*, vol. II, pp. 424–425.

3. Campbell to Breckinridge, March 5, 1865, John A. Campbell Papers, Southern Historical Collection.

4. United States War Department, *War of the Rebellion: Official Records of the Union and Confederate Armies*, ser. I, vol. 46, pt. 2, p. 1292.

5. Ibid., p. 1295.

6. Edward Younger, ed., *Inside the Confederate Government*, p. 203; Burton Harrison to Davis, May 24, 1877, in Dunbar Rowland, ed. *Jefferson Davis, Constitutionalist*, vol. VII, p. 551; Campbell to Speed, August 31, 1865, in "Papers of John A. Campbell," p. 69.

7. United States War Department, *War of the Rebellion: Official Records of the Union and Confederate Armies*, ser. I, vol. 46, pt. 2, p. 1240.

8. John B. Jones, *A Rebel War Clerk's Diary*, vol. II, p. 447. The replies to Breckinridge's circular are to be found in the Louis T. Wigfall Papers, Library of Congress, while Breckinridge's covering letter to Davis, dated March 13, 1865, is in the Frederick M. Dearborn Collection, Houghton Library, Harvard University.

9. Edward Younger, ed., *Inside the Confederate Government*, pp. 202–203.

10. United States Congress, *Journal of the Congress of the Confederate States of America*, vol. IV, pp. 703–706, 713.

11. J. L. M. Curry, *Civil History of the Government of the Confederate States*, p. 106.

12. George G. Vest, "John C. Breckinridge: Recollections of One Who Knew Him in the Prime of His Manhood," Louisville, KY, *Courier-Journal*, June 8, 1875.

13. John B. Jones, *A Rebel War Clerk's Diary*, vol. II, p. 454; Nelson D. Lankford, ed., *An Irishman in Dixie*, pp. 60–61.

14. Sarah Woolfolk Wiggins, ed., *The Journals of Josiah Gorgas, 1857–1878*, p. 158.

15. Fannie Walker Miller, "The Fall of Richmond," p. 305.

16. John B. Jones, *A Rebel War Clerk's Diary*, vol. II, p. 455.

17. Nelson D. Lankford, ed. *An Irishman in Dixie*, pp. 47–48.

18. Edmund Kirke, *Down in Tennessee and Back by Way of Richmond*, pp. 269 ff.

19. William C. Davis, *Davis*, pp. 601–602; Varina Davis, *Jefferson Davis, Ex-President of the Confederate States of America*, vol. II, pp. 574–577.

20. John B. Jones, *A Rebel War Clerk's Diary*, vol. II, p. 460.

21. Campbell to Horace Greeley, April 26, 1865, p. 6; Campbell to Speed, August 31, 1865, "Papers of John A. Campbell," p. 67; Campbell to Curtis, July 20, 1865, "Open Letters," p. 953.

22. Campbell to Greeley, April 26, 1865, in "Papers of John A. Campbell," p. 64.

23. Breckinridge to Zebulon Vance, March 21, 1865, Governors Papers, Zebulon B. Vance, North Carolina Department of Archives and History.

24. Glenn Tucker, *Zeb Vance, Champion of Personal Freedom*, pp. 390–393.

25. John B. Jones, *A Rebel War Clerk's Diary*, vol. II, p. 463.

26. Fannie Walker Miller, "The Fall of Richmond," p. 305.

27. United States War Department, *War of the Rebellion: Official Records of the Union and Confederate Armies*, ser. I, vol. 46, pt. 3, p. 1371. Lee to Agnes Lee, April 1, 1865, in Clifford Dowdey and Louis A. Manarin,

eds., *Wartime Papers of Robert E. Lee*, p. 924, says "I...will be compelled to visit Richmond the first moment I can."

28. William H. Parker, *Recollections of a Naval Officer, 1841–1865*, p. 349.

29. Harrison to Davis, May 24, 1877, in Dunbar Rowland, ed., *Jefferson Davis, Constitutionalist*, vol. VII, pp. 547–548.

30. W. H. Swallow, "Retreat of the Confederate Government from Richmond to the Gulf," pp. 596–597.

31. Samuel J. T. Moore, Jr., *Moore's Complete Civil War Guide to Richmond*, p. 120.

32. John H. Reagan, *Memoirs, with Special Reference to Secession and the Civil War*, p. 198; John A. Campbell, *Recollections of the Evacuation of Richmond, April 2d, 1865*, p. 4; Edward Younger, ed., *Inside the Confederate Government*, p. 205; John H. Reagan account in undated clipping, Virginia Clay Scrapbook, Clement C. Clay Papers, Duke University Library.

33. John B. Jones, *A Rebel War Clerk's Diary*, vol. II, p. 465; United States War Department, *War of the Rebellion: Official Records of the Union and Confederate Armies*, ser. I, vol. 46, pt. 3, p. 1378.

34. Dallas Tucker, "The Fall of Richmond," pp. 155–156; H. W. Bruce, "Some Reminiscences of the Second of April, 1865," p. 207; Amelia Gorgas, "The Evacuation of Richmond," p. 110; Nelson D. Lankford, ed., *An Irishman in Dixie*, p. 82.

35. Mallory Recollections, June 1865, Stephen R. Mallory Papers, Southern Historical Collection.

36. John H. Reagan, "Flight and Capture of Jefferson Davis," pp. 148, 151; W. T. Walthall, "The True Story of the Capture of Jefferson Davis," p. 99; George Davis to William T. Walthall, September 4, 1877, in W. T. Walthall, "The True Story of the Capture of Jefferson Davis," p. 124; William H. Parker, *Recollections of a Naval Officer, 1841–1865*, pp. 349–350.

37. John B. Jones, *A Rebel War Clerk's Diary*, vol. II, p. 466; Edward Younger, ed., *Inside the Confederate Government*, p. 205; Fannie Walker Miller, "The Fall of Richmond," p. 305.

38. W. H. Swallow, "Retreat of the Confederate Government from Rich-

mond to the Gulf," p. 597; George Davis to Walthall, September 4, 1877, in W. T. Walthall, "The True Story of the Capture of Jefferson Davis," pp. 124–125; United States War Department, *War of the Rebellion: Official Records of the Union and Confederate Armies*, ser. I, vol. 46, pt. 3, pp. 1378–1379; Virginia Clay-Clopton, *A Belle of the Fifties: Memoirs of Mrs. Clay, of Alabama*, pp. 244–245.

39. Charles C. C. Coffin, *The Boys of '61*, p. 506.

40. Rembert Patrick, *The Fall of Richmond*, pp. 42–44; John A. Campbell, *Recollections of the Evacuation of Richmond, April 2d, 1865*, p. 5; William C. Davis, *Breckinridge: Statesman, Soldier, Symbol*, p. 503.

41. Nelson D. Lankford, ed., *An Irishman in Dixie*, p. 84 n.

42. Edward Younger, ed., *Inside the Confederate Government*, p. 205; John Leyburn, "The Fall of Richmond," p. 93; William H. Davies, in *Life and Reminiscences of Jefferson Davis, by Distinguished Men of His Time*, pp. 42–43.

43. John Leyburn, "The Fall of Richmond," pp. 92–96.

44. Warren Spencer, ed., "A French View of the Fall of Richmond: Alfred Paul's Report to Drouyn de Lhuys, April 11, 1865," pp. 181–182.

45. Mallory Recollections, Stephen R. Mallory Papers, Southern Historical Collection.

46. William H. Parker, *Recollections of a Naval Officer*, p. 352.

47. Rembert Patrick, *The Fall of Richmond*, p. 34; Peter H. Mayo Recollections, Southern Historical Collection.

48. Mallory Recollections, Stephen R. Mallory Papers, Southern Historical Collection; Lewis E. Harvie to St. John, January 1, 1876, "Resources of the Confederacy in 1865," pp. 110–111; William C. Davis, *Breckinridge: Statesman, Soldier, Symbol*, p. 505.

49. Davis to Varina Davis, April 5, 1865, in Dunbar Rowland, ed., *Jefferson Davis, Constitutionalist*, vol. VI, p. 533.

50. William H. Parker, *Recollections of a Naval Officer, 1841–1865*, pp. 352–353.

51. William H. Parker, "The Gold and Silver in the Confederate States Treasury," p. 305.

52. Fannie Walker Miller, "Fall of Richmond," p. 305; E. T. Watehall, "Fall of Richmond, April 3, 1865," p. 215; Dallas Tucker, "The Fall of Richmond," pp. 157–158; Mary B. Maltby, *Mary Cyrene Breckinridge*, p. 8.

53. Sallie B. Putnam, *Richmond during the Confederacy*, p. 364; Leeland Hathaway Recollections, Southern Historical Collection.

54. Clement Sulivane, "The Fall of Richmond, I: The Evacuation," in Robert U. Johnson and Clarence C. Buel, eds., *Battles and Leaders of the Civil War*, vol. IV, pp. 725–726.

55. United States War Department, *War of the Rebellion: Official Records of the Union and Confederate Armies*, ser. I, vol. 46, pt. 3, p. 594; Charles C. C. Coffin, *The Boys of '61*, p. 506.

56. Clement Sulivane, "The Fall of Richmond, I," p. 726.

57. R. T. W. Duke, "Burning of Richmond," p. 135.

58. T. C. De Leon, *Four Years in Rebel Capitals*, p. 359; Rembert Patrick, *The Fall of Richmond*, pp. 44–52; Mary B. Maltby, *Mary Cyrene Breckinridge*, p. 8; Charles C. C. Coffin, *The Boys of '61*, p. 506.

Chapter Three

1. H. W. Bruce, "Some Reminiscences of the Second of April, 1865," p. 209.

2. Except where otherwise cited, this account of the train ride to Danville, and the comments on the cabinet members aboard, are taken from Mallory Recollections, Mallory Papers, Southern Historical Collection. An edited version of this account appeared in *McClure's Magazine*, XVI (December 1900, January 1901), as "The Last Days of the Confederate Government," but in most instances the original document has been used since it contains material omitted from the published version.

3. John H. Reagan, *Memoirs, with Special Reference to Secession and the Civil War*, p. 198.

4. Anna Trenholm Diary, April 2, 1865, George A. Trenholm Papers, South Caroliniana Library.

5. Beverly Wellford Diary, April 2, 1865, White, Wellford, Taliaferro, and Marshall Family Papers, Southern Historical Collection.

6. H. W. Bruce, "Some Reminiscences of the Second of April, 1865," p. 209; John S. Wise, *The End of an Era*, p. 415.

7. Mallory Recollections, Stephen R. Mallory Papers, Southern Historical Collection.

8. Edward Pollock, *Illustrated Sketch Book of Danville, Virginia; Its Manufactures & Commerce*, pp. 51–52.

9. Anna Trenholm to My Darling Children, April 4, 1865, George A. Trenholm Papers, South Caroliniana Library. J. Frank Carroll, *Confederate Treasure in Danville*, p. 84, is the only source that says that Trenholm actually vomited as soon as his ambulance left the station, but no source is given, and the book is so careless with sources and so confuses and jumbles events, that it is unwise to accept much on its authority alone without corroboration from other sources.

10. Robert Douthat Meade, *Judah P. Benjamin, Confederate Statesman*, p. 313; John H. Brubaker, III, *The Last Capital*, p. 19.

11. William C. Davis, *Jefferson Davis, the Man and His Hour*, p. 607; Dunbar Rowland, ed., *Jefferson Davis, Constitutionalist*, vol. VI, p. 538.

12. John S. Wise, *The End of an Era*, p. 415.

13. Danville, *Weekly Register*, April 7, 1865.

14. Anna Trenholm to My Dear Children, April 4, 1865, George A. Trenholm Papers, South Caroliniana Library.

15. Davis to the People of the Confederate States of America, April 4, 1865, in Dunbar Rowland, ed., *Jefferson Davis, Constitutionalist*, vol. VI, pp. 529–531.

16. Jefferson Davis, *Rise and Fall of the Confederate Government*, vol. II, p. 677.

17. John H. Burrill to his parents, April 4, 1865, John H. Burrill Papers, Civil War Times Illustrated Collection, United States Army Military

History Institute. This rumor of Davis leaving Richmond in a dress, for which the Burrill letter is the only currently known source, is not to be confused with the later much publicized accusations that followed his May 10 capture, which is dealt with in Chapter 12.

18. Joseph B. Anderson, manuscript narrative, "President Jefferson Davis in Danville, Va. April 3–10, 1865," Special Collections, University of Virginia Library; James Elliott Walmsley, "The Last Meeting of the Confederate Cabinet," p. 338.

19. John H. Brubaker III, *The Last Capital*, p. 32.

20. Anna Trenholm to My Dear Children, April 4, 1865, George A. Trenholm Papers, South Caroliniana Library.

21. William H. Parker, "The Gold and Silver in the Confederate States Treasury," p. 306; William H. Parker, *Recollections of a Naval Officer, 1841–1865*, p. 354; Micajah H. Clark, "The Last Days of the Confederate Treasury and What Became of Its Specie," p. 545.

22. Micajah Clark's statement of the total treasury bullion has been printed many times but will be most readily found in Otis Ashmore's "The Story of the Confederate Treasure" (p. 135). The estimate of the Richmond banks specie comes from Otis Ashmore's "The Story of the Virginia Banks Funds"(p. 186).

23. New York, *Times*, January 6, 1882.

24. Mallory Recollections, Stephen R. Mallory Papers, Southern Historical Collection.

25. William H. Parker, *Recollections of a Naval Officer, 1841–1865*, pp. 354–355.

26. Ibid., p. 354; R. H. Fleming Diary, April 4, 1865, Washington and Lee University.

27. Mallory Recollections, Stephen R. Mallory Papers, Southern Historical Collection.

28. W. H. Swallow, "Retreat of the Confederate Government from Richmond to the Gulf," p. 598.

29. Wellford Diary, April 2–9, 1865, White, Wellford, Taliaferro, and Marshall Family Papers, Southern Historical Collection.

30. Mallory Recollections, Stephen R. Mallory Papers, Southern Historical Collection.

31. William Preston Johnston to Varina Davis, April 12, 1865, Edwin M. Stanton Papers, Library of Congress.

32. John H. Brubaker, _The Last Capital_, p. 27.

33. C. E. L. Stuart to Davis, February 10, 1862, Letters Received, Confederate Secretary of War, record group 109, National Archives; Harrison to William Preston Johnston, June 19, 1867, Mason Barret Collection, Tulane University; New York _Citizen_, April 27, 1867.

34. J. H. Averill, "Richmond, Virginia. The Evacuation of the City and the Days Preceding It," p. 269; Mallory Recollections, Stephen R. Mallory Papers, Southern Historical Collection.

35. Moses Hoge to Francis Lawley, August 14, 1897, Pierce Butler Papers, Tulane University.

36. William Preston Johnston to Rosa Johnston, April 8, 1865, Mason Barret Collection, Tulane University.

37. Davis to Beauregard, April 4, 1865, p. 529, and Davis to Johnston, April 5, 1865, p. 532, in Dunbar Rowland, ed., _Jefferson Davis, Constitutionalist_, vol. VI.

38. Davis to Varina Davis, April 5, 6, 1865, in Dunbar Rowland, ed., _Jefferson Davis, Constitutionalist_, vol. VI, pp. 532–534.

39. Humphrey Marshall to Davis, January 6, 1884, Jefferson Davis Papers, Museum of the Confederacy.

40. _Memorials of the Life, Public Services, and Character of William T. Sutherlin_, pp. 13–17.

41. B. Boisseau Bobbitt, "Our Last Capital," p. 337.

42. Mallory Recollections, Stephen R. Mallory Papers, Southern Historical Collection.

43. _Memorials of the Life, Public Services, and Character of William T. Sutherlin_, pp. 13–17.

44. Mallory Recollections, Stephen R. Mallory Papers, Southern Historical Collection.

45. W. H. Swallow, "Retreat of the Confederate Government from Richmond to the Gulf," p. 599.

46. Edward Pollock, *Illustrated Sketchbook of Danville, Virginia,* pp. 55–57.

Chapter Four

1. Breckinridge to St. John, May 16, 1871, in Dunbar Rowland, ed., *Jefferson Davis, Constitutionalist,* vol. VII, pp. 356–357.

2. St. John to Davis, July 14, 1873, in Dunbar Rowland, ed., *Jefferson Davis, Constitutionalist,* vol. VII, p. 354.

3. Festus P. Summers, ed., *A Borderland Confederate,* pp. 95–98; M. W. Venable, "On the Way to Appomattox—War Memories," p. 303; Parke Rouse, Jr., ed., *When the Yankees Came: Civil War and Reconstruction on the Virginia Peninsula,* pp. 88–89. The Rouse book, an edition of the memoir of George B. West, dates this episode as Friday April 7, but being written thirty-six years after the fact, it clearly confuses the date.

4. Clifford Dowdey and Louis A. Manarin, eds., *Wartime Papers of R. E. Lee,* pp. 930–931.

5. Joseph Packard, "Ordnance Matters at the Close," p. 228.

6. St. John to Davis, July 14, 1873, in Dunbar Rowland, ed., *Jefferson Davis, Constitutionalist,* vol. VII, p. 355.

7. United States War Department, *War of the Rebellion: Official Records of the Union and Confederate Armies,* ser. I, vol. 46, pt. 3, p. 1389, and vol. 47, pt. 3, p. 767.

8. Campbell to Joseph R. Anderson, April 7, 1865, in John A. Campbell, "Evacuation Echoes," pp. 351–353; Robert Saunders, Jr., *John Archibald Campbell, Southern Moderate, 1811–1889,* pp. 181–185.

9. Michael B. Ballard, *A Long Shadow,* p. 58.

10. W. G. Bean, ed., "Memoranda of Conversations between General Robert E. Lee and William Preston Johnston," p. 479.

11. Joseph Packard, "Ordnance Matters at the Close," p. 229.

12. United States War Department, *War of the Rebellion: Official Records of the Union and Confederate Armies,* ser. I, vol. 46, pt. 3, p. 1388.

13. Clifford Dowdey and Louis A. Manarin, ed., *Wartime Papers of Robert E. Lee,* pp. 931–932.

14. John S. Wise, *The End of an Era,* pp. 444–447.

15. Montgomery, AL, *Daily Advertiser,* October 10, 1865.

16. Constance Harrison, *Recollections Grave and Gay,* p. 208.

17. *Memorials of the Life, Public Services, and Character of William T. Sutherlin,* p. 17; Varina Davis to Davis, April 7, 1865, in Dunbar Rowland, ed., *Jefferson Davis, Constitutionalist,* vol. VI, p. 539.

18. Edward Pollock, *Illustrated Sketch Book of Danville, Virginia,* pp. 57–59.

19. Mallory Recollections, Stephen R. Mallory Papers, Southern Historical Collection.

20. Davis to Johnston, April 10, 1865, in Dunbar Rowland, ed., *Jefferson Davis, Constitutionalist,* vol. VI, pp. 542–543; Fairfax Harrison, ed., *The Harrisons of Skimino,* p. 228.

21. *Memorials of the Life, Public Services, and Character of William T. Sutherlin,* p. 17; Edward Pollock, *Illustrated Sketchbook of Danville, Virginia,* pp. 63–64.

22. Sarah Woolfolk Wiggins, ed., *The Journals of Josiah Gorgas, 1857–1878,* p. 159; Edward Younger, ed., *Inside the Confederate Government,* p. 206.

23. New York, *Herald,* July 4, 1865.

24. Hoge to Lawley, August 14, 1897, Pierce Butler Papers, Tulane University.

25. Edward Pollock, *Illustrated Sketch Book of Danville, Virginia,* p. 60.

26. Anna Trenholm Diary, April 10, 1865, George A. Trenholm Papers, South Caroliniana Library.

27. J. H. Averill, "Richmond, Virginia. The Evacuation of the City and the Days Preceding It," p. 269.

28. B. Boisseau Bobbitt, "Our Last Capital," p. 339.

29. Stories and legends of lost treasure from the Virginia bank funds began to surface shortly after the war and persist to the present. All are based on thin evidence and a lot of speculation, some of it wild. J. Frank

Carroll, in *Confederate Treasure* (pp. 126 ff), suggests that $196,000 in silver was left behind, later hidden by Danville's citizens, and its whereabouts kept a secret thereafter through a conspiracy of silence that included, even many years later, an unwillingness to retrieve the silver. The whole story, in its many versions, rests on unsupported supposition and the sort of flimsy logic that characterizes most stories of lost treasure, and it can safely be dismissed. The citizens of Danville and the stragglers from the army there on April 10 thought nothing of plundering government warehouses. That they would scruple at taking Confederate silver seems inconsistent at best. That they would for years afterward know where a horde of money lay but refuse to reclaim it even during the hard years of Reconstruction is ridiculous. Moreover, the notion of there being any discrepancy between the amount in the Treasury that left Richmond and that later accounted for in disbursements rests solely on an approximate recollection by Walter Philbrook some seventeen years after the fact. Perhaps the best statement of what is in any event a very weak argument will be found in Carroll's *Confederate Treasure*, a confused pastiche, much of it innocently plagiarized from other sources, which still presents a rather full portrait of Treasury affairs in Danville until the author gets to the speculations on lost treasure.

30. New York, *Herald*, July 4, 1865; Danville, *Register*, January 22, 1939.

31. Mallory Recollections, Stephen R. Mallory Papers, Southern Historical Collection; Fairfax Harrison, ed. *The Harrisons of Skimino*, p. 230.

32. Montgomery, AL, *Daily Advertiser*, October 10, 1865, and February 25, 1886.

33. Mallory Diary, April 10, 1865, Stephen R. Mallory Papers, Southern Historical Collection.

34. Davis to J. M. Walker, April 10, 1865, in Dunbar Rowland, ed., *Jefferson Davis, Constitutionalist*, vol. VI, p. 543.

35. Fairfax Harrison, ed., *The Harrisons of Skimino*, pp. 230–231.

36. Harrison to Varina Davis, April 12, 1865, Edwin M. Stanton Papers, Library of Congress.

37. J. H. Averill, "Richmond, Virginia. The Evacuation of the City and the Days Preceding It," p. 269.

38. Anna Trenholm Diary, April 10, 1865, George A. Trenholm Papers, South Caroliniana Library.

39. Burke Davis, *The Long Surrender*, p. 61.

40. Edward Pollock, *Illustrated Sketch Book of Danville, Virginia*, pp. 61–62; J. H. Averill, "Richmond, Virginia. The Evacuation of the City and the-Days Preceding It," pp. 269–271.

41. Edward Younger, ed., *Inside the Confederate Government*, p. 206; Wellford Diary, April 11, 1865, Southern Historical Collection.

42. Mallory Recollections, Stephen R. Mallory Papers, Southern Historical Collection.

43. William Preston Johnston to Varina Davis, April 12, 1865, Edwin M. Stanton Papers, Library of Congress.

44. S. S. Lee to Clifton R. Breckinridge, April 6, 1865, in possession of the author.

45. Leeland Hathaway Reminiscences, Southern Historical Collection.

46. Thomas L. Rosser Memoirs, Thomas L. Rosser Papers, University of Virginia; Jedediah Hotchkiss Diary, April 12, 1865, Jedediah Hotchkiss Papers, Library of Congress.

47. Jedediah Hotchkiss Diary, April 12, 1865, Jedediah Hotchkiss Papers, Library of Congress.

48. United States War Department, *War of the Rebellion: Official Records of the Union and Confederate Armies*, ser. I, vol. 46, pt. 3, p. 1394.

Chapter Five

1. Anna Trenholm Diary, April 11, 1865, George A. Trenholm Papers, South Caroliniana Library; Mallory Recollections, Stephen R. Mallory Papers, Southern Historical Collection.

2. New York, *Herald*, July 4, 1865.

3. William Preston Johnston to Rosa Johnston, April 22, 1865, Mason Barret Collection, Tulane University; William Preston Johnston to Varina Davis, April 12, 1865, Harrison to Varina Davis, April 12, 1865, Edwin M. Stanton Papers, Library of Congress.

4. Mallory Recollections, Stephen R. Mallory Papers, Southern Historical Collection.

5. W. H. Swallow, "Retreat of the Confederate Government from Richmond to the Gulf," pp. 599–600.

6. Royce G. Shingleton, *John Taylor Wood, Sea Ghost of the Confederacy*, p. 150.

7. Mallory Recollections, Stephen R. Mallory Papers, Southern Historical Collection; Varina Davis to Jefferson Davis, April 7, 1865, Jefferson Davis Papers, Duke University Library.

8. United States War Department, *War of the Rebellion: Official Records of the Union and Confederate Armies*, ser. I, vol. 46, pt. 3, p. 1393.

9. William Preston Johnston to Varina Davis, April 12, 1865, Edwin M. Stanton Papers, Library of Congress.

10. Alfred B. Roman, *The Military Campaigns of General Beauregard in the War between the States 1861 to 1865*, vol. II, pp. 390–392.

11. Ibid., p. 394; Joseph E. Johnston, *Narrative of Military Operations*, pp. 396–397.

12. Robert E. Lee, *Recollections and Letters of General Robert E. Lee*, pp. 136–137.

13. John Taylor Wood Diary, April 12, 1865, John Taylor Wood Papers, Southern Historical Collection.

14. William Preston Johnston to Rosa Johnston, April 12, 1865, Mason Barret Collection, Tulane University.

15. Joseph E. Johnston, *Narrative of Military Operations*, pp. 397–398.

16. Mallory Recollections, Stephen R. Mallory Papers, Southern Historical Collection; Joseph E. Johnston, *Narrative of Military Operations*, pp. 396–398.

17. Joseph E. Johnston, *Narrative of Military Operations*, p. 398.

18. Jefferson Davis, *Rise and Fall of the Confederate Government*, vol. II, pp. 679–680.

19. Mallory Recollections, Stephen R. Mallory Papers, Southern Historical Collection.

20. John H. Reagan, *Memoirs, with Special Reference to Secession and the Civil War*, p. 199.

21. Mark L. Bradley, *This Astounding Close: The Road to Bennett Place*, p. 142.

22. Mallory Recollections, Stephen R. Mallory Papers, Southern Historical Collection.

23. John H. Reagan, *Memoirs, with Special Reference to Secession and the Civil War*, p. 199.

24. Alfred B. Roman, *The Military Campaigns of General Beauregard in the War between the States 1861–1865*, vol. II, p. 395; Joseph E. Johnston, *Narrative of Military Operations*, p. 399; John H. Reagan, *Memoirs, with Special Reference to Secession and the Civil War*, p. 200, and Reagan to Davis, December 12, 1880, in Dunbar Rowland, ed., *Jefferson Davis, Constitutionalist*, vol. VIII, pp. 536–537, are the only sources for the cabinet vote after Johnston's presentation. Reagan provides the most information but also makes himself the most active, and it must be noted that, especially in his *Memoirs*, he frequently shows faulty recollection, as when he says he was the youngest member of the cabinet, whereas he was in fact two years older than the secretary of war.

25. Mallory Recollections, Stephen R. Mallory Papers, Southern Historical Collection; Joseph E. Johnston, *Narrative of Military Operations*, p. 400.

26. Jefferson Davis, *Rise and Fall of the Confederate Government*, vol. II, pp. 681–682.

27. Wood Diary, April 13, 1865, John Taylor Wood Papers, Southern Historical Collection; Fairfax Harrison, ed., *The Harrisons of Skimino*, pp. 232–233.

28. W. H. Swallow, "Retreat of the Confederate Government from Richmond to the Gulf," p. 600.

29. Mallory Recollections, Stephen R. Mallory Papers, Southern Historical Collection.

30. W. H. Swallow, "Retreat of the Confederate Government from Richmond to the Gulf," pp. 599–600.

31. Mallory Recollections, Stephen R. Mallory Papers, Southern Historical Collection.

32. Fairfax Harrison, ed., *The Harrisons of Skimino*, pp. 259–260 n; Royce G. Shingleton, *John Taylor Wood, Sea Ghost of the Confederacy*, p. 160. It was no doubt a garbled report of this plan that later led to the mistaken belief that Davis had ordered the Confederate commerce raider *Shenandoah* to be waiting off the Florida coast to take him to safety. John H. Reagan, "Flight and Capture of Jefferson Davis," p. 150.

33. Davis to Varina Davis, April 14, 1865, in Dunbar Rowland, ed., *Jefferson Davis, Constitutionalist*, vol. VI, p. 545.

34. Micajah H. Clark, "The Last Days of the Confederate Treasury," pp. 542–543; Wellford Diary, April 15–16, 1865, White, Wellford, Taliaferro and Marshall Family Papers, Southern Historical Collection.

35. Davis to John C. Hendren, April 15, 1865, in Dunbar Rowland, ed., *Jefferson Davis, Constitutionalist*, vol. VI, pp. 545–546; Micajah H. Clark, "The Last Days of the Confederate Treasury," p. 545.

36. George G. Dibrell to W. T. Walthall, April 3, 1878, in Dunbar Rowland, ed., *Jefferson Davis, Constitutionalist*, vol. VIII, p. 148, and April 9, 1878, p. 160, and William C. P. Breckinridge to Walthall, April 3, 1878, pp. 152–154.

37. Mallory Recollections, Stephen R. Mallory Papers, Southern Historical Collection; John H. Reagan, *Memoirs, with Special Reference to Secession and the Civil War*, p. 200; Fairfax Harrison, ed., *The Harrisons of Skimino*, p. 235; Micajah Clark, "Last Days of the Confederate Treasury," pp. 542–544; Wellford Diary, April 15–16, 1865, White, Wellford, Taliaferro, and Marshall Family Papers, Southern Historical Collection.

38. Anna Trenholm Diary, April 15, 1865, George A. Trenholm Papers, South Caroliniana Library.

39. Fairfax Harrison, ed., *The Harrisons of Skimino*, pp. 236–237.

40. John H. Reagan, "Flight and Capture of Jefferson Davis," p. 152.

41. Breckinridge to Alfred Iverson, April 15, 1865, John C. Breckinridge Papers, Duke University.

42. Given Campbell, Memorandum of a Journal Kept Daily During the Last March of Jefferson Davis, April 15, 1865, Library of Congress.

43. James M. Morgan, *Recollections of a Rebel Reefer,* p. 235.

44. Mallory Recollections, Stephen R. Mallory Papers, Southern Historical Collection.

45. W. H. Swallow, "Retreat of the Confederate Government from Richmond to the Gulf," p. 600.

46. Michael B. Ballard, *A Long Shadow,* p. 89.

47. Given Campbell, Memorandum, April 15–17 [16], 1865, Library of Congress.

48. Anna Trenholm Diary, April 16, 1865, George A. Trenholm Papers, South Caroliniana Library; Mallory Recollections, Stephen R. Mallory Papers, Southern Historical Collection.

49. Fairfax Harrison, ed., *The Harrisons of Skimino,* pp. 239–241; Mallory Recollections, Stephen R. Mallory Papers, Southern Historical Collection.

50. United States War Department, *War of the Rebellion: Official Records of the Union and Confederate Armies,* ser. I, vol. 47, pt. 3, pp. 801, 803.

51. It has been common to assert that Johnston wired Davis and asked him to send someone to counsel, and that Davis selected Breckinridge and Reagan. Reagan himself says this in *Memoirs,* p. 201, and also in Reagan to Davis, December 12, 1880, in Dunbar Rowland, ed., *Jefferson Davis, Constitutionalist,* vol. VIII, p. 537. As is frequently the case with Reagan's recollections, his memory is faulty. Johnston's April 16 telegram is clearly addressed to Breckinridge. Moreover, in *Rise and Fall,* vol. II, p. 683, Davis does not say that the telegram came to him but only that Johnston asked Breckinridge to come and that Davis himself sent Reagan along.

52. Joseph E. Johnston, in *Narrative of Military Operations* (p. 404), mistakenly says that he did not wire for Breckinridge to come until the

evening of April 17, and only after a day of negotiations with Sherman. Michael B. Ballard, in *A Long Shadow* (p. 93), states that Beauregard had suggested that Johnston ask the secretary of war to come, thinking that having Breckinridge present would shield Johnston in case the talks took a direction unpleasing to Davis. The sources he cites, however, say nothing at all on this point, and Beauregard's own memoir is silent, merely paraphrasing what Johnston said in his own *Narrative* (cited above).

53. United States War Department, *War of the Rebellion: Official Records of the Union and Confederate Armies*, ser. I, vol. 43, pt. 3, p. 806.

54. Michael B. Ballard, *A Long Shadow*, p. 84; United States War Department, *War of the Rebellion: Official Records of the Union and Confederate Armies*, ser. I, vol. 43, pt. 3, pp. 791–792; Mark L. Bradley, *This Astounding Close*, pp. 146–147, 333 n.

55. United States War Department, *War of the Rebellion: Official Records of the Union and Confederate Armies*, ser. I, vol. 43, pt. 3, p. 806.

56. Breckinridge to Vance, April 17, 1865, Governors Papers, Zebulon Vance, North Carolina Department of Archives and History.

57. W. H. Swallow, "Retreat of the Confederate Government from Richmond to the Gulf," p. 601.

58. Mark L. Bradley, *This Astounding Close*, pp. 165–166.

59. Ibid., p. 167.

60. Rufus R. Wilson, ed., *Lincoln among His Friends*, p. 361.

61. Mark L. Bradley, *This Astounding Close*, pp. 160–161; William T. Sherman to Joseph Webster, April 17, 1865, Brooks D. Simpson and Jean V. Berlin, eds., *Sherman's Civil War: Selected Correspondence of William T. Sherman, 1860–1865*, p. 863.

62. Joseph E. Johnston, *Narrative of Military Operations*, p. 404.

63. United States War Department, *War of the Rebellion: Official Records of the Union and Confederate Armies*, ser. I, vol. 47, pt. 3, p. 807.

64. Joseph E. Johnston, *Narrative of Military Operations*, p. 404.

65. "Captain Ridley's Journal," *Confederate Veteran*, p. 99.

66. Except where otherwise cited, this account of the negotiations is based on Mark Bradley's excellent account in *This Astounding Close*, pp. 170–178.

67. William T. Sherman, *Memoirs*, vol. II, pp. 352–353. John S. Wise, in *The End of An Era*, 449–453, told a story, some thirty-seven years after the fact, that Breckinridge was outraged when Sherman only offered them one drink, and later declared that the Yankee general was a "hog" for not sharing his liquor more freely. Wise was not present, but said Johnston told him the story in 1880, though neither Johnston nor Sherman ever made reference to the episode. It is third hand at best, in a book that is otherwise filled with inaccuracies due to failing memory, and on its own does not deserve credence. But it soon became a part of the literature and lore of the Civil War and is more responsible than anything else for the persistent misconception that Breckinridge was a heavy drinker. Within a few years of the appearance of Wise's book, other old Confederates absorbed his anecdote into their own accounts, as for instance that of Virginia congressman John Goode in 1907, who also was not present and almost certainly borrowed the story from Wise (Mark L. Bradley, *This Astounding Close*, p. 341 n), and later a 1930s newspaper account cited in Stanley Horn, *The Army of Tennessee*, p. 427.

68. Sherman to Grant, April 18, 1865, in Brooks D. Simpson and Jean V. Berlin, eds., *Sherman's Civil War*, p. 864.

69. United States War Department, *War of the Rebellion: Official Records of the Union and Confederate Armies*, ser. I, vol. 47, pt. 3, pp. 806–807.

70. Joseph E. Johnston, *Narrative of Military Operations*, p. 405.

71. Sherman to Grant, April 18, 1865, in Brooks D. Simpson and Jean V. Berlin, eds., *Sherman's Civil War*, pp. 863–864.

72. William C. Davis, *Breckinridge: Statesman, Soldier, Symbol*, pp. 512–513; J. Stoddard Johnston, "Sketches of Operations of General John C. Breckinridge, No. 3," p. 389.

73. Alfred B. Roman, *The Military Operations of General Beauregard in the War between the States 1861–1865*, vol. II, p. 398. Sherman to Grant,

April 18, 1865, in Brooks D. Simpson and Jean V. Berlin, eds., *Sherman's Civil War*, p. 864.

74. Sherman to Ellen Sherman, April 22, 1865, in Brooks D. Simpson and Jean V. Berlin, eds., *Sherman's Civil War*, pp. 871–872.

75. United States War Department, *War of the Rebellion: Official Records of the Union and Confederate Armies*, ser. I, vol. 47, pt. 3, p. 831.

76. Sherman to Johnston, April 21, 1865, in Brooks D. Simpson and Jean V. Berlin, eds., *Sherman's Civil War*, p. 870.

77. No actual account of what Breckinridge said is known to survive, and only brief hints are given by Sherman and Johnston in their memoirs, with a somewhat more explicit general description in J. Stoddard Johnston's "Operations of General Breckinridge" article cited above. However, several items specifically discussed, and the fact that Sherman took action on them, can be interpolated from comments in his April 18, 1865, letter to Grant, in Brooks D. Simpson and Jean V. Berlin, eds., *Sherman's Civil War* (pp. 863–864), and since all parties seem to agree that Breckinridge did the talking on civil issues, it is thus assumed that these arguments were made by him and not Johnston. The views attributed to him are those he is known to have expressed on other occasions, thus it seems not unreasonable to expect that he would have represented the same thoughts to Sherman.

78. Breckinridge's surmise is inferred from the statement of his close friend J. Stoddard Johnston in "Sketches of Operations" that Breckinridge had influenced the document, for he would only have heard such detail from Breckinridge himself. Johnston's guess that Sherman already had his terms in mind appears in Johnston's *Narrative of Military Operations* (p. 405).

79. Gideon Welles Diary, April 25, 1865, Gideon Welles Papers, Library of Congress.

80. United States War Department, *War of the Rebellion: Official Records of the Union and Confederate Armies*, ser. I, vol. 47, pt. 3, pp. 243–245.

81. Sherman to Johnston, April 21, 1865, in Brooks D. Simpson and Jean V. Berlin, eds., *Sherman's Civil War*, pp. 869–870.

82. John S. Wise, *The End of an Era*, p. 453.

83. Sherman to Grant, April 18, 1865, Brooks D. Simpson and Jean V. Berlin, eds., *Sherman's Civil War*, p. 863, and Sherman to Ellen Sherman, April 18, 1865, p. 867.

84. Mark L. Bradley, in *This Astounding Close* (pp. 174ff), argues that Johnston's contribution to the agreement has been overlooked and that the final terms bear his "unmistakable stamp." In perhaps the only weakness in this otherwise outstanding study, Bradley goes to some lengths to establish a dominant role for Johnston that simply does not match either the sources or the context. No sources other than Johnston himself give him credit for any of the contents of the cartel, and after the war the general became one of the chief authors of Confederate "lost cause" fiction in his claims for what he had done, or would have done. Reagan's initial draft of discussion points presented at the Greensboro cabinet meeting reflected common peace concerns that came not from Johnston, nor likely even from Reagan himself though he would claim them, but which were in discussion by Breckinridge, Campbell, Hunter, even Lee and others, for months earlier. Nor is there credible evidence that in pushing Davis for a more comprehensive negotiation at Greensboro, Johnston had it in mind for himself to go beyond matters dealing strictly with the armies in his own negotiations. As for the terms proposed by the Confederates at Durham Station, Bradley omits any mention (pp. 142–143) of those drafted by Reagan at the meeting in Greensboro—for which Reagan himself seems to provide credible witness—and then in discussing the April 18 meeting with Sherman, he says that the draft delivered from Reagan during the conference had been "dictated" to the postmaster by Johnston (p. 167), as if to suggest that Johnston himself was their author, when in fact Johnston merely says in his *Narrative of Military Operations*, p. 404, that Reagan was reducing to writing the substance of the terms that Johnston and

Sherman had agreed upon the day before. At that, Johnston is probably exaggerating, since he indicates that everything that would appear in the final memorandum the next day had been agreed upon on April 17 excepting the issue of amnesty for Davis and the cabinet. That is not how Sherman remembered the day, and the fact is that the draft Reagan sent on April 18—supposedly dictated by Johnston—bore little resemblance to the final memorandum but was in places almost word for word what Reagan submitted to the Greensboro cabinet several days before. Johnston had a lifelong penchant for exaggerating his own importance, and in this instance Bradley seems to have believed him. Others at the time felt that Breckinridge exerted the greater influence in the discussion, and since so many of the points in the final memorandum are concerns he had been raising for months, it seems probable that his influence was as great as Johnston's, and likely far greater.

85. Sherman to Henry W. Halleck, April 18, 1865, Brooks D. Simpson and Jean V. Berlin, eds., *Sherman's Civil War,* p. 866.

86. W. H. Swallow, "Retreat of the Confederate Government from Richmond to the Gulf," p. 602; Eliza McHatton Ripley, *Social Life in Old New Orleans, Being Recollections of My Girlhood,* p. 288.

87. William T. Sherman, *Memoirs,* vol. II, p. 353.

88. Sherman to Ellen Sherman, April 22, 1865, Brooks D. Simpson and Jean V. Berlin, eds., *Sherman's Civil War,* p. 872.

Chapter Six

1. Bradley, *This Astounding Close,* pp. 180–181; United States War Department, *War of the Rebellion: Official Records of the Union and Confederate Armies,* ser. I, vol. 47, pt 3, p. 809, and vol. 53, p. 418.

2. United States War Department, *War of the Rebellion: Official Records of the Union and Confederate Armies,* ser. I, vol. 47, pt. 3, pp. 810–811.

3. Davis to Breckinridge, April 18, 1865, Dunbar Rowland, ed., *Jefferson*

Davis, Constitutionalist, vol. VI, p. 548, and Breckinridge to Davis, April 19, 1865, p. 551.

4. Anna Trenholm Diary, April 17, 1865, George A. Trenholm Papers, South Caroliniana Library; Mallory Recollections, Stephen R. Mallory Papers, Southern Historical Collection.

5. Fairfax Harrison, *The Harrisons of Skimino,* p. 240; Varina Davis, *Jefferson Davis, Ex-President of the Confederate States of America,* vol. II, p. 627.

6. Given Campbell, Memorandum, April 18, 1865, Library of Congress. Campbell says they rode all night, in fact, though Mallory and other sources indicate there was something of an overnight stop in Concord.

7. Burton Harrison, Extract from A Narrative, written not for Publication, September 1877, Confederate States of America Records, Center for American History. This is an extract from the full text later published in November 1883 in *Century Magazine* and again in Fairfax Harrison, ed., *The Harrisons of Skimino* (pp. 225 ff), from a version annotated by Davis, but there are a few variations in wording, and this being the earliest extant holographic copy, though a fragment, it is used here.

8. Mallory Recollections, Stephen R. Mallory Papers, Southern Historical Collection.

9. Lynchburg, *Daily Virginian,* August 31, 1866; Burton Harrison, Extract, Confederate States of America Records, Center for American History; William Johnston to Davis, March 29, 1882, in Dunbar Rowland, ed., *Jefferson Davis, Constitutionalist,* vol. IX, pp. 157–158; Joseph G. Fiveash, "When Mr. Davis Heard of Lincoln's Death," p. 366.

10. Mary C. Courtney, Days of the Confederacy, n.d., in possession of John R. Riddler.

11. W. H. Swallow, "Retreat of the Confederate Government from Richmond to the Gulf," p. 603.

12. The best eyewitness account of this episode appears to be E. A. Alston's July 31, 1866, letter in the Lynchburg, *Daily Virginian,* August 31, 1866. Sources vary as to whether the telegram was read aloud before,

during, or after Davis's brief speech, and by whom. In Harrison's Extract, he says it came beforehand, and Johnston read it afterward. Fiveash, in "When Mr. Davis Heard of Lincoln's Death" (p. 366), says it came just as Davis was starting to speak, and Johnston read it. Basil W. Duke, in "After the Fall of Richmond" (p. 161), says that Davis himself read the telegram during his brief address. W. H. Swallow, in "Retreat of the Confederate Government from Richmond to the Gulf" (p. 603), says it was read by someone else when Davis concluded. The earliest known account is Lewis F. Bates's May 30, 1865, testimony at the assassination conspirators' trial, in Ben Pitman, *The Assassination of President Lincoln and the Trial of the Conspirators* (pp. 46–47), in which he says that Davis read the telegram himself during his speech, though much of Bates's testimony is discredited since he did not witness the event. Stephen R. Mallory's June 1865 Recollections (Southern Historical Collection) does not mention the speech at all but says the telegram came within an hour of their arrival in Charlotte and before the cabinet had dispersed to their separate lodgings, which suggests that they were all still together for some reason, most likely Davis's speech. Davis himself, in *Rise and Fall of the Confederate Government* (II, p. 683), makes no mention at all of his making a speech but says he got the telegram as he dismounted. In William Johnston's letter to Davis (March 29, 1882, in Dunbar Rowland, ed., *Jefferson Davis, Constitutionalist*, IX, p. 158), he says the telegram was delivered as Davis finished. The bulk of the testimony would suggest that it came while Davis was speaking but at or very near the end of his remarks and was read just after he closed. Virtually all sources say that Davis made no public comment on the news.

13. Basil W. Duke, "After the Fall of Richmond," p. 161.

14. Mallory Recollections, Stephen R. Mallory Papers, Southern Historical Collection.

15. William Preston Johnston to Adam Rankin Johnson, March 14, 1898, in Adam R. Johnson, *The Partisan Rangers of the Confederate States Army*, pp. 271–272.

16. John Oliver to James A. Wilcox, May 18, 1865, entry 38, record group 110, National Archives.

17. Ben Pitman, *The Assassination of President Lincoln and the Trial of the Conspirators*, p. 47.

18. Burton Harrison, Extract, Confederate States of America Records, Center for American History.

19. William C. Davis, *Jefferson Davis, the Man and His Hour*, p. 130.

20. Fairfax Harrison, ed. *The Harrisons of Skimino*, pp. 242–243; Anna Trenholm Diary, April 19, 1865, George A. Trenholm Papers, South Caroliniana Library.

21. Alfred J. Hanna, *Flight Into Oblivion*, pp. 47–48.

22. Burton Harrison, Extract, Confederate States of America Records, Center for American History.

23. Mary C. Courtney, Days of the Confederacy, n.d., in possession of John R. Riddler.

24. William Preston Johnston to Rosa Johnston, April 22, 1865, Mason Barret Collection, Tulane University.

25. Mrs. James A. Fore, "Cabinet Meeting in Charlotte," p. 66.

26. Anna Trenholm Diary, April 19, 1865, George A. Trenholm Papers, South Caroliniana Library.

27. Davis to Beauregard, April 20, 1865, in Dunbar Rowland, ed., *Jefferson Davis, Constitutionalist*, vol. VI, pp. 553, 555, and Davis to Howell Cobb, April 21, 1865, pp. 556–557.

28. Wood Diary, April 20, 1865, John Taylor Wood Papers, Southern Historical Collection.

29. Breckinridge to Beauregard, April 19, 1865, John C. Breckinridge Papers, in possession of Walter Agard.

30. United States War Department, *War of the Rebellion: Official Records of the Union and Confederate Armies*, ser. I, vol. 47, pt. 3, pp. 814, 818–819, 828–829.

31. New York, *Herald*, July 4, 1865; Varina Davis, *Jefferson Davis, Ex-President of the Confederate States of America*, vol. II, pp. 628–629; Ben

Pitman, *The Assassination of President Lincoln and the Trial of the Conspirators*, p. 47; United States War Department, *War of the Rebellion: Official Records of the Union and Confederate Armies*, ser. II, vol. 8, pt. 3, p. 855.

32. Joseph T. Durkin, ed., *John Dooley, Confederate Soldier: His War Journal*, pp. 197–198.

33. George Davis to Davis, April 22, 1865, in Dunbar Rowland, ed., *Jefferson Davis, Constitutionalist*, vol. VI, p. 577.

34. Mrs. James A. Fore, "Cabinet Meeting in Charlotte," p. 66.

35. Micajah H. Clark, "The Last Days of the Confederate Treasury and What Became of Its Specie," p. 543.

36. The cabinet responses to Davis will be found in United States War Department, *War of the Rebellion* (ser. I, vol. 47, pt. 3, pp. 821 ff). All except Breckinridge's and Mallory's are dated April 22. Mallory's actually carries the date April 24, but in opening he refers to Davis calling for these opinions at the cabinet discussion of the previous day, which had been April 22, so Mallory presumably just misdated his document. Breckinridge was probably too busy to get to his until after midnight on the day he arrived, April 23, consistent with his old habit of working very late.

37. Davis to Varina Davis, April 23, 1865, in Dunbar Rowland, ed., *Jefferson Davis, Constitutionalist*, vol. VI, pp. 561–562, and Davis to Armistead Burt, April 23, 1865, p. 562.

38. Fairfax Harrison, ed., *The Harrisons of Skimino*, p. 243.

39. Ibid., p. 243.

40. United States War Department, *War of the Rebellion: Official Records of the Union and Confederate Armies*, ser. I, vol. 47, pt. 3, pp. 821–831.

41. Clement Dowd, *Life of Zebulon B. Vance*, pp. 485–487. Mark L. Bradley, in *This Astounding Close* (p. 348 n 55), raises the issue of when Vance had this passage with Davis and the cabinet, establishing that it could have happened no later than April 25, and no earlier than April 23, the

date of this cabinet meeting. The latter best fits the course of known events, since Davis approved Johnston's terms on April 24.

42. William Preston Johnston to A. D. Garnett, September 19, 1865, Mason Barret Collection, Tulane University.

43. H. C. Binkley, "Shared in the Confederate Treasure," p. 88; Joseph T. Durkin, ed., *John Dooley, Confederate Soldier,* p. 198.

44. Basil W. Duke, "After the Fall of Richmond," pp. 161–162.

45. United States War Department, *War of the Rebellion: Official Records of the Union and Confederate Armies,* ser. I, vol. 47, pt. 3, p. 831.

46. John H. Reagan, "Flight and Capture of Jefferson Davis," p. 150; W. C. P. Breckinridge to Walthall, April 3, 1878, in Dunbar Rowland, ed., *Jefferson Davis, Constitutionalist,* vol. VIII, p. 154.

47. Joseph E. Johnston, *Narrative of Military Operations,* p. 410.

48. United States War Department, *War of the Rebellion: Official Records of the Union and Confederate Armies,* ser. I, vol. 47, pt. 3, pp. 834–835.

49. Ibid., pp. 835–836; John H. Reagan, "Flight and Capture of Jefferson Davis," p. 150; W. C. P. Breckinridge to Walthall, April 3, 1878, in Dunbar Rowland, ed., *Jefferson Davis, Constitutionalist,* vol. VIII, p. 154.

50. Mallory Recollections, Stephen R. Mallory Papers, Southern Historical Collection; United States War Department, *War of the Rebellion: Official Records of the Union and Confederate Armies,* ser. I, vol. 47, pt. 3, pp. 836–837.

51. United States War Department, *War of the Rebellion: Official Records of the Union and Confederate Armies,* ser. I, vol. 47, pt. 3, pp. 836, 839; Joseph E. Johnston, *Narrative of Military Operations,* p. 411.

52. James H. Carson, Grasshopper Springs in 1865, manuscript in possession of Craig M. Morisak.

53. Tench Tilghman Diary, April 20, 1865, Southern Historical Collection.

54. Edward Younger, ed., *Inside the Confederate Government,* p. 207; Wellford Diary, April 25, 1865, Southern Historical Collection; Minutes of

meeting of John C. Breckinridge and others, April 25, 1865, Rives Family Papers, Virginia Historical Society.

55. William Preston Johnston to Rosa Johnston, April 26, 1865, Mason Barret Collection, Tulane University; Wood Diary, April 24, 1865, John Taylor Wood Papers, Southern Historical Collection.

56. Josiah Gorgas, Extracts from My Notes Written Chiefly Soon After the Close of the War, ca. 1878, in Dunbar Rowland, ed., *Jefferson Davis, Constitutionalist,* vol. VIII, p. 332; Joseph Wheeler, "Loyal to the Last, Part I," p. 20.

57. Edward Younger, ed., *Inside the Confederate Government,* p. 207.

58. Mrs. James A. Fore, "Cabinet Meeting in Charlotte," pp. 66–67.

59. Joseph Wheeler, "Loyal to the Last," pp. 20, 66.

60. Dibrell to Johnston, April 9, 1878, in Dunbar Rowland, ed., *Jefferson Davis, Constitutionalist,* vol. VIII, pp. 160–161.

61. John H. Reagan, "Flight and Capture of Jefferson Davis," p. 153.

62. Wellford Diary, April 24–25, 1865, Southern Historical Collection; Edward Younger, ed., *Inside the Confederate Government,* pp. 206–207; R. G. H. Kean to Jubal Early, November 15, 1873, "Resources of the Confederacy in February, 1865," p. 57; United States War Department, *War of the Rebellion: Official Records of the Union and Confederate Armies,* ser. I, vol. 47, pt. 3, p. 842.

63. Edward Younger, ed. *Inside the Confederate Government,* p. 207.

64. Sarah Woolfolk Wiggins, ed., *The Journals of Josiah Gorgas, 1857–1878,* p. 162.

65. United States War Department, *War of the Rebellion: Official Records of the Union and Confederate Armies,* ser. I, vol. 47, pt. 3, p. 847; New York *Herald,* July 4, 1865. Sarah Woolfolk Wiggins, ed., *The Journals of Josiah Gorgas, 1857–1878,* p. 162, entry for April 30, 1865, confirms that Davis learned at least in broad terms of Johnston's surrender before leaving Charlotte.

66. Mary C. Courtney, Days of the Confederacy, n.d., in possession of John R. Riddler.

67. Joseph T. Durkin, ed., *John Dooley, Confederate Soldier,* p. 198.

68. New York, *Herald,* July 4, 1865.

69. Mary C. Courtney, Days of the Confederacy, n.d., in possession of John R. Riddler.

Chapter Seven

1. Mallory Recollections, Stephen R. Mallory Papers, Southern Historical Collection.

2. Basil W. Duke, "After the Fall of Richmond," p. 162.

3. Francis R. Lubbock, *Six Decades in Texas,* p. 566; Anna Trenholm Diary, April 26, 1865, George A. Trenholm Papers, South Caroliniana Library.

4. Reagan to Davis, December 12, 1880, in Dunbar Rowland, ed., *Jefferson Davis, Constitutionalist,* vol. VIII, p. 537; John H. Reagan, *Memoirs, with Special Reference to Secession and the Civil War,* p. 209.

5. Anna Trenholm Diary, April 26, 1865, George A. Trenholm Papers, South Caroliniana Library; Trenholm to Davis, April 27, 1865, in Dunbar Rowland, ed., *Jefferson Davis, Constitutionalist,* vol. VI, pp. 564–565, and Davis to Trenholm, April 28, 1865, p. 565.

6. Katherine W. Springs, *The Squires of Springfield,* pp. 235–236.

7. Dibrell to William Preston Johnston, April 9, 1878, in Dunbar Rowland, ed., *Jefferson Davis, Constitutionalist,* vol. VIII, p. 161.

8. Tench Tilghman Diary, April 27, 1865, Southern Historical Collection.

9. Basil W. Duke, "After the Fall of Richmond," p. 162.

10. Clark to Varina Davis, October 6, 1890, Varina Davis, *Jefferson Davis, Ex-President of the Confederate States of America,* vol. II, p. 587; Micajah H. Clark, "Retreat of the Cabinet from Richmond," p. 294; Mallory Recollections, Stephen R. Mallory Papers, Southern Historical Collection.

11. Basil W. Duke, "After the Fall of Richmond," p. 162.

12. Michael B. Ballard, *A Long Shadow,* p. 119.

13. Mallory Recollections, Stephen R. Mallory Papers, Southern Historical Collection.

14. John H. Reagan, *Memoirs, with Special Reference to Secession and the Civil War,* pp. 209–210.

15. New York, *Herald,* July 4, 1865; Dibrell to William Preston Johnston, April 9, 1878, in Dunbar Rowland, ed., *Jefferson Davis, Constitutionalist,* vol. VIII, p. 161; Given Campbell, Memorandum, April 28, 1865, Library of Congress.

16. Breckinridge to Hampton, April 28, 1865, "Last Letters and Telegrams of the Confederacy—Correspondence of General John C. Breckinridge," p. 105.

17. Given Campbell, Memorandum, April 28, 1865, Library of Congress.

18. Dallas, *Morning News,* April 30, 1897; John Hendren to Davis, April 5, 1865, in Dunbar Rowland, ed., *Jefferson Davis, Constitutionalist,* vol. VI, p. 531.

19. Given Campbell, Memorandum, April 29, 1865, Library of Congress.

20. Mallory Recollections, Stephen R. Mallory Papers, Southern Historical Collection.

21. Joseph Wheeler, "Loyal to the Last," p. 66.

22. Tench Tilghman Diary, April 30, 1865, Southern Historical Collection.

23. Undated April 1967 clipping from a Union County, South Carolina, newspaper, in files of Jefferson Davis Papers, Rice University.

24. W. H. Swallow, "Retreat of the Confederate Government from Richmond to the Gulf," p. 604.

25. Given Campbell, Memorandum, May 1, 1865, Library of Congress.

26. Varina Davis to Davis, April 28, 1865, in Dunbar Rowland, ed., *Jefferson Davis, Constitutionalist,* vol. VI, pp. 566–567.

27. Joseph Wheeler, "Loyal to the Last," p. 66.

28. Mallory Recollections, Stephen R. Mallory Papers, Southern Historical Collection; Dibrell to William Preston Johnston, April 9, 1878, in

Dunbar Rowland, ed., *Jefferson Davis, Constitutionalist*, vol. VIII, p. 161; W. H. Swallow, "Retreat of the Confederate Government from Richmond to the Gulf," p. 604.

29. Mallory Recollections, Stephen R. Mallory Papers, Southern Historical Collection.

30. United States War Department, *War of the Rebellion: Official Records of the Union and Confederate Armies*, ser. I, vol. 49, pt. 1, p. 346 ff.

31. Mallory Recollections, Stephen R. Mallory Papers, Southern Historical Collection; Dibrell to William Preston Johnston, April 9, 1878, in Dunbar Rowland, ed., *Jefferson Davis, Constitutionalist*, vol. VIII, p. 161; W. H. Swallow, "Retreat of the Confederate Government from Richmond to the Gulf," p. 604; New York, *Herald,* July 4, 1865.

32. Given Campbell, Memorandum, May 3 [2], 1865, Library of Congress.

33. Mrs. Charles Iverson Graves Reminiscences, Charles Iverson Graves Papers, Southern Historical Collection.

34. William H. Parker, *Recollections of a Naval Officer, 1841–1865*, pp. 355–356. Except where otherwise noted, this account of the movements of the treasure train and the midshipmen comes from Parker, pp. 356 ff.

35. Graves Reminiscences, Charles Iverson Graves Papers, Southern Historical Collection.

36. R. H. Fleming Diary, April 15, 1865, Washington and Lee University.

37. Ibid., April 17–19, 1865.

38. Graves Reminiscences, Charles Iverson Graves Papers, Southern Historical Collection.

39. R. H. Fleming Diary, April 20, 1865, Washington and Lee University. William H. Parker, in *Recollections of a Naval Officer, 1841–1865* (p. 359), says that he did not remove the specie from the train in Augusta, but his memory is often faulty in his memoirs, while Fleming's diary says explicitly that the money was moved to a bank vault.

40. John F. Wheless to William Jones, February 10, 1882, "The Confederate Treasure—Statement of Paymaster John F. Wheless," p. 139.

41. Graves Reminiscences, Charles Iverson Graves Papers, Southern Historical Collection.

42. Eliza Frances Andrews, *The War-Time Journal of a Georgia Girl, 1864– 1865*, p. 187.

43. R. H. Fleming Diary, April 26–29, 1865, Washington and Lee University.

44. William H. Parker, *Recollections of a Naval Officer, 1841–1865*, p. 364.

45. F. E. Richardson to Walthall, August 26, 1878, in Dunbar Rowland, ed., *Jefferson Davis, Constitutionalist*, vol. VIII, p. 263.

46. Samuel Ferguson Diary, May 3 [2], 1865, in Dunbar Rowland, ed., *Jefferson Davis, Constitutionalist*, vol. VIII, p. 250.

47. William H. Parker, *Recollections of a Naval Officer, 1841–1865*, pp. 364– 365; Wheless to Jones, February 10, 1882, "The Confederate Treasure," p. 140; William H. Parker, "The Gold and Silver in the Confederate States Treasury," p. 309.

48. Ferguson Diary, May 3[2], 1865, in Dunbar Rowland, ed., *Jefferson Davis, Constitutionalist*, vol. VIII, pp. 250–251.

49. Duke to Walthall, April 6, 1878, in Dunbar Rowland, ed., *Jefferson Davis, Constitutionalist.*, vol. VIII, p. 159.

50. William H. Parker, *Recollections of a Naval Officer, 1841–1865*, p. 365.

51. Ibid., pp. 366–368.

52. W. C. P. Breckinridge to Walthall, April 3, 1878, in Dunbar Rowland, ed., *Jefferson Davis, Constitutionalist*, vol. VIII, p. 152.

53. Basil W. Duke, "After the Fall of Richmond," pp. 162–163.

54. Ferguson Diary, May 3 [2], 1865, in Dunbar Rowland, ed., *Jefferson Davis, Constitutionalist*, vol. VIII, pp. 250–251.

55. W. C. P. Breckinridge to Walthall, May 3, 1878, in Dunbar Rowland, ed., *Jefferson Davis, Constitutionalist*, vol. VIII, p. 191.

56. Dibrell to William Preston Johnston, April 9, 1878, in Dunbar Rowland, ed., *Jefferson Davis, Constitutionalist*, vol. VIII, p. 161.

57. Except where otherwise cited, this account of the Abbeville meeting comes from Basil W. Duke, "After the Fall of Richmond," pp. 163– 164, which is the fullest account.

58. Dibrell to William Preston Johnston, April 9, 1878, in Dunbar Rowland, ed., *Jefferson Davis, Constitutionalist*, vol. VIII, pp. 161–162.

59. Ibid., p. 162, and Dibrell to Walthall, April 3, 1878, pp. 148–149.

60. Samuel W. Ferguson, "Another Account by Gen. S. W. Ferguson," p. 264.

61. Lee to Davis, April 20, 1865, Clifford Dowdey and Louis A. Manarin, eds., *Wartime Papers of R. E. Lee*, p. 939.

62. Samuel W. Ferguson, "Another Account by Gen. S. W. Ferguson," p. 263.

63. Dibrell to William Preston Johnston, April 9, 1878, in Dunbar Rowland, ed., *Jefferson Davis, Constitutionalist*, vol. VIII, p. 162.

64. W. C. P. Breckinridge to Walthall, April 3, 1878, in Dunbar Rowland, ed., *Jefferson Davis, Constitutionalist*, vol. VIII, p. 152.

65. W. C. P. Breckinridge to Walthall, April 3, 1878, in Dunbar Rowland, ed., *Jefferson Davis, Constitutionalist*, vol. VIII, p. 154; W. C. P. Breckinridge, in *Life and Reminiscences of Jefferson Davis*, p. 386.

66. Duke to Walthall, April 6, 1878, in Dunbar Rowland, ed., *Jefferson Davis, Constitutionalist*, vol. VIII, p. 159.

67. Basil W. Duke, *A History of Morgan's Cavalry*, p. 575.

68. Duke to Walthall, April 15, 1878, in Dunbar Rowland, ed., *Jefferson Davis, Constitutionalist*, vol. VIII, p. 171.

69. Ibid.; Jefferson Davis, *Rise and Fall of the Confederate Government*, vol. II, pp. 692–694; Davis to William Preston Johnston, n.d. [1878], Arthur Marvin Shaw, ed., "A Letter by Jefferson Davis Relating to Events Preceding His Capture," p. 32.

70. W. C. P. Breckinridge to Walthall, April 3, 1878, in Dunbar Rowland, ed., *Jefferson Davis, Constitutionalist*, vol. VIII, p. 152.

71. Duke to Walthall, April 15, 1878, in Dunbar Rowland, ed., *Jefferson Davis, Constitutionalist*, vol. VIII, p. 171.

72. W. C. P. Breckinridge to Walthall, May 3, 1878, in Dunbar Rowland, ed., *Jefferson Davis, Constitutionalist*, vol. VIII, p. 190, and Duke to Walthall, April 6, 1878, p. 158; Basil W. Duke, *A History of Morgan's Cavalry*, p. 575.

73. W. C. P. Breckinridge to Walthall, May 3, 1878, in Dunbar Rowland, ed., *Jefferson Davis, Constitutionalist*, vol. VIII, p. 192.

74. Duke to Walthall, April 6, 1878, in Dunbar Rowland, ed., *Jefferson Davis, Constitutionalist*, vol. VIII, p. 159.

75. W. C. P. Breckinridge to Walthall, May 3, 1878, in Dunbar Rowland, ed., *Jefferson Davis, Constitutionalist*, vol. VIII, pp. 191–192, and Dibrell to Walthall, April 3, 1878, p. 150.

76. W. C. P. Breckinridge to Walthall, April 3, 1878, in Dunbar Rowland, ed., *Jefferson Davis, Constitutionalist*, vol. VIII, p. 153, and May 3, 1878, p. 189, Ferguson Diary, May 3 [2], 1865, p. 251.

77. Ferguson Diary, May 3 [2], 1865, in Dunbar Rowland, ed., *Jefferson Davis, Constitutionalist*, vol. VIII, p. 251.

78. That Davis agreed to this seems implicit in his course thereafter, and the next day Breckinridge, in a message to Davis, made reference to the "opinions" he had expressed to the president the previous evening. United States War Department, *War of the Rebellion: Official Records of the Union and Confederate Armies*, ser. I, vol. 49, pt. 2, p. 1277.

79. Arthur Marvin Shaw, ed., "A Letter by Jefferson Davis Relating to Events Preceding His Capture," p. 33.

80. W. C. P. Breckinridge to Walthall, May 3, 1878, in Dunbar Rowland, ed., *Jefferson Davis, Constitutionalist*, vol. VIII, p. 189.

81. United States War Department, *War of the Rebellion: Official Records of the Union and Confederate Armies*, ser. I, vol. 47, pt. 3, p. 861.

82. Mallory to Davis, May 2, 1865, in Dunbar Rowland, ed., *Jefferson Davis, Constitutionalist*, vol. VI, p. 586; Mallory Recollections, Stephen R. Mallory Papers, Southern Historical Collection.

83. William H. Parker, *Recollections of a Naval Officer, 1841–1865*, pp. 366, 368–369.

84. United States War Department, *War of the Rebellion: Official Records of the Union and Confederate Armies*, ser. I, vol. 49, pt. 2, p. 1277.

85. New York, *Times*, January 6, 1882.

86. Basil W. Duke, "After the Fall of Richmond," p. 164.

87. Given Campbell Memorandum, May 3, 1865, Library of Congress; Michael B. Ballard, *A Long Shadow*, p. 127; Harrison to Davis, May 24, 1877, in Dunbar Rowland, ed., *Jefferson Davis, Constitutionalist*, vol. VII, p. 548.

88. Robert Gilliam, "Last of the Confederate Treasury Department," p. 424.

89. Mallory Recollections, Stephen R. Mallory Papers, Southern Historical Collection.

90. Dibrell to Davis, April 3, 1878, in Dunbar Rowland, ed., *Jefferson Davis, Constitutionalist*, vol. VIII, pp. 150–151, and Dibrell to William Preston Johnston, April 9, 1878, p. 162.

91. John H. Reagan, *Memoirs, with Special Reference to Secession and the Civil War*, p. 210.

92. Francis R. Lubbock, *Six Decades in Texas*, p. 567.

93. John W. Headley, *Confederate Operations in Canada and New York*, pp. 433–435; John H. Reagan, *Memoirs, with Special Reference to Secession and the Civil War*, p. 212.

94. William C. Davis, *Breckinridge: Statesman, Soldier, Symbol*, p. 520; Davis to William Preston Johnston, April 5, 1878, Breckinridge Family Papers, Library of Congress.

95. Ferguson Diary, May 4 [3], 1865, in Dunbar Rowland, ed., *Jefferson Davis, Constitutionalist*, vol. VIII, p. 251, and Richardson to Walthall, August 26, 1878, p. 263.

Chapter Eight

1. Mallory Recollections, Stephen R. Mallory Papers, Southern Historical Collection.

2. Given Campbell, Memorandum, May 3, 1865, Library of Congress.

3. Pierce Butler, *Judah P. Benjamin*, p. 362.

4. Benjamin to Penina Kruttschnitt, July 22, 1865, Pierce Butler Papers, Tulane University.

5. Jefferson Davis, *Rise and Fall of the Confederate Government*, vol. II, p. 364.

6. John H. Reagan, *Memoirs, with Special Reference to Secession and the Civil War*, p. 211.

7. Micajah H. Clark, "The Last Days of the Confederate Treasury and What Became of Its Specie," p. 544; W. H. Swallow, "Retreat of the Confederate Government from Richmond to the Gulf," p. 605.

8. Dibrell to Walthall, April 3, 1878, in Dunbar Rowland, ed., *Jefferson Davis, Constitutionalist*, vol. VIII, pp. 148–149.

9. R. Thomas Campbell, ed., *Midshipman in Gray*, p. 191.

10. M. E. Robertson, "President Davis's Last Official Meeting," pp. 293–294.

11. There would later be some controversy over whether or not the cavalry was promised pay during the May 2 conference with Davis. Certainly Dibrell believed it to be so, but his recollections after the fact are often mistaken.

12. Micajah H. Clark, "The Last Days of the Confederate Treasury and What Became of Its Specie," p. 546; Joseph M. Broun, "The Last Confederate Payroll," p. 202. The latter source is virtually identical to Broun, "Last Confederate Payroll," but is published from the original manuscript and contains a few differences in wording.

13. Basil W. Duke, "After the Fall of Richmond," p. 164.

14. United States War Department, *War of the Rebellion: Official Records of the Union and Confederate Armies*, ser. I, vol. 49, pt. 2, p. 1277.

15. Ibid., p. 1278.

16. Breckinridge to Johnston, December 9, 1865, Basil W. Duke Papers, Southern Historical Collection; Micajah H. Clark, "The Last Days of the Confederate Treasury and What Became of Its Specie," p. 547.

17. Mary House Lane, Some Incidents of the Civil War as Related by an Eye Witness, 1925, in Ralph L. Hobbs, *The Fate of the Two Confederate Wagon Trains of Gold*, pp. 9–10.

18. Basil W. Duke, "After the Fall of Richmond," pp. 164–165; Basil W. Duke, *Reminiscences of General Basil W. Duke, C.S.A.*, p. 389.

19. United States War Department, *War of the Rebellion: Official Records of the Union and Confederate Armies*, ser. I, vol. 49, pt. 2, p. 1278.

20. Ferguson Diary, May 5 [4], 1865, in Dunbar Rowland, ed., *Jefferson Davis, Constitutionalist*, vol. VIII, p. 251.

21. Joseph M. Broun, "The Last Confederate Payroll," p. 202. This reminiscence is confused in some respects, and the interpretation given here seems to be the only one that fits the context.

22. Lane, Some Incidents of the Civil War, pp. 10–11; William H. Parker, "The Gold and Silver in the Confederate States Treasury," p. 311.

23. Dibrell to William Preston Johnston, April 9, 1878, in Dunbar Rowland, ed., *Jefferson Davis, Constitutionalist*, pp. 162–163.

24. Eliza Frances Andrews, *The War-Time Journal of a Georgia Girl*, pp. 190–192.

25. Mallory Recollections, Stephen R. Mallory Papers, Southern Historical Collection.

26. William C. Davis, ed., *Diary of a Confederate Soldier: John S. Jackman of the Orphan Brigade*, p. 167.

27. Eliza Frances Andrews, *The War-Time Journal of a Georgia Girl*, pp. 201–202.

28. M. E. Robertson, "President's Davis's Last Official Meeting," pp. 295–296.

29. W. L. Wittich, "Escort to President Davis," p. 263.

30. Eliza Frances Andrews, *The War-Time Journal of a Georgia Girl*, pp. 193–196, 198.

31. Mallory Recollections, Stephen R. Mallory Papers, Southern Historical Collection.

32. Mallory to Davis, May 2, 1865, in Dunbar Rowland, ed., *Jefferson Davis, Constitutionalist*, vol. VI, p. 586, and Davis to Mallory, May 4, 1865, pp. 586–587; W. H. Swallow, "Retreat of the Confederate Government from Richmond to the Gulf," p. 605.

33. Virginia Clay-Clopton, *A Belle of the Fifties*, p. 246.

34. John H. Reagan, *Memoirs, with Special Reference to Secession and the Civil War,* pp. 214–216; William Y. Thompson, *Robert Toombs of Georgia,* pp. 217–218. In his *Memoirs* Reagan suggests that both Toombs and Davis here uttered magnanimous expressions about each other. It is faintly possible that Davis might have done so, but utterly out of character for Toombs.

35. Eliza Frances Andrews, *The War-Time Journal of a Georgia Girl*, p. 202.

36. Mallory Recollections, Stephen R. Mallory Papers, Southern Historical Collection.

37. United States War Department, *War of the Rebellion: Official Records of the Union and Confederate Armies*, ser. I, vol. 49, pt. 2, p. 1277.

38. Eliza Frances Andrews, *The War-Time Journal of a Georgia Girl*, p. 205.

39. M. E. Robertson, "President Davis's Last Official Meeting," pp. 295–296.

40. Jefferson Davis, *Rise and Fall of the Confederate Government*, vol. II, p. 695.

41. William C. Davis, ed., *Diary of a Confederate Soldier,* p. 167; M. F. Robertson, "President Davis's Last Official Meeting," p. 296.

42. United States Congress, *Journal of the Congress of the Confederate States of America,* IV, pp. 588, 593; John Echols to Cooper, February 22, 1865, Felix H. Robertson Compiled Service Record, record group 109, National Archives.

43. William C. Davis, *Diary of a Confederate Soldier,* p. 167; Eliza Frances Andrews, *The War-Time Journal of a Georgia Girl,* pp. 193, 195, 199.

44. M. E. Robertson, "President Davis's Last Official Meeting," pp. 296–297.

45. John H. Reagan, "Flight and Capture of Jefferson Davis," pp. 150–152.

46. Jefferson Davis, *Rise and Fall of the Confederate Government*, vol. II, pp. 696–697.

47. Michael B. Ballard, *A Long Shadow*, p. 132.

Chapter Nine

1. Micajah H. Clark, "The Last Days of the Confederate Treasury and What Became of Its Specie," pp. 545, 548; Varina Davis, *Jefferson Davis, Ex-President of the Confederate States of America,* vol. II, pp. 864–865.

2. New York, *Herald,* July 4, 1865.

3. Given Campbell, Memorandum, May 4, 1865, Library of Congress; Jefferson Davis, *Rise and Fall of the Confederate Government,* vol. II, p. 695.

4. Harrison to Davis, May 24, 1877, Dunbar Rowland, ed., *Jefferson Davis, Constitutionalist,* vol. VII, p. 549.

5. M. E. Robertson, "President Davis's Last Official Meeting," p. 291.

6. Eliza Frances Andrews, *The War-Time Journal of a Georgia Girl,* pp. 204–205.

7. M. E. Robertson, "President Davis's Last Official Meeting," p. 298.

8. Eliza Frances Andrews, *The War-Time Journal of a Georgia Girl,* p. 206.

9. *Illustrated London News,* July 22, 1865.

10. M. E. Robertson, "President Davis's Last Official Meeting," p. 297.

11. John W. Headley, *Confederate Operations in Canada and New York,* p. 437.

12. Micajah H. Clark, "The Last Days of the Confederate Treasury and What Became of Its Specie," p. 545.

13. Eliza Frances Andrews, *The War-Time Journal of a Georgia Girl,* pp. 204–205.

14. Gary W. Gallagher, ed., *Fighting for the Confederacy,* p. 552; Edward Porter Alexander, *Military Memoirs of a Confederate,* p. 617.

15. Eliza Frances Andrews, *The War-Time Journal of a Georgia Girl,* pp. 206–207.

16. M. E. Robertson, "President Davis's Last Official Meeting," p. 296; Joseph Wheeler, "Loyal to the Last, Part I," p. 68.

17. Eliza Frances Andrews, *The War-Time Journal of a Georgia Girl,* p. 206.

18. William C. Davis, ed., *Diary of A Confederate Soldier,* p. 168.

19. John F. Wheless, "The Confederate Treasure," p. 141.

20. Basil W. Duke, "After the Fall of Richmond," p. 165.

21. M. E. Robertson, "Jefferson Davis's Last Official Meeting," p. 298.

22. Mrs. Clay Stacker statement, September 13, 1910, in William Couper, *The V.M.I. New Market Cadets*, p. 195.

23. Micajah H. Clark, "The Last Days of the Confederate Treasury and What Became of Its Specie," pp. 545–549.

24. Ibid., p. 549; John F. Wheless, "The Confederate Treasure," pp. 140–141.

25. Micajah H. Clark, "The Last Days of the Confederate Treasury and What Became of Its Specie," pp. 550–552.

26. Basil W. Duke, *Reminiscences of General Basil W. Duke, C.S.A.*, p. 390.

27. Micajah H. Clark, "The Last Days of the Confederate Treasury and What Became of Its Specie," pp. 547, 552–553; Reagan to Davis, n.d., Varina Davis, *Jefferson Davis, Ex-President of the Confederate States of America*, vol. II, p. 865. John H. Reagan, *Memoirs, with Special Reference to Secession and the Civil War*, p. 216.

28. Joseph M. Broun, "Last Confederate Payroll," p. 202; Micajah H. Clark, "The Last Days of the Confederate Treasury and What Became of Its Specie," p. 553.

29. Breckinridge to Chiefs of Bureaus and Personnel of the War Department, May 4, 1865, Jeremy F. Gilmer Papers, Museum of the Confederacy.

30. General Order No—, May 4, 1865, John C. Breckinridge Papers, in possession of author.

31. That Breckinridge and Ferguson had such a discussion is implicit in Ferguson's speech to his brigade later that evening, as reported in F. E. Richardson to Walthall, August 26, 1878, in Dunbar Rowland, ed., *Jefferson Davis, Constitutionalist*, vol. VII, p. 265.

32. John H. Reagan, *Memoirs, with Special Reference to Secession and the Civil War*, p. 213; Micajah H. Clark, "The Last Days of the Confederate Treasury and What Became of Its Specie," p. 553.

33. Ferguson Diary, May 5 [4], 1865, in Dunbar Rowland, ed., *Jefferson Davis, Constitutionalist*, vol. VIII, pp. 251–252, and Richardson to

Walthall, August 26, 1878, pp. 264–266; L. C. McAllister, "Disbanding of President Davis's Escort," p. 25.

34. Ferguson Diary, May 6 [5], 1865, in Dunbar Rowland, ed., *Jefferson Davis, Constitutionalist*, vol. VIII, p. 252, and Richardson to Walthall, August 26, 1878, p. 265, and G. W. Tunstall to Davis, March 29, 1888, X, pp. 60–62; L. C. McAllister, "Disbanding of President Davis's Escort," p. 25.

35. Samuel W. Ferguson, "Another Account by Gen. S. W. Ferguson," p. 264.

36. Basil W. Duke, "After the Fall of Richmond," p. 165.

37. Richardson to Walthall, August 26, 1878, in Dunbar Rowland, ed., *Jefferson Davis, Constitutionalist*, vol. VIII, p. 266; United States War Department, *War of the Rebellion: Official Records of the Union and Confederate Armies*, ser. I, vol. 49, pt. 2, p. 955; "Federal Veterans at Shiloh," p. 104; Otis Ashmore, "The Story of the Confederate Treasure," pp. 137–138.

38. Richardson to Walthall, August 26, 1878, in Dunbar Rowland, ed., *Jefferson Davis, Constitutionalist*, vol. VIII, p. 266.

39. William C. Davis, ed., *Diary of a Confederate Soldier*, p. 168; Louisville, KY, *Courier-Journal*, May 8, 1867; Basil W. Duke, "After the Fall of Richmond," p. 165.

40. Eliza Frances Andrews, *The War-Time Journal of a Georgia Girl*, p. 217.

41. Ibid., p. 223; Milford Overly, "Escort to President Davis," p. 122.

42. William C. Davis, *Diary of a Confederate Soldier*, p. 168.

43. Basil W. Duke, *A History of Morgan's Cavalry*, p. 577.

44. W. C. P. Breckinridge to W. R. Bringhurst, September 23, 1892, "Unwritten History Worth Preserving," p. 534; Lexington, KY, *Morning Herald*, May 28, 1900; "Maj. Clay Stacker," p. 656; P. N. Harris, "Interesting Reply to a Question," p. 296; Basil W. Duke, "After the Fall of Richmond," p. 166; Basil W. Duke, *A History of Morgan's Cavalry*, pp. 577–578; W. R. Bringhurst, "Survivor of President Davis's Escort," p. 369; H. G. Damon, "The Eyes of General Breckinridge," p. 380.

Chapter Ten

1. Varina Davis to Davis, May 1, 1865, and n.d., in Dunbar Rowland, ed., *Jefferson Davis, Constitutionalist*, vol. VI, pp. 589–590.

2. John H. Reagan, *Memoirs, with Special Reference to Secession and the Civil War*, p. 212; Davis to Reagan, August 21, 1877, Jefferson Davis–John H. Reagan Collection, Dallas Historical Society; Wood Diary, May 4–5, 1865, John Taylor Wood Papers, Southern Historical Collection.

3. Given Campbell, Memorandum, May 4, 1865, Library of Congress.

4. Michael B. Ballard, *A Long Shadow*, p. 135.

5. Micajah H. Clark, "The Last Days of the Confederate Treasury and What Became of Its Specie," p. 553; John H. Reagan, *Memoirs, with Special Reference to Secession and the Civil War*, pp. 213–214.

6. Micajah H. Clark, "The Last Days of the Confederate Treasury and What Became of Its Specie," p. 553.

7. Davis to William Preston Johnston, n.d. [1878], in Arthur Marvin Shaw, ed., "A Letter by Jefferson Davis Relating to Events Preceding His Capture," p. 33.

8. Micajah H. Clark, "The Last Days of the Confederate Treasury and What Became of Its Specie," pp. 553–554.

9. John H. Reagan, *Memoirs, with Special Reference to Secession and the Civil War*, p. 217.

10. Given Campbell, Memorandum, May 6, 1865, Library of Congress; Wood Diary, May 6, 1865, John Taylor Wood Papers, Southern Historical Collection.

11. W. T. Walthall, "The True Story of the Capture of Jefferson Davis," pp. 109–110; Fairfax Harrison, ed., *The Harrisons of Skimino*, p. 254 n.

12. W. T. Walthall, "The True Story of the Capture of Jefferson Davis," p. 110; Fairfax Harrison, ed., *The Harrisons of Skimino*, p. 253.

13. Fairfax Harrison, ed., *The Harrisons of Skimino*, pp. 247–250; Harrison

to ?, May 2, 1865, in Dunbar Rowland, ed., *Jefferson Davis, Constitutionalist*, vol. VI, pp. 587–588.

14. Leeland Hathaway Recollections, Southern Historical Collection.

15. United States War Department, *War of the Rebellion: Official Records of the Union and Confederate Armies*, ser. I, vol. 49, pt. 2, p. 1277.

16. Fairfax Harrison, ed., *The Harrisons of Skimino*, pp. 251–253; Leeland Hathaway Recollections, Southern Historical Collection.

17. Fairfax Harrison, ed., *The Harrisons of Skimino*, pp. 246, 248; Leeland Hathaway Recollections, Southern Historical Collection.

18. Leeland Hathaway Recollections, Southern Historical Collection; Fairfax Harrison, ed., *The Harrisons of Skimino*, pp. 251–253.

19. Leeland Hathaway Recollections, Southern Historical Collection.

20. William Preston Johnston to Walthall, July 14, 1877, in "Letter from Colonel William Preston Johnston, Late Aid to President Davis," p. 119; Given Campbell, Memorandum, May 7, 1865, Library of Congress. Hereafter Campbell's Memorandum lumps all subsequent dates under the heading of May 7.

21. Fairfax Harrison, ed., *The Harrisons of Skimino*, pp. 254–255.

22. William Preston Johnston to Walthall, July 14, 1877, in "Letter from Colonel William Preston Johnston," p. 119.

23. Ibid. Fairfax Harrison, ed., *The Harrisons of Skimino*, pp. 255–257.

24. David Pierson to William H. Pierson, May 9, 1865, Pierson Family Papers, Kountz Collection, Tulane University.

25. Johnston to Walthall, July 14, 1877, in "Letter from Colonel William Preston Johnston," p. 120; Fairfax Harrison, ed., *The Harrisons of Skimino*, pp. 255–257, 259 n; W. T. Walthall, "The True Story of the Capture of Jefferson Davis," p. 110; John H. Reagan, *Memoirs, with Special Reference to Secession and the Civil War*, pp. 218–219; Lubbock to Walthall, August 2, 1877, "Letter from Ex-Governor Lubbock, of Texas, Late Aid to President Davis," p. 122; Given Campbell, Memorandum, May 7, 1865, Library of Congress.

26. Johnston to Walthall, July 14, 1877, in "Letter from Colonel William Preston Johnston," p. 120.

27. Fairfax Harrison, ed., *The Harrisons of Skimino*, pp. 257, 259–260 n; Wood Diary, May 10, 1865, John Taylor Wood Papers, Southern Historical Collection; Austin, TX, *Statesman*, July 21, 1904; John H. Reagan, *Memoirs, with Special Reference to Secession and the Civil War*, p. 219.

28. Fairfax Harrison, ed., *The Harrisons of Skimino*, p. 257 and n.

29. Ibid., p. 260 n; John H. Reagan, "Flight and Capture of Jefferson Davis," p. 127; John H. Reagan, *Memoirs, with Special Reference to Secession and the Civil War*, p. 220; Varina Davis, *Jefferson Davis, Ex-President of the Confederate States of America*, vol. II, p. 638.

30. Wood Diary, May 10, 1865, John Taylor Wood Papers, Southern Historical Collection; Fairfax Harrison, ed., *The Harrisons of Skimino*, pp. 257–258.

31. Fairfax Harrison, ed., *The Harrisons of Skimino*, p. 260 n; Chester Bradley, "Was Jefferson Davis Disguised as a Woman When Captured," pp. 243ff; W. T. Walthall, "The True Story of the Capture of Jefferson Davis," p. 111; Wood Diary, May 10, 1865, John Taylor Wood Papers, Southern Historical Collection.

32. Fairfax Harrison, ed., *The Harrisons of Skimino*, pp. 258–259, 260 n; Harrison to Davis, September 1877, Dunbar Rowland, ed., *Jefferson Davis, Constitutionalist*, vol. VII, p. 589; W. T. Walthall, "The True Story of the Capture of Jefferson Davis," p. 111; Davis to W. M. Green, May 8, 1872, St. Louis, *Post-Dispatch*, January 22, 1937; Account by George M. Munger, n.d., J. B. Munger, *Munger Book*, pp. 475–476; William C. Davis, *Jefferson Davis, the Man and His Hour*, p. 637.

33. Leeland Hathaway Recollections, Southern Historical Collection; Varina Davis, recollection of capture, n.d., Jefferson Davis Papers, Tulane University; Lubbock to Walthall, August 2, 1877, "Letter from Ex-Governor Lubbock," p. 123; Fairfax Harrison, ed., *The Harrisons of Skimino*, p. 264.

34. Munger account, J. B. Munger, *Munger Book*, p. 476.

35. United States War Department, *War of the Rebellion: Official Records of the Union and Confederate Armies*, ser. I, vol. I, pt. 1, pp. 536–537; John-

ston to Walthall, July 14, 1877, "Letter from Colonel William Preston Johnston," pp. 120–121; Lubbock to Walthall, August 2, 1877, "Letter from Ex-Governor Lubbock," p. 123; John H. Reagan, "Flight and Capture of Jefferson Davis," p. 155; Leeland Hathaway Recollections, Southern Historical Collection.

36. Given Campbell, Memorandum, May 7, 1865, Library of Congress; Fairfax Harrison, ed., *The Harrisons of Skimino*, pp. 259 n, 263.

37. William Preston Johnston to Rosa Johnston, July 7, 1865, Mason Barret Collection, Tulane University.

38. Stephen B. Barnwell, *The Story of an American Family*, p. 216.

39. Johnston to Walthall, July 14, 1877, "Letter from Colonel William Preston Johnston," p. 119.

40. Wood Diary, May 10, 1865, John Taylor Wood Papers, Southern Historical Collection; John Taylor Wood, "Escape of the Confederate Secretary of War," p. 110.

41. Fairfax Harrison, ed., *The Harrisons of Skimino*, pp. 264–265; Leeland Hathaway Recollections, Southern Historical Collection; Varina Davis, *Jefferson Davis, Ex-President of the Confederate States of America*, vol. II, pp. 642–644.

42. Jefferson Davis, *Rise and Fall of the Confederate Government*, vol. II, p. 703.

43. Basil W. Duke, "Last Days of the Confederacy," in Robert V. Johnson and Clarence C. Buel, eds., *Battles and Leaders of the Civil War*, vol. 4, p. 766.

44. Garnett to William Preston Johnston, September 10, 1865, Johnston to Garnett, September 19, 1865, Mason Barret Collection, Tulane University.

45. Fairfax Harrison, ed., *The Harrisons of Skimino*, p. 266.

Chapter Eleven

1. Myrta Lockett Avary, *Recollections of Alexander H. Stephens*, pp. 99–124, passim.

2. Pleasant A. Stovall, *Robert Toombs: Statesman, Speaker, Soldier, Sage,* pp. 286–307.

3. John H. Reagan, *Memoirs, with Special Reference to Secession and the Civil War,* p. 211; John Taylor Wood, "Escape of the Confederate Secretary of War," p. 110; Benjamin to Kruttschnitt, July 22, 1865, Pierce Butler Papers, Tulane University.

4. Benjamin to Kruttschnitt, July 22, 1865, Pierce Butler Papers, Tulane University; John Taylor Wood, "Escape of the Confederate Secretary of War," p. 110; Wood Diary, May 11, 1865, John Taylor Wood Papers, Southern Historical Collection.

5. Alfred J. Hanna, *Flight into Oblivion,* pp. 207–208.

6. John Taylor Wood, "Escape of the Confederate Secretary of War," p. 111; Benjamin to Kruttschnitt, July 22, 1865, Butler Papers, Tulane University.

7. John Taylor Wood, "Escape of the Confederate Secretary of War," p. 111; Stephen B. Barnwell, *The Story of an American Family,* p. 209.

8. W. H. Swallow, "Retreat of the Confederate Government from Richmond to the Gulf," p. 606.

9. Ibid. Clifton R. Breckinridge to Breckinridge, May 13, 1874, Breckinridge Family Papers, Library of Congress; United States War Department, *War of the Rebellion: Official Records of the Union and Confederate Armies,* ser. I, vol. 49, pt. 2, p. 719.

10. Cincinnati, *Enquirer,* April 10, 1868. This article, titled "The Close of the Revolution—One Day With John C. Breckinridge," is the earliest known published account of Breckinridge's journey written by a participant, and is signed only "M." It contains suggestions indicating that it is excerpted from a fuller account, and it was republished from its first appearance in the Columbus, GA, *Sun and Times* of an unknown date. It specifically lists those in the party as given here in the text except for W. H. Swallow, failing to identify only two members, the writer himself and their guide, who he describes as "a prominent citizen." The initial "M" fits none of those named, but the writer

does describe himself as the only one of the party who had been paroled—which eliminates the civilian Swallow—and says that he had known Breckinridge well for at least a decade, and indicates that he was well acquainted with the appearance of the other cabinet members. The only other soldier known to have accompanied the party during this period was Lieutenant Draughton S. Haynes (see below), who by this time would very likely have been paroled, but he does not fit the rest of the description that implies long association with Breckinridge and the cabinet. However, Lieutenant Colonel Wilson had been released from a Union prison and exchanged just before the fall of Richmond, had known Breckinridge for years, and was with him and the cabinet throughout the journey from Richmond. Moreover, Wilson did write an account of the flight in 1868 (James Wilson to Breckinridge, August 1, 1868, Breckinridge Family Papers, Library of Congress), confessing that he was tempted to embellish their adventures in the manner of the fictional Baron Munchausen. The letter in which he mentions having written an account was written at least four months after the probable first appearance of this article in the *Sun and Times*, however, and then Wilson said that he could not release it to the world until after Breckinridge was dead. Yet the flavor and style of the article are not unlike Wilson's own jocular writing, raising the possibility that he was in fact the author of the article—which in fact shows no signs of embellishment of fact. Moreover, the "M" byline certainly could stand for "Munchausen." In the absence of more conclusive evidence to the contrary, then, it is assumed that Wilson is the probable author.

11. W. H. Swallow, "Retreat of the Confederate Government from Richmond to the Gulf," p. 606; Sutton S. Scott, "Glimpses of Two Noteable Confederates, Soon After the Fall of Richmond," undated clipping from the *Sunny South*, in Sutton S. Scott Notebook, Alabama Department of Archives and History.

12. John Taylor Wood, "Escape of the Confederate Secretary of War," p. 111.

13. Draughton Stith Haynes, *The Field Diary of a Confederate Soldier*, pp. 39–42; Dr. John S. Carbonne to the author, September 26, December 3, 1997. The binoculars are now in the possession of Dr. Carbonne.

14. W. H. Swallow, "Retreat of the Confederate Government from Richmond to the Gulf," p. 606.

15. Ibid., p. 607; Cincinnati, *Enquirer*, April 10, 1868.

16. Cincinnati, *Enquirer*, April 10, 1865.

17. W. H. Swallow, "Retreat of the Confederate Government from Richmond to the Gulf," p. 607.

18. Draughton Stith Haynes, *The Field Diary of a Confederate Soldier*, p. 40.

19. Alfred J. Hanna, *Flight into Oblivion*, pp. 105–106; H. G. Damon, "The Eyes of General Breckinridge," p. 380.

20. Wood Diary, May 15, 1865, John Taylor Wood Papers, Southern Historical Collection; John Taylor Wood, "Escape of the Confederate Secretary of War," p. 111.

21. New York, *Herald*, May 15, 1865.

22. Wood Diary, May 16, 1865, John Taylor Wood Papers, Southern Historical Collection; Mary Breckinridge Kirkland, telephone conversation with author, July 4, 1971.

23. Hereafter, unless otherwise cited, material is drawn from Breckinridge to John W. Breckinridge, July 1865, in possession of Breckinridge, Thomas Dunlap, IL, a letter written in diary format covering the escape journey; and from Wood Diary, May 16, 1865 ff, John Taylor Wood Papers, Southern Historical Collection. The Breckinridge letter has been published in Alfred J. Hanna, ed., "The Escape of Confederate Secretary of War John Cabell Breckinridge as Revealed by His Diary," pp. 323–333.

24. J. J. Dickison to Dear Sir, October 1884, Mary Elizabeth Dickison, *Dickison and His Men. Reminiscences of the War in Florida*, pp. 211, 224–225.

25. Ibid., pp. 225–226.

26. John Taylor Wood, "Escape of the Confederate Secretary of War," p. 111.

27. United States Naval War Records Office, *Official Records of the Union and Confederate Navies in the War of the Rebellion*, ser. I, vol. 17, p. 853; Cincinnati, *Enquirer*, May 28, 1865.

28. Tench Tilghman Diary, May 10–22, 1865, Southern Historical Collection.

29. Alfred J. Hanna, *Flight into Oblivion*, pp. 114–116; William C. Davis, *Jefferson Davis, the Man and His Hour*, p. 652.

30. Alfred J. Hanna, *Flight into Oblivion*, pp. 117–118.

31. United States War Department, *War of the Rebellion: Official Records of the Union and Confederate Armies*, ser. I, vol. 47, pt. 3, pp. 651–656.

32. Otis Ashmore, "The Story of the Virginia Banks Funds," pp. 171 ff; Augusta, GA, *Chronicle*, February 27, 1970; Lewis Shepherd, "The Confederate Treasure Train," pp. 257–258.

33. New York, *Times*, May 27, 1865.

34. Thomas P. Ochiltree to ?, n.d. [August 20, 1867], clipping from unidentified newspaper in Breckinridge Family Papers, Library of Congress.

35. Proclamation, May 30, 1865, clipping in Sallie Johnson Breckinridge Scrapbook in possession of Peter Ten Eyck, New York.

36. John Taylor Wood, "Escape of the Confederate Secretary of War," p. 112.

Chapter Twelve

1. Virginia Clay Diary, May 24, 1865, Clement C. Clay Papers, Duke University.

2. James P. Jones, ed., "Your Left Arm: James H. Wilson's Letters to Adam Badeau," pp. 243–244; W. T. Walthall, "The True Story of the Capture of Jefferson Davis," pp. 116–117.

3. Joseph Wheeler, "Loyal to the Last, II," pp. 26, 64–65.

4. The literature on the dress and hoopskirt stories is considerable. Davis himself did not even discuss it in *Rise and Fall of the Confederate Government,* and his point of view is perhaps best represented on his behalf in Walthall, "The True Story of the Capture of Jefferson Davis," pp. 117–118. Varina Davis, in *Memoir* (vol. II, pp. 640–641, 648–649) alludes to it briefly. Denials by Pritchard's men include James Parker's letter in the Nashville *Union and American* (June 26, 1873), while Major Charles Hudson of the Fourth Michigan, by his own account the first officer to ride into the Davis encampment, wrote an 1875 account that, though confirming Davis did have on the raglan and shawl and accepting that Varina intended it as a disguise, makes clear there were no dresses or bonnets or hoopskirts (undated clipping attached to Harrison, Extracts, Confederate States of America Records, Center for American History). J. B. Munger's account appears in *Munger Book* (pp. 475–476), and while mentioning the raglan and shawl, he does not assert that Davis was attempting to pose as a woman, only that at first Munger would have mistaken him for one but for his boots. The fullest study of the matter is in Chester Bradley's "Was Jefferson Davis Disguised as a Woman When Captured?," pp. 248 ff.

5. William C. Davis, *Jefferson Davis, the Man and His Hour,* pp. 646–647.

6. Benjamin to Kruttschnitt, July 22, 1865, Pierce Butler Papers, Tulane University.

7. Robert Douthat Meade, *Judah P. Benjamin, Confederate Statesman,* pp. 319–320.

8. Ibid., pp. 320–321; Alfred J. Hanna, *Flight into Oblivion,* pp. 199–200.

9. Cincinnati, *Enquirer,* May 31, 1865.

10. Breckinridge's map of Florida is now in the collections of the Museum of the Confederacy in Richmond, VA.

11. John Taylor Wood, "Escape of the Confederate Secretary of War," p. 112.

12. New Orleans, *Tribune*, June 3, 1865.

13. Breckinridge to Dickison, June 26, 1865, in Mary Elizabeth Dickison, *Dickison and His Men*, p. 227.

14. Cincinnati, *Enquirer*, June 25, 1865.

15. William H. Parker, "The Gold and Silver in the Confederate States Treasury," p. 313; Dickison to Dear Sir, October 1884, in Mary Elizabeth Dickison, *Dickison and His Men*, p. 226; John Taylor Wood, "Escape of the Confederate Secretary of War," p. 114.

16. Fairfax Harrison, ed., *The Harrisons of Skimino*, p. 262; William H. Parker, "The Gold and Silver in the Confederate States Treasury," p. 313.

17. John Taylor Wood, "Escape of the Confederate Secretary of War," pp. 115–116; Wilson to Breckinridge, August 1, 1868, Breckinridge Family Papers, Library of Congress.

18. Edgefield, SC, *Advertiser*, June 6, 1865.

19. At this point, Breckinridge's letter in diary form and Wood's diary get out of synch by one day. It appears that either Breckinridge inadvertently added a day to the actual ocean voyage or Wood mistakenly added an extra day to their coastal trip. Given Wood's estimate that they made slow progress of 15 to 20 miles a day along the coast, it is more likely that they would not have reached the Boca Ratones until late on June 7, as his diary states. It should be added that Breckinridge's account was written a month later, in July, though almost certainly from notes kept during the trip, while it is equally likely that Wood's existing diary, which is in much too good a state of preservation to have endured the exposure and repeated soakings of the journey, is a later work based on or simply copying notes made at the time. Thus both documents, which are otherwise in wonderful agreement, contain the potential for an inadvertent after-the-fact error in dating.

20. John Taylor Wood, "Escape of the Confederate Secretary of War," p. 116.

21. The sole source for this episode at Fort Dallas is John Taylor Wood, "Escape of the Confederate Secretary of War" (pp. 116–118). Wood's Diary makes no mention of it other than to say that they obtained

some provisions, and Breckinridge's diary letter also says nothing about being chased and fighting with the tories. None of the accounts that they gave to newspaper correspondents after their arrival in Cuba mention it, either. In telling the story of the escape to Burton Harrison in 1866, Breckinridge also did not speak of it apparently (Fairfax Harrison, ed., *The Harrisons of Skimino*, pp. 262–263). Wilson's August 1, 1868, letter to Breckinridge (Breckinridge Family Papers, Library of Congress) regarding the journey says nothing about it, and the oral account that Wood gave to William Parker early in 1893, some months before his "Escape" article appeared, also seems to have made no mention of such an encounter (William H. Parker, "The Gold and Silver in the Confederate States Treasury," p. 313). It seems strange that all of these other accounts would omit such a dramatic episode, especially since they all cover the piracy and the storm, and most also mention the subsequent near loss of Wood overboard. Moreover, Wood's "Escape" article in almost all other respects follows his diary rigorously, sometimes verbatim, with few if any signs of real embellishment. Thus this single episode stands out all the more, and it has to be considered at least possible that Wood simply invented it to make his article even more dramatic. Breckinridge was dead and could not gainsay, while Russell, O'Toole, and Ferguson, even if literate, had faded into obscurity and were not likely to be *Century Magazine* readers. Unquestionably the fugitives did stop at Fort Dallas and obtain provisions. Beyond this, one can do no more than raise a question about how much more than that bare fact can be accepted from Wood's account.

22. John Taylor Wood, "Escape of the Confederate Secretary of War," pp. 118–120. Here again Wood offers a story that appears in none of the other accounts by participants and not in his own diary, saying that after leaving Fort Dallas, a large schooner appeared and chased them for some time. Attempting to elude it in the shallow reefs, says Wood, led to the difficulty in their passage to the Atlantic, and forced them to jettison most of their provisions. It seems improbable, not least because he says the boat came up behind them from the north, yet that

was the very direction they had come themselves, from the northern tip of the bay. Thus, if there was any schooner up there already, they would have had to pass it on their way south long before this point in their trip. His own diary indicates a routine passage down the bay, and so does Breckinridge's, leading to the conclusion that this chase was almost certainly an embellishment. Nevertheless, statements in Breckinridge's diary and a couple of other reliable accounts make it clear that when out in the Gulf they were once again short on provisions, and so Wood's account in his article about their jettisoning or otherwise ruining some of their food is apparently accurate.

23. New Orleans, *Tribune*, July 4, 1865.

24. Thomas D. Jeffress, in "Escape of Breckinridge and Benjamin" (pp. 26–27), gives a highly fanciful and inaccurate account of the journey, which is nevertheless almost certainly based on a genuine interview Jeffress had with Breckinridge in 1874, but the passage of thirty-six intervening years greatly warped Jeffress's recollection, for he had Breckinridge and Benjamin escaping together, and claims that the general described the ocean voyage as "two days and three nights of the most delightful and propitious weather." Consequently, while it has some interesting comments, the Jeffress article has not been used in this study.

25. John Taylor Wood, "Escape of the Confederate Secretary of War," pp. 121–122.

26. J. Stoddard Johnston, "Sketches of Operations of General John C. Breckinridge, No. 3," pp. 390–391; William H. Parker, "The Gold and Silver in the Confederate States Treasury," p. 313.

27. John Taylor Wood, "Escape of the Confederate Secretary of War," p. 122; Fairfax Harrison, ed., *The Harrisons of Skimino*, pp. 262–263.

28. Boston, *Transcript*, June 22, 1865.

29. [John Cahill], "The Escape of J. C. Breckinridge," clipping from unidentified ca. 1900 issue of the St. Louis, *Globe-Democrat*, Breckinridge Family Papers, Library of Congress; John Taylor Wood, "Escape of the Confederate Secretary of War," p. 125.

30. Alfred J. Hanna, *Flight into Oblivion*, p. 200; Robert Douthat Meade, *Judah P. Benjamin, Confederate Statesman*, pp. 320–321; Benjamin to Kruttschnitt, July 22, 1865, Pierce Butler Papers, Tulane University. Unless otherwise cited, the balance of this account of Benjamin's voyage is drawn from his July 22 letter, Hanna, *Flight* (pp. 200–208), and Meade, *Benjamin* (pp. 322–325).

31. Benjamin to Kruttschnitt, August 1, 1865, Pierce Butler Papers, Tulane University.

32. Ibid.

33. Ibid., September 29, 1865.

34. Benjamin to James A. Bayard, August 30, 1865, James A. and Thomas F. Bayard Papers, Historical Society of Delaware.

35. Alfred J. Hanna, *Flight into Oblivion*, pp. 210–223, passim.

Aftermath Notes

1. John Cahill to Breckinridge, August 10, September 14, 1871, Breckinridge Family Papers, Library of Congress.

2. New York, *Herald*, June 27, 1865; Eliza Ripley, *Social Life in Old New Orleans*, p. 288.

3. Eliza McHatton Ripley, *Social Life in Old New Orleans*, p. 128; Mary B. Maltby, *Mary Cyrene Breckinridge*, p. 8. The only known original print of the Havana photo is in the Sallie Johnson Breckinridge Scrapbook in possession of Peter Ten Eyck, New York.

4. New York, *Herald*, June 27, 1865.

5. Washington, *Daily National Intelligencer*, June 29, 1865.

6. Ibid.; New York, *Herald*, June 29, 1865.

7. Breckinridge to Dickison, June 26, 1865, in Mary Elizabeth Dickison, *Dickison and His Men*, p. 227.

8. Ibid.; New York, *Herald*, June 27, 1865; Breckinridge to Wood, Sep-

tember 17, 1865, John Taylor Wood Papers, Southern Historical Collection; Alfred J. Hanna, *Flight into Oblivion*, p. 267.

9. Steve Sands to the author, April 6, 1984. Information on Richard Russell supplied by Steve Sands of Marietta, GA.

10. Breckinridge, testimonial, July 7, 1865, in possession of Louisa Hill, New York, NY.

11. New York, *Tribune*, July 18, 1865; New York, *Herald*, June 27, 1865.

12. Wilson to Breckinridge, August 1, 1868, Breckinridge Family Papers, Library of Congress.

13. William C. Davis, "'The Conduct of Mr. Thompson'," pp. 4–7, 43–47.

14. Breckinridge to Catherine Carson, November 13, 1865, Breckinridge Family Papers, Library of Congress.

15. Littleton B. Washington, Memoir of Judah Benjamin, November 11, 1897, copy in possession of Douglas Gibboney, Carlisle, PA.

16. For Breckinridge's postwar years, see William C. Davis, *Breckinridge: Statesman, Soldier, Symbol*, pp. 549 ff.

17. For Davis's postwar years see William C. Davis, *Jefferson Davis, the Man and His Hour*, pp. 640 ff.

18. Louisville, *Courier-Journal*, October 16, 1870.

BIBLIOGRAPHY

Sources for the story of the collapse of the Confederate government and the flight of its leaders are myriad and of varying quality. The pioneering work on the subject is A. J. Hanna's *Flight into Oblivion*, which after more than sixty years still makes delightful reading. It remains a pertinent source of material nowhere else available, though somewhat dated and containing numerous errors. Michael Ballard's 1988 *A Long Shadow: Jefferson Davis and the Final Days of the Confederacy* corrects Hanna in many respects and offers much that is new, though perhaps it lacks the atmosphere of its earlier counterpart. Both should be used in any further reading on the subject. Burke Davis's *The Long Surrender* is less satisfying and casts a wider net but is still occasionally useful.

Biographical studies of the principal protagonists are cited in the notes, but here it should be mentioned that the most recent and authoritative studies of the Confederate president are William C. Davis's *Jefferson Davis, The Man and His Hour* and William J. Cooper's *Jefferson Davis*. The latter is thin on the period covered in the present work but very full for Davis's career in general, while the former devotes more attention to the last days in office. For the secretary of war the standard work is William C. Davis's *Breckinridge: Statesman, Soldier, Symbol*, while the best work on the secretary of state is still Robert Douthat Meade's *Judah P. Benjamin, Confederate Statesman*. The secretary of the navy has had one capable biography, Joseph T. Durkin's *Stephen R. Mallory, Confederate Navy Chief*. The best source for Postmaster General John H. Reagan remains his *Memoirs, with Special Reference to Secession and the Civil War*, though being written at the end of a long life, it is considerably embellished and inaccurate in places. No adequate biography of the secretary of the Treasury exists, but Ethel S. Nepveuz's *George Alfred Trenholm and the Company That Went to War 1861–1865* has some limited use. Similarly, there is no biography of Attorney General George Davis. Rembert W. Patrick, in *Jefferson Davis and his Cabinet*, however, provides good general background on all the cabinet members.

The evacuation of the capital is briefly, though ably, handled in Rembert W. Patrick's *Fall of Richmond*, while the Johnston-Sherman surrender negotiations are wonderfully illuminated in Mark L. Bradley's *This Astounding Close: The Road to Bennett Place*. Jefferson Davis's own *Rise and Fall of the Confederate Government* is largely disappointing, leaving purposely unsaid almost as much as it says. His wife's memoir (*Jefferson Davis, Ex-President of the Confederate States of America. A Memoir by His Wife*) adds much more flesh to the story, especially of the last days of the flight and their capture. For the story of the myth of Davis being in woman's clothing when taken, Chester Bradley's *Journal of Mississippi History* article remains the best source. The affairs of the fleeing government in its various stops have been handled in a considerable number or articles and short works, and those that have been useful are cited in the notes. The literature on the Treasury is perhaps the most extensive of all, but much of it is of questionable value. J. Frank Carroll's *Confederate Treasure in Danville* can be useful, though the information is flawed and must be handled carefully. William H. Parker's *Recollections of A Naval Officer, 1841–1865* is a standard source for the involvement of the Naval Academy midshipmen in guarding the treasure. Still the best account is Micajah Clark's 1881 article in the *Southern Historical Society Papers*, while the story of the separate treasure of the Virginia banks is competently dispensed with in Otis Ashmore's 1918 *Georgia Historical Quarterly* article. Ralph L. Hobbs's *Fate of the Two Confederate Wagon Trains of Gold* also contains information not otherwise available.

A surprising number of first-person accounts on the flight of the government, the treasure trains, the collapse in Washington, and the rest of the story presented here appeared in the issues of the *Confederate Veteran* over the years of its publication from 1892 to 1932. Many have been useful, but it must be emphasized that almost all must be handled carefully, for several were written more than fifty years after the fact by very aged men, and some are little better than fancy replacing lost memory. The articles in the earlier *Southern Historical Society Papers* are in the main more reliable.

Primary Sources

MANUSCRIPTS

Alabama Department of Archives and History, Montgomery
  Sutton S. Scott Notebook

Center for American History, University of Texas, Austin
  Confederate States of America Records

Charleston Museum, Charleston, South Carolina
  Aiken Rhett Collection

Dallas Historical Society, Dallas, Texas
  Jefferson Davis–John H. Reagan Collection

Historical Society of Delaware, Wilmington
  James A. and Thomas F. Bayard Papers

Duke University Library, Durham, North Carolina
  John C. Breckinridge Papers
  Clement C. Clay Papers
  Jefferson Davis Papers

Filson Club, Louisville, Kentucky
  John C. Breckinridge Papers

Houghton Library, Harvard University, Cambridge,
Massachusetts
  Frederick M. Dearborn Collection

Library of Congress, Washington, D.C.
  Breckinridge Family Papers
  Given Campbell, Memorandum of a Journal Kept Daily
    During the Last March of Jefferson Davis

Causten-Pickett Papers
Jedediah Hotchkiss Papers
Edwin M. Stanton Papers
Gideon Welles Papers
Louis T. Wigfall Papers

Museum of the Confederacy, Richmond, Virginia
    John C. Breckinridge's map of Florida
    Jefferson Davis Papers
    Jeremy F. Gilmer Papers

National Archives, Washington, D.C.
    Record Group 109
        Letters Received, Confederate Secretary of War
        Misc. Register of Letters and Telegrams Received, Army of
            Northern Virginia 1862–1863, chapter VIII, volume 232
        Secretary of War, Register of Letters Received, February
            1864–April 1865, chapter IX, volume 31
        Robertson, Felix H., Compiled Service Record
    Record Group 110
        Entry 38

North Carolina Department of Archives and History, Raleigh
    Governors Papers
        Zebulon B. Vance

Rice University, Houston, Texas
    Jefferson Davis Papers project archives

South Caroliniana Library, University of South Carolina,
Columbia
    George A. Trenholm Papers

Southern Historical Collection, University of North Carolina,
Chapel Hill
    John A. Campbell Papers
    Basil W. Duke Papers
    Charles Iverson Graves Papers
    Leeland Hathaway Recollections
    Stephen R. Mallory Papers
    Peter H. Mayo Recollections
    Tench Tilghman Diary
    White, Wellford, Taliaferro, and Marshall Family Papers
    John Taylor Wood Papers

Tulane University, New Orleans, Louisiana
    Mason Barret Collection
    Pierce Butler Papers
    Jefferson Davis Papers
    Pierson Family Papers, Kountz Collection

United States Army Military History Institute, Carlisle,
Pennsylvania
    John H. Burrill Papers, Civil War Times Illustrated
        Collection

University of Virginia Library, Charlottesville
    Joseph B. Anderson, "President Jefferson Davis in Danville,
        Va. April 3–10, 1865"
    Thomas L. Rosser Papers

Virginia Historical Society, Richmond
    Rives Family Papers

Washington and Lee University, Lexington, Virginia
    R. H. Fleming Diary

MANUSCRIPTS IN PRIVATE HANDS

Walter Agard, Madison, Wisconsin
  John C. Breckinridge Papers

William C. Davis, Roanoke, Virginia
  John C. Breckinridge Papers

Douglas Gibboney, Carlisle, PA
  Littleton B. Washington Papers

Craig M. Morisak, Whittier, California
  James H. Carson, Grasshopper Springs in 1865

Katherine Breckinridge Prewitt, Mt. Sterling, Kentucky
  John C. and Clifton R. Breckinridge Papers

John R. Riddler, Tyler, Texas
  Mary C. Courtney, Days of the Confederacy

Peter Ten Eyck, New York, New York
  Sallie Breckinridge Johnson Scrapbook

Breckinridge Thomas, Dunlap, Illinois
  John C. Breckinridge Letter, July 1865

NEWSPAPERS

Augusta, GA, *Chronicle*, 1970

Austin, TX, *Statesman*, 1904

Boston *Transcript*, 1865

Cincinnati, *Enquirer*, 1865, 1868

Dallas, *Morning News*, 1897

Edgefield, SC, *Advertiser,* 1865

Danville, VA, *Register,* 1939

Danville, VA, *Weekly Register,* 1865

Lexington, KY, *Morning Herald,* 1900

London, *Illustrated London News,* 1865

Louisville, KY, *Courier-Journal,* 1867, 1870, 1875

Lynchburg, VA, *Daily Virginian,* 1866

Montgomery, AL, *Daily Advertiser,* 1865, 1886

Nashville, TN, *Union and American,* 1873

New Orleans, LA, *Tribune,* 1865

New York, *Citizen,* 1867

New York, *Herald,* 1865

New York, *Times,* 1865

St. Louis, *Post-Dispatch,* 1937

Washington, D.C., *Daily National Intelligencer,* 1865

Washington, D.C., *Evening Star,* 1861

LETTERS, DIARIES, MEMOIRS,
AND OFFICIAL COMPILATIONS

Alexander, Edward Porter. *Military Memoirs of a Confederate.* New York, 1907.

Andrews, Eliza Frances. *The War-Time Journal of a Georgia Girl, 1864–1865.* New York, 1908.

Avary, Myrta Lockett, ed. *Recollections of Alexander H. Stephens.* New York, 1910.

Campbell, John A. *Recollections of the Evacuation of Richmond, April 2d, 1865.* Baltimore, 1880.

Campbell, R. Thomas, ed. *Midshipman in Gray.* Shippensburg, PA, 1997.

Clay-Clopton, Virginia. *A Belle of the Fifties: Memoirs of Mrs. Clay, of Alabama.* New York, 1905.

Crist, Lynda Lasswell, and Mary Seaton Dix, eds. *The Papers of Jefferson Davis, Volume 5, 1853–1855.* Baton Rouge, 1985.

Davis, Jefferson. *Rise and Fall of the Confederate Government.* 2 vols. New York, 1881.

Davis, Varina. *Jefferson Davis, Ex-President of the Confederate States of America. A Memoir by His Wife.* 2 vols. New York, 1890.

Davis, William C., ed. *Diary of a Confederate Soldier: John S. Jackman of the Orphan Brigade.* Columbia, SC, 1990.

De Leon, T. C. *Four Years in Rebel Capitals.* Mobile, 1890.

Dickison, Mary Elizabeth. *Dickison and His Men. Reminiscences of the War in Florida.* Louisville, 1890.

Dowdey, Clifford, and Louis A. Manarin, eds. *Wartime Papers of R. E. Lee.* Boston, 1961.

Duke, Basil W. *A History of Morgan's Cavalry.* New York, 1906.

——. *Reminiscences of General Basil W. Duke, C.S.A.* New York, 1911.

Durkin, Joseph T., ed. *John Dooley, Confederate Soldier: His War Journal.* Georgetown, DC, 1945.

Gallagher, Gary W., ed. *Fighting for the Confederacy: The Personal Recollections of General Edward Porter Alexander.* Chapel Hill, NC, 1989.

Harrison, Constance. *Recollections Grave and Gay.* New York, 1912.

Harrison, Fairfax, ed. *The Harrisons of Skimino.* N.p., 1910.

Haynes, Draughton Stith. *The Field Diary of a Confederate Soldier.* Darien, GA, 1963.

Headley, John W. *Confederate Operations in Canada and New York.* New York, 1906.

Johnson, Adam R. *The Partisan Rangers of the Confederate States Army.* Louisville, 1904.

Johnston, Joseph E. *Narrative of Military Operations.* New York, 1874.

Jones, John B. *A Rebel War Clerk's Diary at the Confederate States Capital.* 2 vols. Philadelphia, 1866.

Kirke, Edmund. *Down in Tennessee and Back by Way of Richmond.* New York, 1864.

Lankford, Nelson D., ed. *An Irishman in Dixie: Thomas Conolly's Diary of the Fall of the Confederacy.* Columbia, SC, 1988.

Lee, Robert E. *Recollections and Letters of General Robert E. Lee.* New York, 1904.

Life and Reminiscences of Jefferson Davis, by Distinguished Men of His Time. Baltimore, 1890.

Longstreet, James. *From Manassas to Appomattox.* Philadelphia, 1896.

Lubbock, Francis R. *Six Decades in Texas.* Austin, 1900.

Memorials of the Life, Public Services, and Character of William T. Sutherlin. Danville, VA, 1894.

Morgan, James M. *Recollections of a Rebel Reefer*. Boston, 1917.

Parker, William H. *Recollections of a Naval Officer, 1841–1865*. New York, 1883.

Phillips, Ulrich B., ed. *The Correspondence of Robert Toombs, Alexander H. Stephens, and Howell Cobb*. Washington, 1913.

Putnam, Sallie B. *In Richmond during the Confederacy*. New York, 1867.

Reagan, John H. *Memoirs, with Special Reference to Secession and the Civil War*. New York, 1906.

Ripley, Eliza McHatton. *Social Life in Old New Orleans, Being Recollections of My Girlhood*. New York, 1912.

Roman, Alfred B. *The Military Operations of General Beauregard in the War between the States 1861 to 1865*. 2 vols. New York, 1884.

Rouse, Parke, Jr., ed. *When the Yankees Came: Civil War and Reconstruction on the Virginia Peninsula*. Richmond, 1977.

Rowland, Dunbar, ed. *Jefferson Davis, Constitutionalist: His Letters, Papers and Speeches*. 10 vols. Jackson, MS, 1923.

Rubinfine, Joseph. *C.S.A. List No. 69*. Pleasantville, NJ, n.d.

Sherman, William T. *Memoirs*. 2 vols. New York, 1875.

Simpson, Brooks D., and Jean V. Berlin, eds. *Sherman's Civil War: Selected Correspondence of William T. Sherman, 1860–1865*. Chapel Hill, NC, 1999.

Summers, Festus P., ed. *A Borderland Confederate*. Pittsburgh, 1962.

United States Congress. *Journal of the Congress of the Confederate States of America.* 7 vols. Washington, 1904.

United States Naval War Records Office. *Official Records of the Union and Confederate Navies in the War of the Rebellion.* 31 vols. Washington, 1894–1920.

United States War Department. *War of the Rebellion: Official Records of the Union and Confederate Armies.* 128 vols. Washington, 1880–1901.

Wiggins, Sarah Woolfolk, ed. *The Journals of Josiah Gorgas, 1857–1878.* Tuscaloosa, AL, 1995.

Wilson, Rufus R., ed. *Lincoln among His Friends.* Caldwell, ID, 1942.

Wise, John S. *The End of an Era.* Boston, 1902.

Woodward, C. Vann, ed. *Mary Chesnut's Civil War.* New Haven, CT, 1981.

Younger, Edward, ed. *Inside the Confederate Government: The Diary of Robert Garlick Hill Kean.* New York, 1957.

ARTICLES

Averill, J. H. "Richmond, Virginia. The Evacuation of the City and the Days Preceding It." *Southern Historical Society Papers,* XXV, 1897, pp. 267–273.

Bean, W. G., ed. "Memoranda of Conversations between General Robert E. Lee and William Preston Johnston." *Virginia Magazine of History and Biography,* LXXIII, October 1965, pp. 474–484.

Binkley, H. C. "Shared in the Confederate Treasure." *Confederate Veteran*, XXXVIII, March 1930, pp. 87–88.

Bobbitt, B. Boisseau. "Our Last Capital." *Southern Historical Society Papers*, XXXI, 1903, pp. 334–339.

Bringhurst, W. R. "Survivor of President Davis's Escort." *Confederate Veteran*, XXXIV, October 1926, pp. 368–369.

Broun, Joseph M. "The Last Confederate Payroll." *Civil War History*, VII, June 1961, pp. 201–204.

——. "Last Confederate Payroll." *Confederate Veteran*, XXV, June 1917, p. 258.

Bruce, H. W. "Some Reminiscences of the Second of April, 1865." *Southern Historical Society Papers*, IX, May 1881, pp. 206–211.

Campbell, John A. "Evacuation Echoes." *Southern Historical Society Papers*, XXIV, 1896, pp. 351–353.

"Captain Ridley's Journal." *Confederate Veteran*, III, April 1895, p. 99.

Clark, Micajah H. "The Last Days of the Confederate Treasury and What Became of Its Specie." *Southern Historical Society Papers*, IX, November–December 1881, pp. 542–556.

——. "Retreat of the Cabinet from Richmond." *Confederate Veteran*, VI, July 1898, pp. 293–294.

Cleveland, Henry W. "Robert Toombs." *Southern Bivouac*, New Series, I, January 1886, pp. 449–459.

Damon, H. G. "The Eyes of General Breckinridge." *Confederate Veteran*, XVII, August 1909, p. 380.

Duke, Basil W. "After the Fall of Richmond." *Southern Bivouac,* New Series, II, August 1886, pp. 156–166.

——. "Last Days of the Confederacy." Robert V. Johnson and Clarence C. Buel, eds., *Battles and Leaders of the Civil War,* New York, 1887, vol. IV, pp. 762–67.

Duke, R. T. W. "Burning of Richmond." *Southern Historical Society Papers,* XXV, 1897, pp. 134–138.

"Federal Veterans at Shiloh." *Confederate Veteran,* III, April 1895, pp. 104–105.

Ferguson, Samuel W. "Another Account by Gen. S. W. Ferguson." *Confederate Veteran,* XVI, June 1908, pp. 263–264.

Fiveash, Joseph G. "When Mr. Davis Heard of Lincoln's Death." *Confederate Veteran,* XV, August 1907, p. 366.

Fore, Mrs. James A. "Cabinet Meeting in Charlotte." *Southern Historical Society Papers,* XLI, September 1916, pp. 61–67.

Gilliam, Robert. "Last of the Confederate Treasury Department." *Confederate Veteran,* XXXVII, November 1929, pp. 423–425.

Gorgas, Amelia. "The Evacuation of Richmond." *Confederate Veteran,* XXV, March 1917, pp. 110–111.

Hanna, Alfred J. "The Escape of Confederate Secretary of War John Cabell Breckinridge as Revealed by His Diary." *Register of the Kentucky Historical Society,* XXXVII, October 1939, pp. 323–333.

Harris, P. N. "Interesting Reply to a Question." *Confederate Veteran,* V, June 1897, p. 296.

Jeffress, Thomas D. "Escape of Breckinridge and Benjamin." *Confederate Veteran,* XVIII, January 1910, pp. 26–27.

Johnston, J. Stoddard. "Sketches of Operations of General John C. Breckinridge, No. 3." *Southern Historical Society Papers*, VII, October 1879, pp. 385–392.

Jones, James P., ed. "Your Left Arm: James H. Wilson's Letters to Adam Badeau." *Civil War History*, XII, September 1966, pp. 230–245.

"Last Letters and Telegrams of the Confederacy—Correspondence of General John C. Breckinridge." *Southern Historical Society Papers*, XII, March 1884, pp. 97–105.

"Letter from Colonel William Preston Johnston, Late Aid to President Davis." *Southern Historical Society Papers*, V, March 1878, pp. 118–121.

"Letter from Ex-Governor Lubbock, of Texas, Late Aid to President Davis." *Southern Historical Society Papers*, V, March 1878, pp. 122–124.

Leyburn, John. "The Fall of Richmond." *Harper's New Monthly Magazine*, XXXIII, June 1866, pp. 92–96.

"Maj. Clay Stacker." *Confederate Veteran*, XVI, December 1908, p. 656.

Mallory, Stephen R. "The Last Days of the Confederate Government." *McClure's Magazine*, XVI, December 1900, pp. 99–107, and January 1901, pp. 239–248.

McAllister, L. C. "Disbanding of President Davis's Escort." *Confederate Veteran*, XIII, January 1905, p. 25.

Miller, Fannie Walker. "The Fall of Richmond." *Confederate Veteran*, XIII, July 1905, p. 305.

"Open Letters." *Century Magazine*, XXXVIII, October 1889, pp. 950–954.

Overly, Milford. "Escort to President Davis." *Confederate Veteran*, XVI, March 1908, pp. 121–123.

Packard, Joseph. "Ordnance Matters at the Close." *Confederate Veteran*, XVI, May 1908, pp. 227–229.

"Papers of John A. Campbell." *Southern Historical Society Papers*, XLII, September 1917, pp. 3–81.

Parker, William H. "The Gold and Silver in the Confederate States Treasury." *Southern Historical Society Papers*, XXI, 1893, pp. 304–313.

Reagan, John H. "Flight and Capture of Jefferson Davis." *Annals of the War Written by Leading Participants North and South.* Philadelphia, 1879, pp. 147–159.

"Resources of the Confederacy in 1865—Report of General I. M. St. John, Commissary General." *Southern Historical Society Papers*, III, March 1877, pp. 97–111.

"Resources of the Confederacy in February, 1865." *Southern Historical Society Papers*, July 1876, pp. 56–63.

Robertson, M. E. "President Davis's Last Official Meeting." *Publications of the Southern History Association*, V, July 1901, pp. 291–299.

Shaw, Arthur Marvin, ed. "A Letter by Jefferson Davis Relating to Events Preceding His Capture." *Georgia Historical Quarterly*, XXXI, March 1947, pp. 31–33.

Shepherd, Lewis. "The Confederate Treasure Train." *Confederate Veteran*, XXV, June 1917, pp. 257–259.

Spencer, Warren, ed. "A French View of the Fall of Richmond: Alfred Paul's Report to Drouyn de Lhuys, April 11, 1865."

Virginia Magazine of History and Biography, LXXIII, April 1965, pp. 178–188.

Sulivane, Clement. "The Fall of Richmond, I: The Evacuation." Robert U. Johnson and Clarence C. Buel, eds., *Battles and Leaders of the Civil War*, New York, 1887, vol. IV, pp. 725–726.

Swallow, W. H. "Retreat of the Confederate Government from Richmond to the Gulf." *Magazine of American History*, XV, June 1886, pp. 596–608.

Tucker, Dallas. "The Fall of Richmond." *Southern Historical Society Papers*, XXIX, 1901, pp. 152–163.

"Unwritten History Worth Preserving." *Confederate Veteran*, VIII, December 1900, pp. 534–535.

Venable, M. W. "On the Way to Appomattox—War Memories." *Confederate Veteran*, XXXII, August 1924, pp. 303–304.

Watehall, E. T. "Fall of Richmond, April 3, 1865." *Confederate Veteran*, XVII, May 1909, p. 215.

Wheeler, Joseph. "Loyal to the Last, Part I." *Civil War Times Illustrated*, XXXVIII, February 2000, pp. 20, 66–68, and "Part II," March 2000, pp. 20–23, 26, 64–68.

Wheless, John F. "The Confederate Treasure—Statement of Paymaster John F. Wheless." *Southern Historical Society Papers*, X, March 1882, pp. 137–141.

Wittich, W. L. "Escort to President Davis." *Confederate Veteran*, XVI, June 1908, p. 263.

Wood, John Taylor. "Escape of the Confederate Secretary of War." *Century Magazine*, XLVII, November 1893, pp. 110–123.

Secondary Sources

GENERAL WORKS, BIOGRAPHIES, AND MONOGRAPHS

Ballard, Michael B. *A Long Shadow: Jefferson Davis and the Final Days of the Confederacy*. Jackson, MS, 1986.

Barnwell, Stephen B. *The Story of an American Family*. Marquette, IL, 1969.

Bradley, Mark L. *This Astounding Close: The Road to Bennett Place*. Chapel Hill, NC, 2000.

Brubaker, John H., III. *The Last Capital*. Danville, VA, 1979.

Butler, Pierce. *Judah P. Benjamin*. Philadelphia, 1907.

Carroll, J. Frank. *Confederate Treasure in Danville*. Danville, VA, 1996.

Coffin, Charles C. C. *The Boys of '61*. Boston, 1886.

Cooper, William J. *Jefferson Davis*. New York, 2000.

Couper, William. *The V.M.I. New Market Cadets*. Charlottesville, VA, 1933.

Curry, J. L. M. *Civil History of the Government of the Confederate States*. Richmond, 1901.

Davis, Burke. *The Long Surrender*. New York, 1982.

Davis, William C. *Breckinridge: Statesman, Soldier, Symbol*. Baton Rouge, 1974.

——. *Jefferson Davis, the Man and His Hour*. New York, 1991.

Dowd, Clement. *Life of Zebulon B. Vance*. Charlotte, NC, 1897.

Durkin, Joseph T. *Stephen R. Mallory, Confederate Navy Chief*. Chapel Hill, NC, 1954.

Hanna, Alfred J. *Flight into Oblivion*. Richmond, 1938.

Hobbs, Ralph L. *The Fate of the Two Confederate Wagon Trains of Gold*. Winnsboro, SC, 1976.

Horn, Stanley. *The Army of Tennessee*. Norman, OK, 1952.

Maltby, Mary B. *Mary Cyrene Breckinridge*. Georgetown, KY, 1910.

Meade, Robert Douthat. *Judah P. Benjamin, Confederate States-man*. New York, 1943.

Moore, Samuel J. T., Jr. *Moore's Complete Civil War Guide to Rich-mond*. Richmond, 1973.

Munger, J. B. *Munger Book. Something of the Mungers, 1639–1914*. N.p., 1915.

Nepveux, Ethel S. *George Alfred Trenholm and the Company that Went to War 1861–1865*. Charleston, 1973.

Patrick, Rembert. *The Fall of Richmond*. Baton Rouge, 1960.

———. *Jefferson Davis and his Cabinet*. Baton Rouge, 1944.

Pitman, Ben. *The Assassination of President Lincoln and the Trial of the Conspirators*. Cincinnati, 1865.

Pollard, E. A. *The Lost Cause*. New York, 1866.

Pollock, Edward. *Illustrated Sketch Book of Danville, Virginia; Its Manufactures & Commerce*. Danville, VA, 1885.

Saunders, Robert, Jr. *John Archibald Campbell, Southern Moderate, 1811–1889*. Tuscaloosa, AL, 1997.

Shingleton, Royce G. *John Taylor Wood, Sea Ghost of the Confeder-acy*. Athens, GA, 1979.

Springs, Katherine W. *The Squires of Springfield*. n.p., n.d.

Stovall, Pleasant A. *Robert Toombs: Statesman, Speaker, Soldier, Sage*. New York, 1892.

Thompson, William Y. *Robert Toombs of Georgia*. Baton Rouge, 1966.

Tucker, Glenn. *Zeb Vance, Champion of Personal Freedom*. Indianapolis, 1965.

ARTICLES

Ashmore, Otis. "The Story of the Confederate Treasure." *Georgia Historical Quarterly*, II, September 1918, pp. 119–138.

——. "The Story of the Virginia Banks Funds." *Georgia Historical Quarterly*, II, December 1918, pp. 171–197.

Bradley, Chester. "Was Jefferson Davis Disguised as a Woman When Captured?" *Journal of Mississippi History*, XXXVI, August 1974, pp. 243–268.

Davis, William C. "'The Conduct of Mr. Thompson'." *Civil War Times Illustrated*, IX, May 1970, pp. 4–7, 43–47.

Walmsley, James Elliott. "The Last Meeting of the Confederate Cabinet." *Mississippi Valley Historical Review*, VI, December 1919, pp. 336–349.

Walthall, W. T. "The True Story of the Capture of Jefferson Davis." *Southern Historical Society Papers*, V, March 1878, pp. 97–118.

INDEX

Alabama, 53, 82, 128, 213
Alabama, CSS, 12, 385
Alexander, General Edward Porter, 269, 341
amnesty proclamations, 348, 382, 386, 393
Andrews, Eliza, 256, 257, 269–70, 281, 392
Andrews, Judge Garnett, 216, 218
Arkansas, 52
Arkansas, CSS, 344
Army of Northern Virginia. *See* Lee, General Robert E.
Army of Tennessee, 22, 24, 49, 113, 147. *See also* Johnston, General Joseph E.

Bank of North Carolina, 177–78, 195
Bank of Virginia, 207, 340–41
Barnwell, Senator Robert W., 309

Barnwell, Captain Stephen, 315
  escapes with Wood, 308–9, 317–19
Barnwell, Major Thomas Osborn, 319
Bates, Lewis, 172–73, 177
  described, 172, 176
Battle of Stones River, 261
Beauregard, General P. G. T., 14, 23, 91
  calls for reinstatement of, 16
  evacuation of Greensboro, 143, 145
  hatred for Davis, 5, 128, 129, 394
  peace talks and, 151, 162, 169
  reports of desperate situation, 128–29, 130, 135
Benedict, Ann, 88
Benjamin, Judah P.:
  in Charlotte, 176, 178, 179
  in Danville, 77, 83, 84–85, 90, 92, 114

Benjamin, Judah P. (*continued*)
  Davis and, 14–15, 28, 30, 136, 141,
    185, 224, 380
    escape with, 236–41, 243–45
  death of, 392
  described, 13–15, 58, 90, 379–80
  escape prospects, 114, 205, 330,
    379–80
  evacuation of Richmond, 55–56,
    58, 62–63
  financial worth, post-war, 206
  in Greensboro, 132, 136, 139–40
    evacuation, 146, 148–49
  imperturbability of, 55–56, 58,
    71–72, 139–40, 204, 318,
    377–81
  on Lee's surrender, 114
  peace movement and, 43
  on the presidential train, 71–72,
    73, 117, 118
  on the presidential wagon train, 204
  Sherman-Johnston agreement and,
    182, 185–86, 189
  strikes out on his own, 243–45,
    316–19, 353–56, 374–81
    in the Bahamas, 378–80
    on the *Blonde*, 374–76
    in Cuba, 380
    destination, 244–45, 355–56
    disguises, 316–17, 319, 354,
      355, 375–76
    encounters with Federals, 355,
      375–76
    in England, 381, 391–92
    indictments, 342
    Leovy and, 244, 245, 316–19
    route, 317–19, 332, 333, 353–54
    storms at sea, 377–78, 379
    with Tresca, 355–56, 374–79
    in the Virgin Islands, 380–81
  at the War Department, 11, 12, 14
  war's aftermath, 391–92

Bird, Mrs. Edgeworth, 324
Blonde, 374–76
Bragg, General Braxton, 222, 226
  Breckinridge and, 22–25, 210, 261
  on the cause as lost, 227–28
  Davis and, 209–10
    escape of, 260, 269
    payment and, 271, 273, 275
  Robertson and, 261, 262
  Smith and, 235
Bragg, Thomas, 315
Bratton, Dr. James, 206
Breckinridge, Cabell, 95, 182
  father's escape and, 279, 283, 321,
    327, 331
  sent home by father, 333, 338,
    339, 357
Breckinridge, Clifton, 182
  arrest of, 325–26
  in Danville, 121–22, 124
  father's escape and, 279, 283,
    320–21
  in Richmond, 62, 66
Breckinridge, General John C.:
  arrest warrant for, 20–21
  Bragg and, 22–25, 210, 261
  as candidate for president, 19
  in Danville, 121–24
  Davis (*see* Davis, Jefferson,
    Breckinridge and)
  death of, 394
  as de facto leader of the
    Confederacy, 114, 117, 142,
    146, 330–31
  described, 17–26, 148, 159–60, 373
    as handsome, 208, 270
    by Hathaway, 122
    by Lee, 106
    post-war, 387–88, 394
  disenchanted states and, 52–54
  escape prospects, 205
  escape, 284–85, 320–74

aliases, 322–24, 336
almost recognized, 322–23,
    326, 331–32, 348
along the Florida coast, 359–67
crossing the Ocmulgee, 327–29
destination Cuba, 364, 367–72
encounters with Federals,
    361–63, 370–71
in the Florida swamps,
    333–37, 341–48
at Fort Dallas, 364–67
on the Indian River, 348,
    356–59
kindness in Florida, 336
last official act during, 342–43
luck, 328–29
members of his party, 320–21,
    331, 333, 335–36
on the *No Name*, 363–73
as pirate, 362–64
route, 320, 324–25, 329–35
safe in Cuba, 372–74, 387–91
severe storms, 356, 357, 368–70
as sole remaining government
    official, 330–31
to and on the St. John's River,
    335–37, 341–47
surrender in the Trans-
    Mississippi, 343
and voracious insects, 341,
    356–57, 358, 364, 367
Wilson's melodramatic
    retelling of, 391
evacuation of government:
    from Abbeville, 233–41
    from Charlotte, 193–200
    from Greensboro, 142–48
    from Richmond, 54–69, 95
    as sole remaining official,
        330–31
    from Washington, 275–81
financial worth, post-war, 207

as general, 21–23, 69, 151, 159
indictments against, 46, 284, 342
Johnston-Beauregard report and,
    130–36
peace plan and (*see* peace
    talks, Johnston's plan)
joins the Confederacy, 21
Lee and (*see* Lee, General Robert
    E., Breckinridge and)
legacy of, 397–400
Lincoln and, 20, 155
    assassination of, 155–56, 167
opposition to the war, 20, 21,
    28–35, 130–36, 144, 159–60,
    343
partisan warfare and, 38, 46, 48,
    105, 123, 147, 162–63,
    187–88, 399
as possible successor to Davis, 23
Robertson and, 261–62
as senator from Kentucky, 20
slavery and, 18, 19, 20, 103–4
surrender terms, 102–9, 123–24,
    136–39
    Johnston-Sherman
        negotiations, 150–68,
        398–99
telegram from Lee, 3–4
as vice president, 18, 19–20, 167
at the War Department, 23–27
    archives (*see* Kean, Robert)
war's aftermath, 397–400
    amnesty, 386, 392–93
    back in Kentucky, 393–94
    in Cuba, 387–91
    death of, 394
    in England, 391–93
    eulogy for Lee, 396–97
    health, 387–88, 394
    reconciliation, 388–89, 394
    sending fellow escapees
        home, 389–91

Breckinridge, Mary, 387
    fall of Richmond, 61, 67, 69
Breckinridge, Colonel William C. P.,
    144, 190, 199
    on the cause as lost, 222, 225–33
    as Davis's escort, 248, 252, 253,
        270, 288
    as decoy, 276, 278–84
    disbands troops, 284–85
Britannia, HMS, 379, 380
Broun, Joseph, 248–49
Brown, Governor Joseph, 52, 211
    arrest of, 315
Bruce, Eli M., 61, 67
Bruce, Congressman Horatio, 91–92
    and the presidential train, 70, 74
Buchanan, James, 18
Burnett, Henry, 45, 261
Burt, Armistead, 184, 213–14, 215,
    220
Butler, Sampson, 331, 332

Cahill, John, 373
Campbell, Major Andrew, 282–85
Campbell, Captain Given, 147, 199
    and Davis's capture, 307, 311
    as Davis's escort, 206, 210, 212,
        233, 235, 256, 288–90,
        295–96
        payment, 289
        reduced in number, 266–68,
            287
Campbell, John A., 26, 28
    fall of Richmond, 51–52, 56, 61
    truce talks and, 28–32, 38–39, 42,
        45
        Lincoln and, 51–52, 79,
            102–5, 109, 123–24
Canada, 391, 393
Caperton, Allen, 45

centennial celebration, 394
Charlotte, North Carolina,
    Confederate government in,
        171–200
    accommodations, 171–72, 176, 177
    Breckinridge seeking Davis,
        169–70, 178–80
    after Federal rejection of peace
        agreement, 193–200
    archives, 198–99
    escape route, 197
    evacuation of Charlotte,
        197–200
    hopeless situation, 195–200
    Johnston's surrender, 193–99
    leadership of escort, 198
    rejection of escape plans,
        193–94
    resignation and withdrawal,
        197
    steadfast brigades, 194,
        197–98
    Virginia deputation, 196
Lincoln assassination, 173–77
    reception, 172–73
Sherman-Johnston agreement,
    180–92
speech from Davis, 172–74
stragglers and parolees, 178–79,
    182–83, 194, 196
Chesnut, General James, 26
Clark, Micajah H., 182
    as acting treasurer, 265–75, 289,
        338–40
    in Danville, 87, 91
    Davis's escape and, 244, 255, 276,
        287–88
    evacuation of Greensboro, 143, 145
    on the presidential wagon train,
        204, 238
Clay, Clement C., 60, 315, 350, 351

Clay, Henry, 18, 19, 275
Clay, Lieutenant James B., Jr., 275,
    282, 320–21
  arrest of, 325–26
Clay, Virginia, 349
Cleburne, Patrick R., 25
Columbine, USS, 335
Confederate cause:
  as hopeless, 28, 32–48 (*see also*
      Breckinridge, General
      John C.)
  leader of, 6 (*see also* Davis,
      Jefferson)
  seceding states, 52–53, 103, 384
  Southern sentiment against, 52,
      82, 125
  winter of 1864–1865, 4–5
Confederate government. *See also*
    Davis, Jefferson
  archives, 198–99, 262, 399–400
      (*see also* Kean, Robert,
      evacuations of archives)
  bureaucracy and, 2, 89, 271, 274
  capture of officials, 313–16, 330,
      374, 381–83
    Davis (*see* Davis, Jefferson,
        capture of)
  congress (*see* Congress,
      Confederate)
  in Danville (*see* Danville, Virginia,
      Confederate government in)
  evacuation of Richmond, 48, 54–65
  firing on Fort Sumter and, 1–2
  in Greensboro (*see* Greensboro,
      North Carolina, Confederate
      government in)
  last address from a member of,
      388–89
  last official act of, 342–43
  Lee and (*see* Lee, General
      Robert E.)

presidential train (*see* presidential
    train)
presidential wagon train (*see*
    presidential wagon train)
Confederate military, 6. *See also*
    specific units and individuals
  Davis and, 6, 7, 16
  final shots fired by, 366–37
  honorable peace and, 48–49
  last to surrender, 388
  Lee's view of, 3–4, 39–43
  navy, 12, 59, 66, 382, 385
  in Danville, 87–88
  partisan warfare:
    Benjamin on, 185
    Breckinridge on, 38, 46, 48,
        105, 123, 147, 162–63,
        187–88, 399
    Davis on, 80–83
    Ferguson on, 228–29
    Lee on, 229
    Mallory on, 186
  pay for, 86, 143, 235, 248–53
  prominent battles, 4, 21–22
  proposal to enlist slaves in, 24–25,
      42, 160
Congress, Confederate, 5, 25
  impotent opposition to Davis in,
      9, 15–16, 34–35, 43–46
  peace movement, 36–48
  Robertson and, 261
Conolly, Thomas, 62
Cook family, 345–46
Cooper, General Samuel, 71, 77, 88,
    140
  in Charlotte, 177, 196, 197–98
  evacuation from cities:
    Danville, 113, 116
    Greensboro, 146, 148–49
    Richmond, 55–56, 57
Courtney, John C., 173–74, 199

Courtney, Mary, 173, 177, 199–200
Cuba:
  arrest of Confederates fleeing to,
    336–37
  Benjamin reaches, 380
  Breckinridge's party escapes to,
    367–74
Curry, Captain John, 374–75

Danville, Virginia, Confederate
  government in, 74–124
  accommodations at, 75, 89–90
  arrival at, 74–75
  Davis proclamation in, 74–84
    as delusional, 79–84
    "demoralized Union" and, 78,
      79
    dissemination of, 83–84
    Lincoln and, 79–80
    on loss of Richmond, 77–78,
      84
    partisan conflict, 80–83
    reaction to, 84, 92
    to Virginians, 78–80, 84
  defenses of, 88, 92, 93
  evacuation of, 113–19
    Breckinridge after, 121–24
    chaos after, 120–21, 123, 145
    government operation, 77, 84–85,
      88–89
    lack of information, 75, 76–77,
      90–94
  Lee's surrender, 110–16
  as navy town, 87
  Red House scouts, 93–95, 107
  as temporary capital, 76
  treasury train in, 76, 85–87
  waiting in, 90–94
Danville Railroad, 54, 56, 59–62, 71.
  See also presidential train
  Federals cutting the line, 99

Danville *Register,* 83
Davis, George:
  arrest of, 316, 330, 374, 381–83
    release, 385
  as attorney general, 11
    resignation, 197
  in Charlotte, 178
  in Danville, 84–85, 114, 117
  death of, 392
  evacuation of Richmond, 58, 60
  financial worth, post-war, 207
  in Greensboro, 132, 140, 146
  Sherman-Johnston agreement and,
    182, 186
Davis, Jefferson:
  army and, 6, 7
  Benjamin and, 14–15, 28, 30, 136,
    141, 185, 224, 236–41
    strikes out on his own, 243–45
  blamed for Southern misfortune,
    126
  bodyguards for, 147
  Breckinridge and:
    appointment to War
      Department, 23–27
    brigade commanders and,
      225–33, 399
    evacuation of Richmond,
      54–65
    in Georgia (*see* Georgia,
      presidential wagon train
      on the run)
    opposition to the war, 28–35,
      130–36, 144
    peace negotiations and,
      34–48, 52–54, 136–39,
      187–88, 189
    safety of Davis, 46, 141–42,
      167–68, 192–99, 224–41
  cabinet of, 10–15, 23–27, 110–11,
    132–39, 152, 178
  last consultation with, 224, 259

resignations from, 197, 202,
257–58
Sherman-Johnston agreement
and, 181–92, 197
capture of, 286–312
captive to Macon, 309–11
comments on, 311–12
concern for family, 301–4, 312
danger from marauders, 294,
298–99, 301
disguised as a woman myth,
302–4, 351–53
identification of Davis, 305–6
personal effects of Davis, 340
plundering, 301, 304–7
Pritchard's troopers and,
299–310
reports of, 317, 329–30, 332,
338
reunited with Varina, 288–91,
294–95, 320
route of escape, 297–98
size and pace of wagon train,
295–97, 311–12, 320
Varina and, 301–4, 351–52
death of, 396
described, 5–10, 15, 25–26, 30–31
Confederate posterity,
397–400
as delusional, 79–84, 128–29,
133, 182, 200, 249
on the run, 113–14, 117, 121,
147, 148, 150, 204,
219–20, 226, 232, 255
sense of humor, 89, 209
dictatorial powers of, 9, 10–13, 52,
211, 224
escape (*see* Georgia, presidential
wagon train on the run in)
fatalism of, 50–51, 110–11, 147
financial worth, post-war, 207
foreign governments and, 7, 81

indictments against, 46, 342
Johnson and, 175, 180, 310, 350
last official meeting as president,
262
Lincoln assassination and, 170,
173–77
blame for, 309–10, 349–50, 386
obsession with Confederate cause,
7–10, 15, 29–30, 34, 44, 50,
269
opposition to, 5, 8, 9, 15–16,
23–24, 34–35, 43–46
outdoors on horseback, 150, 204–5
palace coup possibilities against,
37, 48
partisan warfare and, 80–83
peace talks and (*see* peace talks)
on the presidential train (*see*
presidential train)
on the presidential wagon train
(*see* presidential wagon train)
in prison, 311, 349–53, 382
in chains, 349, 351, 353, 380,
396
release, 386, 394
war's aftermath, 384–86, 388
refuses to consider surrender,
36–48
Danville proclamation and,
74–84
Johnston-Beauregard report
and, 128–36
leaves Charlotte, 193–200
Lee's surrender and, 110–14,
127–30
note to Sherman, 136–39
Sherman-Johnston agreement,
169–92
Trans-Mississippi situation
and, 298
refuses to leave the country,
223–33

Davis, Jefferson (*continued*)
  reward for, 243, 309–10, 318
  sycophants of, 9, 11, 14–15, 16,
    30, 136, 209–10
  Trans-Mississippi and (*see* Trans-
    Mississippi Department
    (General E. Kirby Smith))
  war's aftermath, 397–400
    death, 396
    as martyr, 396, 397
    memoirs of, 395
    in prison, 384–86, 388, 394,
      396
    rebuilding his life, 394–95, 396
    recriminations, 393–94
  wife of (*see* Davis, Varina)
Davis, Joseph, 97
Davis, Varina, 126, 127, 177, 254
  capture of (*see* Davis, Jefferson,
    capture of)
  children of, 292, 294, 303
  communications with husband, 75,
    91, 171, 292
    continuation of the cause,
      210–11, 286
    Lee's surrender, 111–12
    prepares for the worst, 142–43
    Sherman-Johnston agreement,
      182–84
  dangers to wagon train of, 288–95
  escape plans, 211, 286, 291
  escapes from Richmond, 50–51,
    55
  financial support for, 338–39
  Harrison and (*see* Harrison,
    Burton, Varina Davis and)
  on husband as president, 5–6, 269
  release of, 351
  reunited with husband, 288–91,
    294–95
  on the treasure train, 214–15

Davis, Varina Anne "Winnie," 294
Davis, Major W. J., 250–51
Davis, Warren, and family, 209
Dawkins, James B., 334
Dawson, Major Oscar, 331
  escapes with Breckinridge, 321,
    327
Dibrell, General George G., 143–44,
    254, 269
  on the cause as lost, 226–34
  as Davis's escort, 194, 199, 203,
    205, 206, 212, 220, 221
  refuses Davis's orders, 245,
    247–48, 250
Dickison, Colonel J. J., 333–36, 389
Dickson, Alexander, 154
Douglas, Stephen A., 19
Duke, General Basil W., 172, 178,
    184, 190, 191
  on the cause as lost, 225–32
  as Davis's escort, 199, 220, 248, 260
    slow pace, 201, 203–4,
      221–22, 311
    steadfastness, 194, 252, 253,
      276, 288
  disbanding of troops, 277, 279–85
  treasure train and, 221, 237–38
    payment to troops from,
      249–53, 270–74

Early, General Jubal, 22, 261
Echols, General John, 261
Eighth Texas Cavalry, 256–57,
    260–62
Elzey, General Arnold, 246, 247, 255,
    257, 258, 269
Emancipation Proclamation, 29, 80,
    103–4, 163–64, 187
Everhart, Rev. George, 177
Ewell, General Richard, 60–61, 68

Ferdinand, Archduke, 191

Ferguson, General Samuel W., 172, 184

   on the cause as lost, 225–32, 234

   as Davis's escort, 194, 199, 220, 221, 241, 252, 253, 288

   rebellion in the ranks of, 247, 248, 270, 276–80

Ferguson, Tom, 390–91

   escapes with Breckinridge (*see* Breckinridge, John C., escapes)

Fifth United States Colored Cavalry, 260–61

Fifty-Sixth Alabama Cavalry, 256

Finegan, General Joseph, 318, 320, 332, 333

First Kentucky "Orphan" Brigade, 225, 281

First Wisconsin Cavalry, 299, 300, 305

Fleming, Midshipman R. H., 216–18

Florida, 53, 245

   Benjamin in (*see* Benjamin, Judah P., strikes out on his own)

   Breckinridge in (*see* Breckinridge, General John C., escapes)

   Davis's escape plans, 142, 233, 240, 252, 263, 307

Florida Rail Road, 334

Forrest, General Nathan Bedford, 144, 228, 263, 284, 298

Fort Capron, Florida, 357–58

Fort Dallas, Florida, 364–67

Fort Lafayette, New York, 360, 383

Fort Monroe, Virginia, 351, 380, 394

Fort Pulaski, Georgia, 374

Fort Sumter, South Carolina, 1–2

Fort Warren, Massachusetts, 351

Fourteenth Amendment, 386

Fourth Michigan Cavalry, 299–311

Freemasons, 293

Fry, General Birkett D., 217

Gamble, Robert, 354–55

Garrett, A. Y. P., 311

Gary, General Martin, 212

Georgia, 52–53, 82, 128, 211, 213

   Davis's escape in (*see next entry*)

Georgia, presidential wagon train on the run in, 242–85

   appeals to "Southern gentlemen," 248–49

   Benjamin departs, 243–45

   Breckinridge's actions, 275–83

   capture of Davis (*see* Davis, Jefferson, capture of)

   civilian reception, 246–47, 254–55, 258

   convinced of need for, 225–36

   decoys, 276, 279–84

   diminished presidential authority, 244, 245

   disbanding the government, 262–64, 267, 275

   discharged troops, 247, 255, 257, 274–85

   disguise of Davis, 287

   "every man for himself," 248, 256–58, 262, 269–70, 275

   family of Davis, 259

   grand visions for the Trans-Mississippi, 263–64

   leaves Abbeville, 233–41

   Mallory departs, 236, 257–58

   payment of troops, 248–53, 266–75

   personal danger to Davis, 258–59

   possible routes, 235, 240, 252, 263, 287, 291, 297–98

   prospects for, 205

Georgia, presidential wagon train on
    the run in (*continued*)
    rebellion of the ranks, 247–52,
        259, 276–78
    reducing the size of, 266–68,
        287–88
    rioting, 254, 256–57, 262
    Robertson and, 260–62
    scouts for, 242, 246
    unites with Varina, 288–99
    in Washington, 254–81, 291–93,
        340–41
    in Woodstock, 279–85
    Yankee troops and, 242–43, 245,
        256, 258, 260, 278, 281–85,
        291
Georgina, HMS, 379
Giles, Jane, 208–9
Gilliam, Robert, 238
Gorgas, General Josiah, 26, 49, 61
    in Charlotte, 196, 197
    in Danville, 88, 113–14
Graham, Senator William A., 52, 53,
    153
Grant, General Ulysses S., 42, 138,
    166, 207
    overtakes Lee, 95–107
    presidential train and, 71
    siege of Richmond and, 4, 48–50
    surrender of Lee, 107–9
Graves, Charles Iverson, 214–18
Graves, Captain W. P., 112
Greensboro, North Carolina,
    Confederate government in,
    125–49
    Beauregard's report, 128–29, 130,
        135
    "cabinet car" accommodations,
        125, 128, 139–41
    evacuation of, 142–49
        civil disintegration and, 144–45

Lee's stragglers or escapees
    and, 147
    plan for, 144, 146
    Johnston's report, 129–36
    last orders to, 206
    surly welcome, 125–27
    Yankee raiders and, 126, 139, 141
Griffith, William, 2

Hampton, General Wade, 154, 158,
    196, 197, 205
    Breckinridge's orders to, 206
    refusal to surrender, 155, 194,
        195
Harris, Congressman Thomas A.,
    337, 376
Harrison, Burton, 42, 89, 185, 236,
    238
    in Charlotte, 172, 176, 177
    in Danville, 110, 111
        evacuation, 113, 117–20
    in Greensboro, 125
        evacuation, 146, 148–49
    on the road to Charlotte, 150,
        171
    Varina Davis and, 50, 55, 182,
        184, 210, 247, 254, 259,
        288–94
        capture of, 295–302, 305,
            311–12
    financial support for, 339
Hathaway, Leeland, 67, 122, 350
    Davis's capture and, 292, 293, 295,
        306–7
Haynes, Lieutenant Draughton S.,
    324, 327, 329, 331
Helen (Davis's children's nurse),
    302–3
Hoge, Dr. Moses, 90, 114
Howell, Margaret, 292

Hunter, R. M. T., 11, 23
  arrest of, 315
  Confederate succession and, 37–38
  truce talks and, 28, 36–37, 45, 79

Illustrated London News, 268

James River fleet, 59, 66, 87–88
Jefferson, Thomas, 113
Johnson, Andrew, 180
  amnesty proclamations, 348, 382,
    386, 393
  described, 175
  hatred for Davis, 175, 310, 350
  rejection of Johnston's plan, 193
Johnson, General Bushrod, 97
Johnson, Waldo, 45
Johnston, General Joseph E., 14, 23,
  113
  evacuation of Greensboro,
    143–44
  hatred for Davis, 5, 129, 135, 151,
    394, 395
  hopes of uniting with Lee, 32, 42,
    48–49, 76, 91, 101, 102, 105
  Lee's stragglers or escapees and,
    147, 163, 178–79
  peace negotiations (*see* peace talks,
    Johnston's plan)
  reinstatement of, 16
  reports on desperate situation,
    129–36
  retreat from Sherman, 126, 128
  surrender of, 193–99, 398–99
    aftermath of, 254, 255, 274,
      277, 278, 286, 315
Johnston, William, 172, 174
Johnston, Colonel William Preston,
  17, 22, 106, 209, 238

capture of Davis and, 295, 297,
  299–300, 304–8, 311, 351
  in Charlotte, 175, 176, 177, 196
  in Danville, 88, 113, 126
  Davis's escape and, 242, 260, 288
  payment during, 289
  evacuation of Richmond, 55, 60
  in Greensboro, 126, 127, 130, 146
  on the presidential train, 73, 121
Jones, Cadwallader, 154–55
Jones, James, 299
Jones, John B., 26–27
Juarez, Benito, 191

Kean, Robert, 26, 32, 42, 43, 77, 88
  evacuations of archives, 262,
    399–400
  from Charlotte, 198–99
  from Danville, 114, 116, 120
  from Greensboro, 145–46
  from Richmond, 56, 59–60
Kentucky, 20–21, 23, 45–46, 393–94
Ku Klux Klan, 393

Lane, Colonel A. J., 324
Lawton, General Alexander R.,
  95–96, 101, 271, 272, 274, 279
  as Davis's escort, 260, 264
Lee, General Robert E., 396
  Breckinridge and, 22, 106
  appointed as secretary of war,
    27
  eulogy for Lee, 396–97
  evacuation of Richmond and,
    32–35, 40, 54–66
  meetings between, 100,
    101–2, 105–6
  messages to, 3–4, 39–43
  peace negotiations, 34–48

Lee, General Robert E. (*continued*)
  on the run from Union forces,
    95–107
  death of, 396–97
  as general-in-chief, 16–17, 37,
    63–64, 108
  hopes for uniting with Johnston,
    32, 42, 48–49, 76, 91, 101,
    102, 105
  lack of information about, 75,
    90–100, 107
  on partisan warfare, 229
  supplies for, 95–108
  surrender of, 107–16, 122–24, 269,
    398
    formal notification of, 127–30
    Grant and, 107–9
    news of, reaches Danville,
      110–16
    on parole, 130, 315
    prelude to, 95–107
    Sayler's Creek disaster and,
      101, 105, 107, 110, 112
Leovy, Henry, 210, 292, 340
  Benjamin and, 244, 245, 316–19
Lesley, Major John, 354
Lincoln, Abraham, 173, 396
  assassination of, 155–56
    blame for, 156, 167, 174–76,
      309–10, 349–50, 385, 386
    implications of, for the South,
      175, 176, 180, 350, 387
    informing Davis, 170, 173–77,
      179–80
    keeping quiet about, 156, 159
    peace negotiations and,
      155–56, 157
    war's aftermath and, 384–86
  Breckinridge and, 20, 155
  on Davis, 168
  described, 7
  election of, 19

reelection of, 4, 8, 79
truce talks and, 29, 30, 79–80
  Campbell and, 51–52, 79,
    102–5, 109, 123–24
West Virginia and, 79–80
Lincoln, Mary, 155
Livingston, Daniel, 331
Lomax, General Lunsford L., 124
Longstreet, General James, 100
Louisiana, 52
Lubbock, Francis, 146, 351
  in Charlotte, 176
  Davis's capture, 299–300, 304–6
  Davis's escape, 240–41, 260, 289
  evacuation of Richmond, 55, 56,
    58, 60
  on the presidential train, 73, 113

McCardell, Lieutenant William,
  335–36
  Confederate commission of,
    342–43
McLaws, General Lafayette, 267
McLeod, H. A., 375–79
McNeil, Captain Archibald, 354–55
Mallory, Stephen R.:
  arrest of, 316, 330, 335
    incarceration, 360, 382
    release, 385
  Benjamin and, 14–15, 30
  in Charlotte, 174, 178
  in Danville, 86–87, 93
    evacuation, 114, 116–17
  Davis's escape and, 239, 242–43,
    255, 256, 259, 260
  death of, 392
  desperate situation and, 131–39,
    150, 224
  evacuation of Richmond, 54–55,
    58–59, 64, 65
  financial worth, post-war, 206

in Greensboro, 126, 139
  evacuation, 145, 146, 147
Lee's surrender and, 112–13
on the presidential train, 70–75
on the presidential wagon train,
    194, 201, 203, 204–5, 208, 213
as secretary of the navy, 12
  resignation, 236, 257–58, 270
Sherman-Johnston agreement and,
    181, 182, 186
treasury train and, 86–87, 214,
    220–21, 223
Marshall, Congressman Humphrey,
  92
Mayo, Mayor John, 58, 60, 61, 68
Means, Lieutenant Edward C., 215
Memminger, Christopher G., 11, 315
Messick, Jack, 292
Mexico, 191, 193, 194, 258, 297
Miles, General Nelson, 351
Miller, Fannie Walker, 2–3, 26, 40,
    49–50
  fall of Richmond, 59–60, 66, 67
Minegerode, Rev. Charles, 56–57
Mississippi, 52, 297
Missouri, 45–46, 82
Monroe, Winder, 292
Morehead, Governor John, 125, 146
Morgan, James, 147
Mosby, Colonel John S., 82
Moseley, Lewis, 331, 333
Moses, Major R. J., 274
Moss, David, 249, 251, 254
Munger, Corporal George, 301–4,
    353
Murphy, Private P., 342, 343–45

Naval Academy midshipmen:
  discharge of, 221
    Davis's request to return to
      their posts, 245

as treasure train guards, 58–59, 62,
    66, 85–87, 122, 143, 214–21
  payment, 272–73
Neptune, USS, 371
New York *Herald*, 332, 391
New York Times, 342
Ninth Kentucky Cavalry, 147
No Name, 363–73, 387, 389
North Carolina, 52, 53–54, 82
  surrender terms and, 104–5, 124,
    153, 185, 189–90
Northrop, General Lucius B., 25, 26,
    95

Oladowski, Colonel Hypolite, 271,
    273
O'Toole, Sergeant Joseph, 335–36,
    342, 399. *See also* Breckinridge,
    John C., escapes
  going home from Cuba, 389, 391
Owens, Colonel Samuel, 335

Packard, Lieutenant Joseph, 106
Palmer, Colonel William, 212, 282
Parker, Captain William H.:
  Davis and, 222–24, 235–36
  evacuation of Richmond, 59, 62,
    64, 65, 66
  as guard of treasure train, 85–87,
    122, 202, 214–21
  payment to troops, 272–73
Patrick Henry, CSS, 59
peace talks:
  Campbell and, 28–32, 38–39, 42,
    45, 51–52, 102–5
  Davis's sabotaging of, 28–35, 80,
    136–39, 152, 176, 180
  at Hampton Roads, 28–32,
    36–37, 43, 79–80, 137, 164,
    180

peace talks (*continued*)
  Johnston's plan, 136–39
    agreement by Sherman and
      Johnston, 167–68
    Breckinridge, Sherman and,
      150–68
    considered by Davis and
      cabinet, 180–92
    Davis's acceptance, 192
    Federal rejection of, 193–200
    Lincoln assassination and,
      170, 174–76
    reaching Davis, 169–80
    Sherman's response, 164–66
  Lincoln's assassination and,
    155–56, 157
  officers and wives scheme, 33–34,
    43, 80
  Vance and, 52–54, 153–55, 158
Perrin, T. C., 214
Pfifer, William, 181, 197
Philbrook, Walter, 86–87, 237
Pierce, Franklin, 6, 10
presidential train, 70–143
  abandonment of, 142–43 (*see also*
    presidential wagon train)
  in Danville (*see* Danville, Virginia,
    Confederate government in)
  Davis on, 73–75, 119–20
  earlier train wrecks and, 74
  Grant's army and, 71
  in Greensboro (*see* Greensboro,
    North Carolina, Confederate
    government in)
  Mallory's view of, 70–75
  occupants of, 70–74
  other trains following, 76, 121
  soldiers on top of, 120
  towns along the way, 74
presidential wagon train:
  assembly of, 142–43

  in Charlotte (*see* Charlotte, North
    Carolina, Confederate
    government in)
  in Georgia (*see* Georgia,
    presidential wagon train on
    the run in)
  leaves Greensboro, 142–49
  on the road to Charlotte, 149–50,
    169–71
  through South Carolina (*see* South
    Carolina, presidential wagon
    train on the run through)
Preston, General William, 26
Princeton University, 18
Pritchard, Lieutenant Colonel
    Benjamin D., 327, 328, 350
  capture of Davis, 299–310, 351–53
Putnam, Sallie, 67

Rains, General Gabriel, 117–18
  daughter of, 119
Randolph, George W., 12
Reagan, John:
  capture of, 300, 306, 330
    incarceration, 350–51
    release, 382, 385
  in Charlotte, 178, 179
  in Danville, 75, 77, 88–89, 113,
    116
  Davis's escape and, 224, 236, 240,
    244, 255–56, 258–60, 263,
    287
    disbanded troops, 275, 276
    looters, 239
    on making haste, 240, 295, 311
    Varina's wagon train, 289–90
  death of, 392
  escape prospects, 205
  evacuation of Richmond, 56, 58
  financial worth, post-war, 206–7

in Greensboro, 132, 140, 146
Johnston's report and, 132–37
at peace negotiations, 152, 155,
    156, 169
    draft proposal, 158–61, 166
as postmaster general, 12–13
on the presidential train, 72, 116,
    117, 118, 120
on the presidential wagon train,
    202, 205–6
as secretary of the treasury, 202,
    221, 251, 265–66
    payment of troops, 249, 250,
    271–75
Sherman-Johnston agreement and,
    182, 183, 186–87, 192, 193
Reconstruction, 183, 385
hopes for, 124, 157, 161–62
Rhett, Robert Barnwell, 8, 397
avoiding arrest, 315
as dissident, 5, 9, 16
Richardson, F. E., 220, 277–78
Richmond, Virginia:
burning of, 61, 66–69, 77
Davis on loss of, 77–78, 84
as doomed, 48–50, 53
evacuation of, 31–35, 40, 46–47,
    54–69, 95, 126
    rumors concerning Davis and,
    83
Lee's army defending, 3–4, 22
looting in, 58, 65–67, 123, 145
significance of, 47
*Rise and Fall of the Confederate
    Government* (Davis), 395
Robertson, Felix, 260–62
Robertson, J. J., and family, 246–47,
    255, 259–60, 262, 267–68, 272,
    341
Rosser, General Thomas, 124
Lee's surrender and, 112, 122–23

Russell, Corporal Richard, 335–36,
    342, 399. *See also* Breckinridge,
    General John C., escapes
going home from Cuba, 389–90,
    391

St. John, General Isaac M., 95–96,
    101, 106, 107, 274, 279
Saltville atrocity, 260–62
Sauls, George, 345–48
Scott, Sutton S., 322–23
Second Florida Cavalry, 335–36
Seddon, James A., 12, 17
arrest of, 315
Seminoles, 362
Semmes, Admiral Raphael:
in Danville as general, 88, 93
evacuation of Richmond, 55, 59, 66
Semple, James A., 274, 338
Seventh South Carolina Cavalry, 68
Seward, William, attempt to
    assassinate, 155, 167, 170
Shenandoah, CSS, 382, 385
Sherman, General William T., 42,
    49, 102, 104, 138
Johnston's surrender and, 193–97
military victories of, 4, 126, 128,
    143
peace talks with Johnston (*see*
    peace talks, Johnston's plan)
slavery:
Breckinridge and, 18, 19, 20
Davis and, 8
Emancipation Proclamation, 29,
    80, 103–4, 163–64, 187
military service and, 24–25, 42,
    160
Missouri Compromise, 113
surrender terms and, 103–4, 136,
    156, 160, 163–64, 187

Smith, E. Kirby. *See* Trans-
    Mississippi Department
    (General E. Kirby Smith)
Smith, Gustavus W., 24, 315–16
Smith, Governor William, 58, 113,
    123, 124, 196
South Carolina, 52
South Carolina, presidential wagon
    train on the run through,
    201–47
    in Abbeville, 213–14, 221–41
    Bragg's opinion, 209–10
    brigade commander's view,
        225–33
    cavalry escort, 201, 203–6, 221–24
    civilian reception, 202, 204–9,
        213–14, 218–19
    Davis's escape, 233–41
    enemy knowledge of, 212–13
    escape prospects, 205
    financial prospects, 206–7
    impediments to, 222, 224
    Parker's opinion, 222–24
    route for, 203, 233
    slow pace, 201, 203, 208, 222, 225
    treasure train and, 214–21
    Varina's letter, 210–11
    Wheeler's marauders, 208
    Yankee units shadowing, 201, 205,
        211–12, 220, 239
Southern Telegraph, 2
Southside Railroad, 54, 99–101, 106
Speed, James, 165
Springs, Colonel A. B., and family,
    201–3
Stacker, Clay, 282
Stark, Major Thomas, 341
Stephens, Alexander H., 21
    arrest of, 313–14, 330
        incarceration, 350–51
        release, 382, 384, 385

Davis and, 8
    death of, 392
    leaves the government, 5
    truce talks and, 28, 29, 79
Stoneman, General George, 212,
    214, 216
Stuart, Charles E. L., 13–14, 27, 126,
    200
    described, 89
    on the presidential wagon train,
        213, 266
Summer, Colonel A. G., 336, 337
Sutherlin, Major William T., and
        family, 75, 89, 90, 92, 110–13,
    118
Swaim, Governor David, 153
Swallow, W. H., 55, 93, 141, 147–48
    escapes with Breckinridge, 321,
        326–27, 329
    on the presidential wagon train,
        213

Tallahassee, CSS, 12, 385
Taylor, General Richard, 203, 213,
    228
    surrender of, 263, 276, 284, 298,
        388
Taylor, Colonel Walter, 68
Tennessee, 46, 52, 82
Texas, 52, 184–85, 194, 297, 346. *See
    also* Trans-Mississippi
    Department
Thirteenth Amendment, 163, 187
Thirty-Sixth Alabama Cavalry, 290
Thompson, Jacob, 391–92
Thompson, Robert M., 321
Thorburn, Colonel Charles, 256, 318
    Davis's capture and, 307
    Davis's escape and, 142, 260, 297
    payment during, 289

Tilghman, Tench, 195, 203
  treasure train, 337, 338, 339
Toombs, Robert, 23, 24, 280
  avoiding arrest, 313–15, 382–83
  Davis and, 254, 258
  as government dissident, 5, 9,
    10–11
Trans-Mississippi Department
    (General E. Kirby Smith), 51,
    111, 129, 144, 235, 240, 258, 297
  expectations for, 128, 184–85,
    188–89, 211, 244, 263–64,
    267, 276, 287
    Treasury and, 265–66, 273
  Hampton and, 194
  reality in, 298, 346
  speculation about, 398
  surrender in, 284, 343, 346, 388
Transylvania University, 18
treason indictments, 384–86, 394
treasure train, 122, 143, 202, 223
  Bragg and, 235
  Clark and, 265–75, 289, 337–40
  contents of, 85–86, 251, 253
  in Danville, 76, 85–87
  Davis's escape and, 237–38, 241,
    265–66
  Duke and, 237–38, 249–53
  evacuation of Richmond, 58–59,
    62, 65, 66
  government collapse and, 337–40
  odyssey of, 214–21
  payment of troops from, 235,
    248–53, 266–75, 339
Trenholm, Anna, 73
  in Danville, 75, 84, 115–16
  on the presidential train, 120
Trenholm, George A., 188
  arrest of, 316, 330
    incarceration, 374
    release, 382, 385

as cipher, 11–12
in Danville, 75, 77, 86–87
death of, 392
financial worth, post-war, 207
in Greensboro, 125, 143, 146
illness of, 75, 143
  on the presidential train, 73,
    115–16, 117
  on the presidential wagon train,
    146, 149, 170, 199, 202
  severity of, 176, 182, 316
  treasure train and, 86–87
resignation of, 202
Tresca, Captain Frederick, 355–56,
    374–79
Tupper, Rev. H. A., 268
Tyler, Robert, 26

Van Benthuysen, Captain Watson,
    and brother, 290
  treasure train and, 337–40
Vance, Governor Zebulon, 127, 196
  arrest of, 315
  peace movement and, 52–54,
    153–55, 158
  Sherman-Johnston agreement and,
    188–90
  state capital and, 169–70
Vaughn, General John, 199, 222, 254,
    269
  on the cause as lost, 226–34
  looters formerly under, 340–41
  refuses Davis's orders, 245,
    247–48, 250
Vest, George G., 45
Virginia, 36, 52, 53, 54, 82, 196
  Davis's proclamation and, 78–80,
    84
  surrender terms and, 103–5, 124,
    185

Vizetelly, Frank, 268
Volunteer, 89

Walker, Mayor James, 75
Walker, Leroy P., 12, 17, 26, 315
Wallace, General William H., 207
Wardlaw, Judge Benjamin, 331, 332
Warthen, Colonel Richard, 324
Watie, General Stand, 346, 388
Watts, Thomas, 315
Wauchula, 336, 337
Weill, Abram, 176
West Point, 6
West Virginia, 79–80
Wheeler, General Joseph, 197, 212,
    235
  capture of, 350–51
  escape of, 270
  marauders of, 208
  Saltville atrocity and, 260–61
Wheless, John, 217
  paying the troops, 271–73
White, William, 202
Whitten, Dr., 321–23
Wigfall, Louis T., 45, 258, 270
  avoiding arrest, 315

Wilson, Colonel James, 68, 95
  escapes with Breckinridge (*see*
      Breckinridge, John C.,
      escapes)
  in exile, 391
Wilson, General James H., 291, 322
  Davis and, 310–11, 349–52
Wise, Lieutenant John S., 74, 110,
    111
Withers, Colonel Robert, 84, 88
Wood, John Taylor, 55, 73, 238
  in Charlotte, 176, 177, 178, 196
  Davis's capture, 299–301
  Davis's escape, 260, 289, 297
  escape of, 307–9, 317–20
    Breckinridge and (*see*
        Breckinridge, General
        John C., escapes)
  in exile, 391
  in Greensboro and, 125, 126–27,
    130, 139, 146

Yulee, Senator David, 335, 338, 339,
    340, 354